THE COMPLETE CHRISTIAN PILGRIM

THE COMPLETE CHRISTIAN PILGRIM

Guide to 250 sacred and historic places every Christian should see

HOWARD KRAMER

Published by **The Complete Pilgrim, LLC**

Cover Design and Typesetting: JD Smith Design

Cover Photo: Church of the Holy Sepulchre, Jerusalem, Israel

ISBN 978-1-7325081-3-2

For Carla

TABLE OF CONTENTS

ACKNOWLEDGMENTS

It is with deep gratitude that I would like to acknowledge the following people for all of their support in my endeavors, not just for this book, but for the many years I have labored on *The Complete Pilgrim*.

First and foremost, I want to thank my family. Thank you Carla for your patience, and for your continued support and encouragement of my dreams even after everything. Thank you Emily and Natalie, not just for your support, but for putting up with all of my crazy vacation itineraries, and also for your many hours of uncompensated research assistance.

Thanks to my mother, Rita Kramer, one of the earliest supporters of *The Complete Pilgrim* project, for your enthusiasm since day one; and to my father, Arthur Kramer, who knew decades before I did that I should have pursued a career in something history related. Well, better late than never.

A huge thanks to my sister Jill, who was not only one of the first people to encourage me to begin posting my work online, but who has also put in countless hours of work into *The Complete Pilgrim* from writing to photo editing.

A very special thanks to my dear friend Rebecca Cantrell, without whom I probably would not have had the courage to publish; and for introducing me to Jane Dixon-Smith, who has done such a masterful job of designing and laying out my books for me.

Also thanks to Kris McInerny, who helped me launch my website, and who helps me to maintain it even though she has been retired for years. I know that you've been undercharging me Kris!

Finally, a big shout-out to all the folks at FPC Marietta, especially the writer's support group; for supporting me in every way, for giving me an amazing forum, and for helping me become more involved in the community. You guys are the best!

INTRODUCTION

Christianity as an independent faith is one of the oldest and largest institutions in the history of humankind. Although divided among dozens of major denominations and hundreds if not thousands of sub-denominations, there were approximately 2.2 billion Christians in the world at the time of this writing, representing approximately 29% of the global population. Despite being of one faith, the world's billions of Christians express their faith in countless ways that affect everything from religious practices to cultural traditions.

These differences, which span both the far reaches of the globe as well as thousands of years of history, are expressed in a bewildering variety of architecture. The world is home to millions of Christian churches, cathedrals, chapels and shrines. They come in all sizes, shapes and ages. And for nearly two thousand years, the greatest and most important of these have been magnets for countless pilgrims.

Over the last twenty-five years, I have had the pleasure and privilege of visiting perhaps five hundred of the most sacred and historic Christian pilgrimage destinations on Earth. Arguably my greatest pilgrimage took place in late 2017. It began on October 31 in Wittenberg, Germany, where I attended the 500th anniversary celebration of Martin Luther's 95 Theses and the start of the Protestant Reformation. From there I travelled to Israel, where I visited virtually all of the hallowed sites of both the Old and New Testaments.

Religious pilgrimage and history-related travel is my life's passion. In the last five years it has manifested itself in the travel blog *The Complete Pilgrim* (www.thecompletepilgrim.com), which I am excited to say is on track this year to receive two hundred thousand visitors. In 2018 *The Complete Pilgrim* was expanded to written form with the release of *The Complete American Pilgrim*, and is now continuing with *The Complete Christian Pilgrim*.

It is my hope that *The Complete Christian Pilgrim* will engender an interest in Christian history, spiritual renewal among those who are religious, and an interest in faith among those who are not. Most importantly, I hope that it will instill its readers with a greater interest in a love for travel and a desire to more fully understand the spiritual complexity of the world in which we live.

Methodology

The process of selecting 250 must-see sites of Christian interest around the world was extremely challenging. With dozens of major denominations and over two hundred countries with Christian populations to consider, I estimate that there are somewhere between eight and sixteen million church buildings in the world. And then there are countless other places, including many museums, that don't qualify as houses of worship but are undoubtedly of Christian interest.

During my initial review I started with a list of about a thousand destinations that could easily be included in this work. In order to narrow down the field, five factors were considered for each location:

1) Is the site already a widely recognized pilgrimage destination, with a substantial number of annual visitors; 2) Was the site critical as a religious center or a major point from which Christianity expanded into new areas; 3) Is anybody buried at the site of particular Christian or historical importance; 4) Is there an artifact or document of great Christian importance associated with or located at the site; and 5) Was the site the location of an important event in Christian history.

Obviously, this was a highly subjective process. I truly hope that I did not understate any particularly worthy location, or worse, overlook one altogether. Whether or not I succeeded in getting it right I leave up to the reader. But in one thing I know I did fail, and that was my futile effort to rank these sites in order of importance. Having abandoned this attempt early in the process, I instead grouped the sites geographically, the best solution I could come up with.

Traveler Cautions

This book references Christian religious sites all over the world. The majority are historic churches still in operation, and most of these can be found in major cities. That said, accessibility can be a significant problem with many of these locations, both in terms of getting to a site and in terms of ramps and other facilities for visitors with physical handicaps. This is especially true in less developed countries where many of the most important Christian sites are to be found. *The Complete Pilgrim* strongly urges its readers who are uncomfortable with certain modes of long distance travel or who have physical limitations to thoroughly research their visit to any of these sites well in advance.

Similarly, while visiting virtually any open church is generally safe, a number of them, especially some very old ones, are located in rough neighborhoods, or even countries which are not particularly welcoming to Christian pilgrims. Again, *The Complete Pilgrim* strongly urges its readers to review safety warnings in advance, such as on the United States Secretary of State website, and avoid areas that may pose a significant threat to tourists. Even in very safe cities, travelers should always take basic safety precautions when sightseeing.

When this book was in production, every effort was made to insure that all visitor information was as accurate and up-to-date as possible, and all information contained herein was deemed reliable as of the completion of writing in 2019. However, in the 36 months or so from the beginning of the writing process to the final edits, there were so many changes to opening hours, worship times and occasionally admission fees that it became too time consuming to update.

Instead, addresses and website information have been included whenever possible. The latter, which were generally up to date and operational at the time of this writing, typically have all necessary visitor and contact information (author's note – websites change frequently, and many are not secure; readers may wish or need to verify website information independently). It is therefore up to the reader to investigate relevant visitor information. In any event, *The Complete Pilgrim* and its writers are not responsible for visitor information. Visitors and pilgrims to all sites in this book are advised to verify any and all visitor information prior to travel.

The Complete Pilgrim reminds all of its readers that the many different denominations of Christianity have many different styles of worship and cultural traditions. While the doors of most churches in the world are open to almost anybody, there are occasional exceptions, especially during hours of worship and on certain holidays. Be respectful of the religious practices of others, and double check hours of worship before you go.

Note on Church Ages

There is no information that is more confusing in this book than the age of churches. There are very few churches discussed in this book that are completely original buildings. Moreover, dating of early churches is often extremely inaccurate. In general, there are many factors that could be considered:

- Date that the congregation, parish, diocese or community (such as a monastery) was founded
- Date that construction began on the original church
- Date that construction on the original church was substantially completed
- Date that the original church was consecrated
- Date that the original church was totally completed
- Date that construction began on the current church
- Date that construction on the current church was substantially completed
- Date that the current church was consecrated
- Date that the current church was totally completed
- Etc.

Obviously dating churches, especially early churches, is a convoluted process. In some cases the completion of the largest cathedrals took centuries, during which time older sections may have undergone renovations while the newer sections were still under construction! Depending on the criteria used, many churches claim to be the 'oldest' in a region or within a denomination. For the purposes of this book, the focus is on the current building, with a nod to the completion of any earlier buildings.

Accuracy of Contents

Finally, a word about the accuracy of the contents of this book. Every effort was made to ensure the accuracy of information about each and every site in this book. As of the time of this writing, the author had personally visited approximately seventy of these destinations and wrote based on first-hand observations supplemented as needed by research. For those religious sites not personally visited, writing was based on thorough research from reliable sources both online and in print.

If any part of this book is found to be in error, or some information of significance has been omitted, *The Complete Pilgrim* encourages its readers to reach out to us at our website (www.thecompletepilgrim.com) with any suggestions. Upon confirmation, changes may be made accordingly at the discretion of the author. A new edition of this volume will likely be issued sometime late in 2021.

TIMELINE OF CHRISTIAN HISTORY

Origins of Christianity

c. 4 BC – Birth of Jesus of Nazareth

c. 29 – Start of the Ministry of Jesus of Nazareth

c. 33 – Crucifixion & Resurrection of Jesus of Nazareth; Death of Judas Iscariot; Founding of the Church; James the Lesser becomes the first Patriarch of Jerusalem; Stephen becomes the first martyr of Christianity

c. 36 – Conversion of Paul

c. 42 – Christianity established in Egypt; Mark the Evangelist becomes the first Patriarch of Alexandria

44 – Persecutions of Herod Agrippa; Death of James the Greater; Scattering of the Apostles

c. 45 – Christianity established in Northern Syria; Peter becomes the first Patriarch of Antioch

46-49 – First Journey of Paul

c. 50 – Council of Jerusalem, attended by Peter, James the Lesser, Paul and Barnabas; Peter goes to Rome and John goes to Ephesus, possibly with Mary; Peter becomes first Patriarch of Rome

50-52 – Second Journey of Paul

- Paul probably writes *Thessalonians I & II* during this period

53-57 – Third Journey of Paul

- Paul probably writes *Corinthians I & II, Galatians, Philippians and Philemon* during this period

c. 54 – Death of Mary the Mother of Jesus

58-62 – Fourth Journey of Paul

- Paul probably writes *Romans* during this period

c. 62 – Death of James the Lesser; Simeon I becomes the second patriarch of Jerusalem

64 – Great Fire of Rome; Christians blamed and persecuted by the emperor Nero; Peter is crucified; Linus succeeds him as the second Patriarch of Rome

66 – Beginning of the Great Revolt in Judea

- Paul probably writes *Colossians* around this time; undated letters attributed to Paul's later life include *Ephesians, Timothy I & II and Titus*

c. 67 – Death of Paul

c. 68 – Death of Mark

- Mark completes the *Gospel of Mark* in the later years of his life

70 – Destruction of Jerusalem and the Temple; Ignatius becomes Patriarch of Antioch

73 – Final stand of the Jews at Masada; end of the Great Revolt

c. 84 – Death of Luke

- Luke completes the *Gospel of Luke and the Book of Acts* in the later years of his life
- Undated letters of *James, Peter I & II, Hebrews and Jude* probably completed in the second half of the 1st century AD

c. 85 – Death of Matthew

- Matthew completes the *Gospel of Matthew* in the later years of his life

88 – Clement I becomes the Patriarch of Rome

c. 95 – John imprisoned on the Isle of Patmos

- John completes the *Gospel of John, the Book of Revelation and possibly the letter of John* while in exile

c. 105 – Death of John, believed to be the last surviving Apostle

Christianity in the Roman Era

132 – Beginning of the Bar Kokhba Revolt

136 – End of the Bar Khokba Revolt; Jerusalem is completely destroyed; Jewish nation ceases to exist in the Holy Land

c. 136 – By this time, centers of Christianity have emerged in Antioch, Alexandria and Rome

c. 200 – Position of Bishop of Rome receives the additional title of 'Pope' around this time

202 – Emperor Septimus Severus issues edict suppressing Christianity in the Roman Empire

222 – Anti-Christian riots in Rome

257 – Emperor Valerian issues edict suppressing Christianity in the Roman Empire

c. 300 – Armenia becomes the first nation to be largely Christianized

303 – Beginning of the Great Persecution of Diocletian; greatest tribulation of Christians in the Roman Empire since Nero

c. 310 – Anthony establishes the first Christian monastery in Egypt

311 – Great Persecution of Diocletian officially ends; Donatist Schism of the Christians who remained faithful

312 – Battle of Milvian Bridge

313 – Edict of Milan legalizes Christianity

318 – Beginning of the Arian heresy; Arius of Alexandria denies divine nature of Christ

321 – Christian Sabbath changed from Saturday to Sunday

325 – First Council of Nicaea – Church formally organized as an institution; Rome, Alexandria, Antioch and Jerusalem recognized as patriarchal seats of the Church; Arian Heresy is condemned; writing of the original Nicene Creed

326 – Empress Helena makes a pilgrimage to the Holy Land and formally recognizes many places and relics of Christian interest

329 – First Basilica of St. Peter built in Rome

331 – Constantine commissions creation of the first Bibles; he has pagan temples sacked and looted

335 – Church of the Holy Sepulcher built in Jerusalem

336 – Athanasius of Alexandria exiled for opposing Arianism

346 – Athanasius restored; Church factions establish an uneasy truce

359 – Eastern Church in Seleucia becomes pro-Arian

360 – Nicene Creed updated to become pro-Arian

372 – Martin, Bishop of Tours, establishes the first hermit community in the west

381 – First Council of Constantinople – Arianism is permanently condemned; Nicene Creed finalized

391 – Theodosius makes Christianity the official religion of Roman Empire

404 – The Vulgate, or Latin Bible, is completed

c. 426 – Berber Christians refuse to accept the central authority of Rome

428 – Nestorius, Patriarch of Constantinople, establishes Nestorian Christianity teaching divine and human natures of God were separate

431 – Council of Ephesus – Nestorianism condemned; Assyrian Churches break away from the Orthodox-Catholic Church

449 – Idea of Monophysitism, that Christ is a single divine nature, begins to spread through Church

451 – Council of Chalcedon - Monophytism condemned; Oriental Churches break away from the Orthodox-Catholic Church

454 – Kingdom of Axum in Ethiopia accepts Coptic Church and leadership of Alexandria

476 – End of Roman Empire in the west

Christianity in the Early Middle Ages

c. 480 – Nestorianism reaches India

484 – Early cracks begin to appear between the church leaders of Constantinople and Rome

489 – Nestorian Christians forced out of Egypt and become established in Persia

491 – Armenian Church becomes independent of the Orthodox-Catholic Church

c. 500 – Clovis I of France converts to Catholic Christianity; many other Germanic kingdoms at this time have adopted Arianism

526 – Dionysius Exiguus establishes tables for the dates of Easter and the Anno Domini (AD) system of dating

529 – Benedict establishes a monastery at Monte Cassino and creates the Benedictine Rules

536 – Ethiopia becomes independent of the Orthodox-Catholic Church

552 – Rift between Coptic and Orthodox-Catholic Christians in Egypt

553 – Second Council of Constantinople

589 – Death of Arian Visigothic king Leovigild; Council of Toledo declares Spain to be Catholic

597 – Augustine evangelizes among Anglo-Saxons in England

603 – Lombards in Italy converted to Roman Catholicism

637 – Muslims conquer the Holy Land and Jerusalem

660 – Third Council of Constantinople

664 – Celtic Christianity replaced by Catholicism

678 – Peace treaty between the Islamic Caliphate and the Byzantine Empire

692 – Episcopal council asserts the Patriarch of Constantinople is equal to the Pope; Pope rejects the decision

711 – Muslims conquer Spain

722 - Boniface becomes the first bishop of Germany

726 – Byzantine Empire bans the veneration of icons

731 – Bede begins his writings in England

732 – Arab armies halted at the Battle of Poitiers in France

756 – Formation of Papal states under the protection of Carolingians

768 – Laity lose right to participate in Papal elections

771 – Charlemagne becomes ruler of the Franks; Papacy requests his aid against the Lombards

778 – Charlemagne defeats the Muslims in Spain

781 – Christianity introduced to China

782 – Saxony converted to Christianity

787 – Second Council of Nicaea – Allows veneration of icons

800 – Pope crowns Charlemagne the first Holy Roman Emperor

807 – Caliph grants protection of Christian holy places in Jerusalem

863 – Beginning of missionary journeys of Cyril and Methodius; First mission to Serbia

869 – Moravia converted to Christianity

875 – Cyril & Methodius undertake mission to Kiev

c. 900 – Bulgaria converted to Christianity

c. 973 – Bohemia converted to Christianity

988 – Kievan Russia converted Christianity

1000 – Hungary converted to Christianity

Christianity in the Later Middle Ages

1009 – Church of the Holy Sepulcher in Jerusalem is desecrated by Muslims

1031 – Beginning of the Christian Reconquista in Spain

1054 – Final schism between Rome and Constrantinople; Pope and Patriarch excommunicate each other

1075 – Pope Gregory VII declares the absolute authority of the Papacy

1076 – Seljuk Turks capture Jerusalem

1085 – Christians in Spain conquer Toledo

1095 – Byzantine Empire appeals to Pope for aid against Muslim invaders; Urban II calls for a Crusade

1096 – First Crusade; Christians attack Jewish communities throughout Europe

1099 – Crusaders retake Jerusalem; rebuild Church of the Holy Sepulcher

1100 – Kingdom of Jerusalem founded

1113 – Order of the Hospital of St. John of Jerusalem (Hospitallers) founded

c. 1118 – Order of Christ and the Temple of Solomon (Templars) founded

1148 – Crusade extended to include the Reconquista in Spain

1149 – Church of the Holy Sepulcher is rededicated

1187 – Battle of Hattin; Crusaders are badly defeated; Muslim forces under Saladin retake Jerusalem

1191 – Crusade of Richard I; Crusaders recover Acre

1192 – Treaty between Richard I and Saladin; Church issues edicts condemning Cathars in France

1204 – Catholic soldiers of the Fourth Crusade sack Orthodox Constantinople

1209 – Crusade against the Cathars

1210 – Order of Friar's Minor (Franciscans) founded

1212 – Children's Crusade disastrously results in many Christian children sold into slavery

1220 – Order of Preachers (Dominicans) founded

1233 – Beginning of the Inquisition in Toulouse, France

1248 – Christians in Spain conquer Seville

1255 – Roman Inquisition authorizes the use of torture on heretics and non-believers

1271 – Marco Polo rediscovers 'long lost' Nestorian Christians during his travels in Central Asia

1274 – Council of Lyons establishes regulations for the election of the Pope

1291 – Crusaders are driven from Acre; end of the Crusader Kingdoms

1302 – Unam Sanctam declares the supreme authority of the papacy

1305 - Papacy relocates to Avignon in France

1312 – Templars accused of heresy and dissolved throughout much of Europe; many are killed

1324 – German emperor refutes papal authority and is excommunicated

1348 – Black Plague spreads throughout Europe; disillusion with the Roman Catholic Church and the Papacy becomes widespread

Christianity in the Renaissance

1366 – England refuses to pay Papal taxes; John Wycliffe challenges papal supremacy

1378 – Babylonian Captivity; rival Popes exist in Rome and Avignon

1380 – John Wycliffe translates the Bible into English; Rise of the Lollards in England

1384 – Death of John Wycliffe

1387 – Lithuania converted to Christianity

1398 – Jan Hus begins lecturing in Prague; rise of the Hussites

1415 – Jan Hus burned for heresy; John Wycliffe posthumously declared a heretic

1417 – End of the Babylonian Captivity; Papacy returns to Rome

1419 – Defenstration of Prague; Hussites revolt against Catholics; beginning of Hussite Wars

1431 – Joan of Arc burned for heresy in France; Hussites win a string of victories against the Church

1439 – Catholic and Orthodox Christians briefly reunite, with Rome as seat of the Church

1448 – Russian Orthodox Church becomes independent but still in communion with Constantinople

1453 – Ottomans conquer Constantinople and rename it Istanbul; final end of the Roman Empire; the great church, Hagia Sofia, is converted into a mosque

1455 – First printed Bibles published by Gutenberg in Germany

1483 – Beginning of the Spanish Inquisition; Sistine Chapel in Rome completed

1492 – Fall of Grenada; end of the Reconquista in Spain; First voyage of Columbus; first Christian activity in the Americas

1494 – Dominican friar Savonarola establishes a theocracy in Florence

1498 – Savonarola is burned at the stake

1506 – Beginning of construction of new St. Peter's Basilica in Rome; Ulrich Zwingli ordained as a priest

1507 – Martin Luther ordained as a priest

1508 – Papacy grants Spain and Portugal religious authority in the New World

1514 – Beginning of forced mass conversions to Christianity among native peoples in the Americas

1517 – Luther writes the 95 Theses

1519 – Luther summoned to Rome to answer charge of heresy

1521 – Diet of Worms; Luther excommunicated

1525 – Prussia becomes a Protestant state; Catholic mass banned in Zurich

1529 – Papacy attempts to reconcile with German princes; Pope refuses to annul the marriage of Henry VIII of England to Catherine of Aragon

1531 – Protestant states begin to band together to oppose the Catholic Holy Roman Empire

1533 – Henry VIII of England is excommunicated

1534 – Henry VIII breaks away from the Roman Catholic Church; Church of England founded; Denmark becomes Lutheran; Luther translates the Bible into German; Founding of the Jesuit Order in Rome

1535 – Calvin writes the Institutes of the Christian Religion

1541 – Geneva adopts Calvinism; Catholic missionary Francis Xavier arrives in Southeast Africa

1542 – Francis Xavier arrives in India

1545 – Council of Trent; Beginning of the Counter-Reformation; Waldensian Protestants massacred in France

1549 – Introduction of the Protestant Book of Common Prayer in England; Huguenot Calvinists in France have become a significant portion of the population; Francis Xavier arrives in Japan

1550 – Jesuit missionaries arrive in Brazil

1551 – Francis Xavier arrives in China

1552 – Death of Francis Xavier

1553 – Roman Catholicism briefly restored in England under Mary Tudor

1555 – Protestants persecuted in England

1561 – John Knox introduces Reformed Christianity in Scotland

1562 – Beginning of Wars of Religion in France

1572 – St. Bartholomew's Day Massacre; thousands of Protestants in France martyred

1598 – Edict of Nantes restores Catholic Church in France; Huguenots flee in large numbers

1602 – Protestants in Central Europe are persecuted

1615 – Franciscan missionaries arrive in Canada

1618 – Bohemian Protestants revolt against the Holy Roman Empire; beginning of Thirty Years War

1620 – Puritans arrive in the New World and establish a religious colony at Plymouth, Massachusetts

1625 – Denmark joins war against Holy Roman Empire

1630 – Sweden joins war against Holy Roman Empire

1636 – France joins war against Holy Roman Empire

1644 – Roman Catholic forces defeated in Central Europe

1648 – Peace of Westphalia ends the Thirty Years War

Christianity in the Colonial Era

1649 – Oliver Cromwell and the Puritans come to power in England; Charles I executed

1649 – Maryland issues laws promoting religious tolerance

1656 – Virginia extends voting rights to all free men regardless of religion

1661 – Quakers hold their first meeting in Rhode Island

1685 – Renewed persecution of Protestants in France; Huguenots flee to South Carolina; James II, a Catholic, becomes King of England

1692 – Edict of Toleration issued for Catholics in China

1692 – Salem Witch Trials in the American colony of Massachusetts

1697 – Holy Roman Empire begins taking territory back from the Ottomans; Jesuit missionaries arrive in California

1700 – First Baptist Association formed in Rhode Island

1701 – Act of Establishment bans Catholics from the English throne

1702 – Huguenots revolt against the French monarchy

1711 – Christopher Wren completes St. Paul's Cathedral in London

1712 – Last execution for witchcraft in England

1741 – Scots-Irish Presbyterians begin immigrating to America

1742 – Handel writes *Messiah*

1748 – First Lutheran synod in the colonies in Philadelphia

1772 – Papacy suppresses the Jesuit Order

1789 – *Declaration of the Rights of Man* supports the idea of freedom of religion

1791 – *Bill of Rights* guarantees freedom of religion in the United States

1806 – End of the thousand-years-old Holy Roman Empire

1807 – Freedom of religion instituted in France; English Protestant missionaries reach China

1814 – English Protestant missionaries reach New Zealand

1825 – Joseph Smith founds Mormonism in New York

1834 – End of the Inquisition as an institution of the Roman Catholic Church

1843 – Russian Orthodox Church establishes missions in Alaska

1847 – Mormons reach Salt Lake City

1854 – Papacy declares Mary the Mother of Jesus free of original sin

1858 – Bernadette Soubirous sees an apparition of the Virgin Mary in Lourdes, France

1872 – Prussia enacts laws curbing the activities of the Catholic Church

1877 – Russia declares war on the Ottoman Empire, ostensibly over Christian rights

1878 – Salvation Army founded in England

1895 – Anti-Christian riots in China

1915 – One million Armenian Christians massacred or deported by Turkey

1916 – D.W. Griffith's *Intolerance* becomes the first major film to depict Jesus of Nazareth

1917 – Russian Revolution; over a thousand Orthodox priests are martyred over the next few years

1920 – Holy Land mandated to Britain and France

1922 – Soviet Union begins suppression of organized religion in Eastern Europe

1929 – Lateran Accords signed by Benito Mussolini guaranty independence of Vatican City

1933 – Nazis take power in Germany; tens of thousands of clergymen, mostly Catholic, are persecuted or murdered over the next twelve years; millions of Jews and other civilians are slaughtered in the Holocaust

Christianity in the Modern Age

1945 – Nag Hammadi library discovered in Egypt; it contains long lost Gnostic Christian texts

1946 – Dead Sea Scrolls, containing oldest known Biblical writings, discovered in Qumram

1947 – Billy Graham launches his ministry and first Crusade in the United States

1948 – Creation of independent state of Israel; Israel War of Independence; founding of the World Council of Churches in Geneva, Switzerland

1950 – Mother Teresa founds Missionaries of Charity in Calcutta, India

1962 – Second Vatican Council begins; it results in many changes in Roman Catholic traditions and practices, including the use of vernacular languages in worship

1963 – March on Washington led by the Reverend Dr. Martin Luther King Jr.; he delivers the famous *I Have a Dream* speech

1964 – First Papal visit to the Holy Land in the modern era; possibly the first since Peter in the 1st century

1965 – Roman Catholic and Eastern Orthodox Churches issue joint declaration initiating dialogue between the two institutions for the first time in centuries; Shrine of the Book constructed in Jerusalem to house ancient Biblical texts

1969 – Basilica of the Annunciation completed in Nazareth

1970 – Orthodox Church in America founded in communion with other Eastern Orthodox Churches

1974 – Haile Selassie, the last Christian emperor of Ethiopia, is deposed

1978 – John Paul II becomes first non-Italian Pope of the Roman Catholic Church since the 15th century

1988 – Persecution of Christians in Soviet Union largely ends after seven decades

2004 – *The Passion of the Christ* becomes the most successful film ever made about the life of Jesus

2013 – Benedict XVI becomes the first Pope to voluntarily resign in nearly six centuries; Francis becomes the first Pope to come from the Americas

2014 – Widespread persecution of Assyrian Christians in Iraq during the region's occupation by the forces of ISIS

HOLY LAND

1. CHURCH OF THE HOLY SEPULCHRE

Shuk ha-Tsaba'im Street, Christian Quarter, Jerusalem, Israel

Alternate/Full Names: Church of the Resurrection, Church of the Anastasis
Denomination: Roman Catholic, Greek Orthodox, Armenian Apostolic (sacred to most Christians)
Dates: 335 (originally completed), 1149 (current building completed)
Web: www.custodia.org/en/sancutaries/holy-sepulchre (official Catholic website)

The Church of the Holy Sepulchre is, for the vast majority of the world's Christians, the most sacred place on Earth. Contained within its walls are the final Stations of the Cross, including the traditional locations where Jesus of Nazareth was crucified and where he was buried. Millions of Christians from around the world flood into Jerusalem's Old City every year for the chance to worship in this church. Jointly overseen by the Catholic, Orthodox and Armenian churches, it is held in trust for Christians of every denomination.

The pivotal event of the life of Jesus of Nazareth was his Crucifixion and Resurrection. These events, commemorated during the Christian Holy Week on Good Friday and Easter Sunday respectively, are the most sacred days on the Christian calendar. Naturally, the sites of these events have been highly venerated since the earliest days of the Church. After the legalization of Christianity in the Roman Empire in the 4th century, a new interest was taken in its holy places. The greatest and most important of these, without question, was the Holy Sepulchre in Jerusalem.

Over the centuries, Jerusalem and the Holy Sepulchre came under the control of a long succession of conquerors. The church was largely destroyed during the early years of Islamic rule but rebuilt by Crusaders in the Middle Ages. After the Muslim reconquest of Jerusalem in

1187, it was promised by Saladin that the Christian pilgrims would be permitted to continue to visit the city. The Holy Sepulchre was allowed to remain standing, and Saladin's promise has largely been honored down through the centuries.

Today, with Jerusalem firmly under control of the Israeli government, Christians of all denominations are now free to visit the Holy Sepulchre year-round. After centuries of squabbling, an agreement known as the Status Quo was reached in the 18th century. The Supulchre is now under the joint jurisdiction of the Roman Catholic Church, the Greek Orthodox Church and the Armenian Apostolic Church, all of whom have a sitting patriarch in Jerusalem.

Of Interest: The Church of the Holy Sepulchre dominates what is believed by many to be the ancient hill of Golgotha. A huge structure crowned with a massive dome, the true size of the church is difficult to ascertain from the outside due to its strange layout and the crowding of nearby buildings, not to mention its relatively humble entrance. The famous "immovable ladder", which has remained in the same place for nearly three hundred years, can be seen over the entryway. The church interior is a magnificent labyrinth of chapels, halls and rooms decorated with a wealth of artifacts and artwork that reflect numerous contributions over many centuries. Most of the points of interest are directly related to Christ's death, including the last five of the fourteen Stations of the Cross. They include the place where he was stripped of his garments (10), where he was nailed to the cross (11), where the cross was erected (12) and the spot where his body was prepared for burial (13). The highlight of the church is the Holy Sepulcher itself (14), where Jesus was laid to rest in the donated tomb. The Sepulcher consists of an enclosed stone shrine located directly beneath the great dome. The cave where Jesus was believed to be buried can be found here.

2. CHURCH OF ST. ANNE & VIA DOLOROSA

Lion's Gate Street, Muslim Quarter, Jerusalem, Israel

Denomination: Roman Catholic (sacred to many Christians)
Dates: c. 5th century (originally completed), 1138 (current building completed)
Web: www.itraveljerusalem.com/ent/church-st-anne (tourism website) & www.theviadolorosa.org (official website)

The Church of St. Anne is one of the oldest mostly intact churches in Jerusalem. According to tradition it stands on the site of the birthplace of Mary, the Mother of Jesus. It also roughly marks the starting point of the Via Dolorosa, or the "Way of Sorrows". This series of streets marks the traditionally accepted route that Jesus walked on his way to the Crucifixion, and terminates at the Church of the Holy Sepulchre in the Christian Quarter.

There are several Biblical traditions associated with the Church of St. Anne. The more commonly known one is that the home of Joachim and Anna, the parents of Mary and the maternal grandparents of Jesus, was located on or near the site. Another is that this was once the site of the Pool of Bethesda of New Testament fame. While there is little evidence for the former, archaeological research does support the latter. A Byzantine-era basilica stood on the site as early as the 5th century.

The current church was constructed in the 12th century by the Crusaders. Just out in front of the Church of St. Anne is the traditional gathering spot for pilgrims starting the Via Dolorosa walk. Over the centuries there have been a number of different routes marking the Way of Sorrows, but the current route wasn't fixed until the 18th century. Its course runs past nine of the Fourteen Stations of the Cross.

The first two Stations of the Cross, located close to St. Anne's, mark places where the trial of Jesus took place. The next seven stations alternatively mark places where Jesus fell (stations 3, 7, and 9) and where he encountered various citizens including his mother Mary (stations 4, 5, 6 and 8). The route is well marked, and thousands of pilgrims walk the Via Dolorosa every day. A formal Roman Catholic procession, led by Franciscan monks, takes place on Fridays.

Of Interest: The Church of St. Anne is one of Jerusalem's best surviving examples of Crusader architecture. One of the piers of the Pools of Bethesda still survives on the grounds of the church. An altar stands over the grotto where tradition holds that Mary was born. The church is currently overseen by a missionary organization known as the White Fathers. The nine Stations of the Cross along the Via Dolorosa are all commemorated with either small shrines or full-on churches. These include the Church of the Condemnation, the Church of the Flagellation, and the Church of Ecce Homo.

---

3. CATHEDRAL OF ST. JAMES

Armenian Orthodox Patriarchate Street,
Armenia Quarter, Jerusalem, Israel

Alternate/Full Name: Saints Jacobs Armenian Cathedral
Denomination: Armenian Apostolic
Dates: c. 5th century (originally completed), 1142 (current building completed)
Web: https://armenian-patriarchate.com/st-james-cathedral (official website)

The Cathedral of St. James is the seat of the Armenian Patriarch of Jerusalem and is the heart of the city's Armenian quarter. Dedicated to both St. James the Greater and St. James the Lesser, it is one of the oldest churches in the city and one of the most important Oriental Orthodox churches in the world. St. Thaddeus and St. Bartholomew, founders of the Armenian Apostolic Church, are also honored here.

A church has stood on this spot at least as far back as the 5th century. It honored the two Apostles who were most closely associated with the city. The first was James the Just, brother of Jesus and the first Patriarch of Jerusalem, who is typically equated with the Apostle James the Lesser. The second was James the son of Zebedee, brother of John, who was martyred here in the mid-1st century. The original church was destroyed by Persian invaders in the 7th century and rebuilt in the Middle Ages.

The Armenian Church separated from the Catholic-Orthodox Church in 554, and an independent Patriarchate of Jerusalem has been maintained ever since. Other than periods when the cathedral came under the jurisdiction of outsiders, including Muslims and Catholic Crusaders, St. James' has served as the headquarters of the Patriarchate. Unlike Jerusalem's other major churches, access to the Cathedral of St. James is limited and typically only open to the public during the afternoon worship.

Of Interest: The Cathedral of St. James is considered by many to be among Jerusalem's most beautiful and exotic churches. The exterior, with its unusual round-peaked roof and minaret-like clock tower, is best appreciated from a more distant vantage point than is available at the main entrance. The church is home to a number of relics as well as a wealth of artwork. Some of the finest iconic paintings in Jerusalem can be found here. Among the cathedral's treasures is the patriarchal throne, used by the Armenian Patriarch on special occasions. It stands upon what is believed to be the original gravesite of James the Lesser.

---

4. CHRIST CHURCH

Armenian Orthodox Patriarchate Street 55,
Armenian Quarter, Jerusalem, Israel

Denomination: Episcopal Church in Jerusalem and the Middle East
Dates: 1849 (completed)
Web: www.cmj-israel.org (official website)

Christ Church is the historic church of the Anglican Communion in Jerusalem. It claims the distinction of being the oldest church building in the Holy Land that is not of Catholic or Orthodox origin. Christ Church was among the most politically important churches in the region during the early 20th century, when Jerusalem was governed under the British Mandate.

The Anglican Church became established in what was then Palestine in the 1840s. Christ Church, the first major church to be constructed in the Holy Land by one of the major western powers, was completed in 1849. For the next half century it served as the seat of the city's Anglican bishop, and for nearly seventy years doubled as the home of the British consulate.

Christ Church was the center of British religious life in Jerusalem until St. George's Cathedral was completed. The seat of the diocese was relocated to St. George's in 1899. Nevertheless Christ Church remains an active house of worship. Thanks to its excellent location just inside the Jaffa Gate, it is also a popular first stop for English-speaking pilgrims to the Old City.

Of Interest: Christ Church is a large, Colonial-era structure located just inside the Jaffa Gate right across the street from the Tower of David. It is part of a complex that includes a guest house and a visitor's center. Despite its age and the fact that it survived significant turbulence throughout its history, the magnificent building looks almost new. In honor of the church's long ties to the local Jewish community, the interior of Christ Church is adorned with numerous symbols of Judaica in both objects and artwork, including a traditional menorah displayed before a replica of a Torah ark.

---

5. CHURCH OF THE REDEEMER

Muristan Street, Jerusalem, Israel

Alternate/Full Name: Lutheran Church of the Redeemer
Denomination: Lutheran
Dates: c. 11th century (originally completed),

1898 (current building completed)
Web: www.elcjhl.org/elcjhl-ministries/congregations/jerusalem (official website)

The Church of the Redeemer is simultaneously the oldest traditional Protestant church standing in the Holy Land as well as the newest church standing within the walls of the Old City. Completed in the late 19th century, it is the seat of the Evangelical Lutheran Church in Israel. The Church of the Redeemer is home to two of Jerusalem's best kept secrets: its bell tower, with some of the best views of the Christian Quarter; and a recently opened subterranean archaeology exhibit with some of Jerusalem's oldest ruins.

German colonists began arriving in the Holy Land in the 1860s and 1870s, establishing themselves first at Haifa and later at Jerusalem. During this time the Ottoman Empire gifted a site in the Christian Quarter of Jerusalem to Kaiser Wilhelm I of Germany. This site had formerly been home to a series of earlier churches on land granted from the Caliph Harun al-Rashid to Charlemagne more than a thousand years earlier.

Wilhelm sponsored the construction of the Church of the Redeemer and personally attended its dedication in 1898. At the time of its completion it was the first and only fully Protestant, non-Anglican church in Jerusalem. It has since served as the seat of the Lutheran Church in the Holy Land. During the 1970s, part of the area beneath the church was excavated by archaeologists. In 2012 this site was opened up as a small archaeological park run by the church.

Of Interest: The Church of the Redeemer is a magnificent colonial-era structure that stands just a short distance from the Church of the Holy Sepulchre in the heart of the Old City's Christian Quarter. The bell tower, one of the highest points in the city, offers a spectacular view of the Holy Sepulchre and its dome. The church interior is spacious and beautiful if a bit utilitarian. Beneath the church is an archaeological site with excavated ruins dating back to the Roman and Crusader eras. The archaeological site is open to the public.

---

6. ABBEY OF THE DORMITION & COENACULUM

Har Tsiyon Street, Mount Zion, Jerusalem, Israel

Alternate/Full Name: Abbey of Hagia Maria Sion
Denomination: Roman Catholic & Formerly Roman Catholic (sacred to many Christians)
Dates: Abbey - c. 415 (originally completed), 1910 (current building completed) & Coenaculum - c. 1200 (completed)
Web: www.dormitio.net (official website) & www.itraveljerusalem.com/ent/the-last-supper-room (tourism website)

The Abbey of the Dormition and the Coenaculum are a pair of neighboring shrines on Mt. Zion that are of great interest to many Christians. The former stands on a site traditionally held to be the location where Mary the Mother of Jesus died and from where she subsequently ascended to Heaven. The latter is home to several rooms of Judeo-Christian interest, including what is believed to be the Upper Room, where Jesus may have dined with his Apostles at the Last Supper.

The Last Supper is one of the pivotal and most famous events of the New Testament. While the actual location of the Last Supper is unknown, tradition has placed it on Mt. Zion, which at the time was inside the city walls and part of the wealthy district. The Dormition of Mary, while not mentioned in the Bible, is a very ancient tradition also associated with Mt. Zion. The location where both buildings now stand has been sacred to Christians since at least Roman times.

A Byzantine church stood where the Abbey of the Dormition now stands at least as far back as the 5th century. Destroyed during the Persian invasion, it was rebuilt in the Middle Ages and again in the early 20th century. The Coenaculum is one of the oddest religious sites in a city of odd religious sites. This former church and mosque is sacred to Christians, Muslims and Jews. On the lower level is a burial vault believed to contain the Tomb of David. On the upper level is a large hall where Christians believe the Last Supper took place. The Coenaculum is currently under the jurisdiction of the Israeli government.

Of Interest: Both the Abbey of the Dormition and the Coenaculum are located south of the Zion Gate just outside of the Old City walls. The abbey church is a relatively modern building with magnificent golden artwork decorating its interior. Stairs lead down to a crypt beneath the church where the Dormition of Mary is said to have taken place. The Coenaculum houses David's Tomb in the lower level and the Room of the Last Supper in the upper level. The Room of the Last Supper is accessible up a back staircase and across the roof of the tomb. The hall where the Last Supper is said to have taken place is gothic and sparse, leaving visions of the New Testament meal up to visitor's imaginations.

---

7. ST. GEORGE'S CATHEDRAL & GARDEN TOMB

Nablus Road 20, Jerusalem, Israel

Denomination: Episcopal Church in Jerusalem and the Middle East (sacred to many Protestants)
Dates: Cathedral - 1898 (completed) & Garden Tomb - 1867 (identified)
Web: www.j-diocese.org & https://gardentomb.com (official websites)

St. George's Cathedral is the seat of the Anglican Church in Israel. It was among the earliest major Protestant churches in Jerusalem to be situated outside of the Old City walls. The seat of the Anglican bishop in the Holy Land, the Cathedral of St. George has been closely associated with the Garden Tomb since the late 19th century. To this day the Garden Tomb remains under the care of the Anglican Church in Jerusalem.

The Garden Tomb is a site on the north side of Jerusalem outside of the Old City Walls that is considered to be an alternate location for the Crucifixion of Jesus. While the Church of the Holy Sepulchre has been the traditional site for pilgrims for at least seventeen centuries, the Garden Tomb location, identified in 1867, fits the Biblical narrative much more closely. Belief in the Garden Tomb location as the actual site of the Crucifixion has been gaining ground among Christians, especially Anglicans and Protestants, in recent years.

Despite nearly two thousand years of tradition, the evidence that the Crucifixion took place at the current site of the Church of the Holy Sepulchre is not conclusive. In the mid-19th century, researchers began investigating the odd rock formations north of the Damascus Gate. One formation of whitish rock with natural cavities bears a striking resemblance to a skull. Moreover, it overlooks the route of an old Roman road leading away from the city. While it is impossible to know with certainty if this was the true Golgotha, or Place of the Skull, no other reasonable alternative has been identified.

In 1894, the Anglican Church purchased a site that incorporated an area that included an excellent vantage of the skull rock as well as an ancient Jewish Tomb. While it is highly unlikely that this was the true sepulcher of Jesus, it is nevertheless an excellent example of the sort of tomb in which someone in the 1st century might have been buried. The tomb, the garden and the view of the skull are now all part of the Garden Tomb site.

Of Interest: The Cathedral of St. George is located outside the walls not too far from the Garden Tomb. The cathedral blends several architectural styles, with stonework that makes the buildings look much older than they are. Within the building is a feature unusual in Anglican churches: a bath large enough to perform full immersion baptisms. The Garden Tomb is as different an experience from the Holy Sepulchre as can be imagined. Consisting of a large, well-sculpted garden, there are copses of trees and bush-lined paths leading to quiet, contemplative spots. A covered seating area offers a magnificent view of the skull-like rock that may be ancient Golgotha. Nearby, carved into the side of the rock, is an ancient tomb that may date the 1st century. The tomb has a small entrance, inside of which is a room with a stone table where the body of the occupant would have been laid out. A sign on the inside of the door reads "He is not here... for He is risen!"

---

8. MOUNT OF OLIVES

Mount of Olives, East Jerusalem, Israel

Alternate/Full Name: Mount Olivet
Denomination: General Christian
Web: https://mountofolives.co.il (official website)

The Mount of Olives is one of the most famous landmarks of the Bible. Home to a sprawling, ancient Jewish cemetery, this hill overlooking the Old City of Jerusalem is sacred to both Jews and Christians. A number of major events mentioned in the New Testament took place on the Mount of Olives. Not surprisingly the mountain is covered with churches and Christian shrines commemorating these events (note that the Chapel of the Ascension and the Garden of Gethsemane are covered in their own sections).

In the weeks leading up to the Crucifixion, virtually every event in the final days of the ministry of Jesus took place either in Jerusalem or on the Mount of Olives. He raised Lazarus in Bethany on its eastern slope, spent the night before his arrest in the Garden of Gethsemane on its western slope, and ascended to Heaven from its peak. The Olivet Discourse, with its prophecy of destruction, was delivered here.

The Mount of Olives has been a sacred place of pilgrimage to Christians since the 1st century, especially in the years after the Great Revolt and destruction of Jerusalem at the hands of the Romans. Churches have been springing up all over its slopes since the days of the Byzantine Empire. According to local tradition, Mary the mother of Jesus was buried here, if only for a brief time. Moreover, no other place offers such a spectacular view of the Old City and the Temple Mount than the peak of this historic hill.

Of Interest: The Mount of Olives is dotted with many churches, shrines and Biblical tombs. Much of the hill is covered with a sprawling, ancient Jewish cemetery which contains the Old Testament burial sites of Absolom, Zechariah, Haggai and Malachi, just to name a few. The great golden-domed church that dominates the western slope is the Russian Orthodox Church of Mary Magdalene, which honors Jesus' most famous female disciple. Along the road between Jerusalem's Lion's Gate and the hill is the Tomb of the Virgin Mary, one of the places where the mother of Jesus may have been buried after her death.

---

9. CHURCH OF ALL NATIONS & GARDEN OF GETHSEMANE

El-Mansuriya Street, Mount of Olives, East Jerusalem, Israel

Alternate/Full Names: Church of the Agony, Basilica of the Agony
Denomination: Roman Catholic (sacred to most Christians)
Dates: c. 4th century (originally completed),
1924 (current building completed)
Web: www.custodia.org/en/sanctuaries/gethsemane (official website)

The Church of All Nations is one of the many magnificent churches that grace the western slope of the Mount of Olives. Located next to the Garden of Gethsemane, it stands on the site where Jesus is believed to have prayed the night of his arrest. The olive trees in front of the church are at least a thousand years old, possibly much older, and are the descendents of a grove that dates back to before the Christian era.

The final events leading up to the arrest of Jesus took place on the Mount of Olives. After the Last Supper, Jesus came to the Garden of Gethsemane with his disciples Peter, James and John. It was here that he prayed in desperation to God to take away his coming tribulation; where he sweated blood in agony; where he was betrayed by Judas; and where, finally, he was arrested by the priests and soldiers of the Temple.

Of all of the places mentioned in the New Testament, there are few that are known with such certainty as the location of the Garden of Gethsemane. Although it may not be possible to pinpoint the exact spot where the agony or arrest of Jesus took place, it was probably on or fairly close to where the remaining olive grove still stands. The area has been visited by pilgrims since the earliest days of Christianity, and may in fact have been a regular meeting place for Christians even before the Great Revolt.

Of Interest: The Church of All Nations is a modernish Neo-Byzantine building that stands on the site of several earlier churches. It is so named because contributions for the construction of the church came from Catholic communities all over the world. The church enshrines an exposed rock that is believed to be the exact spot where Jesus prayed with his apostles before he was arrested. The grove of olive trees just outside of the church is a verifiable remnant of the Garden of Gethsemane of Jesus' day. The current trees have been dated back to the 11th century. It is one of the most peaceful, prayerful places in Jerusalem.

---

10. CHAPEL OF THE ASCENSION

Rub'a el-Adawiya Street, Mount of Olives, East Jerusalem, Israel

Denomination: Formerly Roman Catholic
(sacred to most Christians)
Dates: c. 4th century (originally completed),
1150 (current building completed)
Web: https://info.goisrael.com/en/chapel-of-the-ascension-60821
(tourism website)

The Chapel of the Ascension at the top of the Mount of Olives is chronologically the last of the major holy sites associated with the life of Jesus. While it has been in use as a mosque for centuries, Saladin granted Christians access to the shrine in perpetuity, and it remains first and foremost a Christian holy place. The chapel is venerated by Christians and Muslims, both of whom recognize it as the site of the Ascension of Jesus to Heaven.

A few weeks after the Crucifixion and Resurrection, Jesus returned to the hills east of Jerusalem where he spent the final days of his time on Earth. According to the New Testament, he made appearances in the area, including upon the Mount of Olives. While the Bible is unclear as to exactly where the Ascension of Jesus took place, the most popular tradition is that it occurred at the peak of the hill.

Christians have revered this spot as the location of the Ascension since the Roman era. An early shrine commemorating this event was located in a cave on the hill's lower slopes, kept secret out of fear of persecution. The Byzantines erected a church on the site in the 4th century. This first incarnation of the chapel was unique among early Byzantine churches in that it was constructed with an open ceiling in honor of the Ascension.

The chapel did not fare well over the centuries. It was destroyed twice, once by the Persians and once by the Muslims. It was rebuilt in the 12th century by the Crusaders, but seized by Saladin during his conquest of Jerusalem in 1187. As a gesture of goodwill he permitted Christian pilgrims to continue to visit the chapel, who were coming anyway. This arrangement has been honored to the present day, and the mosque continues to welcome Christian visitors more than eight centuries later.

Of Interest: The Chapel of the Ascension is located at the highest point of the Mount of Olives. The current shrine largely dates from the Crusader period, but incorporates elements of earlier Byzantine- and Persian-era shrines, as well as later additions contributed by Muslim rulers. The shrine is enclosed within a walled compound which incorporates the chapel as well as a crypt. Nobody is exactly certain who if anyone is buried inside this mysterious tomb. Within the sparse interior of the small, octagonal shrine is an odd relic: the Ascension Rock. It has an impression of a footprint which some believe was made by Jesus at the moment of his departure.

11. ISRAEL MUSEUM & SHRINE OF THE BOOK

Derech Ruppin Boulevard 11, Jerusalem, Israel

Denomination: Public Museum
Dates: 1965 (opened)
Web: www.imj.org.il (official website)

The Israel Museum is the national museum of the State of Israel and one of the world's greatest repositories of Biblical artifacts. A sprawling world-class complex, no other museum in Israel boasts so large or diverse a collection of antiquities and art. Designed to capture the immense, grandiose history of this ancient land and its people, it is home to an exceptional collection of artifacts of Christian interest. Among its many exhibits are archaeological treasures that can be directly tied to the New Testament and early Christianity, as well as some of the oldest surviving Biblical writings.

It has been suggested that it is impossible to dig up a shovel full of dirt in the Holy Land without uncovering some ancient artifact or bit of archaeological ruin. In the 19th and early 20th centuries, expeditions sponsored by governments and universities from around the world descended on the Holy Land intent on uncovering the secrets of the Biblical world.

In 1925, James Henry Breasted, an archaeologist and professor at the University of Chicago, was visiting Palestine when he learned that there was no proper institution for the preservation, study, display and storage of the region's antiquities. Working with John D. Rockefeller Jr., who supplied substantial funds for the project, Breasted saw to the establishment of an archaeology museum in Jerusalem. In 1938, the Palestine Archaeological Museum, also known as the Rockefeller Museum, was opened. It became the official repository for many of the Holy Land's greatest finds. Since 1948, it has also been home to the Israel Department of Antiquities and Museums.

In the 1960s, it was decided that a more modern and much larger facility was needed. The Israel Museum was established as the country's national museum, designed to house and display not only the best pieces of the huge archaeological collection, but also exhibits on Jewish art and culture. The old Rockefeller Museum is now run as an annex of the Israel Museum, which has become one of the most popular museums in the entire Middle East.

Of Interest: The Israel Museum is a sprawling masterpiece of modern architecture that occupies a twenty-acre site in West Jerusalem. While the main focus is on Judaica, there is a huge collection of Christian artifacts, some pieces of great New Testament importance, mostly on display in the archaeological wing. These include, among other things, the Sarcophagus of Herod the Great, the Ossuary of Caiaphas the High Priest and the Pilate Stone. The latter is the only absolutely authoritative contemporary mention of any of the major New Testament figures. Another popular exhibit for Christian visitors is a spectacular, sprawling scale model of Jerusalem during the Second Temple Period which had formerly been on display at the Jerusalem Holy Land Hotel. The Shrine of the Book houses some of the world's oldest surviving Biblical writings, including the fabled Dead Sea Scrolls.

---

12. TOMB OF LAZARUS

Al-Hardub Street, Al-Eizariya, West Bank

Denomination: Formerly Roman Catholic
(sacred to many Christians)
Dates: c. 4th century (originally completed),
1384 (current building completed)
Web: www.custodia.org/en/sanctuaries/bethany
(official Catholic website)

The Tomb of Lazarus in Al-Eizariya, or Bethany, is one of two burial sites for this famous Christian figure. This one is where Lazarus' body was buried the first time he died, and where Jesus is believed to have raised him from the dead. The other, in Cyprus, is where the body is currently believed to be interred. Both sites have been venerated by Christians since Roman times.

In the last days of his ministry, Jesus made his way to Jerusalem to celebrate Passover. The final stop on his journey was the village of Bethany. There, the sisters Mary and Martha implored Jesus to heal their brother Lazarus, who was recently deceased. Jesus went to the tomb and commanded Lazarus to come forth, which he did. Word of this miracle spread like wildfire, including to nearby Jerusalem. It was this miracle more than anything else that cemented Jesus as a celebrity prior to his arrival in the capital, and why such huge crowds greeted his triumphant entrance into Jerusalem on Palm Sunday.

A church was documented to have stood on the site of the tomb as early as the 4th century. Destroyed by an earthquake a few centuries later, it was replaced by a succession of other churches which were also later destroyed. In 1384 a mosque was built at the site. Although Christians were permitted to worship in the mosque, they cut their own entrance into the tomb in the 16th century. This remains the primary entrance to the tomb for Christian pilgrims to the present day.

Of Interest: The Tomb of Lazarus is among the least developed of all of the sacred Christian sites in the Holy Land. While some pilgrims are disappointed by the lack of a major shrine at the site, others enjoy its sparseness and lack of gaudy trappings. Access to the tomb itself requires a difficult backwards climb down a steep staircase and a crawl through a passage leading to the room where Lazarus' body is believed to have been interred.

---

13. CHURCH OF THE NATIVITY

Manger Square, Bethlehem, West Bank

Alternate/Full Name: Basilica of the Nativity
Denominations: Roman Catholic, Greek Orthodox, Armenian Apostolic (sacred to most Christians)

Dates: c. 330 century (originally completed),
565 (current building completed)
Web: www.custodia.org/en/sanctuaries/bethlehem
(official Catholic website)

The Church of the Nativity stands on the traditional site of the birthplace of Jesus Christ, and is generally regarded as Christianity's second holiest site. The current structure dates in large part to the 6th century and is one of the oldest churches still in use in the world. Like the Holy Sepulchre, the Church of the Nativity is overseen by several major denominations in a complex arrangement that dates back centuries. For many Christians it is the penultimate Christmas pilgrimage destination.

Bethlehem was an important Jewish town long before the birth of Christ. It was the ancestral home of King David and the House of Judah, from whom Jesus was descended. During the reign of Caesar Augustus, sometime around the year 4 BC, Mary and Joseph were required to travel to Bethlehem in order to register for the imperial census. What followed is probably the single most famous narrative in the New Testament: The Nativity of Jesus.

There is no way today to tell with any certainty exactly where the famous inn and manger once stood. However, sometime around the early 2nd century the Romans erected a pagan temple on the site in an effort to discourage Christian pilgrims. This not only failed to deter the Christians from secretly visiting, it inadvertently kept the location well marked. When Helena arrived in the Holy Land in the 4th century looking for holy places upon which to construct shrines, the local Christians showed her exactly where to build.

This first church survived until 529 when it was destroyed in the Samaritan Revolt. It was replaced by a new church based on the original plans and has remained standing ever since. Although the Church of the Nativity remained in Muslim hands from 1187 onwards, Christians were generally allowed to continue to visit. Starting around 1347, the shrine was held in trust by the Franciscans. However, ever since the Orthodox Church was allowed to return to the area in the 16th century, Catholic and Orthodox partisans have bickered over the guardianship of the site. The Church of the Nativity is currently in the joint custody of the Roman Catholic, Greek Orthodox and Armenian Apostolic churches.

After the Six-Day War in 1967, Bethlehem became more accessible to Christians, and pilgrims began flocking back to the Church of the Nativity. In 2002, the Church of the Nativity was the site of a tense standoff between Palestinian gunmen and Israeli military forces. Neither this nor the current political situation in the West Bank has stopped countless determined and enthusiastic pilgrims from coming to this second holiest of Christian destinations.

Of Interest: The Church of the Nativity consists of the main church structure above and the grottoes below, as well as the adjoining St. Catherine's Church. The main church is entered through the tiny Door of Humility, so called because it forces all those entering to bend over low. The interior mostly dates from the Byzantine period, with many embellishments added later, including an oak ceiling donated by King Edward IV of England. A mosaic of the Three Wise Men is the shrine's most famous piece of art. Legend has it that this decoration saved the Church from demolition by the Persians. The main attraction is the Grotto of the Nativity located beneath the Church. Inside, a fourteen-pointed star, symbolizing the Star of Bethlehem and the Stations of the Cross, marks the traditional place where Jesus was born. A Latin inscription reads 'Here Jesus Christ was born to the Virgin Mary'. Fifteen lamps, gifts of various Christian churches, illuminate the sanctuary. Also of note is the neighboring St. Catherine's Church, which is home to the Tomb of St. Jerome as well as the Chapel of the Innocents.

---

14. CHAPEL OF THE SHEPHERD'S FIELD

Belt Sahour, Bethlehem, West Bank

Denomination: Roman Catholic
Dates: c. 5th century (originally completed),
1953 (current building completed)
Web: www.custodia.org/en/sanctuaries/bethlehem-shepherds-field-and-grotto (official website)

The Chapel of the Shepherd's Field stands on the site where, according to tradition, angels announced to shepherds watching their flocks by night that a savior had been born to them. The story of this event is recounted in the Book of Luke in one of the most moving passages in the entire New Testament, and has been celebrated on this spot since Roman times. Many pilgrims who come to Bethlehem find the Chapel of the Shepherd's Field to be a quiet, contemplative alternative to the insane crowds of the Church of the Nativity in the center of town.

According to the Biblical account, on the night that Jesus was born, angels descended from the heavens to bring the good news to the people of Bethlehem. The first to receive the miraculous message were shepherds in the fields nearby. The fact that these poorest of the poor were the ones to receive this great honor would later become symbolic of everything Jesus stood for in his teachings and ministry.

A church was documented to have stood on the site as far back as the 5th century, but like most other early churches of the Holy Land did not survive the area's many invasions and occupations. The current church was only completed in 1953. While some pilgrims choose to visit this church first in order to do things in Biblical order, others come here after visiting the Church of the Nativity in order to recover from the chaos and enjoy a more quiet, reflective moment.

Of Interest: The Chapel of the Shepherd's Field is a relatively small building surrounded by a somewhat undeveloped area so that pilgrims can actually see what's left of the fields and imagine what it was like two thousand years ago. A stone carving of an angel hovers over the main entrance. The interior of the church is decorated with frescoes of the angels and shepherds. It is not uncommon for visitors to find groups of pilgrims here singing Christmas carols regardless of the time of year.

---

15. MONASTERY OF THE TEMPTATION

Mount of Temptation, Jericho, West Bank

Denomination: Greek Orthodox (sacred to many Christians)
Dates: c. 6th century (originally completed),
1895 (current building completed)
Web: www.visitpalestine.ps/where-to-go/city/jericho/sites-attractions-jericho (tourism website)

The Monastery of the Temptation is a relatively recently complex constructed on top of one of Christianity's most ancient sacred sites. According to tradition which dates back at least to the 4th century, the mountain upon which the monastery stands was the location where Jesus spent forty days in the wilderness preparing for his ministry. Although off the beaten path, it remains a destination that die hard Christian pilgrims will go out of their way to reach.

According to the New Testament, right after Jesus was baptized, he headed out into the wilderness, presumably towards the Dead Sea. There he spent forty days fasting and praying. Towards the end of this period, hungry and tired, Jesus was confronted by none other than Satan himself. During this encounter, the devil famously tempted Jesus three times in an effort to get him to change His allegiance. According to locals, Jesus rejected these temptations on this very mountain.

An early monastery stood on this spot at least as far back as the Byzantine era. During the Middle Ages, Crusaders built several new churches here. These were in turn replaced in the 19th century by a new Orthodox monastery. This monastery remains in use, with monks caring for the site and making sure it is available and accessible to visiting pilgrims.

Of Interest: The Monastery of the Temptation clings dramatically to the side of a cliff halfway up the slope of the Mountain of Temptation. Concealed within its walls is a cave where Jesus is believed to have dwelt during his forty day hermitage. The cave now contains a chapel which is the main destination for pilgrims. A cable car provides easy access to the monastery.

---

16. CHURCH OF ST. PHOTINI

Balatah Street, Nablus, West Bank

Denomination: Greek Orthodox (sacred to many Christians)
Dates: c. 4th century (originally completed),
1893 (current building completed)
Web: www.visitpalestine.ps/where-to-go/city/nablus/sites-attractions-nablus (tourism website)

The Church of St. Photini in the Palestinian city of Nablus is home to one of the lesser known treasures of the Bible: Jacob's Well. While this ancient well is almost certainly not the original one dug by the Patriarch Jacob, it has been verifiably dated to the Roman era, and is thus almost certainly the Jacob's Well referred to in the New Testament. Therefore it is likely that Jesus drank from this well, making it one of the most reliable locations connected to the New Testament.

The modern city of Nablus grew out of the ancient town of Shechem, now an archaeological site, closely tied to the family of Abraham. According to the Old Testament, Jacob, the grandson of Abraham, dug a well here, probably sometime around the 17th century BC. The site was revered among ancient Jews as Jacob's Well at least as late as the 1st century.

Sometime during his ministry, Jesus passed through the area. While resting at the well, he met a Samaritan woman and spoke with her of eternal life. This was one of the Biblical passages that would later be used to support the idea that salvation was not exclusively for the Jewish people. According to Eastern Christians, the woman's name was Photini, and she has since been acclaimed as a saint in the Orthodox tradition.

The earliest church to stand on the site was probably completed in the 4th century. However, this building was almost certainly destroyed during the Samaritan uprisings. At least two other churches were erected around or over the well, but these also did not survive the region's turbulent history. The current building dates from 1893.

Of Interest: The Church of St. Photini is a modern building with distinctly eastern elements. The magnificent iconic paintings which cover both the inside and outside of the church are the work of a solitary and very dedicated priest. The main point of interest is the ancient well, which is located in the crypt beneath the main sanctuary. The well itself is thousands of years old, though the retaining walls are more recent. Water can still be drawn from the well by pilgrims with a hand-powered winch, rope and bucket.

---

17. BASILICA OF THE ANNUNCIATION

Al-Bishara Street, Nazareth, Israel

Alternate/Full Name: Church of the Annunciation
Denomination: Roman Catholic (sacred to most Western Christians)
Dates: c. 4th century (originally completed), 1969 (current building completed)
Web: www.custodia.org/en/sanctuaries/nazareth (official website)

The Basilica of the Annunciation is one of the highlights of Christian pilgrimage in the Holy Land. Generally regarded as the third most sacred city for Christians after Jerusalem and Bethlehem, Nazareth may actually be the most fascinating and is in some ways the best preserved. The basilica has the distinction of being the largest Christian shrine in Israel exclusively under the jurisdiction of a single entity, in this case the Roman Catholic Church.

As far as is known, Nazareth did not play a significant role in history prior to the Christian era. In fact, Nazareth was never even mentioned as such in the Old Testament, and may not even have existed as a village until the Second Temple period. Its first appearance in history, and in the Bible, was during the reign of Augustus Caesar. Sometime before 6 BC, Nazareth became home to what would be its most famous couple: Joseph the carpenter and his young wife Mary. It was during their residence here that the first miracle of the New Testament, the Immaculate Conception, took place.

The Bible offers only a brief overview of this pivotal event. According to the New Testament, Mary was informed of her delicate condition by the Archangel Gabriel, though it is uncertain whether the conception took place at this time or earlier. Presumably she spent most of her pregnancy in Nazareth, although the famous birth itself took place in Bethlehem. Joseph and Mary returned to Nazareth after the death of Herod the Great and raised Jesus there.

While the Galilee region was home to many Christian converts during Jesus' life, Nazareth itself remained solidly Jewish for the next three centuries. Christians began to take an active interest in Nazareth as a sacred destination in the 4th century. The first church commemorating Gabriel's visit was built around that time. Nazareth is now a bustling city, one of the largest in Northern Israel, with hundreds of thousands of Christian pilgrims visiting the Church of the Annunciation every year.

Of Interest: The Basilica of the Annunciation is a massive building, dwarfing most other churches in the Holy Land. Constructed in the 1960s, the huge church is actually built around the ruins of the original 4th century Byzantine structure. The Grotto of the Annunciation beneath the church marks the traditional spot of Mary's house. Giant works of art donated by Catholic churches from all over the world depict Mary and the Infant Jesus in every artistic style imaginable. Just outside and partially beneath the church is an exposed archaeological site with some of the city's original Roman ruins and streets. The odds are very good that Jesus and his family walked on these ancient stones.

---

18. CHURCH OF ST. GABRIEL & MARY'S WELL

Anis Kardosh Street, Nazareth, Israel

Alternate/Full Name: Greek Orthodox Church of the Annunciation
Denomination: Greek Orthodox (sacred to most Eastern Christians)
Dates: c. 4th century (originally completed), 1769 (current building completed)

Web: www.nazarethinfo.org/en/attractions/religious-sites/greek-orthodox-church-annunciation (tourism website)

The Church of St. Gabriel is an alternative site to the nearby Roman Catholic basilica as a possible location for the Annunciation. It is recognized as such by the churches of the Eastern Orthodox communion and some other Christian groups as well. It stands close to a structure known as Mary's Well which, while relatively new, draws water from the city's ancient spring, which has been a water source since the Roman era.

Nazareth has been a destination for Christian pilgrims at least as far back as the 4th century. A church has stood on the spot since the Byzantine era. As with most other major shrines in the Holy Land, it was rebuilt on several occasions, including by the Crusaders. The current church was completed in the 18th century.

Mary's Well has been in use on and off over the centuries, and has been closed and reopened on a regular basis. It is uncertain if a well was in active use on this spot in the 1st century. However, the well of Mary's time was probably close by, making this location a possible candidate for the place where the angel Gabriel first appeared to Jesus' mother.

Of Interest: The Church of St. Gabriel is architecturally typical of Orthodox churches built at the height of the Ottoman era. While the exterior is unassuming, the inside is home to a wealth of wonderful artwork depicting images of the Annunciation. The main attraction is a subterranean chamber with access to Nazareth's ancient spring. While it is unknown exactly where the well was located, this spring was undoubtedly the source of the water. Mary's Well, recently reconstructed, has been the subject of archaeological investigations that indicate that a Roman bath house once stood on the site. This location also has access to the city's spring.

19. CHURCH OF THE TRANSFIGURATION

Mt. Tabor, Shibli, Israel

Denomination: Roman Catholic (sacred to many Christians)
Dates: c. 5th century (originally completed), 1924 (current building completed)
Web: www.custodia.org/en/sanctuaries/mount-tabor (official website)

The Church of the Transfiguration, located on Mt. Tabor east of Nazareth, is one of the many lesser known Christian pilgrimage destinations that cover northern Israel. According to tradition, it stands on the site where the Transfiguration of Jesus occurred. One of the pivotal New Testament sites, Mt. Tabor and the Church of the Transfiguration are an integral pilgrimage stop for Christians working their way from Nazareth to the Sea of Galilee.

According to the Biblical account, Jesus travelled to a mountain to meditate with his disciples Peter, James and John. What started out as a prayer to God became a major event. Jesus made a spiritual-physical connection with Heaven, and there he spoke with the great Jewish prophets Moses and Elijah. It was during this historic journey that He was referred to as 'Son' for the first time.

This was the first event as recorded by the Gospels that suggest that Jesus was not just a run-of-the-mill prophet, but something much greater. Early Christians held the site sacred, with a church here dating back as far as the Byzantine period. The current church was completed in 1924, and has since become an integral part of the Christian pilgrimage trail in Northern Israel.

Of Interest: The Church of the Transfiguration is a relatively modern building that incorporates elements of a previous Crusader era church. Sprawling over a large area close to the top of Mount Tabor, it is part of a monastic complex run by the Franciscan order. The focal point of the massive church is a trio of grottoes and related chapels. These chapels represent the three great figures of the Transfiguration: Jesus in the center, Moses to the north and Elijah to the south.

20. CHURCH OF THE BEATITUDES

Route 8177, Mount of Beatitudes, Tabgha, Israel

Denomination: Roman Catholic (sacred to many Christians)
Dates: c. 4th century (originally completed),
1938 (current building completed)
Web: www.custodia.org/en/sanctuaries/tabgha-and-magdala
(official website)

The Church of the Beatitudes is possibly the most popular Christian shrine in the Galilee region. This mountainside church, which offers magnificent views of the Sea of Galilee, stands on the traditional site where Jesus delivered one of the most famous speeches in history, the Sermon on the Mount. Because of this the Church of the Beatitudes is an absolute must see on any Christian pilgrim's itinerary to the area.

The Sermon on the Mount was one of the pivotal events in the life of Jesus of Nazareth. It encapsulated most of His greatest teachings, and has been a foundation of Christian theology for nearly two thousand years. According to tradition based on certain interpretations of the Bible, the sermon is believed to have been delivered on a hillside outside of ancient Capernaum in the vicinity of what is today the city of Tabgha.

Over the course of centuries, many churches commemorating the event have been erected in the area. The best known of these, the current Church of the Beatitudes, was constructed in the 1930s. A gift of the nation of Italy, its chief sponsor was the fascist dictator Benito Mussolini. Despite this, the Church of the Beatitudes is an incredibly popular Christian pilgrimage destination. Recitations of the Sermon on the Mount can be heard hear at most times of the day and in many different languages.

Of Interest: The Mount of Beatitudes, which overlooks Tabgha and Capernaum, was identified by the Byzantines as the location of the Sermon on the Mount in the 4th century. A large, relatively flat and open steppe on the hillside is the traditional location where Jesus delivered his famous oratory. The setting is certainly inspirational enough, and the view of Galilee below is spectacular. The church itself is a relatively small structure surrounded by green lawns and palm trees, giving it the feel of an oasis in the wilderness. The building is octagonal in shape, the eight sides symbolizing the eight Beatitudes.

---

21. CHURCH OF THE PRIMACY OF ST. PETER & CHURCH OF THE MULTIPLICATION

Route 87, Tabgha, Israel

Alternate/Full Name: Church of the Multiplication of Loaves and Fishes
Denomination: Roman Catholic (sacred to many Christians)
Dates: Primacy - c. 4th century (originally completed), 1933 (current building completed) & Multiplication - c. 5th century (originally completed), 1982 (current building completed)
Web: www.custodia.org/en/sanctuaries/tabgha-and-magdala (official website)

The Church of the Primacy of St. Peter and the Church of the Multiplication are a pair of churches in Tabgha which commemorate two of the lesser events of the New Testament. The first, Jesus' declaration of Peter as the Rock upon which the Church would be built; and the second, the Miracle of the Loaves and Fishes. Both of these churches are part of a cluster of historic Christian sites at the northern end of the Sea of Galilee which are popular with pilgrims.

In one of the most dogmatically important moments of the New Testament, Jesus declared that Peter will be the 'Rock upon which the Church will be built'. This statement, as interpreted by the Roman Catholic Church, is the basis for the authority of the Papacy, whose leaders are direct heirs of Peter. Obviously controversial among the other denominations of Christianity, it is nevertheless of paramount important to Catholics, who honored the Biblical passage with a shrine in Tabgha.

Jesus also performed one of his most famous miracles that did not involve healing here. In what has become known as the Feeding of the Multitude, Jesus took two fish and five loaves of bread and from this humble store fed as many as five thousand of his followers, with food to spare. This miracle was perhaps Jesus' greatest expression of caring for the needs of a downtrodden and hungry people.

Both of these Biblical events were identified by early Christians as having taken place along the north shore of the Sea of Galilee, and churches have commemorated both passages since at least the 4th century. The original Church of the Primacy of St. Peter was one of the longest surviving early churches, standing for nearly a thousand years before being replaced during the Crusades. The early Church of the Multiplication was not as lucky, having been destroyed in the 7th century and not rediscovered until more than a thousand years later.

Of Interest: Both the Church of the Primacy of St. Peter and the Church of the Multiplication are relatively recent incarnations which only date back to the 20th century. The Church of the Primacy of Peter, completed in 1933, incorporates the ruins of the original 4th century church. The Church of the Multiplication, completed in 1982, actually had a major renovation recently due to an arson attack in 2015. The floor of the Church of the Multiplication incorporates some ancient Roman-era mosaics, representing some of the oldest surviving Christian artwork in Israel.

---

22. RUINS OF CAPERNAUM ARCHAEOLOGICAL SITE

Route 87, Capernaum, Israel

Denomination: Roman Catholic, Greek Orthodox (sacred to most Christians)
Dates: 1838 (rediscovered)
Web: www.custodia.org/en/sanctuaries/capernaum (official Catholic website)

The Capernaum Archaeological Site is one of Northern Israel's most important Christian ruins and incorporates a number of sacred spots of New Testament interest. Although some of the ruins date from later eras, a lot of the foundations of the ancient Roman-era town have survived and have been excavated over the last two centuries. Capernaum is usually the final stop for Christian pilgrims working their way along the Sea of Galilee.

The ancient city of Capernaum was a focal point of activity in the early stages of Jesus' ministry. During his time in Capernaum Jesus performed a number of miracles of healing here as well as an exorcism. At least four of the Apostles came from Capernaum, including the brothers James and John, and the brothers Andrew and Peter.

Capernaum appears to have maintained a Christian community in the centuries after the Jewish revolts. It may have even provided a link of continuity until Christianity was formally legalized in the Roman Empire. While Capernaum survived and recovered from a number of conquests and natural disasters in ancient times, it seems to have finally been abandoned in the Middle Ages. The ruins were rediscovered by archaeologists in the 19th century, and excavations have been ongoing ever since.

Of Interest: The Ruins of Capernaum are extensive, with much of the site dating from the Roman era. Jurisdiction over the site is split between the Roman Catholic and Greek Orthodox churches, though the entire area is generally open to all visitors. There are two places of particular interest to Christians here. One is the remains of a 4th century synagogue, which lie on top of the ruins of a much earlier synagogue. It is highly likely that Jesus visited the earlier synagogue during his time in Capernaum. Even more interesting perhaps is the remains of the House of Peter. This site, which has been dated to the 1st century, appears to have been used for religious purposes almost since that time. The remains of an octagonal church can also be seen through the glass floor of the house.

23. JEZREEL VALLEY

Derech LeMegiddo, Megiddo, Israel

Alternate/Full Names: Valley of Megiddo, Plain of Megiddo
Denomination: General Christian
Web: www.parks.org.il/en/new/tel-megiddo-national-park (official website)

The Jezreel Valley is the Holy Land's most famous battlefield. Countless armies have fought across this vast, open, and highly strategic valley, from the Egyptians and Canaanites in the 15th century BC to the British and Ottomans during World War I. However, the best-known Biblical conflict at Megiddo has not yet been fought. That honor, according to prophecy, goes to the yet-to-come titanic Battle of Armeggedon, which will presage the return of the Messiah at the end of times. Jezreel Valley is part of the Biblical Tels UNESCO World Heritage Site.

The Jezreel stretches out from the slopes of the Carmel Mountains in the west towards the Jordan River Valley in the east. Its strategic importance has been recognized since the arrival of the area's first inhabitants thousands of years ago. The first great battle to be fought there took place around 1480 BC, when an expeditionary force from Egypt crushed the combined armies of several Canaanite city-states. The Egyptians passed through the area again a few centuries later on their way to fight the Hittites at the Battle of Kadesh.

The most famous Biblical battle to take place at Jezreel occurred sometime around the 12th century BC. During the days of the Judges, the Prophetess Deborah was called upon to defend the northern tribal territories from a marauding Canaanite army. Assisted by Barak, an able general from the tribe of Naphtali, she assembled an army of ten thousand warriors at Mount Tabor on the western side of Megiddo. From there she led the Israelites to victory over the Canaanites. Yet another Biblical battle was fought there between the Kingdom of Judah under Josiah and the Egyptians in the 7th century BC.

Over the course of millenia, virtually every army that has conquered the Middle East passed through the Jezreel at some point: the Assyrians, Babylonians, Persians, Greeks, Seleucids, Romans, Byzantines, Arabs, Crusaders and many others. But these pale in comparison to what is yet to come. According to the Book of Revelation, it is at Tel Megiddo that all the armies of the Earth will be gathered for the final battle of history's final war. Whether or not this cataclysmic event will actually take place remains to be seen.

Of Interest: The Jezreel Valley stretches from Mount Tabor and the hills near Nazareth to the east and Mount Carmel to the west. The word 'Armegeddon' technically refers to Tel Megiddo, a long-inhabited hill that commands a wide view of the valley. On a good day the city of Nazareth is visible from the top. Tel Megiddo and part of the surrounding area have been incorporated into Tel Megiddo National Park. This park includes a number of archaeological sites, including excavations of at least twenty layers of cities that once existed in the area. One of these dates back to the period of King Solomon and includes a large stable complex which may have once housed over four hundred horses. The park also has a museum which tells the history of the area.

---

24. SHRINE OF OUR LADY OF LEBANON

Harissa Road, Harissa, Lebanon

Denomination: Maronite Catholic
Dates: 1907 (completed)
Web: www.ololb.org (official website)

The Shrine of Our Lady of Lebanon is the iconic Catholic church of Lebanon and home to one of the world's most famous Christian statues. Though not the tallest statue of the Virgin Mary in the world, it is arguably the most famous and memorable. Our Lady towers atop a huge pedestal reaching up from a great hill overlooking the

Mediterranean Sea, her arms outstretched in a gesture of blessing and welcome. It is among the most visited tourist sites in Lebanon.

The Maronites of Lebanon are a branch of the Catholic Church that dates back to the Middle Ages and the Crusades. This community, one of the few Catholic Churches in the world that doesn't follow the Roman rite, has survived centuries of warfare and foreign rule, both Islamic and Christian. It continued to exist throughout the entire Ottoman period, despite being a minority even among Middle Eastern Christians.

The shrine was founded in 1904, and the great statue completed in 1907. After World War I, Lebanon became a French Mandate, and the shrine became a popular pilgrimage destination for Western European Catholics. It was visited by Pope John Paul II in 1997. Today it is also a popular pilgrimage destination for Muslims and Druze as well as Christians as both groups also hold the Virgin Mary in reverence.

Of Interest: The statue of the Shrine of Our Lady of Lebanon is a nearly nine-meter high, blindingly white statue crowned with gold. It stands on a great hill towering over the town of Harissa almost a half a mile above sea level. It is arguably the world's second most dramatic Christian statue after Christ the Redeemer in Rio de Janeiro. Behind the statue is the actual church: a huge, modern cathedral that bears a resemblance to an ancient sailing ship, especially at night when it is all illuminated.

---

25. CHURCH OF ST. LAZARUS

Ayiou Lazarou, Larnaca, Cyprus

Denomination: Church of Cyprus (sacred to many Eastern Christians)
Dates: c. 10th century (completed)
Web: http://en.agioslazaros.org.cy (official website)

The Church of St. Lazarus is the most famous and important Christian shrine on the island of Cyprus. The heart of the Church of Cyprus, one of the autocephalous Eastern Orthodox Churches, it is believed to be the site of the final burial of the Biblical Lazarus. It is also home to one of the world's oldest bishoprics outside of Israel, one which according to the New Testament was personally founded by Paul.

Christianity arrived on Cyprus at an extremely early date. Paul, accompanied by Barnabas and Mark, visited the island during his first missionary journey. Because persecution of Christians had not yet spread beyond Judea, Paul met with reasonable success here, including the conversion of the territorial governor. According to tradition, Cyprus was also visited by another distinguished New Testament figure: Lazarus, the man whom Jesus had raised from the dead. Lazarus was undoubtedly the greatest living evidence of Christ's miracles, and his existence was an embarrassment to the ruling elite in Jerusalem.

At some point after the Ascension, it is believed that Lazarus fled for his life to Cyprus, and was later anointed the first Bishop of Larnaka by Paul. He lived there for the rest of his life, and was buried there after his death. His tomb was forgotten for a time, but was rediscovered in the early Middle Ages. The Church of St. Lazarus was built on the site sometime around the year 900.

For many centuries Cyprus was a popular stopping point for pilgrims on their way to the Holy Land by sea. Despite its popularity, the Church of St. Lazarus maintained a low profile for years, a fact that has helped it to survive more or less intact throughout the centuries of foreign occupation. Ever since Orthodox Christians took back control of Larnaka in the 20th century, the Tomb of Lazarus has been one of Cyprus' most popular and visited Christian sites.

Of Interest: The Church of St. Lazarus is a late Byzantine-era structure that has served as the chief Christian shrine of Cyprus for over a thousand years. Its dominant exterior feature is a four-story square bell tower that appears almost more like a pagoda capped with a small cross. The main sanctuary is a combination of plain Byzantine stonework and oversized baroque-era furnishings. An enormous golden chandelier illuminates the main chamber. The major feature of the sanctuary is the gold-bedecked Holy of Holies. The Tomb of Lazarus actually lies in a lower chamber directly beneath this in a cramped space decorated with lamps and censors. The marble sarcophagus bears the inscription "Lazarus, the Friend of Jesus".

MIDDLE EAST

26. BAPTISM SITE OF JESUS

Baptism Road, Al-Maghtas, Jordan

Denomination: General Christian
Dates: c. 3rd century (identified)
Web: www.baptismsite.com (official website)

The Baptism Site of Jesus, sometimes referred to as Al-Maghtas, has become in recent years a popular destination for Christian converts. The reason, obviously, is that many wish to be baptized in the same place that Jesus was nearly two thousand years ago. Located on the far side of the river in Jordan, this ancient sacred site represents both a physical and spiritual transition into the Christian faith.

At the very beginning of his ministry, Jesus went to the River Jordan and presented himself to John the Baptist, a popular ascetic and probable member of the enigmatic group known as the Essenes. John baptized Jesus, though reluctantly as he did not feel he was worthy of performing such an act on the man he believed was the Messiah. This event symbolically marked the beginning of Jesus' ministry.

One of the definitive events in the life of Jesus, the site of his baptism is a natural draw for pilgrims. Long identified by Jews as the place where the Prophet Elijah ascended into Heaven, the same location on the east side of the Jordan River has been recognized as the site of the baptism of Jesus since Roman times. Due to natural disasters and politics, the 'official' site moved on several occasions throughout the centuries, but the original site was rediscovered by archaeologists in the 1990s. Al-Maghtas has been designated as a UNESCO World

Heritage Site.

Of Interest: The Baptism Site of Jesus is actually a recently excavated archaeological site at Al-Maghtas in Jordan. The ruins include ritual bath pools which were fed water by pipes, remains of piers that jutted out into the river and the foundations of some early churches. Modern additions to the site, designed to make access to the river easier, have been designed in an ancient style that blend in with the original construction.

---

27. CHURCH OF ST. GEORGE

King Hussein Street, Madaba, Jordan

Alternate/Full Name: St. George's Greek Orthodox Church
Denomination: Greek Orthodox
Dates: 542 (originally completed), 1894 (current building completed)
Web: www.international.visitjordan.com/wheretogo/madaba (tourism website)

The Church of St. George in the city of Madaba is home to one of the great artistic treasures of the ancient world: the Madaba Map. This map, a 6th century floor mosaic of the city of Jerusalem, is the oldest floor mosaic of its kind in the world. Although it depicts Jerusalem as it would have been during the Byzantine era, it is still the earliest reasonably intact map of Jerusalem ever discovered.

A church has stood on this spot since at least the 6th century. Unlike many other churches of the era, St. George survived both the Byzantine and Muslim invasions. Unfortunately, it did not survive an earthquake which struck the area in the 8th century, at which time the site was abandoned and not rebuilt for over a thousand years.

The ruins of the church were rediscovered in the late 19th century, and while most of the building had long since crumbled, a large portion of the floor mosaics survived. These mosaics included about half of an ancient map of the Holy Land, including the city of Jerusalem. Later, a new church was built over the site, but the floor was preserved as best as possible. Pilgrims and art lovers from all over the world travel here to see this amazing mosaic.

Of Interest: The Church of St. George is a modern building with an unusual open air multi-bell tower. Few come to see the building, however. The Madaba Map is the main attraction. The map displays an amazing amount of detail of the Holy Land in the Byzantine era, thoroughly labeled in Greek. Much of the city of Jerusalem is depicted. The map is fully exposed, protected only by a rope, allowing pilgrims to get a fantastically close look at this ancient artistic treasure.

---

28. CHAPEL OF ST. ANANIAS & STRAIGHT STREET

Bab Sharqi Street, Damascus, Syria

Alternate/Full Names: House of St. Ananias; Street Called Straight, Damascus Straight Street
Denomination: Maronite Catholic (sacred to many Christians)
Dates: c. 5th century (completed)
Web: No website available (tourism info for Syria limited at the time of this writing)

The Chapel of St. Ananias is an ancient cave church that, according to tradition, marks the location where Paul was baptized by Ananias. It is located along the Damascus Straight Street, a pre-Roman axis street that runs the length of the Old City. Both the House of St. Ananias and the Straight Street are prominently mentioned in the New Testament Book of Acts and are part of the Christian pilgrimage tradition in Syria.

Ananias was one of the earliest disciples of the Christian Church. In the years following the Pentecost, he evangelized and baptized new converts in the Syrian city of Damascus. Ananias played a small but pivotal role in early Christian history here. Paul, the great persecutor of the disciples of Jesus, was travelling to Damascus when he received a vision of Jesus and overcome with blindness.

Arriving in the city he was brought to the House of Ananias where he was cured and formally converted. Paul's subsequent time in Damascus was spent proclaiming his new-found faith, for which he was soon chased out of the city. Although he probably never returned to Damascus, Paul has been indelibly tied to the city and the role it played in his conversion since the earliest days of the Church.

Of Interest: Straight Street is largely laid out today as it was over two thousand years ago. Paul almost certainly walked along this street in ancient Roman times. The House of St. Ananias was actually discovered as part of the ruins of a Byzantine era church that was uncovered in the early 20th century. A small chapel displays artwork featuring scenes from Paul's various journeys and ministry. A short distance from the house is the city's ancient Eastern Gate, believed to be the location where Paul fled from Damascus in a dramatic escape over the city wall.

---

29. GREAT MOSQUE OF DAMASCUS

Bein Assourain Lane, Damascus, Syria

Alternate/Full Name: Umayyad Mosque
Denomination: Muslim (sacred to many Christians)
Dates: 715 (completed)
Web: No website available (tourism info for Syria limited at the time of this writing)

The Great Mosque of Damascus is one of the most historic mosques in the Islamic tradition. However, it is sacred to many Christians as well, due to one of the New Testament's most famous relics: the head of John the Baptist. Throughout Christendom, there are many churches and shrines that claim to possess this famous head, and other pieces, of John. However, the reliquary in this ancient Damascus shrine is the most widely recognized. The Great Mosque of Damascus is part of the

Ancient City of Damascus UNESCO World Heritage Site.

John the Baptist was one of the pivotal figures of the New Testament. According to the New Testament, it was he that baptized Jesus of Nazareth at the start of His ministry. A vocal critic of the Jewish authorities under the Romans, his words and actions earned him a martyr's death by beheading. The head was subsequently delivered to the family of Herod, then King of Judea.

Christianity arrived in Damascus at a very early date, perhaps as early as the year 35. It is possible that the Patriarchate of Jerusalem relocated to Damascus for a time in the 1st and 2nd centuries. In the 8th century, Damascus was selected as the capital of the Islamic Caliphate, and an enormous new mosque was constructed there.

Taking a cue from the area's many Byzantine churches, the Muslims decided to sanctify the new mosque with an important relic, and transferred the head of John the Baptist there, possibly from Herod's fortress at Machaerus. Since the arrival of the relic, the Great Mosque of Damascus has not only been one of Islam's pre-eminent religious sites but an important and popular destination for Christian pilgrims as well.

Of Interest: The Great Mosque of Damascus is a spectacular edifice. Constructed before Persian-style architecture came into vogue in the Islamic world, it appears much more like a Byzantine monastic complex than a mosque. One of the minarets of the mosque is dedicated to Jesus of Nazareth. The interior of the mosque is richly decorated, blending Christian and Muslim artistic styles of many periods. The head of John the Baptist is contained in an elaborate white-marble tomb located beneath the great dome. The reliquary is visible through a series of latticework protected openings. The Umayyad mosque is also home to the tomb of one of Islam's greatest heroes: Saladin, the king who retook Jerusalem from the Christian Crusaders in the 12th century.

---

30. CONVENT OF ST. THECLA MA'LULA

Faj Mar Takla, Maaloula, Syria

Denomination: Greek Orthodox (sacred to many Eastern Christians)
Dates: c. 5th century (founded)
Web: https://www.antiochpatriarchate.org/en/page/the-convent-of-st-thecla-ma-lula (official website)

The Convent of St. Thecla Ma'Lula stands over an ancient Christian site, dating perhaps as far back as the mid-1st century. Thecla, an early Church convert, does not appear in the New Testament, but was a prominent figure of Apocryphal Christian literature. She may have been the first woman martyred for the Christian faith. During the years of her persecution, Thecla apparently took refuge in a cave in Maloula. The Convent of Thecla Ma'lula above the cave has been a popular pilgrimage site since at least Byzantine times.

Thecla was a young woman of noble birth, possibly the daughter of a Seleucid prince, who followed Paul, converted to Christianity and adopted a chaste lifestyle. This did not sit well with her betrothed or with her family, who sought to marry her off for political purposes. Despite repeated threats, she refused the marriage.

Thecla was condemned to be burned at the stake for her defiance, but was miraculously saved when a fierce storm doused the flames. After this narrow escape, she departed with Paul to seek safety in Asia Minor. However, once again she became the subject of a nobleman's unwanted attention, and once again she protested her virtue. In punishment, the local authorities confined her with wild beasts. Once again she was saved by a miracle, when the female animals defended her from the males.

Based on these stories, early Christians esteemed Thecla as a paragon of female virtue. According to tradition, she was eventually captured and martyred. At some point before or during the Byzantine era, she began to be venerated as a saint. The site of her cave was identified in Syria near the modern day city of Ma'loula. The Mar Taqla Monastery has been around, in one form or another, since this early era. The local Christian community is one of the world's oldest, and may be the only one to speak Aramaic, the language probably spoken by Jesus of Nazareth.

Of Interest: The Convent of St. Thecla Ma'Lula is an impressive and unusual complex. It is literally built right into the mouth of the cave in which Thecla once took sanctuary from her pursuers. The cave opening is both very wide and tall, and it is actually more like a giant dent in the mountainside. The older portions of the monastery, where the original shrine was located, is actually inside of the cave, its sides and contours melting into the surrounding rock. The entire site is interconnected by a string of narrow alleyways, suspended walkways and underground passages. Behind the monastery, in the remaining space of the cave, is the shrine of Thecla, the highlight of which is an ancient natural spring whose water is sought after by visiting pilgrims.

---

31. RUINS OF THE CHURCH OF ST. SIMEON STYLITES

Route 62, Deir Semaan, Syria

Alternate/Full Name: Cathedral of St. Simeon Stylite
Denomination: Greek Orthodox
Dates: 475 (originally completed)
Web: No website available (tourism info for Syria limited at the time of this writing)

The Church of St. Simeon Stylites was the site of the home of one of early Christianity's most eccentric aesthetics: Simeon the Stylite. So named for his tendency to sit and meditate atop tall columns, Simeon the Stylite distinguished himself as a champion of self-deprivation and went on to be honored as a wise man of the faith. His tomb was once a popular stop for pilgrims on their way to the Holy Land, which they continued to do for many centuries after his death.

Around the year 423, Simeon decided to pursue a life of faith and solitude. After flirtations with both monasticism and isolationism, Simeon decided to eschew tradition and spend his life as a 'hermit' in full view of the local citizenry. Ascending a stone column, he then proceeded to subject himself to all manner of deprivation and hardship. At first he was regarded as a form of entertainment, but as time passed Simeon was taken more seriously. Soon he had a considerable following, and word of his self-imposed tribulations spread.

Later, new pillars were constructed for him, higher and smaller, so that he might make himself even more uncomfortable. As his fame grew, he became so popular that even high Church officials began to seek out his wisdom and blessing. The Byzantine emperor himself eventually came and paid him a visit. By the time of his death, Simeon was one of the most famous figures of his day. An enormous church was constructed around his final pillar, and for many years continued to draw pilgrims to the area.

By the time of the Muslims arrived in the 7th century, Aleppo's importance as a Christian pilgrimage center had waned. Today many Christian scholars now regard the Stylists as eccentrics at best, exhibitionists at worst. Critics of Simeon the Stylite point to the earthquake that destroyed the Church of St. Simeon less than a century after his death as a divine sign that perhaps the Stylites were not great examples. Nevertheless, the ruins of the church still draw a steady stream of the highly devout and the curious.

Of Interest: The Church of St. Simeon Stylites was once among the most magnificent and most visited churches in Syria. However, after it was laid waste by an earthquake in the 6th century, it was abandoned and never rebuilt. Because of this the ruins of the church are in surprisingly good condition. While the great vaulted ceiling and most of the outer walls are long gone, major sections remain, including much of the façade. Archways lead to great vaults and alcoves long open to the sky. The centerpiece of the church is the fabled pillar of St. Simeon, believed to be the last that he sat on and upon which he died. Today, all that is left is the pedestal and the base of the pillar, about two meters in height. (Note - The Church of St. Simeon Stylites was badly damaged during an airstrike in 2016; the state of the ruins was unknown as of the time of this writing)

32. RUINS OF THE HOUSE CHURCH OF DURA EUROPOS

Route 4, Dura Europos, Syria

Denomination: General Christian
Dates: c. 2nd century (originally completed as a house); c. 232 (consecrated as a church)
Web: No website available (tourism info for Syria limited at the time of this writing)

The House Church of Dura Europos, or what remains of it, is possibly the world's oldest known existing Christian church structure. Dating perhaps as far back as the early 2nd century, the House Church was probably abandoned before Constantine legalized Christianity in the empire. On its site is preserved some of the world's earliest Christian artwork, including the oldest known depiction of Jesus Christ. Because it is very far off the beaten path, the House Church of Europos provides a nearly pristine pilgrimage experience, one that few visitors ever get to enjoy.

Dura Europos was an ancient border city along the constantly shifting frontiers of the Roman and Persian empires. Its position along the major trade routes between Aleppo and Ctesiphon made it a natural stepping stone for the spread of Christianity eastward. According to tradition, the Christian community of Dura Europos was founded by Thomas the Apostle or one of his disciples when he passed through the area on his way to Persia in the 1st century.

At some time in the late 2nd or early 3rd century, the Christians of Dura Europos began to assemble in the private residence which would later become known as the House Church. It is uncertain whether these assemblies were at first held in secret, but by 235 at least the Christians seemed to be confident enough to begin decorating the church with Christian artwork. A number of frescoes on the church walls date from around this time, including three featuring episodes from the life of Jesus. These are the oldest artistic depictions of Jesus that have ever been discovered.

Approximately two decades after the church's decoration, the Roman garrison of Dura Europos was overcome by the Sassanids. The local population was killed or driven off, and many of the buildings destroyed. The city was soon abandoned, never to be inhabited again. It is for this reason that the House Church is so well preserved. Between the dry desert climate, the lack of natural disasters, lack of demolition or new construction, and lack of interest by the locals, what the Sassanians failed to destroy in the 3rd century has been preserved to be enjoyed by Christian visitors nearly eighteen-hundred years later.

Of Interest: The Ruins of the House Church are located in the southwestern corner of the Dura Europos archaeological site, not too far from the city gate. The surviving remains of the church consist of several complete walls, a few partial walls and the outlines of the foundation. The most notable features of the ruins are the surviving frescoes. The main fresco is that of the three women visiting the Holy Sepulchre after the crucifixion. One of them is identified by name as Salome. Other frescoes include the Parable of the Shepherd; Jesus walking on water; Jesus healing the sick; Adam and Eve; and David and Goliath.

---

33. CHURCH OF THE HOLY WISDOM (HAGIA SOPHIA)

Sultan Ahmet, Ayasofya Meydani, 34122 Fatih/Istanbul, Turkey

Alternate/Full Names: Church of the Holy Wisdom; Greek Orthodox Patriarchal Cathedral
Denomination: Formerly Greek Orthodox (sacred to most Eastern Christians)
Dates: 537 (completed)
Web: https://ayasofyamuzesi.gov.tr/en (official website)

The Hagia Sophia of Istanbul is the greatest surviving church of antiquity. It is also one of the most spectacular buildings of the ancient world that has survived mostly intact to the present day. Constructed by the Byzantine Empire at its height in the 6th century, the Hagia Sophia became one of five Patriarchal seats of the church, and for a time was the greatest of these. After the Great Schism, the Hagia Sophia was revered as the mother church of all Eastern Christians. Now run as a museum, the Hagia Sofia remains Orthodox Christianity's spiritual heart. The Hagia Sofia of Istanbul is part of the Historic Areas of Istanbul UNESCO World Heritage Site.

In the 4th century, Constantine, one of the greatest emperors in the history of Rome, made several fateful decisions that have had repercussions in the Christian faith ever since. First, he legalized Christianity in the Roman Empire. Second, he moved the imperial capital to Byzantium in what is now Turkey and renamed it Constantinople. In just a few decades, Constantinople grew into one of the largest cities in the world. In recognition of its importance, the city's Christian bishop was elevated to the rank of Patriarch, on par with the Bishop of Rome.

In the early 6th century, the emperor Justinian I decided to build a monumental new church as a symbol of the imperial capital. This church, the Hagia Sophia, was the largest and most spectacular that had yet been constructed. For nearly a thousand years Constantinople remained the capital of the Greek Orthodox world, and the Hagia Sophia its chief church. However, in 1453, the Turks conquered the city, and the Hagia Sophia was appropriated and put to use as a mosque. It remained so until the early 20th century, when it was neutralized by the Turkish government and repurposed as a museum.

Of Interest: The Hagia Sophia of Istanbul is the greatest surviving example of Byzantine architecture. The staggered walls give the outer structure an almost stepped appearance crowned by a great dome with a golden spire. Four towering white minarets were added to the complex in the 15th century after the Hagia Sofia was converted to use as a mosque. The interior of the church is decorated in marble pillaged from throughout the empire. One of the most striking features of the Hagia Sophia is the large number of windows in the place. Few other churches built in the early Middle Ages boasted such an abundance of natural light. Wall-to-wall paintings and mosaics cover nearly every square inch of surface area. Icons of Jesus and the saints abound. Today the church consists mostly of open space used as a museum for the display of religious art and artifacts.

34. CHURCH OF ST. GEORGE

Yavuz Sultan Selim Mahallesi, Dr. Sadik Ahmet Cd. No. 44, 34083 Fatih/Istanbul, Turkey

Alternate/Full Names: Greek Orthodox Cathedral of St. George, Patriarchal Church of St. George
Denomination: Greek Orthodox (sacred to many Eastern Christians)
Dates: 1614 (completed)
Web: www.patriarchate.org/saintgeorge (official website)

The Church of St. George is the seat of the Patriarch of Constantinople. As the senior Patriarchate, St. George's is also the de-facto seat of the entire Eastern Orthodox communion, making it one of the most influential churches in the world. Additionally, it is home to some of Christianity's most ancient relics and treasures, largely what was saved after the Ottoman Empire annexed the city in the 15th century.

The Bishop of Constantinople was elevated to the rank of Patriarch in the early Byzantine era. The Patriarchate, one of only five in the world, was based out of the Hagia Sophia for the better part of nine hundred years. However, after the Ottoman conquest of Constantinople in 1453, the Eastern Orthodox Church lost control of the Hagia Sophia and most of the city's other major churches. Sometime around 1600, the Patriarchate adopted an old convent for use as the new home of the patriarch.

The Church of St. George has had a rough history. It has been ravaged by time, fires and occasional violence and has been rebuilt and renovated on numerous occasions, most recently in 1991. The current church consists of elements from half a dozen incarnations of the church going back to the pre-Ottoman era.

Of Interest: The Church of St. George is surprisingly small considering its importance, probably because it was never intended to play such an important role in the Eastern Orthodox communion. Nevertheless the interior is lavishly appointed and displays some treasures from the earliest days of Christianity. The main item of interest is the Pillar of the Flagellation, which according to tradition was where Jesus was bound when he was being tortured by the Romans. Also here are the relics of two early saints, John Chrysostom and Gregory the Theologian, both of whom contributed significantly to the theology of the Church in the 4th century.

---

35. RUINS OF THE BASILICA OF ST. JOHN

Ataturk Mh., St. Jean Cd., 35920 Selcuk, Turkey

Denomination: Greek Orthodox (sacred to many Christians)
Dates: c. 6th century (originally completed)
Web: www.goturkeytourism.com/things-to-do/8-magnificent-ruins-of-ephesus (tourism website)

The Basilica of St. John in Ephesus occupies a fascinating niche in Christian history. According to tradition, it stands on or near the site of the home of John, the last surviving Apostle, and it is probably where he was buried. It was also almost certainly the location of the last surviving Autograph, the original handwritten scriptures. Little is known about the last days of John, but his presence in Ephesus in the later years of the 1st century made that city a critical center of the early Church.

Ephesus was the seventh largest city in the Roman Empire, with as many as a half million residents at its height. It was one of the most important cities mentioned in the New Testament, and it served as a missionary base for Paul in Western Asia. Paul's letter to the Ephesians was included in the New Testament, and Ephesus is prominently mentioned in the Book of Revelation.

After the dispersion of the Apostles from Judea, John is said to have travelled to Ephesus. Of all of the Apostolic destinations, this one is among the most likely to be correct. John spent most of the second half of his long life in the region, alternatively living here and in exile on the nearby island of Patmos. After the death of the Emperor

Domitian in the year 96, John returned to Ephesus where he spent the rest of his life. He was the only one of the Twelve Apostles not to die as a martyr.

Ephesus remained an important organizational center of the early Church. It was not a patriarchal seat, which is strange considering the city's size and John's presence there, as well as its convenient location about halfway between Rome and Jerusalem. Ephesus was the site of the third ecumenical council in 431, which was called to address the Nestorian Heresy. It was at the Council of Ephesus that the Catholic Church essentially finalized its canon beliefs, reaffirmed the Nicaean Creed as being whole and complete, and outlawed the Nestorians.

An early church or shrine may have been present here as early as the 3rd century, but a full basilica was not completed until the 6th century. This original structure was destroyed at an unknown time several centuries later. However, the location of the tomb has been preserved, and the church ruins remain a popular place of pilgrimage.

Of Interest: The Basilica of St. John is now a magnificent ruin, and has been for over a thousand years. Because it was never rebuilt, what little survives is a rare and excellent example of Byzantine architecture. The location of the tomb is marked by more recent paving stones. Four restored columns stand at the corners of the tomb, making it easy to discern amongst the rubble.

---

36. HOUSE OF THE VIRGIN MARY

Sultaniye Mahallesi, 35922 Selcuk, Turkey

Denomination: Roman Catholic, Muslim (Marian shrine)
Dates: c. 1st century (completed)
Web: www.goturkeytourism.com/things-to-do/8-magnificent-ruins-of-ephesus (tourism website)

The House of the Virgin Mary is an ancient building long held sacred by many Christians. According to tradition, when John the Apostle fled the Holy Land with Jesus' mother in the 1st century, they came to Ephesus, and Mary lived in this house until she died. Many early patriarchs, bishops and other church leaders regularly visited Ephesus to meet with John, the last surviving Apostle, and probably Mary. Today, both Christian and Muslim visitors from all over the world come to visit the humble residence in which Mary is said to have dwelt in her final years, especially in August when the Assumption of the Virgin Mary is celebrated.

After the final departure of Jesus, Mary remained in the company of the Apostles in Judea. Apparently she fled from Judea in her later years, seeking either peace, safety or both. She went in the company of the Apostle John, who was charged by Jesus with her safe keeping. Sometime around the middle of the 1st century they arrived in Ephesus, where she spent the rest of her life in John's care. There is no record of the place or time of her death..

Soon after the fall of the Western Roman Empire, the harbor of Ephesus silted over and most of the city was abandoned. After Ephesus was conquered by the Ottomans, the holy places associated with Mary continued to be venerated by the Muslims. The House of Mary itself was forgotten for some time, until it was rediscovered in the 19th century. A shrine now stands on the site and is an active place of worship for both Christians and Muslims. The House of the Virgin Mary was officially declared to be a Catholic Shrine in the 19th century.

Of Interest: The House of the Virgin Mary is something of an oddity in that it was never demolished or overbuilt with a massive cathedral or mosque. The small brown and grey brick shrine now appears today much as it has for centuries. The building incorporates the original 1st century dwelling as well as an expansion that encloses Mary's Tomb. Behind the house is the Well of Mary, and any visit to the shrine usually includes a drink of the well's curative waters. The interior of the house has four rooms. The bedroom is now used as a small Christian Chapel, and a sitting room has been converted into a small mosque.

37. CHURCH OF THE HOLY WISDOM

Mahmut Celebi Mahallesi, 16890 Iznik, Turkey

Denomination: Formerly Greek Orthodox
Dates: c. 6th century (completed)
Web: www.goturkeytourism.com/things-to-do/christian-sacred-sites-in-turkey (tourism website)

The Hagia Sophia of Nicaea is one of Christianity's lesser known but great historical treasures. It was here in 787 that the Second Council of Nicaea, the last of the original seven ecumenical councils of Christianity, took place. Although not nearly as pivotal an event as the First Council of Nicaea in the 4th century, it is the only surviving original council site. The church and the city both remain important links in Turkey's Christian history.

Asia Minor was one of the first sizeable regions of the Roman Empire to develop a substantial Christian community. At least four of the Apostles, as well as Paul, actively evangelized in Asia Minor in the 1st century. When Constantine chose Byzantium for his new capital, he may have had Asia Minor's Christians in mind. After the legalization of Christianity in the 4th century, Western Asia became the central focus of Christian organizational activity.

In 325 Constantine called for a universal ecumenical council to be held in Nicaea to address the problem of the Arian heresy and other Church issues. It was close to the imperial capital so that the emperor's presence was strongly felt at the meetings. It was also out-of-the-way compared to most of the other major Christian centers, thus limiting the number of bishops and patriarchs who could attend. Less than three hundred were present at the council. This number almost certainly would have been much higher had the council been held in Antioch or even in Ephesus. It would have also guaranteed a higher attendance of the Arian bishops, which was not desired by the council's organizers.

The First Council of Nicaea was one of history's pivotal moments. Among those items discussed were the first version of the Nicene

Creed, the Arian Heresy, the establishment of Easter as a separate holiday from Passover, and the creation of the New Testament. Another ecumenical council took place in Nicaea in 787 in order to address the issue of Iconoclasm. In 1331 Nicaea was conquered by the Ottomans, after which it began to fall into a long decline. Little now remains of its Christian population, and few pilgrims still come to visit the city's Christian holy sites.

Of Interest: The Hagia Sophia in Nicaea was constructed in the 6th century by the Byzantine emperor Justinian I. The Second Council of Nicaea took place within its walls in the 8th century, the first council having taken place in the now-ruined Senatus Palace. The Hagia Sophia of Nicaea evokes the Byzantine architectural style of the early Middle Ages. Unfortunately, it has not been well cared for in the last few centuries due to the emigration of virtually all of Nicaea's Christians. A large part of the ceiling and roof has collapsed. The church still has a few treasures, largely in the form of beautiful artwork on the walls and tile mosaics on the floors.

---

38. CAVE CHURCHES OF CAPPADOCIA

Aydinli Mah, Yavuz Sok. No1, 50180 Goreme/Nevsehir, Turkey

Denomination: Formerly Greek Orthodox
Dates: c. 4th century (founded)
Web: www.goreme.com/goreme-open-air-museum (official website)

The Cave Churches of Cappadocia are among the most unique architectural legacies of Christianity in antiquity. Consisting of a half-dozen magnificent churches carved from volcanic rock, they were once part of a large Christian community that lived here in a vast network of above-ground and underground structures designed to isolate them from the world. Goreme National Park, where the churches are located, is a UNESCO World Heritage Site.

The Goreme area of Cappadocia in Northern Asia Minor has been home to a Christian community since at least the 4th century. The area, which is geologically famous for its fairy chimney rock formations and soft volcanic stone, was an ideal location for the carving of subterranean passages and rooms. Local Christians chose the area for the construction of what was effectively an underground city, hidden from the world and potential persecutors.

Beginning in 4th century, Christians began carving out a vast network of underground tunnels and chambers interconnected with buildings on the surface. Over time the area became a labyrinth and included everything from residences to shops and storehouses. The various complexes also included a number of churches, chapels and burial areas. The caves of Goreme remained in use for many centuries, and most of the site still looks as it did more than a millennium ago.

Of Interest: The Cave Churches of Cappadocia number half a dozen, mostly still in good condition. The standout is undoubtedly the one known as the Church of the Buckle (Tokali Kilise). Consisting of an old church, a new church and a crypt, Tokali Kilise is covered in frescoes depicting scenes and cycles from many books of the Bible, as well as from historic events of early Christianity. Another popular church here is the Dark Church (Karanlik Kilise), which has even better if less extensive artwork. Collectively the Cave Churches of Cappadocia boast some of the best Christian artwork from the Byzantine era.

---

39. ST. NICHOLAS CHURCH

Merkez Mahallesi, 07570 Demre, Turkey

Denomination: Formerly Greek Orthodox
Dates: c. 6th century (completed)
Web: www.goturkeytourism.com/things-to-do/christian-sacred-sites-in-turkey (tourism website)

The St. Nicholas Church was constructed to honor one of early Christianity's greatest champions. Nicholas of Myra, one of the most beloved post 1st-century Church figures, is universally cherished among Catholic, Orthodox and Protestant Christians alike. Few other figures of early Christianity are as venerated as a patron saint or has more churches and cathedrals named in their honor. Today, after being forgotten for centuries, the local Muslim population of Demre is making a major effort to attract Christian pilgrims to this ancient church and restore the city's reputation as the city of Nicholas.

Nicholas was born sometime in the 3rd century in the City of Patara in Asia Minor. As a teenager Nicholas moved to the city of Myra where he pursued theological studies under the tutelage of the city's bishop. As a young man he was ordained as a priest, and much of his early tenure was focused on the survival of the Church during the persecutions of Diocletian. After Constantine's legalization of Christianity, Nicholas went through a transformation from beloved church leader to passionate champion of orthodoxy. Nicholas was among the first Church leaders to strongly reject Arianism.

Nicholas spent much of his life opposing Arianism, which continued to spread and thrive even after its denouncement. His efforts kept much of Asia Minor free of the heresy. Apparently Constantine, who himself ultimately became an Arian Christian, was nevertheless still so impressed with Nicholas that he neither hindered the popular bishop nor forced the Arian view on the Church as a whole. Nicholas died a hero of Christian Orthodoxy sometime in the mid-4th century. Two hundred years later, a great church was erected in his honor in the city of Myra.

Of Interest: The Church of St. Nicholas in Myra, once the seat of one of Asia Minor's most important bishoprics, has been neglected for many years. Originally constructed in the 6th century on the site where Nicholas once lived, the church has been renovated on a number of occasions. By the late 20th century, the church had become a ruin. However, the Turkish Ministry of Culture has recently undertaken a massive restoration effort in conjunction with the Orthodox Patriarchate of Russia. Despite its ancient age and poor condition, a significant portion of the original 6th century structure still exists. The interior of the church still features ancient art and paintings on the walls as well as surprisingly intact tile mosaics on the floor. The highlight of the church is the sarcophagus that once held Nicholas' remains.

40. ST. PAUL'S CHURCH

Sehitkerim Mallallesi, 3407.SK.No:9, 33440 Tarsus/Mersin, Turkey

Denomination: Formerly Greek Orthodox
(sacred to many Christians)
Dates: 1102 (completed)
Web: www.goturkeytourism.com/things-to-do/christian-sacred-sites-in-turkey (tourism website)

St. Paul's Church in Mersin commemorates the birthplace of Saul of Tarsus, who later became Paul of New Testament fame. Although no claim is made as to whether or not this church marks the spot of Paul's birth, residence or any other place of significance in his life, it has become the destination of choice for pilgrims seeking to learn more of the city where he grew up. The church is now preserved by the Turkish government as a museum.

Paul was born into a prominent Jewish family in the city of Tarsus sometime in the early years of the 1st century. Known as Saul, he was raised in Tarsus until a young man, when he moved to Judea. At some point Paul returned to Tarsus, though the Bible offers little information about this visit. Other visits were likely as most of Paul's missionary journeys usually took him to Asia Minor. It is possible he even established a church there.

Christianity probably existed in Tarsus as early as Paul's time, and was certainly practiced by the 3rd century. Persecutions of Christians in the city were recorded around this time. It is uncertain how early the first church was constructed here, but the current St. Paul's Church dates back to the early 1100s. St. Paul's is still a sporadically semi-active church, though run as a museum under the auspices of the Turkish government.

Of Interest: St. Paul's Church forms the core of a number of places of Christian interest in Mersin. The church itself, which looks like it was built much more recently than nine hundred years ago, boasts some very old and beautiful frescoes. Not too far from the church is

St. Paul's Well, believed to be the well used by his family when he lived in Tarsus as a child. Also nearby is the Seven Sleepers Cave where, according to tradition, seven young Christians escaped persecution in the 1st century.

---

41. CHURCH OF ST. PETER

Kucukdalyan Mahallesi, Sen Piyer Cad Haraparasi,
31120 Antakya, Turkey

Alternate/Full Name: St. Peter's Cave Church
Denomination: Formerly Roman Catholic (sacred to many Christians)
Dates: c. 4th century (originally completed), c. 1100 (current building completed)
Web: https://hometurkey.com/en/attractions/cave-church-of-saint-peter (tourism website)

The Church of St. Peter in Antakya, ancient Antioch, is among the world's oldest place of Christian worship still in use. Built into the side of the slope of Mount Starius, it was the seat of the first Christian Patriarchate established outside of the Holy Land. According to tradition, it stands on the spot where Peter the Apostle delivered the first sermon in the city, and it was here that the term 'Christian' was probably used for the first time. The Church of St. Peter is remarkable for the fact that activity in the cave has been dated to the 1st century.

Peter, chief of the Apostles, personally travelled to the city of Antioch, one of the Roman Empire's greatest and most hedonistic cities. He probably arrived there sometime between the years 40 and 45, and soon a Christian community was established there. This community later grew into the Patriarchate of Antioch, a leading center of ancient Church activity. Paul also spent time in Antioch, and it was during his tenure working here that the term 'Christian' was coined by Barnabas. This seemingly minor event was actually a major development in the identity of the Church as an independent entity from Judaism.

The first actual church building in Antioch dates from the time of Peter and consisted primarily of a small cave on the mountainside. The extent of the original structure is uncertain, but it was probably no bigger than a small chapel. Peter apparently worked here for several years before departing for Rome sometime in the middle of the 1st century. Within a century or so, the Patriarchate of Antioch grew so important that the city's bishops eventually established larger church buildings.

Over the years the original church managed to survive the arrival of Islam in the region, and continued to be a stopping point for Christian pilgrims on their way from Asia Minor to the Holy Land. It was expanded and embellished during the Crusader period, and again during the Napoleanic period. For a while it was under the jurisdiction of Capuchin monks who maintained it for use of the local Christians and visitors who still found their way to the ancient shrine. After the breakup of the Ottoman Empire, the Church of St. Peter was taken over by the Turkish government, and it has been run as a museum ever since.

Of Interest: The Church of St. Peter is not only one of the world's oldest church sites, it is also one of the oldest surviving buildings in Antioch. It stands on a ledge on the slope of Mount Starius and affords a wonderful view of the modern-day city. Most of the church is carved into the side of the mountain. An imposing façade was constructed across the entrance centuries ago and largely restored in the 19th century. The church interior, once a small cave, was carved out and extended several times, mostly by the Crusaders. Some of the interior mosaics and frescoes date from the earliest days of the church. An interior tunnel is also thought to date from early Christian times. Numerous tombs have been discovered at the site over the years, both inside and outside the shrine, though the corpses have not been identified.

42. JVARI MONASTERY

Zahesi-Jvari Monastery, Mtskheta, Georgia

Alternate/Full Name: Monastery of the Cross
Denomination: Georgian Apostolic Orthodox
Dates: c. 5th century (founded)
Web: www.georgia.travel/en_us/mtskheta-mtianeti/mtskheta/jvari-monastery (tourism website)

The Jvari Monastery is the most famous Christian site in Georgia (the nation, not the state), and is the heart of the Georgian Orthodox Church. One of the world's oldest largely intact churches, it preserves some of the personal effects of St. Nino, an evangelist who brought Christianity to the area in the 4th century. The monastery is the Georgian Orthodox patriarchal seat and country's most important Christian pilgrimage destination. The Jvari Monastery is a UNESCO World Heritage Site.

The history of Christianity in Georgia, or Eastern Iberia as it was called in ancient times, is closely linked to that of neighboring Armenia. Armenian and Syrian missionaries visited the area as early as the 3rd century. By the 4th century, the region had a substantial Christian population. As in Armenia, Muslims who arrived centuries later never made a serious effort to impose Islam on the area, which was sometimes ruled by a Christian monarch. When the Ottoman Empire decided to persecute the Christians of the Caucasus, the people of Georgia were largely spared thanks to the buffer of Armenia.

Ironically, the long-independent Georgian Orthodox Church, one of the oldest in the world, faced its greatest threat in the 19th century, not by Islam, but by absorption into the Russian Orthodox Church. However, despite a serious effort on the part of the Czars, this attempt largely failed. The Georgian Orthodox Church successfully survived both the Czarist period and the even more dangerous communist period, and did so with flying colors. Georgia was the first Soviet Republic to enjoy free elections, and the people celebrated by flocking back to the holy sites of Mtskheta.

Of Interest: The Jvari Monastery is one of the oldest Christian sites in the Caucasus. It is believed to have been built on the spot where St. Nino established the area's first mission, setting up a cross big enough so that the whole town could see it. The current monastery dates back to around 600, but the original building wasn't much older. Although the church is still standing, much of the outer compound is now a ruin. The church interior, lit by small window slits and candles, is dark and mysterious. The remains of the Cross of St. Nino were discovered when the earlier church was replaced, and have been on display here ever since the 7th century. The tomb of St. Nino is believed to be located somewhere beneath the church.

---

43. ETCHMIADZIN CATHEDRAL

Vagarshapat, Etchmiadzin, Armenia

Denomination: Armenian Apostolic
Dates: 301 (originally completed), c. 6th century (current building completed)
Web: https://armenianchurch.us/essential_grid/holy-etchmiadzin (official website)

Etchmiadzin Cathedral is the oldest surviving church of the oldest surviving denomination of Christianity. Armenia has the honor of being the world's oldest Christian nation, with a population that has somehow managed to remain largely Christian for the better part of fifteen centuries. The city's cathedral is one of the oldest in the world, and houses numerous treasures, including artifacts associated with the Crucifixion and Noah's Ark. The Etchmiadzin Cathedral is part of the Etchmiadzin UNESCO World Heritage Site.

Armenia has a long and rich Christian history that may date as far back as the 1st century. During the Roman era, Armenia remained nominally independent of both the Roman and the Sassanid Empires. It is perhaps for this reason that Christianity was better received in Armenia than elsewhere. Persecutions were rare in Armenia, and many

Christian refugees likely found sanctuary there. In 309 Christianity was recognized as the official state religion of Armenia.

Two years later, Gregory the Illuminator established a church in Etchmiadzin after a vision directed him to do so. This church became the seat of the nation's bishopric, and was later expanded into a much larger cathedral in the 6th century. Throughout this period, though Armenia remained closely tied to the Byzantine Empire, its Christians were largely independent of foreign authority. The region retained its Christian identity despite the long parade of Islamic empires which occupied the region.

The Armenian Christian community survived even during harsh persecutions in the late Ottoman era. While many Armenians did not survive the turbulence of the early 20th century, the Etchmiadzin Cathedral did. It remains to this day the seat of the Armenian Apostolic Church, which is now part of the Oriental Orthodox communion. Home to a number of sacred treasures, it is the most important Christian pilgrimage destination in Armenia.

Of Interest: Etchmiadzin Cathedral is one of the world's oldest churches, with at least part of its structure dating back to the 4th century. However, most of the building was completed in the 6th century. The ancient style borrows somewhat from Byzantine influence but is otherwise uniquely Armenian. The original main building in the center appears more like an old Roman fortification. The unusual central tower is crowned with a conical roof rather than a dome. The cathedral's interior houses a museum in which Christian artwork and artifacts are displayed. One of the cathedral's architectural curiosities is an ancient fire-pit from the site's earlier incarnation as a pagan temple. It has been preserved and is located near the altar. Among the cathedral treasures is the Spear of Destiny and a hunk of wood that supposedly came from Noah's Ark.

44. KHOR VIRAP MONASTERY

H11, Pokr Vedi, Armenia

Denomination: Armenian Apostolic
Dates: c. 5th century (originally completed),
1662 (current building completed)
Web: www.armenia.travel/en/church-and-monastery/khor-virap-monastery (tourism website)

The Khor Virap Monastery is the second most sacred Christian site in Armenia and is closely associated with the events leading up to the Christianization of the country in the 4th century. According to tradition, the monastery stands on the site of a building where Gregory the Illuminator was once imprisoned. It is a very popular pilgrimage destination among Armenian Apostolic Christians.

Although Christianity in Armenia traces its roots back to the Apostle Bartholomew in the 1st century, it was the efforts of St. Gregory the Illuminator that led to the entire nation accepting that faith in the year 301. Gregory, a former advisor to the pagan King Tiridates, was imprisoned and tortured for his faith for thirteen years. During this time he was held in a dungeon on or near the present site of the monastery. He was kept alive by a daily ration of bread provided by a sympathetic citizen.

Later, Tiridates had Gregory released and was himself eventually converted. Shortly thereafter he proclaimed Christianity to be the official state religion of Armenia. In the 5th century, a chapel was built on the site of the dungeon in honor of St. Gregory's years of suffering. The current church was completed in the 17th century.

Of Interest: The Khor Virap Monastery stands on an isolated outcropping of rock some distance from the nearest buildings in the city of Artashat. Mount Ararat of Noah's Ark fame makes a magnificent backdrop to the complex. The church is enclosed by a wall lined with the monastic community's buildings. The interior of the church stands over the ancient dungeon of St. Gregory's incarceration. It is still accessible by a very steep ladder. The name 'Khor Virap' means 'Deep Dungeon', a reference to Gregory's imprisonment.

---

45. ST. THADDEUS MONASTERY

Qareh Kelisa, West Azerbaijan, Iran

Denomination: Armenian Apostolic (sacred to many Eastern Christians)
Dates: c. 7th century (originally completed), 1811 (current building completed)
Web: www.itto.org/iran/attraction/saint-thaddeus-monastery-chaldiran-azerbaijan (tourism website)

The St. Thaddeus Monastery is an isolated church complex tucked away in the hinterlands of Armenia. It is believed to stand on the site of the martyrdom and/or burial of the Apostle Thaddeus (aka Jude). It is revered by members of both the Oriental Orthodox and Assyrian Orthodox Churches. For the last three decades, the monastery has been under the jurisdiction of the Iranian government. The St. Thaddeus Monastery is part of the Armenian Monasteries of Iran UNESCO World Heritage Site.

Thaddeus is among the least well-known of all of the Apostles. The Bible says virtually nothing of him beyond his inclusion in the list of the Twelve. Even his identity is enigmatic. He is only mentioned in two of the gospels, though he is usually identified with the Apostle Jude who does appear in the other two gospels. Nevertheless a popular tradition has grown up around him. According to legend, Thaddeus travelled to Armenia, perhaps in the company of Bartholomew, where he spent the final years of his life until his martyrdom sometime around the year 65.

The belief is very strong that Thaddeus evangelized in the area and that he died here. Of the lesser-known Apostles, the tradition of Thaddeus' tomb here is possibly the most plausible. The real question is, is it the tomb of Thaddeus the Apostle, or actually the tomb of

Thaddeus of Edessa, one of the Seventy Disciples of Jesus, who traveled into the east with the Apostle Thomas. Either way it is the resting place of a very important early church figure.

According to tradition, the first church was built on the site a few years after Thaddeus' death. Over the centuries this was replaced by a series of larger churches. The entire site was completely rebuilt in the 19th century thanks to the generosity of a local Muslim prince. However, in the wake of the 1979 Iranian revolution, the local Christians were driven from the site and told not to return. At the time of this writing a special dispensation was permitted for pilgrims to visit once a year on on St. Thaddeus' feast day.

Of Interest: The Saint Thaddeus Monastery is extremely isolated in every sense of the word. It is located in the extreme northeastern corner of Iran close to the borders of Armenia, Azerbaijan and Turkey. The setting is Biblical, with rolling hills dotted with tents and herds of sheep. Although some claim that a church stood on the site in the 1st century, nothing is left of any other structure on the site prior to the 7th century. The current monastery predominantly dates from the 19th century restoration. The monastic compound consists of a rectangular fortified wall surrounding a beautiful Armenian-style church. Despite its relatively small size, the lonely church dominates the surrounding plain. The exact spot where Thaddeus is buried at the monastery is uncertain.

FAR EAST

46. ST. FRANCIS CHURCH

St. Francis Church Road, Fort Kochi, Kochi, Kerala 682001, India

Denomination: Anglican Church of South India
Dates: 1503 (originally completed),
1516 (current building completed)
Web: www.stfranciscsichurch.com (official website)

St. Francis Church is oldest Christian church in India as well as one of the oldest churches built by any European colonial power in the Far East. It was from here that Christianity began its long march throughout the Indian Subcontinent. Its history includes brushes with famous European explorers as well as numerous colonial wars. It has been part of the Roman Catholic, Dutch Reform and Anglican denominations.

In 1500, a Portuguese fleet arrived off the coast of Southern India, bringing with it a number of missionary priests. Within a few years the first Roman Catholic churches were constructed in and around the city of Cochin, including the St. Francis Church, which was completed in 1503. In 1524, Vasco da Gama died while visiting Cochin, and his body was interred here for a time.

The Church of St. Francis remained an important Catholic site until 1663 when the Portuguese lost their colony to the Dutch. The Dutch subsequently burned down most of the Catholic churches in the region, sparing the St. Francis Church for use as a Dutch Reformed Church. In 1795 the colony changed from Dutch hands to British, and in 1804 the St. Francis Church became part of the Anglican communion. St. Francis is recognized by several Christian denominations as the de-facto Mother Church of India.

Of Interest: The St. Francis Church is a classic example of colonial religious architecture similar to that which can be found in former

Spanish and Portuguese colonies around the world. It has a plain but distinctive white façade with a single entrance above which is one of the oldest public clocks in India. A great stone marker commemorating the church stands directly before the entrance. The church interior has been renovated several times over the centuries to accommodate its changing role. Most traces of the original Roman Catholic décor are long gone in favor of more austere Protestant appointments. The original tomb where Vasco da Gama was once buried is still on display in the church.

---

47. BASILICA OF BOM JESUS

Old Goa Road, Bainguinim, Goa 403402, India

Denomination: Roman Catholic
Dates: 1605 (completed)
Web: www.bomjesus.org (official website)

The Basilica of Bom Jesus is one of the oldest churches in India, and one of that country's most important Catholic pilgrimage destinations. It is the site of the tomb of St. Francis Xavier, one of the greatest Christian missionaries in history. The Basilica of Bom Jesus is part of the Churches and Convents of Goa UNESCO World Heritage Site.

Francis Xavier is credited with introducing Christianity to almost every corner of the Far East. He was born in Spain in 1506 and received his theological training in Paris. By the time he was in his twenties, Francis was part of a close-knit group of clergymen that included a number of men who are counted among the most influential theologians of the 16th century. One of these was Ignatius Loyala, with whom Francis Xavier founded the Society of Jesus in 1534.

In 1540, the King of Portugal requested the aid of the Jesuits in his colonial endeavors. His goal was to make an end-run around the Muslims who were then expanding down the Malay Peninsula. Xavier responded, and the next year he set out. In 1542 he arrived in Goa, which he made the base of his missionary operations. During the next three years he traveled throughout Southern India and Sri Lanka spreading the Gospel. He later visited a number of the Moluccan Islands in eastern Indonesia before returning to Goa, where he remained until 1549. Francis Xavier's missionary work then took him to China and Japan.

In 1552, exhausted from many years of non-stop travel in foreign lands, Francis Xavier died enroute to the island of Shagchuan. His body was returned to Goa. Although none of the countries that Francis Xavier visited was destined to have a Christian majority, many of the communities he founded still exist. At the end of the 16th century, the Basilica of Bom Jesus was constructed in his honor. It is now one of the most popular Catholic pilgrimage destinations in Southern Asia.

Of Interest: The Basilica of Bom Jesus is an absolutely magnificent structure, built at the height of Portuguese power and affluence in the colonial period. The cathedral's impressive façade is distinctly European, but with a touch of classical Indian elements. The interior of the church consists of an enormous vaulted nave constructed in white marble and lavishly trimmed in gold. Much of the wall behind the altar is covered with a large iconic painting of St. Francis Xavier. His body is kept in a silver-bedecked tomb. Francis Xavier's remains, while partly veiled, are still displayed to the public.

---

48. ST. THOMAS BASILICA

38 Santhome High Road, Chennai, Tamil Nadu 600004, India

Alternate/Full Names: St. Thomas Cathedral Basilica, National Shrine of St. Thomas
Denomination: Roman Catholic (sacred to many Christians)
Dates: c. 6th century (originally completed),
1896 (current building completed)
Web: www.archdioceseofmadrasmylapore.in/shrine (official website)

The St. Thomas Basilica in India is one of the most important churches in the Far East and yet one of Christianity's least well-known major shrines. Its fame comes from the fact that Christian community here was likely founded by the Apostle Thomas in the 1st century. Its obscurity is due to its geography, as the community probably had little or no communication with other Christians for the better part of a thousand years.

Thomas was one of the twelve Apostles that accompanied Jesus during his ministry. His disbelief regarding Jesus' Resurrection was one of the most memorable moments in the New Testament. According to tradition, it was because of Thomas' disbelief that he drew the lot that required him to travel to the distant lands of the east. The Apocryphal books of Thomas are among the most extensive, and because of this we have more clues concerning Thomas' later life than some of his fellow Apostles.

There are several variations of the stories of Thomas' travels following the Apostolic Diaspora, not necessarily mutually exclusive. All versions agree that he did go east, spending some time in Syria and Persia before continuing on to India. There is evidence of a Christian community of Syrian origin in India dating possibly as far back as the 2nd century. Thomas may have arrived in India around 52 AD. He lived and preached there for about two decades, outliving most of the other Apostles.

After years of peace, Thomas was chased out of his long-time home and pursued to the top of a mountain where he was caught and pierced through the heart with a lance. After his death, his body was taken back to the town and buried. At some point an early church was built on or near Thomas' grave. This was replaced by a larger shrine around the 6th century. Portuguese explorers discovered the shrine in the 17th century and replaced it with a Catholic church. Thomas' body may have been moved in whole or in part back to Edessa as early as the 4th century, and thence to Ortona in Italy. Today the Basilica of St. Thomas is highly venerated as one of the world's only surviving Apostolic burial sites.

Of Interest: The current St. Thomas Basilica was completed in the 19th century and stands on the site of the former Portuguese colonial church. A beautiful colonial building in blindingly white stone, the focus of the church is entirely on the Apostle Thomas. The main point of interest is a chapel located beneath the main sanctuary, where the sarcophagus of Thomas can still be found. It has not been opened in almost three hundred years, and it is uncertain what may actually still be inside. Some believe that part of Thomas' body is still there, while others believe that it was completely removed and sent to Edessa or Ortona centuries ago. In all likelihood a bit of the body resides in each location. A small museum in the church possesses Christian antiquities which date from the Portuguese period.

---

49. ST. MARY'S CHURCH

Rajaji Salai, Chennai, Tamil Nadu 600009, India

Denomination: Anglican Church of South India
Dates: 1680 (completed)
Web: www.chennai.org.uk/religious-places/churches/st-mary-church (tourism website)

St. Mary's Church is the oldest purpose-built Anglican church in India. A part of the first British settlement on the Subcontinent, St. Mary's has survived virtually intact to the present day. Its antiquity and its graveyard, with a number of interesting burials, has earned it the nickname Westminster Abbey of the East, though this is perhaps a bit of an overstatement. Nevertheless St. Mary's is one of the most important Anglican pilgrimage sites in India.

The first major British settlement in India was established in 1639. While the East India Company quickly constructed Fort St. George and other public buildings to protect its interests, it took a while for them to build an Anglican church here. For nearly four decades, the practice of Anglicanism in the colony took place in a warehouse dining room.

The East India Company finally constructed a church for the colony in the 1670s. The church was constructed so as to resist military attacks and doubled as a barracks when needed. Throughout the time of British rule in India, the St. Mary's had periodic moments in the spotlight. Elihu Yale, who served as governor of the province in the early 18th century, provided a major endowment with which Yale

University in Connecticut was founded. A large number of British statesman and military leaders who served in India are buried here, making its graveyard an interesting historic site.

Of Interest: St. Mary's Church is a beautiful white colonial era structure with walls four feet thick designed to protect it against gun fire. Some of the church appointments, including the altar, came from nearby Catholic churches which had been ransacked. The graveyard, which was restored to its original location in the 19th century, is home to a number of burials of local British interest, including famed artist Elizabeth Gwilim.

---

50. ST. PAUL'S CATHEDRAL

1A Cathedral Road, Kolkata, West Bengal 700071, India

Denomination: Anglican Church of North India
Dates: 1847 (completed)
Web: https://www.wbtourismgov.in/destination/place/st_paul_s_cathedral (tourism website)

St. Paul's Cathedral in Kolkata is the largest Anglican church in India and among the largest in Asia. Located in what was for over a century the capital of British India, St. Paul's was of particular religious and political importance throughout much of the British colonial era. It is part of a cluster of Kolkata's major sites, including a number of museums and the Victoria Memorial, and is among the most visited places in the city.

Over the course of the 19th century, the East India Company established Kolkata as one of the most important centers of trade in India, making it their headquarters and ultimately the capital of their colonial territories. In 1858, when the British Empire annexed India outright, Kolkata became the colonial capital which it remained for over half a century.

By the time the East India Company had reached the height of its power and influence in the early 19th century, the Church of

England had become a prominent institution in India. To serve the large Anglican expat community that had grown up in Kolkata, and in recognition of the colony's political importance, a new cathedral was constructed in the heart of the city. Completed in 1847, it was one of the largest non-Catholic churches in the world outside of Europe.

The cathedral became the seat of one of the most important Anglican dioceses in the Far East, as well as one of the architectural symbols of the city. It stood for exactly one hundred years before the end of British colonial rule in India in 1947. Now part of the Church of North India, it is still an important institution in the Anglican Communion and one of the most important bishoprics in Asia.

Of Interest: St. Paul's Cathedral is among the finest examples of Gothic Revival architecture in the Far East. A gleaming white edifice, it is one of Kolkata's defining landmarks. The traditional cross layout is crowned with an immense bell tower over the transept. The current tower, modeled after one at Westminster Abbey in London, replaced an earlier tower that was destroyed by an earthquake in 1934. The cathedral interior has traditional appointments and stained glass windows, but with a modern, arced exposed ceiling which was originally designed to support the installation of ceiling fans.

---

51. MOTHER HOUSE OF THE MISSIONARIES OF CHARITY

54A Acharya Jagadish Chandra Bose Road, Ripon Street, Kolkata, West Bengal 700016, India

Denomination: Roman Catholic
Dates: 1950 (founded)
Web: www.motherteresa.org/missionaries-of-charity (official website)

The Mother House of the Missionaries of Charity in Kolkata is one of India's most humble and beloved Catholic shrines. This unassuming building, which serves as the global headquarters for one of the world's most famous charitable organizations, is also the site of the tomb of its founder, Mother Teresa. Many who come here to pay tribute to this great Catholic missionary often stay to become missionaries themselves.

Agnes Gonxha Bojaxhiu was born into a poor family in Macedonia in 1910. In her childhood she witnessed the tumultuous upheavals that ravaged the Balkan Peninsula between the world wars. These events had a profound effect on the young Agnes. About ten years after World War I, at the age of eighteen, she committed her life to Christ and joined the Sisters of Loreto, receiving the name Teresa. When her training was complete, Sister Teresa was sent to Calcutta to teach at St. Mary's High School, which she did for nearly two decades.

Over time she became ever more concerned by the desperate poverty that saturated the city. In 1948, she finished teaching and headed for Calcutta's slums. After spending two years doing freelance missionary work, Sister Teresa received Vatican permission to start a new order, the Missionaries of Charity. Teresa and her disciples served the community with great enthusiasm, providing food, medical care, shelter and education to as many people as could find their way to her. By 1965 the order had grown so large that the Vatican designated it an international religious family.

Over the next three decades the missionaries spread across the globe. In 1979, Mother Teresa was awarded the Nobel Peace Prize for her untiring efforts. She continued her work until the very end of her life in 1997. She is recognized around the world as one of the greatest Christians of the 20th century, and is a beloved figure far beyond the Roman Catholic Church. Her body was laid to rest in the Mother House of the Missionaries of Charity in 1997.

Of Interest: The Mother House of the Missionaries of Charity is located in a poor area far from Kolkata's major tourist sites. The building itself is 20th century block construction, and appears more like a small office building than the headquarters of one of the world's great missionary societies. The only outward decoration is a statue of the Virgin Mary located on building's corner. The interior is similarly utilitarian. The heart of the building is a simple courtyard used for both communal gathering and quiet reflection. Just inside from the courtyard is the room where Mother Teresa lies in eternal repose in a simple white marble tomb.

---

52. RUINS OF ST. PAUL'S CATHEDRAL

Calcada de Sao Paulo, Macau, China

Denomination: Roman Catholic
Dates: 1640 (originally completed)
Web: www.macautourism.gov.mo/en/sightseeing/churches/ruins-of-st-pauls (tourism website)

St. Paul's Cathedral was once the largest Christian edifice in the Far East. Destroyed by a fire in the 1800s, its preserved façade has become Macau's most famous, and touristy, site. A destination for Catholic pilgrims who come to explore the region's Christian history, it is also a magnet for other visitors fascinated by the unusual architecture. The Ruins of St. Paul's Cathedral are part of the Historic Centre of Macau UNESCO World Heritage Site.

The Portuguese were the first Europeans to arrive in China, and in 1535 received permission to trade in Macau. About twenty years later, the Portuguese began building the first permanent colony. The Roman Catholic Church soon followed. The famous Jesuit missionary Francis Xavier visited China in 1549 and died there a few years later. In 1576, the Papacy established a diocese for the entire Far East, which included all of China, Japan, Vietnam and Malaysia, with the capital at Macau.

In the late 16th century, Jesuit missionaries in Macau built the first major cathedral in China. Although predated by a few other cathedrals in the Spanish Philippines, St. Paul's Cathedral was the largest and most important Catholic church in the Far East for many years. Macau and its church became an important refuge for Japanese Christians in the wake of persecutions which swept Japan in the early 17th century. Skilled Japanese craftsman helped to complete the cathedral's famous façade.

Macau was steadfastly maintained as a Portuguese colony for hundreds of years, throughout which time it remained the center of Catholicism in China. However, in 1835 a fire swept through St. Paul's Cathedral. Rather than rebuild the old church, a new cathedral was constructed. Practical civic leaders had the façade preserved in memory of Macau's long Catholic history.

Of Interest: St. Paul's Cathedral, or at least its preserved façade, is quite a dramatic site. Perched on top of a tall hill, the cathedral is not fronted by a typical colonial-style plaza, but rather by a grand staircase consisting of 66 stone carved steps. These must be climbed in order to reach the perfectly preserved façade, which has been featured on postcards of the city since the 19th century. The facade is known for its blending of Asian and European artistry in the carving details, courtesy of the early Japanese craftsman who worked on it. Behind the façade virtually nothing remains of the cathedral, although the floor plan is preserved, as are bits of the outer walls. Recent excavations have discovered early Chinese Christian artifacts, as well as relics of both Jesuit missionaries and Japanese martyrs.

---

53. MYEONGDONG CATHEDRAL

74 Myeongdong-gil, Jeodong 1(il)-ga, Jung-ga, Seoul, South Korea

Alternate/Full Name: Cathedral Church of the Virgin Mary of the Immaculate Conception
Denomination: Roman Catholic
Dates: 1898 (completed)
Web: www.mdsd.or.kr/bbs (official website)

Myeongdong Cathedral is the seat of the Roman Catholic Church in Korea. It is also one of the oldest churches in the country, as the government had generally opposed the construction of Christian houses of worship prior to the mid-20th century. The cathedral is now a burial site for martyrs of the Korean church, and has become an important place of pilgrimage as well as a popular tourist destination.

The Korean Peninsula was among the very last places in mainland Asia to see the introduction of Christianity. Although Catholic missionaries had already visited nearby China and Japan in the 17th century, Christianity did not arrive in Korea until 1785. Its establishment here was met with strong resistance and even persecutions. It was more than another century before tepid tolerance by the government permitted the building of churches in the country.

Construction on a major cathedral did not take place until the 1890s, but it was completed quickly and dedicated in 1898. It was for a time the largest building in Korea. The Myeongdong Cathedral has not only been the heart of Roman Catholicism in the country for the last century, it has also been a popular place for political rallies and demonstrations. The cathedral was designated a Korean National Historic Site in 1977.

Of Interest: Myeongdong Cathedral is a huge structure with an enormous bell and clock tower that dominates the surrounding neighborhood. A locally famous statue of Our Lady of Lourdes stands beside the church. A crypt beneath the church houses the remains of nine Christian Korean martyrs who died in the persecutions of the 19th century. A grotto on the property has been hopefully dedicated to the dream of the reunification of the two Koreas.

---

54. TWENTY-SIX MARTYRS MUSEUM AND MONUMENT

850-0051 Nagasaki Prefecture, Nagasaki, 7-8, Japan

Denomination: Public Monument
Dates: 1962 (completed)
Web: www.26martyrs.com (official website)

The Twenty-Six Martyrs Museum and Monument commemorates the massacre of early Christian converts in 16th century Japan. When the Catholic Church tried to expand into Japan, resistance was fierce. The focal point of the persecutions took place in and around the city of Nagasaki, where Christianity had briefly taken root. The Twenty-Six Martyrs Monument is one of the most memorable Catholic shrines in the Far East.

When Portuguese missionaries arrived in Japan in the mid-16th century, it marked the end of Christianity's long, slow progression around Asia. Francis Xavier himself was among the first priests to arrive and to help establish the Church in this distant land. At first Christianity was tolerated, particularly by local warlords who sought Portuguese military assistance in the country's feuds. By 1600, several hundred thousand Japanese citizens had been converted.

Around this time, Japan had become somewhat unified under the Emperor Toyotomi Hideyoshi, who was concerned about the presence of Europeans. He became convinced, not without reason, that Christian missionary efforts allowed the Europeans to gain a foothold among the local population. He banned missionary activities, and a general intolerance ensued. Persecutions followed, and in 1597 twenty-six Christians, including six missionaries and twenty Japanese converts, were publicly crucified. This was later followed by other pogroms, most notably the Great Martyrdom of Nagasaki in 1622.

Eventually Christianity was banned outright in Japan. This situation did not change until the late 19th century, when tentative new missionary efforts arrived along with powerful western navies to back them up. The Twenty-Six martyrs of Japan were canonized in 1862, among the first Christians in the Far East to be so honored. A century later, in the wake of Japan's disastrous war against the United States and the dropping of the second atomic bomb, the Twenty-Six Martyrs Museum and Monument was erected as part of Nagasaki's reconciliation with its past.

Of Interest: The Twenty-Six Martyrs Museum and Monument stands on the site where some of the earliest Japanese Christians gave their lives for their faith. It was constructed in the 1960s as part of the post-war reconstruction of devastated Nagasaki. Architecturally it is a strange concrete structure combining modern, Japanese and Christian elements. It is crowned with two of the oddest, most tree-like bell towers in the world. Twenty-six bronze effigies represent the men and boys crucified here. The museum is home to several exhibits documenting the history of Christianity in Japan. Among the more notable exhibits are letters written by Francis Xavier and statues of the Virgin Mary disguised as Buddhist deities. There are also the famous Treading images, which depict local citizens walking on statues of Jesus and Mary.

---

55. BASILICA OF SANTO NINO

Pilgrim's Center, Osmena Boulevard, Cebu City, Philippines

Alternate/Full Name: Basilica of the Holy Child of Cebu City
Denomination: Roman Catholic
Dates: 1739 (completed)
Web: https://santoninodecebubasilica.org (official website)

The Basilica of Santo Nino is the oldest church in the Philippines as well as one of the oldest in the greater Pacific area. It is home to a number of regionally important church artifacts and icons. The major church of Cebu City, it was from here that Catholicism spread to the rest of the Philippines in the 16th and 17th centuries. Because of this Santo Nino is regarded not only as a popular pilgrimage site but one of the Philippines' most important historic sites as well.

Christianity arrived in the Philippines when Ferdinand Magellan found his way here in 1521. However, his missionary efforts were short-lived, when he and his crew found themselves at odds with a local chieftain, leading to their subsequent deaths. When more Spanish explorers arrived a few decades later, they discovered two treasures that Magellan had left behind: the cross which he had set up in honor of the Church, and a small icon of the Baby Jesus that had been presented to a local leader's wife.

Soon after their arrival, they established the Basilica of Santo Nino in honor of Magellan. As Catholicism grew in the area, so too did the importance of the Basilica. In 1571 the center of Spanish colonial administration was moved to Manila. While its political importance waned, Cebu City remained an important religious center for the country.

The Basilica of Santo Nino is still the Philippines' great historic Christian treasure. Today, after nearly five hundred years, it remains one of the most important churches in the Philippines. Pilgrims continue to flock to Cebu City to see the Cross of Magellan and the Icon of Santo Nino de Cebu, among the most important Christian artifacts in the East Indies.

Of Interest: The Basilica of Santo Nino is an excellent example of 16th century Spanish-colonial architecture. It was one of the largest churches in the Pacific for the better part of a century. The interior of the basilica is impressive and decorative. A large screen behind the main altar displays a collection of artwork and artifacts. The famous Icon of Santo Nino de Cebu occupies the center shelf. Just out in front of the Basilica is a small shrine displaying Magellan's Cross. This cross is actually a replica; what's left of the original is well guarded, to protect it from further abuse by souvenir seekers.

---

56. QUIAPO CHURCH

363 Quezon Boulevard, Quiapo, Manila, Philippines

Alternate/Full Names: Basilica of the Black Nazarene, Parish Church of St. John the Baptist
Denomination: Roman Catholic
Dates: c. 16th century (originally completed),
1984 (current building completed)
Web: www.quiapochurch.com (official website)

The Quiapo Church is the most famous Catholic shrine in the Philippines. It is home to and dedicated to an icon of Jesus, known as the Black Nazarene, to which miracles have been attributed. Located in a suburb of the national capital of Manila, this church is one of the most visited Catholic sites in the country.

The Black Nazarene was actually created by an unknown Mexican woodworker around the turn of the 17th century. According to tradition, there was a fire on board a Spanish galleon that was transporting Augustinian missionaries across the Pacific Ocean. Although the image was blackened by the smoke, it miraculously survived both the fire and the voyage. Upon arrival in the Philippines, the wooden statue was placed in an early mission church in the newly founded capital of Manila.

A number of miracles were credited to the icon, most notably the success of the initial voyage, and the mission church became a place of pilgrimage. Meanwhile, another church, the Quiapo Church, had been established by Franciscans in 1586. The icon was moved here in the 18th century. Although the Quiapo Church was destroyed on several occasions, including by earthquake in the 19th century and by fire in the 20th century, the icon miraculously survived.

During World War II, the statue was credited with protecting the church during the Japanese occupation. In 1975, two priests were murdered here, apparently in a bungled robbery attempt. Fortunately, this did not affect the popularity of the church, which was designated a basilica in 1988. With millions of visitors annually, the Quiapo Church is by far the most popular Catholic site in the Philippines.

Of Interest: The Quiapo Church is the fourth church to stand on the site, and largely dates from the 1920s. The plaza in front of the church can accommodate tens of thousands of worshippers, which gather in huge numbers several times per year. Following a major remodel and expansion in the 1980s, the church interior was modernized, with no columns and minimal obstructions in order to maximize the number of visitors that can be accommodated. The baroque-ish niche behind the altar houses the Black Nazarene. The icon that is on display is the original body of the statue with a replica of the head. The original head rests upon a replica body which is kept beneath the altar.

57. ST. ANDREW'S CATHEDRAL

11 St. Andrew's Road, Singapore, 178959

Denomination: Anglican Church of South East Asia
Dates: 1836 (originally completed), 1862 (current building completed)
Web: https://cathedral.org.sg (official website)

St. Andrew's Cathedral is the seat of the Anglican Church in Singapore and that country's largest Christian place of worship. The second on the site, it was the first major Anglican church constructed east of India. For a while it was home to the only Revere Bell outside of the United States, a gift of the daughter of the famous American silversmith.

Christianity was introduced to Singapore when the British established a major port here in the early 19th century. Land was set aside for the construction of a church soon after the founding of the colony, and an initial church was completed on the site in 1836. In 1843, Maria Balestier, the wife of the American consul and the daughter of Paul Revere, donated an extremely rare Revere Bell to the church.

Structural issues necessitated the demolition of the first church in the 1850s. Because of the growth and importance of the colony, the old church was replaced with a full-on cathedral in 1862. In 1869 St. Andrew's became the seat of a new Anglican diocese which was being separated from the diocese of Calcutta. The cathedral became a national monument of Singapore in 1973.

Of Interest: St. Andrew's Cathedral is a towering white Gothic Revival building with modernish elements. Among the church's treasures are a trio of artifacts from England: the Canterbury Stone, the Coventry Cross and the Coronation Carpet. The first two were gifts of Canterbury Cathedral and Coventry Cathedral in England. The latter was used during the coronation of Britain's current monarch, Elizabeth II. Unfortunately, the famous Revere Bell is no longer in use here or kept here, but can be seen at the National Museum of Singapore.

---

58. EBENEZER CHURCH

95 Coromandel Road, Ebenezer, NSW 2756, Australia

Denomination: Uniting Church in Australia
Dates: 1823 (completed)
Web: www.ebenezerchurch.org.au (official website)

Ebenezer Church is the oldest surviving church building located on the continent of Australia. Founded a little over two centuries ago by some of New South Wales' early settlers, it has been under the jurisdiction of a number of different Protestant denominations over the years. It is currently run as a Uniting Church.

Britain began efforts to settle Australia in earnest in the late 18th and early 19th centuries. Members of one of these small settlements formed a mixed denominational congregation at Ebenezer in 1803. They completed construction of their church in 1823, and the following year it became a Presbyterian institution. However, Anglicans, Methodists and other Christians formed part of the congregation as well.

Ebenezer Church has enjoyed a consistent if quiet existence, serving its community throughout the British Colonial era and beyond. It was renovated and expanded several times in the 20th century. It became part of the newly formed Uniting Church in Australia in the 1970s. Ebenezer Church was listed on the New South Wales State Heritage Register in 1999.

Of Interest: Ebenezer Church is not only Australia's oldest surviving church, it is one of the best examples of early European colonial architecture on the continent. It is a small but stately building, nestled among the graves of a tidy cemetery dating back to the early 1800s. The external vestry was added in the 1950s. Next door to the church is a centuries-old tree where the community's first service was held.

---

59. ST. PAUL'S CATHEDRAL

Flinders Lane & Swanston Street, Melbourne, VIC 3000, Australia

Denomination: Anglican Church of Australia
Dates: 1891 (completed)
Web: https://cathedral.org.au (official website)

St. Paul's Cathedral is one of the oldest cathedrals in Australia as well as one of the largest churches built during the colonial era. Tracing its roots back to one of the continent's earliest Anglican parishes, the cathedral was constructed to accommodate the rapid growth of the colony in the mid-19th century. More recently, St. Paul's has become the seat of the Anglican Primate of Australia.

The first Anglican parish in Melbourne was established in 1835. The city's original cathedral, Old St. James, was completed in 1847. This church, which is still standing and still in use, remained the city's cathedral until the 1890s. Following the Australian gold rush of the 1850s, Melbourne's population grew significantly, and a much larger cathedral was needed

St. Paul's Cathedral was founded on the spot of the city's original parish meeting, and was consecrated in 1891. Work was completed a few decades later. St. Paul's soon became an important site for state occasions, and famously hosted a visit by the Roman Catholic Pope John Paul II in 1986. In 2014 it was designated as the seat of the Anglican Church in Australia.

Of Interest: St. Paul's Cathedral is a classic Gothic Revival church typical of Anglican architecture of the Colonial era. One of the notable features of the exterior are the trio of spires, two over the bell towers and a much larger one over the transept. The interior has several unusual, by Anglican standards, points of interest. One is an eight-pointed Persian tile star that commemorates two Anglican churches in what is now Iran. The other is an immersion font shaped like a cruciform.

60. CHRIST CHURCH

Church Street, Russell 0202, New Zealand

Denomination: Anglican Church of New Zealand
Dates: 1835 (completed)
Web: www.oldchurch.org.nz (official website)

Christ Church is the oldest standing church, and one of the oldest buildings overall, in New Zealand. Constructed in 1835, it was among the first buildings completed in Russell, the earliest major settlement of the New Zealand colony. It was also the first building to be listed on the New Zealand Historic Places Trust.

Although New Zealand was first discovered by Europeans in the 17th century, colonization organized by the British Empire did not start until the early 1800s. Christian missionaries arrived at this time, establishing a foothold for the Anglican Church on the islands. Small Anglican parishes were established in the 1830s.

The first Christian missionaries in the Russell area commuted by boat across the Bay of Islands in order to lead worship in homes until the community built its own church. Fighting between the British and local Maoris occurred near the church in 1845. Although Christ Church was not the first church to be built in New Zealand, it is the oldest that has survived to the present day.

Of Interest: Christ Church is a small, whitewashed structure reminiscent of similar buildings built on the American frontier in the mid-19th century. The church is surrounded by a well groomed cemetery that is home to the graves of some of New Zealand's earliest settlers. Among those buried here is Tamati Waka Nene, a Maori who died during the fighting in 1845.

AFRICA

61. ST. MARK'S CATHEDRAL

19 Al Akbat Church, Qesm Al Attarin, Alexandria, Egypt

Alternate/Full Name: St. Mark's Coptic Orthodox Cathedral
Denomination: Coptic Orthodox Church of Alexandria (sacred to many Eastern Christians)
Dates: 1st century (originally completed), 1819 (current building completed)
Web: www.egypt.travel/en/atractions/coptic-cathedral-of-st-mark (tourism website)

St. Mark's Cathedral is the seat of the Coptic Orthodox Church of Alexandria, one of the five ancient Patriarchal seats of Christianity. It is also regarded as the mother church of the Papal See of Africa by the Coptic Orthodox Church. According to ancient custom, the Patriarch is technically the senior bishop of the continent of Africa. While most of ancient Alexandria is long gone, the current Cathedral of St. Mark is believed to stand on the same site as the original church. The enclave where St. Mark's stands is also home to some other very old churches as well as the tombs of nearly fifty ancient patriarchs, bishops and saints.

Alexandria enjoyed almost a millennium as one of the greatest cities in the Mediterranean world. Founded by Alexander the Great in the 4th century BC, it became the capital of Egypt, then a territorial capital of Rome, and finally one of the five great centers of the early Church. Christianity was first introduced to Alexandria and Egypt by Mark the Evangelist, and many early Christians moved there to avoid persecutions in Judea. During the Great Revolt, it is believed that many Christians fled to Alexandria.

Mark the Evangelist probably lived in Alexandria sometime in the mid-1st century. After a seven year career evangelizing here, he was martyred by being dragged through the streets. His body was interred beneath the city's first church, which he helped to build. The original church was replaced by a new building in the 4th century, though this was destroyed during the Muslim invasion in 641. During the 9th century, Mark's body was smuggled out of Alexandria and taken to Venice, at least in part. The church was destroyed and rebuilt several more times over the centuries. The current incarnation of St. Mark's was completed in 1819.

Of Interest: St. Mark's Cathedral is one of the most sacred shrines in the Coptic Orthodox tradition, and the complex of the Patriarchate of Alexandria where it stands remains one of the city's most venerable institutions. The 20th century building is highly ornate and decorated with a treasure trove of Orthodox artwork and icons. The real historic treasures of the Church, however, are the tombs of the approximately fifty patriarchs who are buried on the site. Among these is a niche for the tomb of St. Mark the Evangelist, although his body was removed long ago. Tradition holds that at least some of Mark's relic, possibly his head, is still entombed here.

---

62. CATHEDRAL OF EVANGELISMOS

111 Al Atarin Mosque, Al Attarin Gharb, Qesm Al Attarin, Alexandria, Egypt

Alternate/Full Name: Holy Church of the Annunciation of the Theotokos
Denomination: Greek Orthodox
Dates: 1856 (completed)
Web: www.egypt.travel/en/regions/white-med/alexandria (tourism website)

The Cathedral of Evangelismos is the seat of the Eastern Orthodox Church in Egypt. Technically, it is one of the patriarchal seats of the Eastern Orthodox communion, a rival claim to the patriarch of the Coptic Church. This rivalry goes back many centuries, and by some accounts all the way back to the schism of the 5th century. Today the two churches in Alexandria tolerate each other in the face of the Muslim majority population of Egypt.

In 451, following the Council of Chalcedon, the Coptic Church of Africa, as well as some other eastern churches, split off from the Catholic-Orthodox Church. Both churches claimed the patriarchal seat of Alexandria, and two lines of patriarchs emerged following the two different traditions. Most local Christians followed the Coptic Church, and claimed all of the city's original holy sites.

The Eastern Orthodox Church in Egypt became an autocephalous church in communion with Constantinople. They maintained their own facilities and began to emerge as an important part of the Eastern Orthodox Community once more during the 19th century. In recognition of this the patriarchate built a magnificent new church, the Cathedral of Evangelismos, in 1856. It remains the seat of the Eastern Orthodox Patriarch of Alexandria to the present day.

Of Interest: The Cathedral of Evangelismos is the newest of the major cathedrals in Alexandria, though in theory it traces back to very ancient beginnings. It has a really beautiful façade that is difficult to architecturally quantify, though it has hints of Spanish Colonial and Gothic elements. The church interior has the look and feel of an ancient Roman basilica, with a touch of something exotically eastern. The walls are covered in magnificent iconic paintings and trimmed in exquisitely executed gold leaf.

---

63. ST. CATHERINE'S MONASTERY

Qesm Sham Ash Sheikh, South Sinai Governate, Feren, Egypt

Alternate/Full Name: Sacred Monastery of the God-Trodden Mount Sinai
Denomination: Greek Orthodox (sacred to many Eastern Christians)
Dates: 565 (founded)
Web: www.sinaimonastery.com (official website)

St. Catherine's Monastery in the Sinai Peninsula is one of the greatest Christian sites of antiquity. It is home to one of the oldest Christian churches still in use: the Chapel of the Burning Bush. It is also home to one of Christianity's most venerable library collections. Located at the base of Mount Sinai, the Chapel of the Burning Bush has been venerated by Christians, Jews and Muslims for thousands of years. Because of this, and because of its out-of-the-way location in the southern Sinai Peninsula, the chapel and monastery have largely escaped the tribulations that have so frequently ravaged the other holy sites of the Middle East. St. Catherine's Monastery is a UNESCO World Heritage Site.

Mount Sinai made its first appearance in Biblical history when Moses found his way there following an arduous trek through the wilderness from Egypt. At the end of his famous forty-day journey, Moses made the acquaintance of the local Bedouins and settled among them as a shepherd. A few years later, Moses chased a stray sheep up the mountain, only to come across a certain fabled Burning Bush. This was followed by the most famous divine audience in history, where God personally ordered Moses to return to Egypt and lead the nation of Israel to freedom.

What followed was one of the most enthralling stories of the Bible. Egypt was devastated by Ten Plagues, the Hebrew slaves were freed, and the Red Sea parted to allow for their escape. Moses then led the Israelites to the foot of Mount Sinai, where they made a great encampment at the base of the mountain. Then came the gift of the Ten Commandments and the episode of the Golden Calf. Finally, in the shadow of God's wrath, the Israelites departed from Sinai, abandoning the sacred mountain sometime around the 14th century BCE.

Nearly two thousand years later, Byzantine Christians began taking an active interest in the holy sites of the Old Testament. Exploratory efforts sponsored by Helena, the mother of the Roman Emperor Constantine, identified Mount Sinai, possibly based on the traditions of the Bedouin nomads who still lived in the area. She ordered a chapel to be constructed here, and over the next few centuries this expanded into a monastery. Emperor Justinian I ordered extensive additions to be made in the 6th century, and much of the monastery dates from that time.

After the rise of the Muslim Caliphate in the 7th century, a special dispensation, attributed by some to Mohammad himself, permitted the Orthodox Church to remain in possession of St. Catherine's Monastery, an agreement which has been more or less honored ever since. Mount Sinai and its environs appear much today as they have for over a thousand years. The isolated location has helped the area remain largely uninhabited and pristine. Although the area is becoming increasingly popular with religious travelers, it is still off the beaten path, and offers one of the world's most unique Christian pilgrimage experiences.

Of Interest: St. Catherine's Monastery is among the most amazing Christian pilgrimage experiences in the world. Parts of the complex date back to the early 4th century and are still in use. The monastery library preserves some of the earliest Christian writings in the world. The Tomb of St. Catherine is here, as well as the Garden of the Burning Bush, home to a possible descendent of the shrub of Biblical fame. The summit of Mount Sinai is reached by the famous Steps of Repentance, 3,750 stone-carved stairs that meander past a series of shrines and memorials, mostly related to the Exodus. The climb begins at St. Catherine's Monastery and runs past the Springs of Moses and Elijah. Towards the top of the mountain are two structures: the Chapel of the Holy Trinity and a small mosque. The latter is located on the site of cave believed to have been used by Moses during his forty days on the mountain.

---

64. MONASTARIES OF ST. ANTHONY AND ST. PAUL THE ANCHORITE

Al Kurimat-Al Zafrana Road, Zafarana, Egypt (Monastery of St. Anthony)

Route 65, Zafarana, Egypt (Monastery of St. Paul the Anchorite)

Denomination: Coptic Orthodox Church of Alexandria
Dates: c. 4th century (founded)

Web: www.egypt.travel/en/attractions/st-anthony-and-st-paul-monasteries (tourism website)

The Monasteries of St. Anthony and St. Paul the Anchorite are among the oldest Christian monasteries in the world. The former is regarded by some to be the first true Christian monastery and credit St. Anthony with being the first true Christian monk. Both monasteries are still in use almost seventeen centuries later, with active orders that continue to practice the original traditions of their founders.

Paul, not to be confused with the 1st century Apostle, first arrived in the Suez region towards the beginning of the 4th century. After being enmeshed in a family squabble over inheritance and witnessing the funeral of a wealthy man whose money meant nothing in the end, Paul renounced his worldly possessions and headed into the desert. He went on to live for decades in a cave, eating a scant diet and wearing clothes made of branches and leaves. Towards the end of his life he befriended a fellow hermit named Anthony. After Paul's death, his disciples constructed a small shrine near the cave where he had lived.

Anthony had actually traveled to the area somewhat earlier than Paul. Like Paul, his family was well off, and he too gave away his possessions in search of a life of poverty. He was active in the Christian politics of the day, and on at least two occasions traveled to Alexandria, once during the persecutions of Maximus and once to confront the Arian heresy. At first he lived alone, but around the year 305 he took on disciples and founded his own monastery. Eventually he left the monastery to return to isolation, and eventually died in his cave in the presence of only a few of his faithful followers.

The area around Zafarana was already a popular place for pilgrims during Anthony's and Paul's lifetimes. As the monastic movement grew throughout the empire, both monasteries became famous examples of ascetic living. After the arrival of Islam, however, both were destroyed and periodically ransacked. St. Anthony's Monastery was reestablished and rebuilt in the 16th century. St. Paul's followed soon afterwards. The current orders were revived at this time.

Of Interest: The Monastery of St. Anthony is an impressive structure, ironically almost the opposite of what Anthony would have wanted. Its five churches and numerous additional buildings are enclosed by a wall, built to keep raiders at bay. Most of the current monastery was built or rebuilt in the 16th century. However the Church of St. Anthony, the main building of the monastery, is much older. The Monastery of St. Paul the Anchorite bears a striking resemblance to St. Anthony's. It was also rebuilt in the 16th century by monks from St. Anthony's, so the architecture is very similar. St. Paul's is somewhat larger, with greater fortifications. The original spring which St. Paul drew water from is still in use. The cave where St. Paul once lived is part of the complex.

---

65. STS. SERGIUS AND BACCHUS CHURCH & HANGING CHURCH

Mari Gerges, Kom Ghorab, Misr Al Qadimah, Cairo, Egypt

Alternate/Full Names: Church of Martyrs Sergius and Bacchus in the Cave & St. Virgin Mary's Coptic Orthodox Church, Church of Mother of God St. Mary in Egyptian Babylon
Denomination: Coptic Orthodox Church of Alexandria
Dates: Sergius and Bacchus - c. 4th century (originally completed), c. 8th century (current building completed) & Hanging – c. 4th century (originally completed), c. 7th century (current building completed)
Web: www.egypt.travel/en/attractions/the-hanging-church (tourism website)

The Church of Sts. Sergius and Bacchus and the Hanging Church are two of the oldest churches in Cairo. Both have important places in Egyptian Christian history. The former is dedicated to two Roman soldiers who were martyred in the 4th century. The latter serves as the residential church of the Coptic Orthodox Patriarch. Both churches are located in the city's old Coptic quarter and together are the major pilgrimage destinations for Coptic Christians.

The Coptic Orthodox Church of Egypt is one of the world's oldest branches of Christianity, having broken away from the Catholic-Orthodox communion in the 5th century. After the Islamic annexation of Egypt in the 7th century, the political center of Egypt moved from Alexandria to Cairo, and the much of the focus of the Church moved here too. In the 690s, the Patriarch Isaac constructed two new churches in Cairo, the Church of Sts. Sergius & Bacchus and the Hanging Church.

The Church of Sts. Sergius & Bacchus was actually constructed on the site of an earlier church which traditionally marked the location where the Holy Family lived in exile during the first few years of the life of Jesus. For many years the consecration of the Coptic popes took place here. The Hanging Church was constructed on top of the walls of the old Roman Fortress, or Babylon Fortress, from which it gets its name. In 1047, the Pope of the Coptic Church permanently relocated to Cairo.

Both churches have survived to the present day, though both have undergone significant reconstructions and restorations over the centuries. Both have also been threatened by sectarian violence in recent years. The two churches are very sacred to all Coptic Christians, but members of other Christian denominations who are visiting Egypt are known to make pilgrimages here as well.

Of Interest: The Church of Sts. Sergius and Bacchus has been rebuilt on numerous occasions, and most of the existing church dates from the Middle Ages and later. A crypt beneath the church supposedly marks the spot where the Holy Family hid out for a time. The Hanging Church also largely dates from the Middle Ages, though it has recently undergone a major restoration. The church literally hangs over the walls of the Babylon Fortress, hence its nickname. The Hanging Church is famous for its magnificent collection of Christian icons collected over a period of more than a thousand years.

66. BASILICA OF ST. AUGUSTINE & RUINS OF THE BASILICA OF PEACE

Chemin de la Basilique St. Augustin, Annaba, Algeria (Basilica of St. Augustine)

Chemin de Musee, Annaba, Algeria (Ruins of the Basilica of Peace)

Denomination: Roman Catholic
Dates: St. Augustine - 1900 (completed) & Peace – c. 5th century (originally completed)
Web: www.gcatholic.org/churches/africa/0332 (Catholic website)

The Basilica of St. Augustine and the nearby ruins of the Basilica of Peace are two of the most historic Christian sites in Northwest Africa. The city of Annaba in Algeria, formerly the Roman metropolis of Hippo Regius, is home to two holy places closely associated with St. Augustine: the Basilica of Peace, where he once served as the city's bishop; and the Basilica of St. Augustine, where a fragment of his relic can be found. So revered is Augustine locally that even the Muslims of Annaba recognize him as one of the city's favorite sons. Despite this, relatively few modern day Christian pilgrims find their way to this ancient historic site.

Augustine of Hippo was born in 354 in Tagaste in what is now Algeria. His mother, Monica, was an extremely pious woman who herself was canonized by the Church. His early life was spent in intellectual and worldly pursuits. At first rejecting Christianity outright, he later embraced Manicheanism, a Gnostic Christian religion condemned by the general church. He spent most of his twenties living unmarried with his mistress, with whom he had a son, and teaching rhetoric in Carthage.

Around the age of thirty Augustine moved to Italy where he converted to Catholicism in 387. The next year he returned to Africa to begin a life of service to the Church. He sold all of his possessions and turned the proceeds over to the poor. In 391 he became a priest, eventually rising to the position of Bishop of Hippo Regus in 396.

He served in this capacity for over thirty years. During this period he authored hundreds of books, letters, commentaries and sermons, many of which survive. His three masterworks, *Confessions*, *On the Trinity* and *City of God*, are all cornerstones of Christian theology.

As Bishop of Hippo Regus, Augustine worked and preached in the city's Basilica of Peace. The basilica, one of the earliest to be built in North Africa, was one of the city's few buildings to survive the onslaught of the Vandals in 430. Augustine died during the Vandal siege of the city, and was buried in a crypt beneath the Basilica of Peace. His body was later moved for safety to Sardinia, and then later to Pavia in Italy. In the 19th century a new basilica was constructed in the city in honor of Augustine, and part of his relic returned there for display for visiting pilgrims.

Of Interest: The Basilica of St. Augustine is located in the city of Annaba. The ruins of the Basilica of Peace, destroyed many centuries ago, are now part of the nearby archaeological site of Hippo Regius. While little is left of Augustine's ancient church, it is easily identified by the foundations of the walls and the bases of the rows of columns. The place where his crypt was once located is identifiable, though nothing is there now. The Basilica of St. Augustine is a relatively recent addition to Annaba. It was built in the late 19th century during the French colonial occupation of Algeria. The sacred highlight is a statue of Augustine, inside of which is contained part of his relic, a gift from the Church of St. Peter in Pavia, Italy.

---

67. BASILICA OF OUR LADY OF PEACE

Rue de St. France, Yamoussoukro, Ivory Coast

Denomination: Roman Catholic
Dates: 1990 (completed)
Web: www.gcatholic.org/churches/africa/1246 (Catholic website)

The Basilica of Our Lady of Peace is one of the largest churches, by some measures *the* largest, in the world. Loosely modeled on St. Peter's

Basilica in Rome, it boasts the largest dome in Africa. The basilica was designed to be a showpiece and tourist draw for the city of Yamoussoukro, at the time intended to be the country's new capital. Despite the exorbitant cost, the basilica has become a source of national pride for the entire country and a testament to Roman Catholicism in West Africa.

French colonists arrived in the area of the Ivory Coast in the mid-19th century, and Christian missionaries soon followed. Many of the colony's residents embraced Christianity at this time. In the post-colonial era, the country's first president, Felix Houphouet-Boigny, endeavored to establish a new national capital at Yamoussoukro. As part of this project, he set about building a great church, the largest ever built, as a tribute to his Roman Catholic faith and as a showpiece to the world.

Construction of the massive edifice took a mere five years, and was completed in 1990. Upon its completion, Felix Houphouet-Boigny donated it to the Roman Catholic Church, and Pope John Paul II himself traveled to the Ivory Coast in order to personally consecrate the new basilica. In the three decades since its completion, the Basilica of Our Lady of Peace has become an architectural symbol of the Ivory Coast, and that country's top pilgrimage destination.

Of Interest: The Basilica of Our Lady of Peace is absolutely massive, but its size ranking is a matter of some debate. The exterior grounds include immense covered colonnades and plazas which can accommodate great crowds. If this is included in the total area of the church, then it is in fact larger than St. Peter's Basilica in Rome. However, if just the interior area is considered, then it would be the 9th largest church in the world, though still the largest in Africa. The main sanctuary is a towering marble affair crowned by one of the world's largest domes. Originally planned to be taller than that of St. Peter's, it was lowered at the request of the Papacy. Nevertheless it is topped off by a tall cross which puts it at more than five hundred feet in height. The interior of the basilica is adorned by some of the finest late-20th century stained glass windows. Houphouet-Boigny's image is worked into the one of the windows as one of the three adoring Magi.

68. CATHEDRAL CHURCH OF CHRIST

29 Marina Street, Lagos Island, Lagos, Nigeria

Alternate/Full Name: Cathedral Church of Christ Marina
Denomination: Anglican Church of Nigeria
Dates: 1869 (originally completed),
1946 (current building completed)
Web: www.thecathedrallagos.org (official website)

The Cathedral Church of Christ is one of the oldest seats of the Anglican Church in Africa and the most important Christian site in Nigeria. It is the location of the tomb of Dr. Samuel Crowther, the first person of African descent to become a bishop of the Anglican Church. The Cathedral Church of Christ is one of Lagos' most important landmarks and a popular pilgrimage destination for visiting Christians.

Nigeria became a crown colony of the British Empire in 1861. Anglican missionaries soon followed. One of these was Samuel Crowther, a former slave freed by the British. Crowther moved to England and committed to study for a life of service in the Church. He was consecrated in Canterbury cathedral in 1864. He then left for Lagos to serve as that city's bishop, which he did until his death in 1891.

The first cathedral in Lagos, and the first Anglican cathedral in West Africa, was completed in 1869. It was replaced in the 20th century by a new much bigger cathedral which was completed in 1946. The Cathedral Church of Christ has served as the seat of the city's Anglican Bishop ever since. The tomb of Dr. Crowther was moved here in 1976.

Of Interest: The Cathedral Church of Christ is a sprawling modernish Gothic structure that looks as though it had been lifted straight out of Victorian England. The towering and memorable clock tower serves as a local city landmark. The interior of the church is huge and stately, memorable for its bright stonework and the large cenotaph that marks the tomb of Dr. Samuel Crowther.

69. ST. GEORGE'S CATHEDRAL & HOLY TRINITY CATHEDRAL

Minilik Square, Addis Ababa, Ethiopia (St. George's Cathedral)
Niger Street, Addis Ababa, Ethiopia (Holy Trinity Cathedral)

Denomination: Ethiopian Orthodox Tewahedo
Dates: St. George's - c. 15th century (originally completed), 1896 (current building completed) & Holy Trinity - 1942 (completed)
Web: No website available (tourism info for Ethiopia limited at the time of this writing)

St. George's Cathedral and the Holy Trinity Cathedral are the major edifices of the Ethiopian Orthodox Tewahedo Church. Both churches are closely tied to the old Ethiopian royal family, and both were constructed in part to commemorate Ethiopia's struggle against Italy during the colonial era. Haile Selassie, the last emperor, was coronated in the former and buried in the latter. Both sites are now highly sacred to Ethiopian Orthodox Christians. St. George is also of religious importance to Rastafarians.

Christianity in Ethiopia can be traced back at least as far as the 3rd century. It was possibly the second national church after that of Armenia to be legally recognized, though it broke away from the mainstream Catholic-Orthodox church in the 5th century. St. George's Cathedral was built on the site of a former church and was completed in 1896. That same year, the ark of the church was carried to victory against Italian invaders at the Battle of Adwa. Some of the last monarchs of Ethiopia, a line that had survived for thousands of years, were crowned here, including Selassie in 1917.

Holy Trinity Cathedral is the seat of the Ethiopian Orthodox Tewahedo Church and a former royal chapel of the imperial family. It was constructed during and immediately after the war of liberation against Italy. It was consecrated just after the Axis powers were driven out of North Africa but while World War II was still raging in Europe. It was one of the largest churches completed in the entire Eastern Hemisphere during the war years.

Of Interest: St. George's Cathedral is unusual in that it was designed as an octagonal structure, a rarity in church architecture. A dome crowns the center of the church. Among the items on display in the church are swords and other weapons that were used in battle against the Italians. Holy Trinity Cathedral is another architectural gem, looking more like a mosque than a traditional church. The stunning interior houses some great artwork, including a depiction of three figures representing the trinity seated on a cloud directly above the main altar. Several members of the imperial family are entombed within the church, including Haile Selassie. Also buried here are the remains of many Ethiopians who were massacred in the war against Italy.

---

70. CHURCH OF OUR LADY MARY OF ZION

Route B30, Aksum, Ethiopia

Denomination: Ethiopian Orthodox Tewahedo
Dates: c. 4th century (originally completed),
c. 17th century (current building completed)
Web: No website available (tourism info for Ethiopia limited at the time of this writing)

The Church of Our Lady Mary of Zion is one of the most historic and sacred churches of East Africa. According to local tradition, this church is the current repository for the Ark of the Covenant, one of the greatest treasures of Judeo-Christianity. Thanks to some convincing historical evidence, the claim is not entirely without merit, despite the fact that this artifact has never been publically shown. Nevertheless Our Lady Mary of Zion is held to be incredibly sacred to members of the Ethiopian Orthodox Tewahedo Church.

According to tradition, the old imperial family of Ethiopia was descended from Menelik I, a son of the ancient Israelite king, Solomon. This tradition goes on to tell of how Solomon sent the Ark to Ethiopia with Menelik for safety, and that it has been in the country's possession ever since. Some consider the Ark's presence here to be responsible for the survival of the Ethiopian dynasty for nearly three thousand years, a dynasty which ended only recently.

Although it is not said where the Ark was kept for most of its history, it was supposedly moved to the Church of St. Mary of Zion when that building was constructed in the 17th century. During the 20th century a new church was constructed next door, the Chapel of the Tablet, to more securely house the Ark. How and when it was moved is a secret. Both the church and the chapel are regarded as major pilgrimage destinations for Ethiopian Christians.

Of Interest: The Church of Our Lady Mary of Zion is actually part of a complex that includes three churches and a monastery. In additional to the original church, which is open to men only, there is a much larger more modern cathedral that accommodates both men and women. The Chapel of the Tablet, where the Ark is supposedly hidden away, is strictly off limits except to the monks who tend it. And of them, only the senior monk of the order is permitted inside the room where the Ark itself is contained, a throwback to the ancient tradition of the Jewish high priest.

---

71. ROCK HEWN CHURCHES OF NEW JERUSALEM

Lalibela, Ethiopia

Denomination: Ethiopian Orthodox Tewahedo
Dates: c. 12th & 13th centuries (completed)
Web: No website available (tourism info for Ethiopia limited at the time of this writing)

The Rock Churches of New Jerusalem are among the most unique religious structures to be found in Africa. This collection of eleven churches was carved out of solid rock by the orders of the Ethiopian king, Lalibela. While this type of spectacular architecture is not unique, the buildings here are arguably the world's best examples of such structures in Christianity. The Rock Hewn Churches of Lalibela are a UNESCO World Heritage Site.

During the Middle Ages, the Menelik dynasty of Ethiopia was briefly interrupted, and it was during this period that a rival ruler, Lalibela, decided to establish his own legacy by constructing churches. The city of Roha was renamed Lalibela in his honor, but he referred to his collection of churches simply as New Jerusalem. The carved churches were mostly completed in his lifetime. However, his dynasty fell apart around the time of their completion. In the ensuing centuries, most of what he had built in Lalibela became abandoned or neglected, with the exception of the churches.

Over the years the small collection of churches became the repository of an ever-increasing collection of icons, treasures and relics. Lalibela remained a Christian stronghold, and the eleven churches were never ransacked or desecrated. A quasi-monastic priesthood has taken care of the carved shrines and their treasures for centuries. On an interesting side note, Lalibela is also home to one of the last surviving remnants of Monophysite Christianity, a heretical movement dating back to the 5th century. Because of its central location and historical importance, Lalibela draws many visitors annually.

Of Interest: The Rock Hewn Churches of New Jerusalem date from the 12th and 13th centuries. Each one is unique in terms of overall structure, size, carving style and decoration. Some of them are carved directly into large rock-faces and incorporate existing caves. Others are freestanding structures, literally hewn from the ground in enormous trenches. Each church also houses its own unique collection of treasures acquired over many uninterrupted centuries. These include very old Bibles and illuminated books, precious icons and crucifixes, and even some jewelry of royal or sacred nature. Some of the churches also boast impressive artwork and wall paintings. The most popular building here is the Church of St. George. This massive structure stands over eighty feet in height, including the pedestal, and viewed from above takes the form of a cross.

72. KISANTU CATHEDRAL

Kisantu Mission, Kisantu, DR Congo

Alternate/Full Name: Our Lady of Seven Sorrows Cathedral
Denomination: Roman Catholic
Dates: 1936 (completed)
Web: www.gcatholic.org/churches/africa/4801 (Catholic website)

The Kisantu Cathedral is one of the largest churches in Central Africa. It is also one of the most important and stable institutions in the area, and serves as a major conduit of health and education services to much of the local population. Constructed by missionaries during the Belgian colonial period, it is not only one of Congo's major churches, but also one of the most popular tourist sites in the entire country.

In 1908, the Congo became a colony of Belgium, and soon after the Catholic Church arrived in force. Missions were established throughout the country, and these set up schools and hospitals. By the mid-20th century, well over half of the country had been converted to Catholicism. Unfortunately, the Catholic Church in the Congo was closely associated with the hated colonial government. When the country achieved its independence in 1960, many locals turned against the Church and a period of persecutions ensued. After a while things calmed down, and the Church went from being a target of the people's ire to their social champion.

This led to a government crackdown on the Catholic Church. Catholics were removed from their posts, religious instruction was banned, pictures of the Pope were destroyed, and even Christmas was cancelled. However, without Church personnel, many government institutions began to fall apart. By 1976 these edicts were reversed, and Catholicism was re-legalized. Kisantu Cathedral remains one of the most important institutions in the Congo as well as one of its most popular tourist destinations.

Of Interest: The Kisantu Cathedral is the largest church in the Democratic Republic of the Congo and one of the most beautiful

Catholic churches in Africa. Located close to the city's famous botanical gardens, it also enjoys a beautiful setting of lawns and palm trees. Built from locally quarried stone and locally produced brick, the exterior is an alluring combination of neo-Gothic and 20th century colonial architecture with just a hint of something exotically African. The interior is reminiscent of the Moorish architecture of Spain and North Africa. Of particular artistic interest are the colorful brick- and tile- geometric patterns that would seem at home in a grand mosque.

---

73. ALL SAINTS CATHEDRAL

Kenyatta Avenue, Nairobi, Kenya

Denomination: Anglican Church of Kenya
Dates: 1952 (completed)
Web: www.allsaintsnairobi.org (official website)

All Saints Cathedral in Nairobi is one of the two preeminent Anglican houses of worship in Kenya, the other being in Mombasa. All Saints in Nairobi is arguably the better known and more visited of the two thanks to its location in the national capital. It is now the seat of the Anglican Church in Kenya and one of the most important Anglican institutions on the East Coast of Africa.

Anglican missionaries began arriving in Mombasa on the Kenyan Coast in the 1840s. Mombasa served as the headquarters of the massive Anglican Diocese of Eastern Equitorial Africa at the height of the Colonial era in the late 19th century. This diocese was later split up, and the focus of Anglican worship in Kenya moved to Nairobi in the early 1900s.

In 1914 it was decided a massive new cathedral was needed in Nairobi to accommodate the growing congregation. Work began on the cathedral while World War I was still raging in Europe, new church construction being an extreme rarity in wartime. Work on the cathedral continued for the next few decades, interrupted only by World War II. It was completed in 1952. It became the seat of the Anglican Church in Kenya in 1974.

Of Interest: All Saint's Cathedral in Nairobi is architecturally one of the most unique churches in Africa. Constructed in the 20th century, it is somewhat Gothic in appearance, with elements that suggest both Moorish and traditional African Influences. The bell towers, which actually jut out from the sides towards the back of the church, have crenellations that give the church a castle-like appearance from certain angles. Another odd feature is the broad awning that runs the entire length of the façade, sheltering the front entrances in a way virtually unknown on other churches.

---

74. CHRIST CHURCH

Benjamin Mkapa Road, Stone Town, Zanzibar City, Tanzania

Denomination: Anglican Church of Tanzania
Dates: 1879 (completed)
Web: www.zanzibaranglican.or.tz (official website)

Christ Church of Stone Town on the island of Zanzibar is one of the oldest Anglican Churches on the East Coast of Africa. It is historically linked to the end of the slave trade in that region. It is also associated with the famous Scottish missionary, David Livingstone. Christ Church is one of the most popular tourist destinations in Stone Town.

The island of Zanzibar was reached by Christian missionaries in the mid-19th century. Zanzibar, which had been a major center of the slave trade dating back to the Middle Ages and possibly earlier, was one of the last places to see an end to the practice. The old slave market was still in existence when Europeans annexed the island. The practice was not fully ended until the time of the American Civil War.

In the 1870s, the remains of the largest slave market in Stone Town was finally cleared to make way for a new cathedral. This cathedral, Christ Church, was completed in 1879. In the century since it has become a primary destination for pilgrims to the island as well as a popular destination for those curious about the history of the African slave trade.

Of Interest: Christ Church is an imposing structure built of coral rock as was common in Stone Town at the time it was completed. The altar of the church stands directly over the location of the former slave market's whipping post. Edward Steere, a bishop of the church and an ardent opponent of slavery, is buried behind the altar. The church also houses a small museum with exhibits on the history of slavery in Zanzibar.

---

75. GREAT CHURCH (GROOTE KERK)

43 Adderley Street, Cape Town City, Cape Town, 8001, South Africa

Denomination: Dutch Reformed
Dates: 1678 (original completion date),
1841 (current building completed)
Web: http://grootekerk.org.za (official website)

The Great Church, or Groote Kerk in Dutch, is one of Southern Africa's oldest church congregations. Something of an oddity in the region, it is possibly the most historic church in Sub-Saharan Africa that is neither Roman Catholic nor Anglican. Founded by Dutch settlers in the 17th century, it remains a Dutch Reformed institution to the present day.

The first European explorers to South Africa were the Portuguese in 1488. However, they did not leave behind a significant colonial or Catholic presence. The area did not come under significant European influence until the arrival of the Dutch in the early 1600s. The Cape Colony was formally established in the 1650s, and missionaries from the Dutch Reform Church soon converted many of the locals to Christianity.

In 1678, the first major church building was constructed in Cape Town, and this remained the preeminent Dutch church in the colony for more than a century and a half. Despite the fact that most of South Africa became a British colony in the 19th century, the Reform congregation survived. The original church was replaced by the current building in 1841.

Of Interest: The Great Church is one of the major historic and architectural landmarks of the city of Cape Town. Although completed in the 19th century, the lack of ornate details on the exterior combined with its grey and white color scheme gives the church a much more modern look. The interior is far more interesting, with a renowned organ that may hold the title of largest in the Southern Hemisphere. Some of the floor stones inside the church are actually old markers from the burial graves of slaves. Simon van der Stel, a governor of the early Dutch colony, is buried here.

---

76. ST. GEORGE'S CATHEDRAL

5 Wale Street, Cape Town, 8001, South Africa

Alternate/Full Name: Cathedral Church of St. George the Martyr
Denomination: Anglican Church of Southern Africa
Dates: 1834 (originally completed), 1909 (current building completed)
Web: http://sgcathedral.co.za (official website)

The Cathedral of St. George is the seat of the Anglican Church in South Africa and politically one of the most important in Sub-Saharan Africa. During the late 20th century, it was a rallying point for those calling for an end to Apartheid. Desmond Tutu, one of the major anti-Apartheid figures, served here as South Africa's first African-born bishop. St. George's Cathedral was named a Provincial Heritage Site in 2014.

The Anglican Church of South Africa was established in the early 19th century as an outpost of the Anglican Church in India. It wasn't until 1834 that Cape Town had its own church. Cape Town became an independent Anglican diocese in 1847, and by the end of the century a new cathedral was needed to accommodate the booming population. St. George's Cathedral was largely completed in 1909.

Throughout the 20th century, the cathedral was the heart of the Anglican community in Cape Town, and politically was the most important church in Southern Africa. In 1986, Desmond Tutu was named archbishop of Cape Town. During his tenure he led many rallies against racial injustice and witnessed the collapse of Apartheid. Because of its role in helping to bring an end to a long injustice, St. George's has been nicknamed the People's Cathedral.

Of Interest: The Cathedral of St. George is huge, a hulking Gothic structure which dominates the surrounding neighborhood. The bell tower houses many bells, including the colony's original namesake bell, Good Hope. St. George's has a wealth of stained glass accounted some of the finest in South Africa. Tucked away beneath the church, in the crypt is, oddly enough, a popular jazz club.

SOUTHEASTERN EUROPE

77. CAVE OF THE APOCALYPSE

Hora 855 00, Patmos, Greece

Alternate/Full Name: Holy Grotto of the Revelation
Denomination: Greek Orthodox (sacred to most Christians)
Dates: c. 4th century (completed)
Web: www.patmos.gr/holy-cave-of-the-apocalypse (official website)

The Cave of the Apocalypse is a sacred site on the island of Patmos, and one of oldest and most holiest sites in Christianity. It was here sometime towards the end of the 1st century that John the Evangelist received his vision of the destruction of the world and the arrival of the New Jerusalem. The Book of Revelation itself confirms Patmos as the location of this event. The entire island has subsequently become something of a super-shrine to John, with monasteries and churches marking the various sites associated with his exile. The Cave of the Apocalypse includes the location where the prophecy was revealed to John. It is part of the Monastery of St. John the Theologian UNESCO World Heritage Site.

John, the last survivor of the original Twelve Apostles, was still actively evangelizing in his eighties. Around the year 95 the Roman authorities arrested him, probably in or near Ephesus, and sent him to Patmos, where he spent approximately eighteen months in exile. While serving his sentence the elderly John received what is undoubtedly the most famous prophetic vision received by any figure in the Bible. In this vision, God laid out for John an extremely thorough, if somewhat confusing, future history of the end of times. John recorded this vision in what would become the Book of Revelation.

Little is known of John for certain after this period. It is possible that he also composed the Gospel of John while in exile here. He almost certainly did not die on Patmos, but probably returned to Ephesus to continue his ministry. The Book of Revelation suggests that John had much work still to do, and he may have lived for perhaps another decade or so. After his death, the tradition of John was maintained by the Christians of Patmos. In time, the island's surviving Greek and Roman temples were torn down, and churches and shrines were erected commemorating John's life and exile.

Between the 6th and 12th centuries Patmos was frequently raided by both Muslim and Christian marauders. For a time the isle was even deserted. Interest in Patmos returned during the 1600s, when the growing Christian community was permitted by the Ottomans to restore the island's sacred places. Most of the current churches and monasteries date from this period. During the 19th century, Patmos was returned to Greek control, and the island underwent a Christian revival. Although out of the way, the island is almost universally revered by all Christians, and pilgrimages are becoming increasingly common.

Of Interest: The Cave of the Apocalypse stands on or near the site of a former ancient temple dedicated to the Greek goddess Artemis. The entrance to the grotto is located inside the walls of a monastery. Near the heart of the monastery there is an ancient, simple door crowned with a fresco of John the Apostle kneeling before Christ as he receives the vision of the Apocalypse. Inside is a small cave, walled off at the mouth, where John lived. The interior is sparsely decorated with a tiny shrine, golden chandelier and candelabra and a few chairs. A waist-high natural shelf in the cave serves as a makeshift altar draped in white. According to tradition, this is the heart of the shrine, where John saw and recorded his visions.

---

78. ST. ANDREW'S CATHEDRAL

Evmilou 4, Patras 262 22, Greece

Denomination: Greek Orthodox (sacred to many Christians)
Dates: 1974 (completed)

Web: www.patrasinfo.com/en/saint-andrews-church-patras (tourism website)

St. Andrew's Cathedral is the largest church in Greece and home to that country's greatest Christian treasure: the remains of the relic of St. Andrew the Apostle. Andrew, who according to tradition was martyred in Patras in the 1st century, is the patron of the city and one of Greece's most venerated saints. While a much earlier church dedicated to St. Andrew is located nearby, the relic of Andrew is now kept in the larger and more accessible 20th century cathedral.

Andrew, the first Apostle chosen by Jesus of Nazareth, is credited with bringing Christianity to parts of the Balkans and Northern Greece. He spent the later years of his life in Greece and Asia Minor, evangelizing in the city of Byzantium, future capital of the Roman Empire. He finally ended up in the city of Patras, where he was arrested and martyred by crucifixion on an X-shaped cross.

Patras has honored St. Andrew since earliest Christian times, and his body was buried there until the 4th century when it was moved to Constantinople. Andrew's relics were subsequently moved to Italy after Crusaders sacked the city in the Middle Ages. Patras was later absorbed into the Ottoman Empire, and the tradition of Andrew fell by the wayside until after Greece regained its independence in the 19th century.

In 1908, work began on a massive new cathedral honoring St. Andrew. As a token of goodwill between the Roman Catholic and Eastern Orthodox churches, the surviving relics of Andrew were returned to Patras in the 1970s and placed in the new building. The Basilica of St. Andrew was completed in 1974 and has been a place of devout pilgrimage ever since.

Of Interest: The Basilica of St. Andrew is a relatively new church. Barely a few decades old, it does not stand on the site of a previous church, though a much earlier church dedicated to Andrew is close by. It does utilize an ancient Byzantine style and is crowned by a magnificent dome. The main treasure of the church of course is the relic of St. Andrew. A reliquary contains parts of his hand and skull, as well as a piece of the cross upon which he was martyred.

79. MONASTERIES OF METEORA

Kalabaka 422 00, Greece

Denomination: Greek Orthodox
Dates: c. 9th century (founded)
Web: www.visitmeteora.travel (official website)

The Monasteries of Meteora are a monastic community which boasts some of the most gravity-defying feats of engineering ever conceived of during the Middle Ages. Constructed to keep the monks out of reach of marauding enemies, these two dozen buildings cling precariously to cliff sides and crown nearly vertical mountains in a show of breathtaking architectural expertise. The Monasteries of Meteora are a UNESCO World Heritage Site.

The first known aesthetics to settle in the area of Meteora probably arrived sometime in the 8th century. These mostly lived solitary lives in the area's countless caves. The first recorded monk at Meteora was named Barnabas, who arrived during the 10th century and established an early church and cloister here. Over the next few centuries additional cloisters were built, and by the 12th century Meteora was fully established as a semi-autonomous monastic state. It became a magnet for religious aesthetics, and over twenty monasteries were established in the region during the late Middle Ages.

A central church was built near the enormous mountain-sized Rock of Doupiani for common worship and use, and a First Monk was chosen as leader of the collective community. Great Meteoron was established in the late 1300s by monks from Mount Athos. Around this time, the looming threat of Islam drove the monks to higher ground. The monks constructed new monasteries higher on the mountainsides. Many of the older and more vulnerable monasteries were abandoned, and by the time the Ottomans arrived, Meteora boasted two-dozen monasteries towering as high as two thousand feet above the surrounding valleys.

The Ottomans apparently took one look at the virtually impenetrable monastery fortresses and decided it was simply easier to leave the monks alone. Unfortunately, the extreme isolation of Meteora's monasteries was also the community's downfall. Effectively cut off from the outside world and new recruits, all but six were abandoned within a century. These now have a collective population of less than a hundred. Nevertheless, the region has enjoyed a surge of new interest in the last few decades, and though new monks are few and far between, pilgrims and other tourists are plentiful.

Of Interest: The community of Monasteries of Meteora sprawls over nine hundred acres and encompasses dozens of mountains. The oldest, largest and most accessible monastery is Great Meteoron. Completed in the 1380s, this extensive complex is a somewhat confused looking jumble of buildings piled onto the top of the original Meteora Mountain. The centerpiece is the Church of the Transfiguration, once the chief place of worship for the entire community. While the monastery is still in active use, it now also functions as a museum. Second in importance is the Varlam Monastery which is even higher and more inaccessible than Great Meteoron. Its superior organization can be attributed to a century and a half of experience in the unusual mountain constructions. The central place of worship here is the 17th century Parish Church of the Three Bishops. There is now a small museum located in the old refectory.

---

80. MONASTERIES OF THE HOLY MOUNTAIN

Mount Athos, Greece

Denomination: Eastern Orthodox (sacred to most Eastern Christians)
Dates: c. 4th century (founded)
Web: www.visitmountathos.eu (official website)

The Holy Mountain, also known as Mount Athos, is one of the most sacred places in Eastern Orthodox Christianity. Home to a collection of monasteries crowded onto a tiny peninsula in northern

Greece, Mount Athos has been a refuge for Orthodox monks since the early days of the Byzantine Empire. Mount Athos is home to twenty monasteries, representing virtually every order and patriarchate of the Eastern Orthodox Church. The tiny, semi-autonomous state around Mount Athos is also one of Europe's best-preserved medieval communities. Mount Athos is a UNESCO World Heritage Site.

According to legend, the inhabitants of Mount Athos were converted to Christianity around the middle of the 1st century by the Virgin Mary herself. The story says Mary discovered the beautiful mountainous peninsula during her journey to Ephesus, subsequently blessing Mount Athos and declaring it to be a haven for Christians. Soon afterwards an earthquake leveled much of the surrounding area, including most of the pagan temples. This prompted many of the locals to convert, and the area has been a Christian stronghold ever since.

Christian communities flourished at Mount Athos as early as the 4th century, and by the end of the 5th century were solidly in control of the area. By the late 9th century the peninsula boasted such a large population of monks and hermits that in 885 the Byzantine emperor issued an edict declaring the place to be a Holy Mountain, for monastic use only. The Chelandariou Monastery was built around this time and was soon followed by the Megisti Lavra Monastery. Eventually the whole area was put under the joint governance of the various orders under the centralized leadership of a First Monk.

Mount Athos continued to prosper for centuries, peaking just before the fall of Constantinople in the 15th century, when it is estimated that upwards of twenty thousand monks inhabited the peninsula. In the year 1430, the Ottoman Empire conquered nearby Thessalonica, and the monks of Mount Athos prudently surrendered rather than suffer assault and potentially devastating occupation. In exchange for heavy taxation, the monasteries were allowed to retain their autonomy. After Greece won its independence from the Ottomans in the 19th century, Mount Athos experienced a renaissance, and is once again the reigning champion of all Orthodox monastic communities.

Of Interest: The Monasteries of the Holy Mountain are isolated on their own peninsula and surrounded by beautiful, pristine wilderness. Each monastery enjoys a unique setting, and architectural styles vary widely. The chief monastery is Great Lavra, the oldest and largest on the peninsula. Founded by the aesthetic Athanasios in the 10th century, the Great Lavra Monastery eventually grew into a small fortress. More than a dozen towers grace the outer walls. Every square inch of space is used, and even the walls and towers have been topped with a dizzying collection of additional buildings, halls and rooms. The main religious sanctuary is the Church of St. Athanasios Athonite. The place is packed with thirty-seven chapels as well. Other highlights include the treasury, which contains a great wealth of art, artifacts and relics; and the library, which contains a large collection of medieval writings.

---

81. CHURCH OF ST. DEMETRIUS & CHURCH OF THE HOLY WISDOM

Agiou Dimitriou, Thessaloniki 546 33, Greece (Church of St. Demetrius)

Agios Sofias, Thessaloniki 546 22, Greece (Church of the Holy Wisdom)

Denomination: Bulgarian Orthodox & Greek Orthodox
Dates: St. Demetrius - c. 4th century (originally completed), 1949 (current building completed) & Holy Wisdom - c. 3rd century (originally completed), c. 8th century (current building completed)
Web: www.thessaloniki.travel/en/exploring-the-city/themed-routes/early-christian-and-byzantine-route (tourism website)

The Church of St. Demetrius and the Hagia Sofia of Thessaloniki are two of the most historic churches in Greece. Both are located in the city of Thessaloniki, home to one of the earliest Christian communities established in Europe. The church was founded here by none other than St. Paul, and two of his Epistles were addressed to the Thessalonians. Together they are part of the Palaeochristian and Byzantine Monuments of Thessaloniki.

Christianity arrived in Thessaloniki sometime in the middle of the 1st century. The community, one of the oldest in the world, built their first churches even before Christianity was legalized in the Roman Empire. The original Hagia Sofia of Thessaloniki may have been erected as early as the 3rd century.

Demetrius was a member of the Christian community in Thessalonica in the early 4th century, and was probably martyred during the persecution of Diocletian. After the legalization of Christianity, Demetrius was named the city's patron saint and a church was built in his honor. Both churches were later badly damaged in fires and other casualties over the years. St. Demetrius was rebuilt in the 7th century, and the Hagia Sofia was rebuilt in the 8th century.

Both churches came under Islamic rule from the 1400s until the early 20th century. During the Great Thessaloniki Fire of 1917, the Church of St. Demetrius was nearly destroyed and the Hagia Sofia was badly damaged. Incidentally, it was during this fire that the synagogue where Paul spoke in the 1st century was also destroyed. Both churches were fully restored after World War II. Today they are among the most important and popular Christian pilgrimage destinations in Northern Greece.

Of Interest: The Church of St. Demetrius is a huge, absolutely magnificent building. Many of the paintings in the church are recreations of those that existed during the Ottoman era. Some of the structure was built using old Jewish tombstones and similar materials pillaged during the Nazi occupation of Greece. While the relic of St. Demetrius is not present, the well where the Romans probably tossed his body is beneath the church. The Hagia Sofia is one of the oldest churches in Greece, with parts of the building dating back to the 3rd century. It served as a mosque for nearly five hundred years. The Hagia Sofia is famous for its mosaics, some of which date back to its reconstruction in the 8th century.

82. ALEXANDER NEVSKY CATHEDRAL

1000 Sofia Center, Sofia, 1000, Bulgaria

Denomination: Bulgarian Orthodox
Dates: 1912 (completed)
Web: www.visitsofia.bg/en/cityinfrastructure/what-to-see/architectural-monuments/the-building-of-st-alexander-nevsky-cathedral (tourism website)

The Alexander Nevsky Cathedral is the seat of the Bulgarian Orthodox Church, one of the autocephalous churches of Eastern Orthodoxy. Named in honor of Alexander Nevsky, the great Russian hero who led the Slavs to victory over numerous enemies, this cathedral purportedly houses some of his relics. It is also one of the largest Orthodox cathedrals in the world and the second largest church to be found in the Balkans.

Bulgaria was the first region of Eastern Europe to be evangelized. The earliest Christian communities in Bulgaria may date as far back as the 1st century, possibly tracing back to the activity of Andrew. Whether or not this is the case, there were certainly Christians in Bulgaria by the 4th century. In 863, missionaries from Constantinople succeeded in converting Boris I, the King of Bulgaria.

At first, the astute king did not necessarily embrace the Orthodox Church, and instead played Rome and Constantinople off against each other in order to get the best deal. Less than a decade later he had one. The Church of Bulgaria became a part of the Eastern Orthodox Church, in communion with the Patriarch of Constantinople, but otherwise politically independent. This became the basis for all future autocephalous churches in Eastern Orthodoxy.

The Bulgarian Church grew quickly, and within a generation most of the country was converted. The country has been Christian ever since and, despite occupation by the Ottoman Empire from the 14th through the 18th centuries, the patriarchate has been continually active since its inception. The Alexander Nevsky Cathedral was erected as the new seat of the Church in 1912.

Of Interest: The Alexander Nevsky Cathedral is absolutely massive. Unlike many other great European cathedrals, which are hemmed in by closely built-out neighborhoods, this cathedral stands in the middle of a huge traffic circle and is easily visible from many directions. The multi-tiered pyramidic white church has yellow tiled roofs below, copper green roofs and domes in the middle and huge golden domes crowning the church and bell tower. Inside the church are two must-see treasures. The first is a case by the altar displaying a bit of bone from Alexander Nevsky. The second is a museum which is home to one of Southeast Europe's finest collections of Orthodox icons.

---

83. RILA MONASTERY

Route 107, Rila, 2643, Bulgaria

Alternate/Full Name: Monastery of St. Ivan of Rila
Denomination: Bulgarian Orthodox
Dates: c. 10th century (founded)
Web: www.rilskimanastir.org (official website)

The Rila Monastery enjoys a special distinction in the Eastern Orthodox Church. Bulgaria was the first Slavic nation to convert to Christianity and was home to the first autocephalous Church that was established in communion with Eastern Orthodoxy. John of Rila was Bulgaria's first ascetic, and by extension the first true monk in Slavic Eastern Europe. The monastery which he founded was the first in Eastern Europe, and it is now the holiest site in Bulgaria. It is revered by many Eastern European Christians as one of the most sacred places in Slavic lands. The Rila Monastery is a UNESCO World Heritage Site.

John of Rila was an important 9th century aesthetic who spent much of his life evangelizing in what is now Bulgaria. He began life as a shepherd, then later became a priest. Finally he chose to live as a hermit, and soon led a small group of devout followers with whom he founded a monastery. During his later years, John of Rila was

Bulgaria's most celebrated holy man, visited by peasants and kings alike who sought his wisdom and blessing. Many miraculous healings were attributed to him.

By the time of his death, John of Rila had become the first truly popular Christian monk of Slavic origin. Although he never technically lived in the monastery (he resided in a cave nearby), it quickly became Bulgaria's most sacred shrine. Vast sums of wealth poured in to make the monastery the jewel of the Bulgarian Church. After a fire in the 19th century, the monastery was rebuilt, even more lavishly than before. With the fall of Communism the Rila Monastery has once again regained its prominence as Bulgaria's most sacred Christian site and one of its most popular tourist destinations.

Of Interest: The original Rila Monastery was largely destroyed by fire in 1833. Most of the current structure dates from the mid-19th century. The grounds are extensive, and the wall and outbuildings enclose an area several acres in size. Residential buildings line the outer walls and include chapels and library facilities. The tall Hrelyu Tower dominates the compound. The centerpiece of the monastery is the church, an architectural hybrid of Slavic and Turkish styles with a large main dome over the central chapel and a number of smaller domes towards the back. The church interior is home to a wealth of decoration and artwork. The tomb of John of Rila lies beneath the Church. The monastery also houses a museum which contains numerous artifacts including the Rafail Cross, which is covered in finely carved Biblical figures.

---

84. DORMITION OF THE THEOTOKOS CHURCH

Rruga Polican-Suhe, Labove e Kryqit, Albania

Alternate/Full Name: St. Mary Church
Denomination: Albanian Orthodox
Dates: c. 6th century (originally completed), 13th century (current building completed)

Web: www.visit-gjirokastra.com/dt_places/labova-of-the-cross (tourism website)

The Dormition of the Theotokos Church is one of the oldest and most historic churches in the Balkans. It traces its roots back to one of the greatest Byzantine emperors, Justinian I. Justinian, who sponsored the construction of many churches in the 6th century founded the Dormition of the Theotokos Church in honor of his mother Vigilantia.

Around the time of its completion, a small piece of the True Cross discovered by St. Helena was placed here, making the church an important and popular pilgrimage destination from its earliest days. It has been substantially rebuilt on several occasions, with much of the current structure dating from the later Middle Ages.

The Dormition of the Theotokos Church was caught up in the politics of post-war Communism, and largely fell into disuse for religious worship in 1967. Efforts to renew both historic and religious interest in the church are currently being promoted. The building has been acknowledged by the government of Albania as a Cultural Monument.

Of Interest: The Dormition of the Theotokos Church is a Byzantine-style medieval church. However it looks far older, and in fact parts of the foundation and other elements of the church do date back to the original construction in the 6th century. The church dome is one of the oldest in southeastern Europe. In addition to the piece of the True Cross, the church is also in possession of a regionally famous icon of the Virgin Mary.

---

85. MONASTERY OF THE PATRIARCHATE OF PEC

Patrijasiska Ulica, Pec, 30000, Kosovo

Denomination: Serbian Orthodox
Dates: c. 13th century (founded)
Web: www.kosovo.net/epatrijarsija.html (official website)

The Monastery of the Patriarchate of Pec is a large complex that serves as the patriarchal seat of the Serbian Orthodox Church. Both the patriarchate and the monastery have been around since the late Middle Ages and have served as important institutions of Christian continuity in the region for centuries. The Patriarchate of Pec is a UNESCO World Heritage Site.

The Serbian Orthodox Church, established in the 13th century, was the eighth autocephalous church of Eastern Orthodoxy to be formed. The monastery was founded around the same time. After moving on several occasions, the seat of the Patriarchate was relocated here permanently in 1291 as the area seemed relatively safer from the threat of invasion. Nevertheless it was closed by the Ottomans from the mid-15th through the mid-16th centuries.

The Serbian Orthodox Church and the monastery weathered nearly five hundred years of Ottoman rule before being fully restored in 1920 following World War I. Although Serbia has been free of Muslim occupation for over a century, the seat of the Serbian Church remains in Pec in neighboring Kosovo. The Patriarchate of Pec was designated a UNESCO World Heritage Site in 2004.

Of Interest: The Monastery of the Patriarchate of Pec consists of an extensive complex which includes four beautiful medieval churches surrounded by lush green forests and hills. Between them they preserve some of the best surviving examples of the regional architecture of the Middle Ages. Almost all of the patriarchs of the Serbian Orthodox Church are buried in the monastic complex.

---

86. CHURCH OF ST. SAVA

Krusedolska 2a, Belgrade, Serbia

Alternate/Full Name: Temple of St. Sava
Denomination: Serbian Orthodox
Dates: c. 13th century (originally completed), 2019 (under construction as of the time of this writing)

Web: www.serbia.com/church-saint-sava-orthodox-heart-belgrade (tourism website)

The Cathedral of St. Sava is one of the largest churches of the Eastern Orthodox Communion in the world. Built to commemorate St. Sava, whose relic was incinerated by the Ottomans on this site in the 16th century, it has in a few short years become one of the most popular tourist attractions and pilgrimage destinations in both Belgrade and Serbia.

Sava was a 13th century ruler who was instrumental in establishing the autocephalous church of Eastern Orthodoxy in Serbia. His later years were spent as the first Archbishop of the Serbian Orthodox Church. He died in 1236 while returning from a pilgrimage to the Holy Land. He was later canonized and went on to become one of the most popular saints in Serbia and the surrounding Balkans.

For centuries Sava's relics were venerated by the people of the Balkans. However, following the outbreak of a Serbian uprising against the Ottoman Empire in 1594, his corpse was brought to Belgrade and burned in retribution. Three hundred years later, after Serbia finally won its independence from the Ottomans, it was decided to honor both their freedom and St. Saba with a massive new church. After being delayed by two World Wars and the Communist era, construction finally began in the 1980s. The church was still under construction as of the time of this writing.

Of Interest: The Cathedral of St. Sava is an absolutely immense Byzantine-Modern structure that towers over the surrounding neighborhood in Belgrade. Although the huge dome was put in place in 1989, parts of the church are still under construction. It will be one of the largest Orthodox churches in the world when it is completed. Modern iconography and works of art adorn the interior in a modest manner. Although his relic is long gone, there is a crypt beneath the church dedicated to St. Sava which is used as a museum featuring exhibits on the saint's life.

87. OSTROG MONASTERY

Ostrog, Montenegro

Denomination: Serbian Orthodox
Dates: c. 17th century (founded)
Web: www.visit-montenegro.com/monastery-ostrog (tourism website)

The Ostrog Monastery is a gravity defying abbey that clings to the side of steep rocky cliff known as Ostroska Greda. Founded in the 17th century, this Eastern Orthodox church is the site of the burial of St. Basil of Ostrog. It is the most popular pilgrimage destination in Montenegro, and one of that country's most famous tourist destinations.

Basil of Ostrog was an Orthodox priest who lived and worked in Montenegro throughout much of the 17th century. He briefly served as a bishop, but spent the later years of his life engaged in the establishment of the monastery at Ostrog. He was later accredited with miracles recognized by Orthodox Christians, Catholics and even the local Muslim population.

The monastery endured a turbulent 20th century, including being badly damaged by fire in the 1920s. During World War II resistance fighters took shelter here. Many of these were later massacred in the town, not by the Nazis, but by a rival faction of resistance fighters. The monastery remained active in the post-war period and is among Montenegro's most popular religious sites.

Of Interest: The Ostrog Monastery is not only of great religious and historic importance to Montenegro. It is also represents an impressive feat of both underground construction and engineering. The complex consists of a series of large buildings, some of which are built directly into the side of a cliff. The oldest sections, which consist of two cave churches, were the only parts of the complex that were spared from a fire. One of these, the Church of the Presentation, houses the relics of St. Basil of Ostrog. A large white cross has been erected on a cliff several hundred feet directly above the main building of the complex.

88. DUBROVNIK CATHEDRAL

Ul. Kneza Damjana Jude 1, 20000, Dubrovnik, Croatia

Alternate/Full Name: Cathedral of the Assumption of the Virgin Mary
Denomination: Roman Catholic
Dates: c. 7th century (originally completed), 1713 (current building completed)
Web: www.dubrovnik-travel.net/dubrovnik-cathedral (tourism website)

The Dubrovnik Cathedral is the great church of the city of Dubrovnik and one of the most magnificent Catholic sites to be found along the Dalmatian Coast. Dubrovnik and its cathedral have seen centuries of pilgrims travelling here to see the Tomb of St. Blaise, an early Christian martyr and one of the Fourteen Holy Helpers of the Roman Catholic Church. The cathedral is a must-see stop for any visitor to the city.

Blaise was one of the truly great heroes of the Church at the turn of the 4th century, and one of the last major pre-Constantine martyrs. Little is known of his early life, except that he was born in Armenia sometime around 270. He is known to have practiced medicine, and was probably part of the Christian community in Armenia prior to its legalization in that country in 301. Although not part of the Roman Empire, Armenia likely suffered at least some fallout from the persecutions of Diocletian.

Blaise, who became bishop of Sabastea around that time, probably looked after Christian refugees fleeing from Rome. Throughout his tenure as bishop, Blaise became known for his care of the sick and infirm. As a physician, most of his work was probably day-to-day care; but miraculous healings were also attributed to him. Crowds came to Blaise from far and wide to seek healing. His most famous miracle was curing a young boy who was choking to death on a fish bone.

In 316, one Agricola, the local governor, launched a violent assault on the Christians of Armenia. Blaise was seized, and when he refused to renounce his faith, was brutally beaten and beheaded. A cult instantly grew up around this popular figure, and he was later named not only a saint but one of the Fourteen Holy Helpers of the Church. His relics were moved to Dubrovnik, probably sometime around the Crusades. His shrine is now among the most venerated Catholic sites on the Dalmatian coast.

Of Interest: The Dubrovnik Cathedral is an 18th century structure that stands on the site of several previous churches, the earliest of which dates back to Roman times. It is a classic baroque building with an intricate façade crowned by a statue of St. Blaise. Built of the same white stone that all of the buildings of the city are famous for, the cathedral is most easily distinguished by its towering and unusual black dome. The cathedral interior houses a number of treasures, including a 15th century gold and silver statue of St. Blaise. A reliquary contains his head, his hands and pieces of his throat. The latter no doubt is in honor of the miraculous saving of the choking boy.

---

89. CATHEDRAL OF ST. DOMNIUS

Ul. Kraj Svetog Duje 5, 21000, Split, Croatia

Denomination: Roman Catholic
Completed: 305 (completed as a mausoleum), c. 7th century (consecrated as a church)
Web: www.visitsplit.com/en/527/cathedral-of-saint-domnius (tourism website)

The Cathedral of St. Domnius is one of the oldest essentially intact cathedrals in the world. Not originally a church, the building was, in fact, the mausoleum of the emperor Diocletian, who ironically was responsible for the last major Roman pogroms against the Christians. The cathedral is named in honor of St. Domnius, one of thousands who died during the brutal persecutions that took place in the early 4th century.

Diocletian was among the most infamous Roman emperors in history, and represented one of the last genuine threats to early Christianity. The later years of his rule were dominated by one of the greatest periods of persecution of Christians ever recorded. Thousands across the empire were tortured and killed, including many leaders of the period. One of these was one Domnius, the bishop of Salona, who was martyred along with seven other Christians, possibly soldiers.

Not too long after Diocletian's death in 311, Christianity was legalized in the Roman Empire. At some point in the ensuing centuries, in an ironic twist, Christians appropriated Diocletian's mausoleum to be repurposed as a church. It was formally consecrated in the 7th century. As an additional victory lap over the hated emperor, the Christians moved the relic of St. Domnius here, probably in the late Roman period.

What has resulted is one of the most historically important churches in the Balkans. The Cathedral of St. Domnius is directly associated with one of the most important events in early Christian history as well as one of the best-known Roman emperors. It is also counted among the world's oldest intact churches, and is one of the most visited parts of the old Roman palace grounds.

Of Interest: The Cathedral of St. Domnius is counted among the world's oldest cathedrals, although it was not actually originally constructed as a church. Diocletian's mausoleum, an impressive Romanesque structure, was completed in 305. It remains in its essentially original condition, with very few updates or renovations. Only the exterior bell tower dates from a significantly later period. The relic of St. Domnius is believed to be kept in the sacristy, though it is possible that it was moved to Rome in the Middle Ages. It is uncertain if Diocletian is still buried on the site.

90. BASILICA OF ST. MARY HELP OF CHRISTIANS

Brezje 72, 4243 Brezje, Slovenia

Alternate/Full Name: National Shrine of Mary Help of Christians
Denomination: Roman Catholic (Marian shrine)
Dates: 1900 (completed)
Web: www.marija.si/en (official website)

The Basilica of St. Mary Help of Christians is the most venerated church in Slovenia. One of Europe's lesser known Marian Shrines, it is associated with a number of miracles that occurred in Slovenia during the 19th century. Today it is one of the most popular pilgrimage destinations in the country.

The history of the shrine only goes back to the early 19th century, when it was constructed as a simple chapel extension off of the local church. Leopold Layer, a local artist, created a painting of Our Lady for the church in 1814. In the 1860s, a number of miraculous healings were reported there. These miracles were attributed to the painting.

By the late 19th century a massive new church was required to accommodate the great number of pilgrims that were coming to see the painting. The church was completed in 1900, and it has been Slovenia's most popular place of Catholic pilgrimage ever since. The church was raised to the status of Basilica Minor in 1988.

Of Interest: The Basilica of St. Mary Help of Christians is a sprawling baroque building, arguably one of the most magnificent in this region of Europe. The exterior features an odd architectural imbalance. To the left towards the rear of the church is the skyscraping bell tower. To the right towards the rear of the church is a side chapel with a magnificent dome that is oddly much shorter than the main building. Together they make for a very unusual view. The titular iconic painting of Mary Help of Christians can be found in the domed chapel. There is also a small building adjoining the church which is home to the Nativity Museum, which displays a collection of Nativity scenes.

ITALY

91. ST. PETER'S BASILICA

Piazza san Pietro, 00120 Vatican City

Alternate/Full Name: Papal Basilica of St. Peter in the Vatican
Denomination: Roman Catholic (sacred to many Christians)
Dates: c. 4th century (originally completed),
1626 (current building completed)
Web: www.vaticanstate.va/content/vaticanstate/en/monument/basilica-di-s-pietro (official website)

St. Peter's Basilica is the great cathedral of Vatican City, the world's smallest sovereign state, and the seat of the Papacy of the Roman Catholic Church. During the Middle Ages the site of Peter's martyrdom and burial became one of the most popular pilgrimage destinations in Europe. This shrine of Peter, which dominates the tiny enclave, draws millions of Catholic pilgrims to Rome every year. It is one of the seven ancient pilgrimage churches of Rome, one of the five Patriarchal Basilicas (representing Constantinople) and one of only four cathedrals in the world to bear the title of Basilica Major. St. Peter's Basilica is part of the Vatican City UNESCO World Heritage Site.

Sometime around the mid-1st century AD, the Apostle Peter traveled to Rome, the greatest city in the western world and capital of the Roman Empire. There he spent the later days of his life preaching and winning converts for the Church. However, in the wake of a terrible fire which destroyed much of the city in the year 64, the Emperor Nero arrested many Christians and cruelly put to them death. Most were sacrificed and devoured by animals in the Coliseum, but Peter was crucified upside-down upon Vatican Hill, where he was later buried with others in a mass grave.

Even from the earliest days of the Church, the symbolic importance of Peter's gravesite was recognized by the Christians of Rome. Shortly after Constantine's legalization of Christianity in the 4th century, a huge church was constructed over the site. Now known as Old St. Peter's Basilica, it stood for over twelve centuries. In the year 800, Charlemagne accepted the title of Holy Roman Emperor from the Pope here. By the time the Crusades were underway, Old Saint Peter's Basilica was showing signs of its age.

During the 1400s it was decided that old St. Peter's would be torn down and completely rebuilt. Despite protests from the local Christian community and the difficulty of having to deal with literally thousands of corpses buried within and beneath the old basilica, work began in 1506. It took more than a century to complete. The Church took full advantage of the proximity and availability of the many great Renaissance artists and architects resident in Italy, including Bernini, Botticelli and Michelangelo. The result was the most spectacular Christian edifice ever built, a claim which remains unchallenged to the present day. On November 18, 1626, the new Basilica of St. Peter was consecrated by Pope Urban VIII. Today it is among the most visited churches on Earth, not only by Catholics but by Christians of every denomination.

Of Interest: St. Peter's Basilica is the grand champion of all of the world's churches in terms of size and splendor. Built during the 16th and 17th centuries, every architectural aspect of St. Peter's Basilica is unrivaled. In front of the Basilica is the immense St. Peter's Square, circumscribed by a massive colonnade and crowned with the statues of a hundred and forty saints. Several giant bronze portals offer entrance to the Basilica. The Holy Door in the center is only opened on special occasions. The interior is an unparalleled work of art. Every inch of the massive sanctuary is overwhelming, from the extensive marble work to the soaring columns to the gilt archways and ceilings. Among the artisans who contributed to its completion were Michaelangelo, who oversaw much of the construction, including the great dome; and Bernini, who designed some of the basilica's greatest interior elements, including the central altar known as the Baldacchino. Beneath the altar and sanctuary, in the Vatican Grotto, St. Peter is buried along with ninety-one Popes and some other historic Church figures. Veronica's Veil, one of the most hallowed of all Christian artifacts, is stored in one of the basilica's chapels.

92. APOSTOLIC PALACE & SISTINE CHAPEL

Viale Vaticano, 00165 Vatican City

Denomination: Roman Catholic
Dates: Palace - 1605 (completed) & Chapel - 1481 (completed)
Web: www.museivaticani.va (official website)

The Apostolic Palace is the best known of the three official residences of the Pope. Adjacent to St. Peter's Basilica, it is one of Europe's most magnificent residences. Many of the most famous painters and artisans of the Renaissance were employed in its construction. The highlight is the Sistine Chapel, the private chapel of the Pope. Millions of tourists pack the Sistine Chapel annually to gawk at Michaelangelo's two masterpieces, *The Creation of Adam* and *The Last Judgement*. The Apostolic Palace is part of the Vatican City UNESCO World Heritage Site.

The Lateran Palace had been donated to the Church in Roman times and had served as the official residence of the popes since the 4th century. However, when the Papacy returned to Rome after the Babylonian Captivity, it was decided that a new home was required for the Popes, a building of such splendor and magnificence that it would have no rival in Europe. It would be a residence befitting the Supreme Pontiff of the Roman Catholic Church.

In the 15th century, work began on the new Apostolic Palace on the Vatican Hill. Throughout Europe, vast sums of wealth were collected for its construction. The artist Rafael designed the palace's reception rooms. Pinturicchio worked on the Borgia Apartments. Donato Bramante laid out the Belvedere Courtyard. And the Sistine Chapel, the holy of holies of Christian art, was created by Michaelangelo.

In the ensuing centuries, the Apostolic Palace was further adorned by the most fantastic collection of Christian art ever assembled. So great was this collection that much of the Apostolic Palace has since been transformed into a museum for the purpose of displaying the Papal treasures. This process began in the 16th century, when the Sistine Chapel opened to the public. The Vatican has since added more than half a dozen new museums and countless galleries, including a number of sculpture museums, a museum of modern religious art, and the famous gallery of maps. Among the palace's contributing artists were Carravaggio, DaVinci, Giotto and Titian. Today the Apostolic Palace is counted among Europe's greatest art museums, beloved of Christians as well as art lovers around the world.

Of Interest: The Apostolic Palace, now largely part of the Vatican Museums, is home to over two dozen galleries, exhibition halls and palace sites. Most of these are interconnected in a sequential series that make them easier to tour. Among the highlights of the collection are the Gregorian Egyptian and Etruscan Museums; the Pinacoteca Art Gallery; and the Ethnological Missionary Museum. The palace sites include the Apartment of St. Pius V, the Borgia Apartment, the Chapel of Nicholas V, the Chapel of Urban VIII, the Room of the Immaculate Conception, the Room of the Chiaroscuri, the Room of the Aldobrandini Wedding, the Sala delle Dame, the Salone Sistino, the Rafael Stanze and the famous Map Room. The highlight is undoubtedly the Sistine Chapel. Every inch of space on the walls and ceiling is covered with paintings and frescoes. Among the highlights are *Christ Giving the Keys to St. Peter*, *Scenes of the Life of Moses*, the *Punishment of Korah* and the *Temptation of Christ*; and of course, the *Creation of Adam* and the *Last Judgement*, both by Michelangelo.

---

93. BASILICA OF ST. JOHN LATERAN & LATERAN PALACE

Piazza di S. Giovanni in Laterano, 4, 00184 Rome, Italy

Alternate/Full Names: Cathedral of the Most Holy Savior and Saints John the Baptist and the Evangelist in the Lateran, Lateran Basilica
Denomination: Roman Catholic (sacred to many Christians)
Dates: 324 (originally completed), 1735 (current building completed)
Web: www.vatican.va/various/basiliche/san_giovanni (official website)

The Basilica of St. John in Lateran was the first of the four basilicas major of the Roman Catholic Church to be built. Because of this St. John's serves as the seat of the Pope in his capacity of the Bishop of Rome. From the 4th through the 17th centuries the Popes ruled a vast Christian empire from the Lateran Palace next door. St. John's is one of the seven ancient pilgrimage churches of Rome, one of five Patriarchal Basilicas (representing Rome) and one of only four cathedrals in the world to bear the distinction of being a Basilica Major. Both the basilica and the Lateran Palace are part of the Vatican City UNESCO World Heritage Site.

When Rome's Christian community was finally able to come out into the open in the 4th century, the number of openly faithful skyrocketed. Around this time, on the east side of Rome, there was a palatial estate that had belonged to the Laterani, one of the most famous and prominent families of the Roman Empire. This ancient estate had been passed down over generations until it was inherited by Fausta, the second wife of the Emperor Constantine. Upon their marriage he assumed possession of the estate. In the year 31 Constantine gifted it to the Bishopric of Rome.

This acquisition, and the subsequent construction of a major new church next door, established the bishop as a major power in the city. Some regard this event as marking the symbolic beginning of what is now known as the Roman Catholic Church. The church's prestige was further raised by the presence of the Scala Sancta, which were presented as a gift to the Bishop of Rome by Helena, the mother of Constantine. According to tradition, these steps came from the governor's palace in Jerusalem, and were climbed by Jesus on his way to trial.

From these humble beginnings, St. John in Lateran grew in importance until it was the seat of all Christian authority in much of Europe. For well over a thousand years, with the brief interruption of the Babylonian Captivity in Avignon, the Popes reigned from the Lateran Palace. The Lateran finally lost its vaunted status in the early 1600s, when Papal activities relocated to the Vatican across town. Nevertheless it retains its formal status as the official church of the Bishop of Rome, which it remains to this day.

Of Interest: The Basilica of St. John in Lateran is one of the most important and sacred churches in the world. Although it was the first of

Rome's great churches to be founded, the original building was badly damaged by fire in the Late Middle Ages, and most of the current structure dates from reconstructions in the 16th and 18th centuries. Although the traditional Roman floor plan was preserved, the basilica is a product of the Renaissance and Baroque eras. The highlight is the Scala Sancta, or Sacred Stairs, which are climbed daily by thousands of pilgrims. The adjacent Lateran Palace is, if less important religiously, perhaps even more important historically. A palace has stood on the site since pre-Christian times, and the ancient Roman structure was used by the Church for well over a thousand years. It too was damaged by fire in the 14th century, but the palace was better preserved during its restoration than the Basilica was. The palace is now home to a museum which houses overflow exhibits from the Vatican.

---

94. BASILICA OF ST. PAUL OUTSIDE THE WALLS

Piazzale San Paolo, 1, 00146 Rome, Italy

Denomination: Roman Catholic (sacred to many Christians)
Dates: 324 (originally completed), 1840 (current building completed)
Web: www.vatican.va/various/basiliche/san_paolo (official website)

The Basilica of St. Paul Outside the Walls, so-called because of its location outside the old city walls of Rome, is yet another of the city's great Christian sites. Aside from its great antiquity, it is home to the grave of Paul, the Christian Apostle to the Gentiles, and perhaps the most influential early Church figure after Peter. St. Paul's is one of the seven ancient pilgrimage churches of Rome, one of five Patriarchal Basilicas (representing Alexandria) and one of only four cathedrals in the world to bear the distinction of being a Basilica Major. The Basilica of St. Paul Outside the Wall is part of the Vatican City UNESCO World Heritage Site.

Paul was one of the most crucial figures in the spread of Christianity in the 1st century. Although he was not one of the Twelve Apostles chosen by Jesus to carry out his ministry, Paul's missionary journeys dominate the second half of the Book of Acts. According to tradition, his final mission took him to the imperial city of Rome, where he was martyred by beheading sometime around year 67. Unlike Peter, Paul's place of burial outside the city was apparently well known and became a place of veneration from the outset.

Shortly after the legalization of Christianity, the emperor Constantine constructed a church over the site of Paul's grave. This church was expanded and embellished many times over the ensuing centuries. Beginning in the year 1215, the Basilica of St. Paul was the home church in exile of the Latin Patriarch of Alexandria. After fires ravaged St. John in Lateran and St. Peter's Basilica was demolished in the 15th century, St. Paul's Basilica became the oldest largely intact church in the city of Rome. Unfortunately, St. Paul's fell victim to fire in 1823, when it was almost completely destroyed by accident during a renovation. It was subsequently rebuilt, based as closely as possible on the design of the earlier church, and reconsecrated in 1855.

During the renovation, the location of Paul's sarcophagus was discovered by Benedictine monks. In 2006 it was excavated and the body examined by Church officials and scientists. To great fanfare, it was announced that the bone fragments within the sarcophagus likely dated to the 1st century. As the site was nearly continually venerated for almost two thousand years, and as the scientific evidence confirmed the antiquity of the remains, the possibility that this was the sepulcher of Paul's corpse is strongly supported. As such, it is considered one of the most important churches in the world, and is a must-see place for Christian pilgrims to the city.

Of Interest: The Basilica of St. Paul Outside the Walls suffered greatly in the fire of 1823. However, the 19th century reconstruction was undertaken with great care and in the spirit of the original. The outside certainly has the look of a Roman-era structure, with marble-faced and columned façade before which stands a solitary statue of St. Paul. Entrance to the church is through a door which incorporates parts of an earlier door built in the 11th century. Another entrance, the Holy Door, is opened only during a Papal declared Jubilee. The church's interior is a breathtaking reproduction of an ancient Roman basilica with a single great nave flanked by columned aisles. The whole is adorned with a variety of mosaics that survived the 19th century fire, as well as newer works. Paul's tomb is located in a marble sarcophagus in a crypt beneath the altar.

---

95. BASILICA OF ST. LAWRENCE OUTSIDE THE WALLS

Piazzale del Verano, 3, 00165 Rome, Italy

Denomination: Roman Catholic
Dates: c. 6th century (completed)
Web: www.gcatholic.org/churches/rome/020 (Catholic website)

The Basilica of St. Lawrence Outside the Walls, so-called because of its location outside the old city walls, is one of the great churches of Rome. Aside from its antiquity, it is home to the tomb of Lawrence, one of the earliest Catholic saints, as well as the possible tomb of St. Stephen. St. Lawrence is one of the seven ancient pilgrimage churches of Rome and one of five Patriarchal Basilicas (representing Jerusalem). The Basilica of St. Lawrence Outside the Walls is part of the Vatican City UNESCO World Heritage Site.

Lawrence of Rome was an important leader of the Church in the mid-3rd century, and one of the very few major Christian figures of the era that anything is known with any certainty. In 258, Lawrence, who was then serving as one of the seven deacons of the Church in Rome, was ordered to turn over all of the Church's wealth to Roman authorities. Instead he distributed all of it to the poor and sick of the city. The Roman prefect was apparently not amused, and had Lawrence put to death by roasting him on a grill.

Lawrence was among the most important Christian leaders honored with a major church in Rome. The emperor Constantine erected a chapel on the site of Lawrence's martyrdom. A full-fledged church was constructed on the site in the 6th century. It is uncertain exactly when the body of Lawrence was interred in the structure, but his burial at the site is believed to date back to this early period. According to tradition, the remains of Stephen the first martyr were later brought to Rome and interred next to Lawrence.

Although not one of the four Basilicas Major of Rome, the Basilica of St. Lawrence Outside the Wall is one of the traditional seven pilgrimage churches of Rome. While it is less important than the four basilicas major, St. Lawrence is older and better preserved, with some of the original structure and artwork still intact. Unfortunately, the church was damaged by bombing during World War II, though it has been fully restored since. The basilica is one of Catholic Rome's less visited sites, a quiet alternative for hard-core pilgrims who wish to avoid the crowds of St. Peter's.

Of Interest: The Basilica of St. Lawrence Outside the Walls largely dates from the Middle Ages, though a core of the original Roman building survives. The façade was mostly rebuilt after World War II when it was badly damaged by bombs. The campanile bell tower to the right of the main church building dates from the 12th century. The main portico entrance is similarly old. The church interior may be one of the best surviving examples of Roman era architecture. Consisting of a simple, central nave flanked by single colonnaded aisles, the white marble and red brick main chamber probably looks much as it did more than a thousand years ago. Some of the early frescoes and artwork survive, including a Roman-era sarcophagus that was recycled for Christian use. The tombs of Lawrence and Stephen are under the main altar. Also buried in the church are St. Hilarius and Pope Pius IX.

---

96. BASILICA OF ST. MARY MAJOR & SHRINE OF OUR LADY OF DIVINE LOVE

Piazza di S. Maria Maggiore, 42, 00100 Rome, Italy (Basilica of St. Mary Major)

Via del Santuario, Castel di Leva, 00134 Rome, Italy (Sanctuary of Our Lady of Divine Love)

Denomination: Roman Catholic (Marian shrine)
Completed: Basilica - c. 5th century (originally completed), 1743 (completed) & Shrine - 1745 (originally completed), 1999 (current building completed)
Web: www.vatican.va/various/basiliche/sm_maggiore (official website)

The Basilica of St. Mary Major and the Shrine of Our Lady of Divine Love are the two great Marian shrines of the city of Rome. Together they constitute two of the seven historic Pilgrimage Churches of Rome. The Basilica of St. Mary Major is one of five Patriarchal Basilicas, representing Antioch, and one of only four cathedrals in the world to bear the distinction of being a Basilica Major. The Shrine of Our Lady of Divine Love is a relative newcomer, but is nevertheless Italy's most popular Marian shrine. The Basilica of St. Mary Major is part of the Vatican City UNESCO World Heritage Site.

One of the very first Marian shrines ever built was the Basilica of St. Mary Major. According to legend, the site of the church on the Esqualine Hill where St. Mary Major now stands was chosen by a freak snowstorm, which had appeared to Pope Liberius in a dream. Despite being damaged in an earthquake in the 14th century, the core of the church essentially dates back to its original construction. Because of this it preserves some of the most ancient architecture and artwork in any church in Rome.

On the opposite end of the timeline is the Shrine of Our Lady of Divine Love. In 1740, a pilgrim was attacked here by a pack of dogs, and was apparently saved by the intervention of the Virgin Mary. A chapel soon arose on the spot, and quickly became Rome's church of choice for prayers of intercession. It became so popular that a full basilica was constructed on the site in the 1990s, making it by far the youngest of Rome's major churches. Because of its popularity among the Roman masses, Pope John Paul II added it to the list of the Seven Pilgrimage Churches of Rome, replacing the Church of St. Sebastian Outside the Walls.

Of Interest: The Basilica of St. Mary Major, while largely dating from later centuries, has preserved some of its Roman-era construction. It is one of the best examples of a true Roman basilica still standing.

Nevertheless there have been many restorations and additions made over the centuries, notably the Renaissance masterpiece Borghese Chapel. There are also splendid mosaics that date back to the 5th century. A number of Popes and other important figures are buried in the church, including the artist Bernini. The Sanctuary of Our Lady of Divine Love is an anomaly among the pilgrimage churches in Rome. Built towards the end of the 20th century, the New Sanctuary is a glass and steel building featuring works of modern art and new age stained glass. The tombs of the Quattrocchis can be found here, a husband and wife who are in the process of being beatified simultaneously.

---

97. CHURCH OF THE JESUITS & CHURCH OF ST. IGNATIUS OF LOYOLA

Via degli Astalli, 16, 00186 Rome, Italy (Church of the Jesuits)

Via del Caravita, 8a, 00186 Rome, Italy (Church of St. Ignatius of Loyola)

Alternate/Full Names: Mother Church of the Society of Jesus, Church of the Most Holy Name of Jesus at the Argentina & Church of St. Ignatius of Loyola Martius
Denomination: Roman Catholic
Dates: Jesuits - 1580 (completed) & St. Ignatius - 1650 (completed)
Web: www.chiesadelgesu.org/la-chiesa & https://santignazio.gesuiti.it/en (official websites)

The Church of the Jesuits and the Church of St. Ignatius of Loyola are a pair of churches in Rome that belong to the Catholic order known as the Society of Jesus. The Jesuits, as they are more commonly known, was the brainchild of Ignatius of Loyala. He established the headquarters of the Jesuits in Rome, and began construction on what is regarded as one of the finest baroque-era churches in Europe, where he was later interred. Later, the order constructed the Church of St. Ignatius of Loyola, named in his honor, as the rectory church of the Romano Collegio. This later became the repository of some of the order's most important relics, as well as the tomb of Robert Bellarmine.

Ignatius of Loyola is among the most colorful Catholic Church figures of the Reformation era. Born in 1491 in Spain on the cusp of the discovery of the Americas, Ignatius spent his twenties as a soldier in service to the Christian armies of the Spanish crown. After a religious awakening in 1521, he decided to devote his life to missionary work. He gathered a number of followers, including his friend Francis Xavier, and in 1534 they founded the Society of Jesus. Ignatius became the order's first General Superior and helped to lead the Church's Counter-Reformation efforts.

In the later years of his life, and throughout the 16th and 17th centuries, the Jesuits went on to become one of the most active organizations in the establishment of churches in Spanish, Portuguese and French colonial territories around the world. He died in Rome in 1556 and was interred in the church he founded.

Robert Bellarmine was born into a prominent Roman family and was nephew to Pope Marcellus II. Most of the first five decades of his life was consumed in studying and teaching throughout Europe. From 1589 onward, Robert Bellarmine became an increasingly important Church figure, both religiously and politically. During this period he was sent as an ambassador to the Catholic League in France, where he witnessed the Siege of Paris during the Wars of Religion. He went on to become both a cardinal and an archbishop. He produced many important writings which later earned him an honored place among the doctors of the Church. He was laid to rest in the chapel of Roman College where he taught for a time as one of its earliest professors.

The Church of the Jesuits in Rome was founded by Ignatius in 1551 and completed in 1584. It was built on the site of an earlier church, the Santa Maria della Strada, where Ignatius had once prayed. The Church of St. Ignatius of Loyola was completed a few decades later, in 1650. Together they represent the two most historic Jesuit churches in Italy, and are still highly honored by members of that order.

Of Interest: The Church of the Jesuits is a great architectural treasure overshadowed by Rome's other historic churches. Lavishly funded, the building was designed and worked on by some of the finest artisans of the Renaissance. Michaelangelo himself worked on it during the early stages of construction. The exterior is attractive and elegant, and the façade definitively baroque. The interior is stunning, with every inch of wall space covered with fine frescoes. The church highlight is the St. Ignatius Chapel, where the order's founder and patron saint is entombed. The Church of St. Ignatius of Loyola was raised in the 17th century as a further tribute to Ignatius. The façade is famous for its ornate masonry and decoration. The interior walls and ceilings boast many works of stunning oil frescoes, including some that depict events in the lives of the early Jesuits. A number of important Jesuit figures are buried in the various chapels here, including Robert Bellarmine.

---

98. CHURCH OF ST. MARY AND THE MARTYRS (PANTHEON)

Piazza della Rotunda, 00186 Rome, Italy

Denomination: Roman Catholic
Dates: 125 (completed as a pagan temple),
609 (consecrated as a church)
Web: www.pantheonroma.com (official website)

The Pantheon is one of the greatest surviving architectural legacies of the Roman Empire. With the original 2nd century building almost completely intact, it has been use as a church for over fourteen hundred years. In addition to its history and antiquity, this building is a treasure trove of Renaissance artwork as well as the site of the tombs of several very prominent Italians.

A temple was known to have stood on this site since the days of Caesar Augustus. Destroyed twice by fires, the current building was completed around 125 under the auspices of the emperor Hadrian. It was used as a pagan temple at least until the fall of the Western Roman Empire, and may have remained in continual use as such all the way until the 7th century when it became the property of the Church.

In 609, the last remaining traces of pagan worship were removed and the building was re-consecrated as a Christian place of worship. It has been continuously in use as an active church ever since. During the

Renaissance it underwent a full renovation under the auspices of some of the greatest artists of the age. By the 19th century, the Pantheon became a symbol of the modern unified Italy, tying the new nation to its ancient Roman and Christian roots. A number of modern Italian kings and other prominent citizens are now entombed here.

Of Interest: The Pantheon is arguably the grandest of ancient Rome's buildings still standing. Not huge by the standards of later cathedrals, it was nevertheless very large by ancient Roman standards. The dome, one of the architectural wonders of the ancient world, is the largest surviving such structure from the Roman Empire. The interior, long cleared of its ancient pagan symbols, has become home to a wealth of art and a number of tombs. The most famous painting is the *Madonna of the Girdle* by an unknown Renaissance artist. Burials include two Italian kings, Umberto I and Victor Emannuel II, as well as the Renaissance master artist, Raphael.

---

99. CHRISTIAN CATACOMBS OF ROME

Rome, Italy (multiple locations)

Denomination: Formerly Roman Catholic
Dates: 1st, 2nd and 3rd centuries (founded)
Web: www.catacombe.roma.it (official website)

The Christian Catacombs of Rome, of which more than a dozen have been rediscovered, are among the oldest intact Christian sites on Earth. Although such underground tomb complexes have been used around the world since antiquity, it was the Christians of Rome and other cities in Italy who raised catacomb building to an art form. From simple entrances scattered along the Roman highways, the Christian catacombs spread like labyrinths, sometimes hundreds of acres in size and many levels deep. Since the 19th century, many catacomb complexes have been rediscovered around Rome, and some of these are now open to the public.

The use of secret underground burial chambers in the area around

Rome dates back at least to Etruscan times. Such practices were continued in early Roman times on a smaller scale. It was not until the early 2nd century that the mass construction of immense labyrinths came into vogue in the area around the imperial capital. Several cultural, religious and logistical needs all seemed to have converged at this time, necessitating a new way to dispose of Rome's dead and ushering in the empire's golden age of catacomb building.

The burial of corpses was becoming popular in the empire in the 2nd century, as opposed to the traditional act of cremation. This was particularly true among the Christian population, who probably influenced the local pagans in this regard. Rome had no room inside the city for such a large number graves, and a law was passed requiring all burials to be moved outside of the walls. For most pagan Romans this meant tombs and graves scattered along the roads and in the countryside outside of Rome. But Christians had additional concerns, including secrecy.

The 2nd and 3rd centuries were a period of great persecution for the Christians of Rome. Underground burials made Christian tombs both less accessible and a less obvious target for vandals. Furthermore, many saints and martyrs were buried in the catacombs in earlier times, and other Christians simply wanted to be buried near them. By the beginning of the 3rd century the use of catacombs had spread throughout the Italian Peninsula. The age of the catacombs began to decline late in the 4th century once Christians could at last move their tombs above ground. A few centuries later the Catacombs of Rome were abandoned entirely, and forgotten until their rediscovery in the late 1500s.

Of Interest: The Christian Catacombs of Rome number over a dozen, of which a few in particular stand out. The Catacombs of Domatilla was possibly the first and among the earliest to be rediscovered, as well as one of the largest and most intact. It is famous for its large, carved-out underground basilica. The Catacombs of San Sebastian, located beneath the Church of San Sebastian Outside the Wall, are among the most visited. The early Christian martyr St. Sebastian was once interred here, and a small statue of the saint created by Bernini marks the former location of his tomb. The Catacombs of San Callisto were among the largest and most prestigious in early Christian times.

Aside from the numerous saints and martyrs who were once entombed there, San Callisto served for a time as the official burial site of the Bishops of Rome, and more than a dozen early Popes were interred there at one time.

---

100. MILVIAN BRIDGE

Ponte Milvio, Rome, Italy

Denomination: Public Bridge
Dates: 115 BC (completed)
Web: www.romeinformation.it/en (tourism website)

The Milvian Bridge has a special place in the history of early Christianity. It was here on October 27, 312 that the Roman Emperor Constantine achieved a great military victory which he attributed to divine intervention. This led directly to his issuance of the Edict of Milan a year later, effectively ending persecution of Christians in the Roman Empire. Amazingly, the Milvian Bridge, one of the world's oldest surviving bridges, is now in its 22nd century and still in use.

In the late 3rd century, the Emperor Diocletian oversaw a turbulent period in Rome's history. In an effort to stabilize the empire, he established the Tetrarchy, at which time four emperors ruled jointly. This unstable system broke down immediately after his death. Within a few years two of the tetrarchs were dead, and the empire was left in the hands of Maxentius in the east and Constantine in the west. Maxentius, with the greater resources and manpower of the east at his disposal, occupied Rome, which was part of the western sphere of influence. Constantine invaded Italy in 312 with an army from Gaul in an effort to dislodge him.

Constantine defeated Maxentius' forces in northern Italy, and then marched southwards to meet his enemy who was entrenched at Rome with a vastly superior force. Constantine's outlook for victory was grim. However, on the eve of the battle, Constantine received a vision instructing him to 'mark the Heavenly sign on the shields of his army'. Taking this to mean the sign of a Christian cross, he had every shield in his army so marked. The next day, Maxentius inexplicably led his army outside of Rome's gates to meet Constantine in open battle. Instead of waiting out what should have been an easy siege, Maxentius' army was routed.

Afterwards, Constantine became the undisputed ruler of most of the Roman Empire. He attributed both his victory and his newly-won throne to the divine intervention of the God of the Christians, and for the first time since the days of Jesus there was a Roman emperor who was genuinely sympathetic to their cause. The next year he issued the Edict of Milan, which guaranteed religious freedom to all people, effectively legalizing the Christian faith. The Milvian Bridge still stands in northern Rome, an architectural testament to this miraculous victory and Roman engineering.

Of Interest: The Milvian Bridge crosses the Tiber River near where it bends eastward on the north side of Rome. It connects two of the city's most ancient roads: the Via Cassia to the north and the Via Flaminia to the south. The original bridge was replaced by the current structure in 115 BC. Its graceful arches and excellent stonework still impress after two thousand years. A tower guards the southern end of the bridge, though this only dates from the 1800s.

---

101. BASILICA OF ST. FRANCIS OF ASSISI

Piazza Inferiore di S. Francesco, 2, 06081 Assisi, Italy

Denomination: Roman Catholic
Dates: 1253 (completed)
Web: www.sanfrancescoassisi.org (official website)

The Basilica of St. Francis of Assisi is the mother church of the Order of Friars Minor and the site of the tomb of its founder, St. Francis. One of the most honored men of his day, he was canonized within two years of his death, a rare achievement. The church served for a time as the headquarters of the Franciscans and as a result Assisi became one of the great centers of Christian learning during the late Middle Ages. The Basilica of St. Francis in Assisi is a UNESCO World Heritage Site.

Francis of Assisi was born into a reasonably well-off family and spent most of his early years alternately enjoying the finer things in life and condemning them. By the time he turned twenty he had already spent much time in various careers, which included service in the military, though he ultimately decided to pursue a life of service with the Church. Following a pilgrimage to Rome, Francis repudiated his family's wealth and turned to a life of poverty. As his first mission he endeavored to restore church buildings in and around Assisi.

In 1209 Francis formalized his personal beliefs into a strict regimen of poverty and sacrifice. He went about the countryside in bare feet preaching the Gospel. Within a year he had a small following and petitioned the Pope to be recognized as an order. His petition was granted, and soon new disciples were flocking to join. Over the next decade Francis worked diligently to continue preaching his message, and new monasteries sprang up all over Europe. In later years Francis went on a journey to the Holy Land, where he preached in Islamic Egypt, fought in the Crusades and visited the Holy Sites of Palestine.

He returned to Italy in 1220, and spent much of the remainder of his life organizing his increasingly popular brotherhood. In 1223 the Rule of the Franciscans was completed. According to tradition, Francis received the Stigmata soon afterwards. By the time he passed away in 1226, he had established one of Christianity's greatest monastic organizations. The friary at Assisi and the basilica that was built there shortly after his death has for the last eight centuries remained the spiritual heart of the order as well as one of the world's most beautiful monasteries. It remains a popular monastic retreat.

Of Interest: The Basilica of St. Francis of Assisi and the neighboring friary crown a low hill overlooking the city of Assisi. The complex consists of an upper and lower basilica, the latter containing his crypt. Among the great artists who contributed their efforts to the church was Giotto Di Bondone. In 1818 St. Francis' stone and iron tomb was disinterred and put on display in the crypt. In addition to Francis, five other important early Franciscans are buried here, including Jacopa dei

Settesoli, a woman who funded much of the Order's early activities. Next door to the basilica is the friary, one of the largest and most magnificent monasteries in Europe. Constructed of white and pink marble, much of the wealth used to improve the friary came from Pope Sixtus IV, who himself had once spent time as a Franciscan. Among the monastery's treasures is one of Europe's largest medieval libraries.

---

102. SAVONAROLA MARKER

Piazza della Signoria, Florence, Italy

Denomination: Public Monument
Dates: c. 20th century (placed)
Web: www.firenzeturismo.it/en (tourism website)

The Savonarola Marker in Florence is a simple plaque that commemorates the execution of Girolamo Savonarola, who led a movement considered to be a precursor to the Protestant Reformation. Savonarola is regarded by many Protestants as a hero and champion of their cause. His martyrdom has only recently been allowed to be officially recognized in Florence.

Girolamo Savonarola was born in Ferrara in 1452 into a well-off middle class family. As a young adult he both studied for a life in the Church while at the same time recognizing that there were inherent problems with Roman Catholicism. Throughout his career he served in a variety of capacities in a number of cities, and by the 1490s was acclaimed by many that knew him as a prophet. By1495 Savonarola was one of the most popular priests in Italy, and he was embraced by the people of Florence as their spiritual leader.

Savonarola led a campaign to cleanse the city of sin and vice, challenging Church officials and eventually the Papacy. He was excommunicated in 1497 and condemned as a heretic in 1498. After his execution by hanging his body was burned and the ashes scattered in the Arno River. Every effort was made to erase Savonarola's memory. However, just a few years after his execution, Reformers in Central

Europe began embracing his ideas. It was not until the 20th century that his martyrdom was finally commemorated on Italian soil.

Of Interest: The Savonarola Marker is a relatively small, simple monument that nevertheless has an honored place among the majestic palaces and Renaissance statues that adorn the Piazza della Signoria. It was placed in this plaza as it was the site of Savonarola's famous Bonfire of the Vanities as well as his martyrdom. The marker is on or close to the exact spot where he was executed.

---

103. FLORENCE CATHEDRAL

Piazza del Duomo, 50122 Florence, Italy

Alternate/Full Name: Cathedral of St. Mary of the Flower
Denomination: Roman Catholic
Dates: c. 4th century (originally completed),
1436 (current building completed)
Web: www.museumflorence.com (official website)

The Florence Cathedral is arguably the definitive architectural masterpiece of the Italian Renaissance. This stunning building, which took well over a century to complete, really set the stage for a revolution in construction engineering that swept Europe in the 15th and 16th centuries. Its dome was the greatest to be completed in Europe since the collapse of the Roman Empire. The Florence Cathedral is now a UNESCO World Heritage Site.

Florence's first church was built in the 4th century under the auspices of St. Ambrose, and it stood for over nine hundred years. By the late Middle Ages, it was falling apart and utterly inadequate to the local Christian community's needs. In the late 13th century it was decided that a new church was needed. The project was overseen by some of the best architects and engineers of the early Renaissance.

After the cathedral was largely completed, work stalled for decades while plans for the massive dome were worked out. The final design was conceived of by Filippo Brunelleschi, who figured out how to build the dome given severe engineering and structural limitations. For his efforts he became known as one of the master architects of the Renaissance. The cathedral was completed in 1436 to great fanfare. It went on to inspire the construction of even greater churches throughout Italy, including the Basilica of St. Peter at the Vatican.

Of Interest: The Florence Cathedral is one of the greatest works of architecture of the Renaissance. It is the product of a number of early Renaissance masters, both architects and artists, with what many people consider to be the world's greatest dome. An immense campanile, almost as tall as the dome, rises up from the plaza in front of the cathedral. Among the countless works of art that adorn the interior are famous paintings depicting events from the Divine Comedy by Dante. Archaeological excavations beneath the church have uncovered early Roman ruins. Several popes are buried in the crypt, along with the dome's architect Filippo Brunelleschi.

---

104. BASILICA OF ST. DOMINIC

Piazza S. Dominico, 13, 40124 Bologna, Italy

Denomination: Roman Catholic
Dates: 1218 (completed)
Web: www.bolognawelcome.com/en/home/discover/places/architecture-and-monuments (tourism website)

The Basilica of St. Dominic is arguably the most famous church in a city packed with amazing churches. It is the site of the Tomb of Dominic, founder of the Dominican monastic order. Established by Dominic himself as the order's headquarters, its location in north central Italy made it easily accessible to the other cities of the region. It remains a religiously important site for members of the Dominican order.

Dominic of Osma is one of the great monastic figures of the Roman Catholic Church, and one of its most controversial saints as well. Born in Spain during the years of the Reconquista, he lived in an age when Catholicism was faced with many challenges, both from competing religions as well as Christian heretical groups. Dominic practically stumbled into history while on a diplomatic mission for the Bishop of Osma. While traveling in Southern France, he had a run-in with the Cathars, a local heretical movement. The encounter left him with a desire to preach against heresy.

In 1215 he founded the Order of Preachers, later known as the Dominicans, with the express purpose of living in poverty, to seek the truth and weed out false teachings in the Church. His organization quickly became one of the most important anti-heretical instruments of the Church, and though Dominic himself did not realize it at the time, he inadvertently set the stage for what later became the Inquisition. After receiving recognition from the Papacy, Dominic established a church in Bologna as his order's headquarters. He died there in 1221.

An implacable foe of heresy, Dominic was known for his fairness and intelligence. The church that he founded in the 13th century is still standing in Bologna. Despite a few additions over the years and renovations in the 18th century, the Basilica of St. Dominic is still essentially intact in its medieval form. Although no longer the headquarters of the Dominicans, it is still that order's most sacred shrine, and historically the most important church building in the city.

Of Interest: The Basilica of St. Dominic is an unassuming place, just as the Dominicans would have known it the 1200s. The brown-brick, fairly simple Romanesque façade is accented by a bell tower added in 1313 and a small plaza in front with a column crowned with a statue of Dominic. The interior is a Renaissance masterpiece. Reworked in the 15th and 16th centuries by Italian artisans which included such luminaries as Michaelangelo, it is a feast of marble, gold leaf and frescoes. Nearly two dozen chapels line the place. The historic highlight of the place is the Chapel of St. Dominic, where the remains of the saint rest in a simple sarcophagus. Adjacent to the church is a small museum holding some of the Dominican's treasures, including the golden reliquary of King Louix IX of France.

105. ARIAN CHURCHES OF RAVENNA

Piazetta degli Ariani, 48121 Ravenna, Italy

Denomination: Formerly Roman Catholic
Dates: c. 5th & 6th centuries (completed)
Web: www.turismo.ra.it/eng/discover-the-area/art-and-culture/unesco-world-heritage (tourism website)

The Arian Churches of Ravenna are among the last surviving architectural remnants of the sect of Christianity that once dominated most of the Christian world. Ravenna, which briefly served as capital of the Roman Empire in the west, is home to over half a dozen essentially intact churches and other Arian Christian sites which date back to the 5th and 6th centuries. This amazing collection of churches includes chapels, baptisteries, churches, and a trio of basilicas. Eight of these buildings are included in the Early Christian Monuments of Ravenna UNESCO World Heritage Site.

The city of Ravenna in Northern Italy was thrust into the world spotlight in the 5th century, when from 402 to 476 it served as the final capital city of the dying western half of the Roman Empire. For another century afterward Ravenna continued to be the chief city of Italy, first as capital of the Kingdom of the Ostrogoths, and later as the administrative center of the Byzantine Empire in the west. It was during these periods that Ravenna acquired its amazing collection of Christian churches and monuments.

One the city's earliest major Christian patrons was Galla Placidia, daughter of the Roman Emperor Theodosius. Under her direction the Church of St. John the Evangelist was constructed. She may have also contributed to the construction of the Baptistry of Neon, as well as the Church of the Holy Cross. The surviving oratory of the latter is now her mausoleum. During the Ostrogoth era, Ravenna became home to competing factions of the Ostrogothic Arian and Latin Orthodox Christians. Each sect constructed their own churches and monuments during this period. The Arians built the Basilica of Sant'Apollinare

Nuovo, which is among the world oldest fully intact Christian-built churches.

In 540 the Eastern Roman Emperor Justinian I conquered Ravenna in his effort to restore the Western Roman Empire. Justinian, a devout Orthodox Christian, crushed the Arian Christian movement throughout Italy. To put his stamp on Ravenna he constructed a pair of hulking churches: the Basilica of San Vitale and the Basilica of Sant'Apollinare in Classe. Both of these basilicas survive intact to the present day. All of the surviving Arian structures were re-consecrated as Orthodox Catholic churches. Justinian's rule marked the last major phase of Ravenna's boom in church building.

Of Interest: Of the historic Arian Churches of Ravenna, the four major pre-Byzantine survivors are the Neonian Baptistry; the Arian Baptistry; the Archbishop's Chapel; and the Basilica of Sant'Apolinare Nuovo. All of these are in very good condition, and together boast some of the best surviving Roman era Christian mosaic works in the world. Justinian's contribution to Ravenna's religious architecture is distinctly eastern in character, especially the Basilica of San Vitale. Completed first, this hulking building appears more like a fortress than a church. This is due in large part to its unusual octagonal layout, with elements reminiscent of the Hagia Sofia in Istanbul. The Basilica of Sant'Apollinare looks similar to the Arian basilica, with decidedly Byzantine elements.

---

106. BASILICA OF ST. ANTHONY OF PADUA

Piazza del Santo, 11, 35123 Padua, Italy

Alternate/Full Name: Pontifical Basilica of St. Anthony of Padua
Denomination: Roman Catholic
Dates: c. 12th century (originally completed),
1310 (current building completed)
Web: www.santantonio.org/it/basilica (official website)

The Basilica of St. Anthony of Padua is one of the largest churches constructed in Italy during the Middle Ages. It was built around an earlier, smaller church containing the tomb of Anthony of Padua, among the greatest theologians and speakers of his age. An important disciple of Francis of Assisi, he distinguished himself by surpassing Francis in church honors and, despite all humility, in popularity. Padua's proximity to Venice made it a natural stopping point for pilgrims ever since its completion.

Anthony of Padua, not to be confused with Anthony the Great of Egypt, is one of Italy's most popular saints. However, for all of his popularity in Italy, he was born in Portugal. Anthony decided to pursue a life of the spirit at an early age. He entered the Abbey of St. Vincent where he served as guest master. After hosting some visiting Franciscans, Anthony decided to join the fledgling order.

Anthony's career with the Franciscans was relatively short. It started out auspiciously, when his ship barely survived a storm at sea by making emergency port in Sicily. After finally arriving in Italy, he was assigned to a small hospice in Forli, a town in the north, where he became known as a speaker. After this he was sent to preach throughout Lombardy, during which time he became close with Francis himself.

Anthony helped to spread the Franciscan order into France, and then later was sent to Rome as an envoy to the Papacy. He unfortunately died of natural causes at the age of 36. According to legend, the church bells of Padua rang by themselves upon Anthony's death. He had one of the fastest canonizations in history, becoming a saint less than a year after his death. By his own request he was buried in the Church of Santa Maria Mater Domini. The enormous basilica dedicated to Anthony was constructed over this site in the 13th century.

Of Interest: The Basilica of St. Anthony of Padua was constructed around the saint's original church in order to accommodate the many pilgrims that began showing up after his death. The cathedral features bits of every architectural style that was in vogue in the 13th century. The exterior is stunning, featuring a main building of western features and a multi-domed roof that would be more at home in the byzantine east. The original Church of Santa Maria Mater Domine was incorporated into the structure. The church interior is exquisitely decorated, with a collection of statues and reliefs executed by Renaissance master

Donatello. Anthony is entombed in the church's Treasury Chapel. His tongue is displayed in a reliquary, so that all pilgrims may pay homage to the saint's skills as an orator.

---

107. ST. MARK'S BASILICA

Piazza San Marco, 328, 30100 Venice, Italy

Alternate/Full Name: Patriarchal Cathedral Basilica of St. Mark
Denomination: Roman Catholic (sacred to many Christians)
Dates: c. 9th century (originally completed),
1092 (current building completed)
Web: www.basilicasanmarco.it (official website)

The Basilica of St. Mark is one of the most important saint shrines in the world. Buried within is St. Mark the Evangelist, one of the authors of the New Testament gospels. Unlike many other New Testament related tombs, the corpse here is probably the real deal. Thanks to the efforts of a few dedicated Christian merchantmen, the city of Venice came into possession of this relic in the 9th century. The spectacular Basilica that was built to showcase the tomb was one of the most richly decorated and costly church buildings constructed in Europe at the time. It remains one of Catholicism's most important sites, and is one of Venice's most popular tourist attractions. The Basilica of St. Mark is part of the Venice UNESCO World Heritage Site.

Mark the Evangelist was an early traveling companion of Paul and Barnabas. After years of working with Paul to spread the Gospel, Mark settled in Alexandria where he became the city's first bishop. At some later point in his life, Mark penned a book on the life of Jesus of Nazareth, a work which was ultimately included in the Bible as one of the primary four Gospels around which the New Testament was formed. Sometime around the year 68 Mark was martyred by a mob led by pagan priests. His body was recovered by his fellow Christians and interred in a church in Alexandria.

During the 7th century, Alexandria was overrun by the armies of

Islam. While the Christians of Egypt were tolerated, they lived under constant threat of harassment and persecution. By the end of the 9th century, a showdown between the Christian west and the Islamic east was looming. Fearing for the security of their beloved relic, the body of Mark, or at least most of it, was exhumed and smuggled out of Egypt by Venetian merchants. Reportedly, the body was hidden inside a crate of pork in order to keep Muslim customs officials from investigating too carefully. It was brought back to Venice after which the city's prestige as a religious center skyrocketed

A massive new basilica was constructed to house the relic. At its height Venice was the wealthiest city in the western world, and huge sums were lavished on the city's basilica. Pilgrims in the hundreds of thousands came to visit the shrine, many on their way to visit the Holy Land. Even after Venice's importance waned in the 16th century, the city remained one of Europe's most important pilgrimage destinations. Today the Basilica of St. Mark remains among the most important and most visited Christian sites in Italy.

Of Interest: The Basilica of St. Mark is a triumph of late Byzantine architecture. Originally constructed in the 9th century, much of the church dates from later restorations. The façade of the church is graced with five large arched entranceways and a high balcony that spans the entire length of the front. The four horses adorning the façade above the central arch are almost two thousand years old, and were brought back as loot from the sacking of Constantinople (actually, the originals are now on display inside the church; those above the gate are replicas). The whole is crowned with a trio of enormous domes. The Basilica's interior is richly decorated, with large portions of the sanctuary gilded from wall to wall. The main altar is partially screened. The tomb which contains St. Mark's relic lies beneath. There is a small museum and treasury inside the church which houses a collection of Christian artifacts.

108. BASILICA OF ST. PETER IN THE GOLDEN SKY

Piazza S. Pietro in Ciel d'Oro, 2, 27100 Pavia, Italy

Denomination: Roman Catholic
Dates: c. 7th century (originally completed), 1132 (current building completed)
Web: www.gcatholic.org/churches/italy/4918 (Catholic website)

The Basilica of St. Peter in the Golden Sky is one of the great Romanesque churches of Northern Italy. It houses the tomb of St. Augustine of Hippo, one of early Christianity's greatest theologians. It has been a popular pilgrimage destination since the 8th century as it is located along one of the major roads to Rome. In addition to Augustine and other relics enshrined here, the basilica's great draw is its fabled gold-leaf dome, one of the most breathtaking pieces of decorative architecture of the Middle Ages.

Augustine of Hippo, one of the four original Doctors of the Church, was among the most influential Christian figures of the late Roman era. Born to a Christian mother and a Pagan father, Augustine's early life is one of history's great studies in religious experimentation. He ultimately embraced Christianity, and some of his ideas, including his thoughts on original sin and the relationship of grace to true freedom, went on to become cornerstones of Christian theology.

Augustine was active at a time when the Roman Empire in the west was crumbling before the onslaught of German invaders. Many of his works, including *City of God*, appear to have been written to address the great changes that were taking place at the time. His later years were spent in Hippo in modern-day Algeria where he served as the city's bishop. Not long after his death, Vandal invaders destroyed Hippo, leaving only the church that Augustine founded standing.

Augustine was interred in his church in Algeria in 430, but the remains were soon moved to Sardinia for safety. They were moved again in 720, when he was reinterred in the Church of Peter in Pavia.

A new church was built over the site in the 12th century. In later years, the corpse was moved several more times, but was returned to Pavia in 1896 after the church underwent a complete renovation. It is one of that city's most popular tourist destinations.

Of Interest: The Basilica of St. Peter in the Sky of Gold is probably one of the most overlooked major churches in Italy. Despite its proximity to Milan, it is somewhat off the beaten tourist path. The current church was completed in 1132 and is among the better examples of Romanesque architecture in Northern Italy. The tomb of Augustine is impressive, and features a stunning reliquary adorned with carved figures and engravings featuring scenes from the Bible and from the saint's life. Also located in the church is the tomb of Boethius, a Christian martyr of the early 6th century. Directly above Augustine's tomb is the fabled 'sky of gold', a half-dome decorated in gold-leaf and mosaics which depict St. Peter before the throne of Christ in Heaven, one of the finest pieces of pre-Renaissance Christian art anywhere.

---

109. CHURCH OF SANTA MARIA DELLE GRAZIE

Piazza di Santa Maria delle Grazie, 20123 Milan, Italy

Denomination: Roman Catholic
Dates: 1497 (completed)
Web: https://legraziemilano.it (official website)

The Church of Santa Maria Delle Grazie is a remnant of a former 15th century Dominican Convent. This church might long ago have been condemned to the dustbin of history if it wasn't for the presence of a painting on the wall of the old convent refectory: Leonardo DaVinci's *The Last Supper*, arguably the most famous work of Christian art in the world. Because of this painting, which miraculously survived bombing during World War II, the Church of Santa Maria Delle Grazie was saved and reconstructed, to the everlasting joy of Christians and art-lovers everywhere. Hundreds of thousands of pilgrims travel to

Milan every year to gape at Leonardo DaVinci's greatest masterpiece. The Church of Santa Maria Delle Grazie is a UNESCO World Heritage Site

To say that Leonardo DaVinci was the defining personality of the Renaissance is an understatement. From art to architecture, engineering to botany, he was a master of all disciplines. Born 1452 in Tuscany not too far from Florence, DaVinci apprenticed in the workshop of Verrocchio where he assisted in painting *Baptism of Christ*. This was just one of the many religious works he would undertake in his lifetime. Other major paintings based on the Bible that he executed include *The Adoration of the Magi* and *The Virgin of the Rocks*.

DaVinci's most famous religious painting is *The Last Supper*. Commissioned by a Dominican convent in Milan, DaVinci painted the enormous mural on the wall of the church refectory. A masterpiece of detail and balance, this enormous painting soon became the wonder of the convent. Visitors sought out the abbey to gaze at what would later be hailed as DaVinci's crowning achievement.

Unfortunately, he did not adequately prepare the painting for a long lifespan. In less than a century it had become so flaked and faded that it was almost unrecognizable. A doorway was callously cut right through the middle of the mural in 1652, though this was later removed. A number of repairs and restorations were undertaken over the years, but these generally made the situation worse. An Allied bombing raid in World War II nearly finished it off. It was not until the late 20th century that experts using the most advanced techniques were finally able to restore the painting to the point where it can now be enjoyed in its nearly original form.

Of Interest: The Church of Santa Maria Delle Grazie is a brown- and beige-brick building consisting of the main church structure as well as elements of the original convent. Most of the church dates from the 1460s, but considerable repairs were necessary after World War II. The interior of the sanctuary is a neo-gothic architectural gem with high vaulted ceilings and exquisite scrollwork throughout. DaVinci's painting *The Last Supper* is located in the refectory on the only wall that was miraculously not destroyed during the war. Its survival was due in large part to the sandbags which had been carefully heaped around it in order to protect it from damage. The painting is very large and dominates the rear wall of the refectory. The painting as it appears now dates largely from the restoration completed in 1999.

---

110. BASILICA OF ST. AMBROSE

Piazza Sant'Ambrogio, 15, 20123 Milan, Italy

Denomination: Roman Catholic
Dates: 386 (originally completed), 1099 (current building completed)
Web: www.basilicasantambrogio.it (official website)

The Basilica of St. Ambrose in Milan is one of the oldest churches in Italy outside of Rome. Originally constructed by Ambrose as the Basilica of Martyrs in the 4th century, it served as a bastion of Catholic-Orthodox Christianity during the turbulent era following the Council of Nicaea. As the site of Ambrose's tomb, it later became an important stopping point for Christian pilgrims traveling in northern Italy. During the Middle Ages, the basilica was also home to several monastic orders. The Basilica of St. Ambrose is regarded as one of the city's most historically important churches.

Ambrose was one of the critical figures of the Catholic Church in the 4th century. Born Aurelius Ambrosius, his father was an important Roman official, and Ambrose originally followed in his footsteps. In his thirties he served as governor of Milan. However, in 374, while mediating between the city's Catholic and Arian factions, Ambrose was entreated to serve as the city's new bishop. Almost overnight he was baptized and ordained, becoming an ardent anti-Arian. Ambrose was later instrumental in crushing the Arian heresy in Northern Italy.

Ambrose was a contemporary of Augustine and his mother Monica, and was involved in Augustine's conversion. During his life he constructed many of Milan's earliest churches, several of which survive. Upon his death in 397, he was entombed in the Basilica of St. Ambrose which he had built. Because the remains were never moved, the relic of Ambrose is one of the best preserved and most easily viewed of virtually any Christian corpse of the Roman period. The

Holy Roman Emperor Louis II, the great-grandson of Charlemagne, was also interred in the church in the 9th century.

Of Interest: The Basilica of St. Ambrose centers around the original 4th century structure with its 12th century Romanesque upgrades. Much of the original floor plan has been preserved. The two adjoining monasteries constructed during the Middle Ages, each boasting its own bell tower, gives the church a slightly off-balance look. Most of the interior elements of the church are stunning, with some portions very ancient. The highlight of the church is the crypt where the bodies of Ambrose and Louis II lie side-by-side.

---

111. TURIN CATHEDRAL

Piazza San Giovanni, 10122 Turin, Italy

Alternate/Full Name: Cathedral of St. John the Baptist
Denomination: Roman Catholic
Dates: c. 600 (originally completed),
1505 (current building completed)
Web: www.duomoditorino.it (official website)

Turin Cathedral is home to one of the most famous and controversial Christian artifacts in the world: the fabled Shroud of Turin. Claimed to be the linen in which Christ's body was wrapped at the time of his burial, it bears the image of a man who suffered death by crucifixion, but as a photo-negative. This artistic feat, thought to be impossible to create by artistic means, at least in pre-modern times, is believed by many to have been divinely wrought. Its home at the Cathedral of St. John the Baptist makes Turin a very popular destination for Christian pilgrims.

The first mention of the Shroud of Turin dates back to 6th century Edessa, where early Christians apparently brought it after fleeing from Jerusalem. This Image of Edessa was mentioned in early writings, including a description of the strange bodily imprint. There is no further mention of the cloth again until it appeared in Constantinople in 944, where it was sent for safekeeping following the Muslim conquest of the Holy Land. The cloth was described in a sermon of the period.

In 1205 the shroud was seized by knights of the Fourth Crusade and brought back to Western Europe. In 1357 it was publicly displayed in Troyes. At first its legitimacy was denounced by both the Church and the local bishop. However the people of Troyes embraced the artifact, and it was soon being presented in other cities of the region to enthusiastic crowds. The Church was forced to change their official position on the Shroud, and soon various factions were fighting for control of the artifact and the right to permanently house it.

Ownership finally came to the House of Savoy, who brought it to Turin in the 15th century. In 1532 the Shroud was damaged during a fire, including being permanently marked by molten silver which burned through it. A poor attempt to repair the Shroud left it further scarred with patches. Since the cathedral's restoration, the artifact has been kept locked away and is now only displayed infrequently. It has been the property of the Papacy since the 1980s, but remains in its home at Turin Cathedral.

Of Interest: Turin Cathedral is mostly only a few centuries old. Much of the original building was damaged by fire in the 16th century. Visually the exterior is a bit odd, with the main church in white stone flanked by an earlier bell tower in deep brown brick. A large expanded wing behind the main altar known as the Chapel of the Shroud houses the Shroud of Turin. The controversial and rarely seen Shroud is one of the most famous artifacts of the Church. The depicted image appears to be a photo-negative. The facial features reflect a traditional image of Jesus of Nazareth, with long flowing hair and prominent beard and mustache. Dark stains appear in the locations where Christ was wounded, including punctures from the Crown of Thorns, his spear wound and the nail-holes where he was crucified. Eight poorly attached patches mark where the Shroud was damaged during the fire.

112. MONTE CASSINO ABBEY

Via Montecassino, 03043 Monte Cassino, Italy

Denomination: Roman Catholic
Dates: c. 6th century (founded)
Web: www.abbaziamontecassino.org (official website)

The Monte Cassino Abbey is regarded by some as the birthplace of international monasticism in Western Europe. It was here in the 6th century that Benedict of Nursia founded the Benedictine Order, created the Benedictine Rule and established the first major monastery in Italy. Since its founding, the Monte Cassino has grown into an immense complex, a masterpiece of architecture in a stunning mountain setting. After fifteen centuries it remains one of the chief centers of the Benedictines and is especially revered by members of that Order, both because of its antiquity as well as due to the fact that Benedict of Nursia is entombed at the site.

The idea of Christian monasticism first appeared in the Eastern Roman Empire in the 3rd century, when men like Anthony set off to live lives of solitude deep in the Egyptian wilderness. But it was another three centuries before Benedict of Nurcia institutionalized the idea and created Christianity's first major international Christian monastic order.

Benedict was born into what was left of the Roman aristocracy at the end of the 5th century. During his teenage years he embraced religious studies with an eye towards a career with the Church. At some point in his twenties he moved to the countryside outside of Rome and began living as a recluse. A few years later he was invited to take over a small abbey that had been under the leadership of his acquaintance Romanus. He held the position for a short period before disagreements with other monks forced him to leave.

Benedict decided to start his own monastic order. By that time he had become somewhat famous and had attracted his own following. Under his leadership thirteen monasteries were built in the area, twelve small ones and a thirteenth for himself and a few followers at Monte Cassino. He also established the Benedictine Rule, a code to guide the growing order so as to give it purpose and to protect it against the petty bickerings he had seen at Romanus' abbey. By the time of his death in the mid-6th century, Benedictine monasteries were springing up all over Europe.

The Monte Cassino Abbey has always been an important center of the Benedictine Order. Unfortunately, Benedict picked a very popular and strategic spot for it, and the abbey has witnessed many conquests and battles throughout its history. It was sacked by the Lombards not too long after Benedict's death, rebuilt in the 8th century, badly damaged by an earthquake in the 14th century, rebuilt again, then sacked once more by Napolean and the French n 1799. The abbey was almost completely destroyed during a five-month siege during World War II, but rebuilt in the decades thereafter. It is now once again an active Benedictine Monastery.

Of Interest: The Monte Cassino Abbey is visually spectacular. Perched high on the slope of the hill known as Monte Cassino, the immense fortress-like complex is surrounded by a dense tree line which shrouds its lower walls. Most of the massive complex dates from its reconstruction in the years after World War II. It houses a vast labyrinth of chapels, libraries, residential areas and an expansive domed basilica. A quartet of cloisters provides easy access from one part of the abbey to another. The abbey's basilica, constructed in 17th century, is a masterpiece of Baroque architecture. The relics of Benedict and his sister Scholastica are interred beneath the main altar. The abbey is also home to an extensive museum which contains more than a dozen galleries filled with artifacts and artwork, including pieces from the abbey treasury.

113. BASILICA OF ST. THOMAS THE APOSTLE

Piazza S. Tommaso, 66026 Ortona, Italy

Alternate/Full Name: Ortona Cathedral
Denomination: Roman Catholic
Dates: 1127 (completed)
Web: www.tommasoapostolo.it (official website)

The Basilica of St. Thomas the Apostle in Ortona is home to what may be part of the relic of the Biblical Thomas. The body of Thomas, who is believed to have died in India sometime in the late 1st century, was eventually returned to the West, though the exact details of this journey are conflicting and unclear. The church itself dates back to the Middle Ages, while the remains of Thomas arrived at a much later date.

According to tradition, St. Thomas spent years traveling throughout the East before ultimately settling in what is now the Chennai area of India. There he was martyred and buried for at least a few centuries. There the story gets confused. At some point in the pre-Islamic area, probably sometime around the 4th century, tradition suggests that the body was returned to Roman territory. Possible destinations included the city of Edessa in Turkey or the Isle of Chios near Greece or both.

In the 13th century at least part of the body made it to Italy. Sometime around the 1350s the relics in Italy, along with what is believed to be the original stone marker, were permanently placed in the Church of St. Thomas in Ortona. Throughout the centuries since, the relics survived numerous sackings of the church. While it is definitely among the lesser known and lesser visited of the Apostolic burial sites, there is nevertheless an ancient pilgrimage route leading to the city known as the Way of St. Thomas that has brought visitors here for many centuries.

Of Interest: The Basilica of St. Thomas is an architecturally unusual church, consisting mostly a brick building only a few centuries old, but with part of it built right over an older stone building. The main façade facing the plaza is actually located on the long side of the building. A copper dome rises from a white, classical base visually at odds with the rest of the building. The interior is much more harmonious and elegant, and simpler. The heavy baroque décor that is often found in other churches of this stature is missing here. The main ornamentation is the tomb of the Apostle Thomas. What is left of the relic of Thomas the Apostle is now kept in a gold and copper reliquary. Part of the skull is kept in a silver bust of the saint.

---

114. BASILICA OF ST. NICHOLAS

Largo Abate Elia, 13, 70122 Bari, Italy

Denomination: Roman Catholic
Dates: 1197 (completed)
Web: www.basilicasannicola.it (official website)

The Basilica of St. Nicholas in Bari is possibly the most popular Christian shrine in Southern Italy. However, other than the fact that St. Nicholas' body was moved here in the 11th century, Bari has virtually nothing to do with the great theologian. However, because Bari is much more accessible to Christians than the Nicholas sites in Turkey, the lion's share of pilgrims traveling to honor the saint come here.

After the Battle of Manzikert in 1071 the victorious Seljuk Turks occupied most of Asia Minor. However, even as the Turks arrived in Myra and started ransacking the city, enterprising sailors from Bari rushed to the cathedral, bullied and drove out the monks, and made off with the body of Nicholas. The act was later semi-officially sanctioned by the Roman Catholic Church, both because it probably saved the relic from destruction, but also because it annoyed the Patriarch of Constantinople.

The city of Bari, meanwhile, had spent more than two centuries under Byzantine occupation, and had just been liberated by the Normans in the same year. In celebration, the people and leaders of Bari received the relic gladly, and an immense cathedral was built to house the corpse. Bari reached its peak during the Crusades, when thousands of Christians passed through Italy's ports on the way to the Holy Land. One of these was Peter the Hermit, who visited the city and preached the First Crusade by the Tomb of St. Nicholas in 1095.

For many Crusaders, Bari was the last European City that they would ever see. As the wars in the Holy Land drew to a close, so too did Bari's importance as a port and its popularity among pilgrims. By the time of the Reformation and the Age of Exploration, Italy was politically shattered. Bari, at the end of the Italian Peninsula, became little more than a backwater. Religious visitors to the basilica slowed to a trickle. This state of affairs continued until the second half of the 19th century, when Bari recovered as a shipping center. The city once again receives many Nicholas-seeking pilgrims.

Of Interest: The Basilica of St. Nicholas is a mix of Byzantine and Gothic designs, due to the availability of both Byzantine and Norman architects in the city at the time of its construction. The white brick cathedral is imposing but austere in appearance from the outside. There are a few relief pictures of Nicholas carved onto the outer walls. A statue of Nicholas, donated by the Russian Orthodox Church in 2003, stands facing the cathedral from across the square. The cathedral interior has a narrow nave and unusual central arches supporting the soaring ceiling. The ceiling was redone in the 17th century in a lavish Renaissance style. Beneath the main church is a smaller chapel and the crypt where the body of Nicholas is kept.

---

115. CATHEDRAL OF SYRACUSE

Piazza Duomo, 96100 Syracuse, Sicily, Italy

Alternate/Full Name: Metropolitan Cathedral of the Nativity of St. Mary
Denomination: Roman Catholic
Dates: c. 7th century (originally completed),
1753 (current building completed)
Web: No official website

The Cathedral of Syracuse is a very old church which stands on a truly ancient sacred site. One of the most famous churches on the island of Sicily, it is closely associated with Lucy, an early Christian martyr and the patron saint of the city. The cathedral is a major landmark of Syracuse and a UNESCO World Heritage Site.

Archaeological investigations indicate that the current site of the cathedral was home to an early pagan temple even before the Greeks arrived in the 8th century BC. A massive temple to Athena was constructed here in the 4th century BC. This building stood throughout the Roman imperial period. In 304 a Christian woman named Lucy was martyred near here during the persecutions instituted by the emperor Diocletian. She was soon venerated as a saint and became a folk hero of the city after Christianity was legalized a few years later.

When Syracuse constructed its cathedral in the 7th century, part of the relic of Lucy was interred inside. The Cathedral of Syracuse has since had a colorful history. From 878 to 1085 it was used as a mosque during the Muslim occupation of the city. It was damaged in an earthquake in the 17th century, and much of the current building dates from a massive restoration afterwards. The Cathedral of Syracuse was designated a World Heritage Site in 2005.

Of Interest: The Cathedral of Syracuse is a hulking baroque edifice that largely dates from the 18th century, though substantial elements of the Medieval cathedral are incorporated into the current building. There are even some surviving columns and other bits from the original Greek temple. The cathedral houses both bodily relics and clothing that belonged to St. Lucy. Several of her ribs are preserved inside a silver statue created by Pietro Rizzo.

---

116. SALERNO CATHEDRAL

Piazza Alfano I, 84125 Salerno, Sicily, Italy

Alternate/Full Name: Cathedral Church of St. Matthew the Apostle

Denomination: Roman Catholic
Dates: 1085 (completed)
Web: www.cattedraledisalerno.it (official website)

Salerno Cathedral is one of the lesser known of Italy's major cathedrals. Nevertheless it has been one of Southern Italy's more popular pilgrimage destinations since the Middle Ages thanks to its great treasure: the relic of St. Matthew, one of the Twelve Apostles of Jesus, who is believed to be buried within. How Matthew's relic got here is very vague, but the tradition is very strong, both for citizens and devout pilgrims.

Matthew was one of the more mysterious of Jesus' main followers. Despite the fact that he authored one of the four primary Gospels of the New Testament, little is known of his life. A tax collector by trade, he was probably among the more educated of the Apostles. There is little tradition, even in the various Apocryphal writings, of where Matthew travelled, and where or how he died. Nevertheless somehow his body made it to Salerno during the Middle Ages.

In the 11th century Robert Guiscard led an army of Norman crusaders to invade Italy. After his conquest of Southern Italy, he established a kingdom and ordered new churches built to help secure his position. One of these was Salerno Cathedral. After its completion the relic of Matthew was placed inside, and it immediately became one of Sicily's most important pilgrimage churches. The building remained largely intact for centuries, until it was badly damaged by fighting in 1943. Salerno Cathedral was repaired in the post-war era and continues to be a popular place of Catholic pilgrimage.

Of Interest: Salerno Cathedral appears as a simple but elegant Romanesque Church with Moorish elements. This is especially apparent in the colonnaded courtyard in front of the church. The interior houses a wealth of stunning architectural details and artwork. This includes colonnades and geometric tile work reminiscent of the Mezquita of Cordoba, as well as baroque-era detailing and flourishes. A museum inside the church is home to historic works of religious art. The magnificent, gilded tomb of St. Matthew is located inside the crypt. Also buried here is Pope Gregory VII.

117. ST. PAUL'S CATHEDRAL & ST. JOHN'S CO-CATHEDRAL

2 Triq San Pawl, Mdina, Malta (St. Paul's Cathedral)
Triq San Gwann, Valletta, Malta (St. John's Co-Cathedral)

Alternate/Full Names: Metropolitan Cathedral of St. Paul, Mdina Cathedral & Conventual Church of St. John
Denomination: Roman Catholic
Dates: St. Paul's - 1705 (completed) & St. John's - 1577 (completed)
Web: www.malta.com/en/attraction/culture/church/st-paul-s-cathedral (tourism website) & www.stjohnscocathedral.com (official website)

St. Paul's Cathedral in Mdina and St. John's Co-Cathedral in Valletta are the joint Archdiocesan cathedrals of the island of Malta. According to tradition, St. Paul's has a history that connects it to the 1st century bishop Publius, while St. John's is closely associates with the knightly Order of St. John, also known as the Hospitallers. Together they represent two of Malta's quintessential Christian pilgrimage sites.

Local tradition has it that the Cathedral of St. Paul stands on what was once the site of the Roman governor's palace of Malta. Publius, who was governor at the time of Paul's stay on the island, became a Christian convert and later a bishop, and may have donated his house for church use. While this has not been verified, the site has been occupied by earlier churches as far back as the Roman era. The current building was completed in the early 18th century.

St. John's Co-Cathedral was constructed by the Hospitallers in the late 16th century as a home church for the Order. It served as the convent church of the Hospitallers from its completion in 1577 until French troops occupied Malta in 1798. Both churches are now listed on the National Inventory of the Cultural Property of the Maltese Islands.

Of Interest: St. Paul's Cathedral is a hulking Baroque structure that towers over the city wall of Mdina and the rest of the city skyline. The façade that faces the square is large and somewhat simple by baroque standards, but conceals a breathtaking interior covered in gold leaf and frescoes. A museum attached to the cathedral contains artifacts from the time it was built. The Co-Cathedral of St. John is a similarly large building, but its relatively small entrance and mish mash of styles on the exterior somewhat conceals this fact. The interior is even more magnificent, at least according to many art aficionados, than St. Paul's, with a sanctuary awash in gold leaf and artwork. Among the many frescoes and works of art here are several by the late Renaissance master Caravaggio, including his *The Beheading of John the Baptist.*

---

118. CHURCH OF ST. PAUL'S SHIPWRECK

St. Lucia's Street, II-Belt, Valletta, Malta

Alternate/Full Name: Collegiate Parish Church of St. Paul's Shipwreck
Denomination: Roman Catholic (sacred to many Christians)
Dates: 1582 (completed)
Web: www.visitmalta.com/en/st-paul-in-malta (tourism website)

The Church of St. Paul's Shipwreck commemorates one of the last events mentioned in the Bible: Paul's shipwreck on the island of Malta. Paul visited the island sometime in the mid-1st century and was instrumental in getting the local Christian community established. Much of the island's Christian history is tied directly to Paul's legacy, and there are a number of places here are associated with events in his life. The Church of St. Paul's Shipwreck is part of the Valleta Old City UNESCO World Heritage Site.

Virtually the entire second half of the Book of Acts is devoted to Paul's legendary missionary journeys. The last chapters recount Paul's final journey to Rome, where he went on to be martyred. Much of this section deals with his accidental visit to Malta sometime around the year 60 AD. While en route to the imperial capital, a terrible storm struck, and Paul's ship was wrecked on the island of Malta.

There he spent three months helping to establish a brand new church. During this period he healed the father of the governor, Publius, who subsequently converted. Paul eventually departed for Rome, leaving behind what would become one of the oldest, continually active Christian dioceses in the world. Publius, who headed the church in Malta after Paul left, went on to a long career, eventually serving as bishop of Athens before being martyred around the year 125.

Paul's unintended visit to Malta was long remembered and celebrated by the local Christian population; but it took another fifteen centuries for the church named in his honor to be built. In the 16th century, relics of Paul were donated from Rome, making the church the most important pilgrimage shrine, if not the most famous church, on the island.

Of Interest: The Church of St. Paul's Shipwreck is small compared to the island's other major churches. Built during the early colonial period, it reflects the styles typical of the era. A large iconic painting of Christ dominates the wall above the main door to the church. The interior is richly appointed with a baroque-era chapel. The shrine contains two pilgrimage-worthy Christian artifacts. The first is the Column of St. Paul, which according to tradition is the column upon which Paul was beheaded. It was brought here from Rome for display in the island where Paul preached so successfully. Also here is the Wristbone of Paul. The rest of him has recently been discovered in a long-lost vault in Rome.

EASTERN EUROPE

119. ST. BASIL'S CATHEDRAL

Red Square, Moscow, Russia, 109012

Alternate/Full Names: Cathedral of Vasily the Blessed, Cathedral of the Intercession of the Most Holy Theotokos on the Moat
Denomination: Russian Orthodox
Dates: 1561 (completed)
Web: https://en.shm.ru/museum/hvb (official website)

The Cathedral of St. Basil the Blessed is one of the great churches of Eastern Orthodoxy and the defining architectural symbol of Russia. It has been hailed as one of the most beautiful churches in the world and is certainly among the most recognizable. It is often thought to be part of the Kremlin, Moscow's great fortress, though it actually stands outside of the Kremlin's walls. Site of the tomb of St. Basil, for which it is named, the cathedral has a history as colorful as its iconic onion domes. St. Basil's Cathedral is part of the Red Square UNESCO World Heritage Site.

St. Basil's Cathedral can trace its origins to two historical events: the death of the Russian holy man known as Basil the Blessed, and the Russian conquest of the Khanate of the Kazars. Beginning in the early 13th century, Moscow had spent the better part of three hundred years under the constant threat of the Tatars. Though Moscow became free in 1480, it was another century before Ivan the Terrible decisively defeated the Kazan Tatars and assumed the title of Tsar of all Russia. The conquest of Kazan in 1552 coincided with the death of Basil the Blessed, a popular Russian holy man.

Basil had become famous for his displays of piety and his charity towards the poor. According to legend he publicly reprimanded Ivan the Terrible over his Christian devotions, an act which apparently earned him the Tsar's respect. In honor of Basil, Ivan commissioned the construction of a new cathedral. The work on the cathedral was completed in a mere six years. According to a very famous but most likely false legend, Ivan was so taken with the beauty of the cathedral that he deliberately blinded the architect so that he would never again create anything so magnificent.

The subsequent history of St. Basil's Cathedral is one of amazing survival. Barely a decade after its completion, the city of Moscow was destroyed by the last major Tatar invasion of the city. Only the area around the Kremlin was spared. The cathedral survived more than half a dozen other invasions and uprisings through the 19th century, including the burning of Moscow before the arrival of Napolean Bonaparte. It even survived the Russian Revolution and Stalin. Today St. Basil's Cathedral is once again the pride of the Russian Orthodox Church and one of the most popular tourist destinations in Russia.

Of Interest: St. Basil's Cathedral is a tented church along the lines of those that were popular in Russia in the 16th and 17th centuries. The exterior is unique even by eastern architectural standards. It appears more like a fairy tale palace than a house of worship. Its pink and white walls are crowned with breathtaking onion domes, each as individually and colorfully decorated as a Faberge Easter egg. The great central spire is crowned by a smaller golden dome and topped with a cross. The interior of the cathedral consists of nine interconnected chapels, each one designed to commemorate one of Ivan the Terrible's victorious battles. Each of these chapels is dedicated to the saint on whose day a particular battle was won. The interior walls and domes display hundreds of paintings and pieces of iconic art. The highlight of the cathedral is the Tomb of St. Basil the Blessed, whose chapel was added to the cathedral a few decades after its completion.

---

120. NOVODEVICHY CONVENT

Novodevichy Passage 1, Moscow, Russia, 119435

Alternate/Full Name: Bogoroditse-Smolensky Monastery
Denomination: Russian Orthodox
Dates: 1524 (founded)
Web: www.novodev.msk.ru (official website)

The Novodevichy Convent is one of the most famous nunneries in Eastern Europe. Founded in the 16th century, many female members of the Russian aristocracy, including some members of the royal family, have served in its ranks. Within its large complex of buildings is the Cathedral of Our Lady of Smolensk, one of the city's most historic churches. The Monastery of Novodevichy is a UNESCO World Heritage Site.

The convent was founded just prior to and during the early years of the reign of the Tsars. Some of the most important rulers of the period, including Vasily III, Ivan the Terrible and Boris Godunov were among its early and prominent patrons. This was due in part to the large number women of the nobility who chose or were forced to become nuns here.

By the time of Peter the Great, the Monastery of Novodevichy was one of the wealthiest and influential religious institutions in Russia. It survived the Napoleanic Wars, the Russian Revolution and World War II, and in 1945 was among the very first Christian possessions to be returned to the control of the Russian Orthodox Church. Since 1994 it has again been in use as a convent. The Monastery of Novodevichy was declared a UNESCO World Heritage Site in 2004.

Of Interest: The Monastery of Novodevichy is a large walled complex of buildings tucked away in the suburbs of the old city center of Moscow. Almost all of the convent's buildings are in nearly original condition despite centuries of turmoil. Part of the complex is run as a branch of the State Historical Museum. The monastery's cemetery, which is just outside the wall, is home to the graves of such Russian luminaries as Anton Checkhov, Sergei Prokofiev and Boris Yeltsin.

121. CATHEDRAL OF THE ANNUNCIATION & CATHEDRAL OF THE DORMITION

Cathedral Square, Moscow, Russia, 103073

Alternate/Full Name: Cathedral of the Assumption (Dormition alternate)
Denomination: Russian Orthodox
Completed: Annunciation - c. 13th century (originally completed); 1489 (current building completed) & Dormition - 1326 (originally completed); 1479 (current building completed)
Web: www.kreml.ru/en-us (official website)

The Cathedral of the Annunciation and the Cathedral of the Dormition are two of the three historic cathedrals that dominate the Kremlin at the heart of Moscow, the third being the Cathedral of the Archangel Michael. The Cathedral of the Annunciation once served as the private chapel of the Tsars when the royal family still resided in Moscow. The Cathedral of the Dormition was the site of royal coronations for the Romanov dynasty for over three hundred years.

Moscow became one of the dominant cities of the Russia in the 14th and 15th centuries, and by the 1460s had become the seat of Russia's most important Grand Duchy. Over the next few decades a massive fortress, the Kremlin, was built to protect the city and house the royal family. This massive complex included three of the largest churches that had yet been built in Eastern Europe.

The Dormition Cathedral, or Cathedral of the Assumption, was completed first in 1479, and is considered to be the mother church of the city. The Cathedral of the Annunciation was completed a decade later. Most royal religious events and state ceremonies were held in these two churches throughout the Tsarist period and some of the imperial period. Both churches suffered during various conflicts, including the Napoleanic Wars and the Russian Revolution.

Both cathedrals were closed throughout the Communist era and repurposed as museums. However, there is an unconfirmed story that during the Nazi onslaught of 1941, a government sanctioned religious service was authorized and held in the Dormition Cathedral to pray for the salvation of the Russian people. Both cathedrals were returned to the control of the Russian Orthodox Church in the 1990s.

Of Interest: Both the Cathedral of the Annunciation and the Cathedral of the Dormition represent some of the earliest examples of traditional Russian Orthodox design. Both churches are large, imposing structures sporting gold leaf trimmed roofs and onion domes. Perhaps because it was finished later, the Cathedral of the Annunciation improved significantly in grandeur over the Cathedral of the Assumption. Iconic paintings and artwork grace both cathedrals in significant quantities, with the most famous work being the *Host of the King of Heaven* in the Cathedral of the Assumption. Also worth noting here is the neighboring Cathedral of the Archangel Michael, the third of the Kremlin's churches, which houses the tombs of most of the Russian Tsars.

---

122. SMOLNY CATHEDRAL

Ploshchad Rastrelli, 1, St. Petersburg, Russia, 191124

Denomination: Russian Orthodox
Dates: 1835 (completed)
Web: www.saint-petersburg.com/cathedrals/smolny-cathedral (tourism website)

Smolny Cathedral is the centerpiece of the Smolny Convent of the Resurrection, a sprawling monastic compound in the heart of Saint Petersburg. Originally intended for an order that included a daughter of Peter the Great, lavish sums were spent on the complex, one of the most spectacular in Russia. At the time of this writing the cathedral and monastery were being prepared for religious use again for the first time in a century.

In 1725, Peter the Great, the first Emperor of Russia, died, and his succession was tumultuous. His daughter Elizabeth, who was not considered a viable candidate for the throne, instead decided to become a nun. Construction began on a massive new convent in St. Petersburg worthy of royalty. However, a coup opened her way to the throne, and Elizabeth became Empress in 1741. Nevertheless she continued to act as a patroness to the convent.

Designed by famed architect Francesco Rastrelli, who oversaw many of St. Petersburg's building projects in the 18th century, the cathedral was not quite complete at the time of Elizabeth's death. Work was finally done in 1835. The complex was closed following the Russian Revolution, and remained largely abandoned for decades. It was finally returned to the Russian Orthodox Church in 2015, and is currently being renovated for use.

Of Interest: Smolny Cathedral is one of St. Petersburg's defining religious landmarks. Standing at the center of the convent, the cathedral and complex consist of a mix of Baroque and Eastern styles. Almost completely unique to the convent is its highly unusual color scheme, which features sky-blue walls and details with white trim crowned in golden crosses. This style on such a large scale is highly unusual in Christian architecture.

---

123. ST. ALEXANDER NEVSKY MONASTERY

Naberezhnaya reki Monastyrki, 1, St. Petersburg, Russia, 191167

Denomination: Russian Orthodox
Dates: 1713 (originally completed),
1790 (current building completed)
Web: www.lavra.spb.ru (official website)

The St. Alexander Nevsky Monastery is a sprawling monastic compound built by Peter the Great as part of his new capital at St. Petersburg. The monastery, named in honor of Russia's popular national hero Alexander Nevsky, was built on what was once thought to be the site of the Battle of the Neva. The hero's relic has been kept at the monastery since the early 18th century.

Alexander Nevsky was a great prince of the Rus who lived in the 13th century. He famously led the Russian people to several major military victories against invaders from Europe, most notably against the Swedes at the Battle of Neva in 1240 and the Teutonic Knights at the Battle of the Ice in 1242. He died a hero of Russia and became a saint of the Eastern Orthodox Church in the 16th century. When Peter the Great became the first Emperor of Russia, he decided to honor Nevsky's legacy in his new capital at St. Petersburg.

The Tsar ordered the construction of the Alexander Nevsky Monastery, one of the largest monasteries ever built. In 1724 the remains of Alexander Nevsky were relocated here from the city of Vladimir. The monastery was constructed on what was once thought to be the site of the Battle of Neva, though this has since been determined to be elsewhere. The monastery was the site of brief fighting during the Russian Revolution. Today it is once again in active use by the Russian Orthodox Church.

Of Interest: The Monastery of Alexander is an absolutely huge Baroque complex located close to the Neva River. The centerpiece is the magnificent yellow and white Alexander Nevsky Cathedral, which stands out spectacularly against the surrounding greenery. The main point of interest, the burial site of Alexander Nevsky, can still be found here. However, his immense and spectacular silver sarcophagus was removed to the State Hermitage Museum years ago.

---

124. ST. ISAAC'S CATHEDRAL & CHURCH OF THE SAVIOR ON SPILLED BLOOD

St. Isaac's Square, 4, St. Petersburg, Russia, 190000 (St. Isaac's Cathedral)

Griboyedov Channel Embankment, 26, St. Petersburg, Russia, 191186 (Church of the Savior on Spilled Blood)

Denomination: Russian Orthodox
Dates: Cathedral - 1858 (completed) & Church - 1907 (completed)
Web: www.saint-petersburg.com/cathedrals (tourism website)

St. Isaac's Cathedral is the great Russian Orthodox cathedral of the city of St. Petersburg. The Church of The Savior on Spilled Blood, completed just a few years later, was built in memory of the Emperor Alexander II, who was assassinated on the site of the church. Together these two massive, stunning churches were among the last major religious building projects undertaken by the Romanov dynasty.

St. Isaac's Cathedral is the largest church in the city and one of the largest Eastern Orthodox cathedrals in the world. Constructed at the height of the rule of the Romanovs, it was designed to cement St. Petersburg's importance among the great European capitals. Throughout the Communist era the church was used as a museum, which it largely remained for the better part of a century. Control of the cathedral was finally returned to the Russian Orthodox Church in 2017.

In 1881, Alexander II, grandfather of Tsar Nicholas II, was assassinated while on his way to a minor military review. In honor of his memory the royal family sponsored the construction of the Church of The Savior on Spilled Blood. The church was largely kept closed during the Communist era, though it was used as a morgue and a storehouse during World War II. The Church of Our Savior on Spilled Blood is now one of the most popular tourist attractions in St. Petersburg, though it is currently unconsecrated.

Of Interest: St. Isaac's Cathedral is an imposing Neoclassical-Byzantine structure with an absolutely tremendous golden dome that can be seen for miles around. Unlike most other major Russian churches, it does not feature classic Eastern-style onion elements, but is rather reminiscent of other major national churches constructed in Central Europe around the same time. The Church of the Savior on Spilled Blood is similarly huge but more traditionally Russian in appearance. Crowned with Faberge-esque onion domes, it is reminiscent of St. Basil's in Moscow. Every inch of the interior is covered in iconic mosaics. It is claimed that this church holds the world record for total square footage of such artwork.

125. TRINITY MONASTERY OF ST. SERGIUS

Sergius Posad, Moscow Oblast, Russia, 141300

Denomination: Russian Orthodox
Dates: 1337 (founded)
Web: www.stsl.ru (official website)

The Trinity Monastery of St. Sergius is one of the most sacred Christian sites in Russia, as well as one of its historically most important monasteries. It has periodically served as the patriarchal seat of the Russian Orthodox Church, and is one of the major religious centers of Eastern Orthodoxy. The Trinity Monastery of St. Sergius is a UNESCO World Heritage Site.

In the mid-14th century a pair of Russian brothers gave up their aristocratic lives in order to seek out a more pious existence as hermits. They established a small chapel in the forest outside of Moscow, and soon they were joined by others. By the early 15th century the Trinity Monastery was one of the largest and wealthiest institutions in Russia. Its close proximity to Moscow and the Russian Orthodox Patriarch made the monastery extremely influential.

Trinity Monastery's most famous resident was the monk Sergius. During the late 1300s, when the fortunes of Russia were at their lowest ebb, Sergius set out to unite the Russian nobles against the Mongols, who still occupied huge swaths of Russian territory. He assembled a large army and led the Russians forces to victory at the Battle of Kulikovo. After his death, Sergius was canonized, and his tomb became one of Russia's most sacred shrines. Over the next two centuries the Church and the Tsars spent lavish sums embellishing the complex. Orthodox pilgrims came by the thousands to pay homage to the relics of Sergius. Massive fortifications were also established around the monastery.

After taking shelter within the monastery in the 1680s, Peter the Great poured money into the place. Beginning in the 18th century, this wealth was slowly sapped by a succession of corrupt governments in search of money and property. First the tsars then later the communists slowly chiseled away at the monastery's holdings. Since the fall of the Soviet government, Russian Christians have passionately re-embraced their heritage, and are returning to the Trinity Monastery of St. Sergius in huge numbers.

Of Interest: The Trinity Monastery of St. Sergius is a massive complex of thickly clustered buildings surrounded by scenic fields and forests. The brilliant white-brick structures are crowned with an assortment of high peaked roofs, towers, golden spires and Russian onion-domes. Among the numerous churches and sundry buildings of the monastery are a quartet of architectural masterpieces: the 15th century Church of the Holy Ghost; the 17th century Church of the Nativity of John the Baptist, added by the Stroganovs; the Church of the Virgin of Smolensk; and the residence of the Patriarch. Trinity Cathedral, built in the 15th century over the ruins of an earlier wooden church, contains the tombs of St. Sergius and St. Nikon. The Assumption Cathedral, the centerpiece of the complex, was built by Ivan the Terrible in the 15th century. Inside is the tomb of Boris Godunov.

---

126. ST. SOPHIA'S CATHEDRAL

Volodymrska Street, 24, Kiev, Ukraine, 01001

Denomination: Ukrainian Orthodox
Dates: c. 1031 (completed)
Web: https://st-sophia.org.ua (official website)

St. Sophia's Cathedral is one of the major architectural landmarks of the city of Kiev and one of the most beautiful churches to be found in Ukraine. Dating from the Middle Ages, the cathedral has endured nearly a millennium of almost constant upheaval, and is one of the oldest surviving churches in the country. While nominally a Ukrainian Orthodox institution, the cathedral was not in use at the time of this writing.

Christianity has probably been around in Kiev since the city's founding in the early Middle Ages. The city's Church of the Tithes, now long gone, was here as early as the 10th century. The Cathedral of St. Sophia was completed around 1031, though the exact date is uncertain. Over the next two centuries, the cathedral was ravaged by war on at least two occasions. The second time, by the Mongols in 1240, left the cathedral in particularly bad shape.

From the 1500s onward, numerous powers fought over Kiev, and the cathedral passed between the control of the Catholic and Orthodox churches. It was seized and closed outright in the 1920s following the Russian Revolution, but subsequently survived seven decades of Communist control. The Cathedral of St. Sophia was declared a UNESCO World Heritage Site in 1990.

Of Interest: St. Sophia's Cathedral is a stunning Byzantine structure with towers crowned by golden onion domes and crosses. Much of the current structure dates from renovations in the 17th and 18th centuries. St. Sophia's boasts magnificent iconic artwork, some of which dates back nearly a thousand years. A number of Kievan monarchs are buried in the cathedral, most notably Yaroslav I, who was the original founder of the church.

---

127. KIEV MONASTERY OF THE CAVES

Lavrska Street, 15, Kiev, Ukraine, 01015

Denomination: Ukrainian Orthodox
Dates: 1051 (founded)
Web: www.lavra.ua (official website)

The Kiev Monastery of the Caves is a medieval monastic complex that began as a tiny community of monks living in a cave here nearly a thousand years ago. From that humble beginning, the monastery has developed into a sprawling complex that almost completely covers a hill overlooking old Kiev. It is, along with nearby St. Sophia's, the city's most historic religious site.

The first monks established a community in Kiev in 1051.

Originally inhabiting local caves, the monks were granted jurisdiction over the entire hill by Iziaslav I, and a cathedral was erected on the site shortly thereafter. By the 12th century, the monastery was among the most important in Eastern Europe. The monastery complex was regularly expanded and renovated until its buildings occupied most of the hill in the 17th century.

The monastery suffered severe damage during World War II, either by the Germans or the Russians, or most likely both, and several of the structures, including the medieval cathedral, had to be rebuilt after the war. For most of the Communist era, the monastery was repurposed for public use. Since the fall of the Soviet Union, the monastery has largely been restored and is once again in religious use. The Kiev Monastery of the Caves was designated a UNESCO World Heritage Site in 1990.

Of Interest: The Kiev Monastery of the Caves complex is enormous, and thanks to its prominent hilltop position easily visible from much of the city. Its buildings exhibit a mix of architectural styles dominated by Byzantine and Baroque construction. The two dominant buildings are the Dormitian Cathedral and the Great Bell Tower. The former is a jaw-dropping, brilliant white structure crowned with more than a dozen golden onion domes. The latter, once among the world's tallest freestanding man-made structures, is easily a contender for Europe's most beautiful Christian bell tower.

---

128. PEOPLE'S SALVATION CATHEDRAL

Strada Izvor, Bucharest, Romania

Denomination: Romanian Orthodox
Completed: 2024 (under construction as of the time of this writing)
Web: www.catedralaneamului.ro (official website)

The People's Salvation Cathedral will soon be the Patriarchal seat of the Romanian Orthodox Church. As of the time of this writing, the cathedral was just consecrated but still under construction. It is anticipated that upon its completion it will the largest church in the world that is within the Eastern Orthodox communion.

During the Ottoman era, Orthodox Christianity was suppressed in the Balkans for many centuries. When Romania achieved independence in the 1870s, the people began calling for the construction of a national cathedral, to celebrate both their freedom and their faith. However, the project was frequently delayed due to unrest in the region and the two World Wars.

Long stalled in the postwar era due to the Communist government, the effort to build a national cathedral was renewed in the 1990s after the collapse of the Iron Curtain. Construction on the cathedral finally began in 2010, and the building was consecrated in 2018. It is anticipated to be completed in 2024.

Of Interest: The People's Salvation Cathedral is an absolutely enormous Neo-Byzantine building. When it is completed, it will be among the largest churches in the world. At over 130 meters in height, it will be the tallest Orthodox church structure anywhere. Although immense, the church interior is somewhat plain, designed to keep attention focused on the altar. The wall behind the altar is nearly covered from floor to ceiling with iconic paintings of the Holy Family and the saints.

---

129. METROPOLITAN CATHEDRAL

Nr. 16, Bulevardul Stefan cel Mare Sfant, Iasi, Romania

Denomination: Romanian Orthodox
Dates: c. 15th century (originally completed),
1887 (current building completed)
Web: https://catedralamitropolitanaiasi.mmb.ro (official website)

The Metropolitan Cathedral of Iasi is the current seat of the Romanian Orthodox Church, one of the autocephalous churches of Eastern Orthodox Christianity. As such it is one of the most important churches in Romania. However, it is anticipated that, upon its completion, the patriarchate will be moved to the new People's Salvation Cathedral in Bucharest.

The city of Iasi has been home to major churches since the late Middle Ages. At least two other churches formerly stood on the site of the cathedral, the White Church and the Presentation Church. The current building was largely completed in the mid-19th century, but much of the church had to be rebuilt after serious construction flaws were discovered leading to a ceiling collapse.

Most of the current building dates from a reconstruction in the 1880s under the patronage of the Romanian monarchs. After its completion, the relics of Paraskeva of the Balkans, a medieval Moldovan saint, were buried here. The cathedral survived both World War II and the Communist era more or less intact. For the time being it remains the spiritual heart of the Romanian Orthodox Church.

Of Interest: The Metropolitan Cathedral is a spectacular Renaissance Revival building with Byzantine elements. There is magnificent iconic artwork throughout the church, including on the exterior. The interior décor of dark stone and gold gives the sanctuary a mysterious and exotic feel. Beneath the church is a museum with exhibits on the history of Christianity in the region.

---

130. ST. MARY'S CATHEDRAL & ST. OLAF'S CHURCH

Toom-Kooli 6, Tallinn, Estonia, 10130 (St. Mary's Cathedral)

Lai 50, Tallinn, Estonia, 10133 (St. Olaf's Church)

Alternate/Full Name: Cathedral of St. Mary the Virgin in Tallinn
Denomination: Lutheran & Baptist
Completed: Cathedral - c. 1219 (originally completed), 1240 (current building completed) & Church - c. 12th century (completed)
Web: www.visitestonia.com/en/where-to-go/tallinn/tallinn-old-town (tourism website)

St. Mary's Cathedral and St. Olaf's Church are the two magnificent, historic churches of old Tallinn. Located in a region dominated by Russian Orthodoxy to the east and Roman Catholicism to the west, these two churches have both been Protestant for many centuries. Both adopted Lutheranism in the years after the Reformation, while the latter went on to change again, embracing the Baptist church.

The Roman Catholic Church arrived in Estonia possibly as early as the 11th century. Both St. Mary's and St. Olaf's had early incarnations that predated the arrival of Danish invaders in 1219. A permanent cathedral was erected to replace St. Mary's in 1240. Later reconstructions notwithstanding, it is the oldest church in Estonia. It was later joined by a permanent structure for the Church of St. Olaf, named in honor of an earlier Norwegian king.

In the 16th century, Estonia was caught up in the Protestant Reformation, and both churches became Lutheran. Both buildings suffered during the ravages of Nazi occupation followed by decades of Communist control. St. Olaf's was famously used by the KGB as a radio tower during the Cold War. After Communism, the cathedral continued to serve as a Lutheran institution while St. Olaf's became a Baptist church.

Of Interest: St. Mary's Cathedral is a stately structure in white crowned with a stunning black spire. Architecturally it is a mix of Gothic and Eastern styles. A number of military heroes are buried within the church, including several who served during the Thirty Years War. St. Olaf's Church is the city's most famous landmark, with a bell tower that absolutely dominates the city skyline. In the late 16th century it was counted among the tallest structures in the world.

---

131. RIGA CATHEDRAL & ST. PETER'S CHURCH

Herdera Laukums 6, Centra Rajons, Riga, LV-1050, Latvia (Riga Cathedral)

Skamu iela, Centra Rajons, Riga, LV-1050, Latvia (St. Peter's Church)

Denomination: Lutheran
Dates: Cathedral - 1211 (completed) & Church - 1746 (completed)
Web: www.doms.lv (official website)

Riga Cathedral and St. Peter's Church are two of the oldest churches in the Baltic region. Both were originally constructed by the Roman Catholic Church and later became Lutheran institutions when much of Northern Europe converted to Protestantism in the wake of the Reformation. The former is now the seat of the Lutheran Archbishop of Riga, and both are among the most important Protestant churches in northeastern Europe.

Christianity did not arrive in Latvia until the Middle Ages, well after the Roman era had ended. The Catholic Church established a presence in Riga in the 11th century, and constructed the city's cathedral in the year 1211. Construction on the Church of St. Peter was also begun around this time, and part of the original church continues to exist to this day.

Throughout the later Middle Ages, Latvia was contested by Catholics from the west and Orthodox Christians from the East, but both of these were pushed aside by the Protestants. Lutheranism was introduced in the 16th century, and within a few decades was the predominant faith of Latvia. Both the cathedral and the church became Lutheran around this time. After many delays, St. Peter's Church was finally completed in 1746.

Of Interest: Riga Cathedral is the one of the largest surviving medieval churches in northeastern Europe. St. Peter's Church mostly dates from later reconstructions, especially after being damaged by artillery during World War II. The dome of the former and the steeple of the latter tower over the city skyline and are among Riga's most memorable landmarks. Inside the Church of St. Peter is one of Latvia's great artistic treasures: an absolutely enormous candelabrum dating from the late 16th century. After being taken as war booty by the Nazis, this candelabrum was finally returned in 2012.

132. VILNIUS CATHEDRAL

Sventaragio g, Vilnius, 01143, Lithuania

Alternate/Full Name: Cathedral Basilica of St. Stanislaus and St. Ladislaus of Vilnius
Denomination: Roman Catholic
Dates: c. 1251 (originally completed),
1783 (current building completed)
Web: www.vilnius-tourism.lt/en/what-to-see/places-to-visit/churches/cathedral-basilica (tourism website)

Vilnius Cathedral is the one of the most important Roman Catholic churches in the Baltics. In the face of Orthodox Russia to the East, Lithuania's rulers were staunch defenders of the Catholic Church, especially Prince Casimir, the only member of the Polish royal family to be honored with sainthood. During his brief life, he won a reputation both for his piety and his outspoken defiance against the Turkish hordes then encroaching in Eastern Europe. His tomb in Vilnius Cathedral is one of the most popular pilgrimage sites in the Baltics.

The short-lived Casimir Jagiellon was among the most famous members of Polish royalty in history. A crown prince and heir to the thrones of Poland and Lithuania, Casimir had a reputation for piety and extreme fasting, and possibly lived a life of voluntary chastity as well. He grew up in the tumultuous decades which followed the Ottoman conquest of Constantinople and their subsequent threat to Christendom in Eastern Europe.

When his uncle the king of Hungary was killed in battle against the Turks, Casimir jumped at the chance to fight against the Ottomans, and remained a staunch opponent of Islam for the remainder of his brief life. He died of tuberculosis in 1484 at the age of 25. He was buried in Vilnius Cathedral, which was at the time the royal seat of the joint kingdom. By popular demand Casimir was canonized and his tomb became the most important site of Catholic pilgrimage in the Baltics.

Vilnius Cathedral itself has a fascinating history. Founded in the mid-13th century, it was constructed on the site of an earlier pagan temple. However, a few years later, the local residents reverted to paganism, and the church was put to use for the worship of a pagan deity. In 1387 Lithuania officially became Christian, and a new cathedral was constructed. This burned down a few years later, and was finally replaced by the present structure in the 18th century.

Of Interest: Vilnius Cathedral served for many years as a royal church. Much of the structure dates from 18th century. The magnificent façade is designed in the manner of an ancient Greek temple, and is adorned by both statues and engraved figures. The building is crowned with statues of Sts. Casimir, Stanislaus and Helena. Directly in front of the cathedral is a slightly leaning minaret-like bell tower crowned by a dome, steeple and cross. The Chapel of St. Casimir inside the cathedral showcases the Prince's reliquary amidst magnificent marble work and statuary. In addition to Casimir, a number of other Polish and Lithuanian royals and luminaries are interred here as well. Also of note is a fresco depicting Jesus, which may date as far back as the 13th century.

---

133. HILL OF CROSSES

Jurgaiciai, Sialiai, 81439, Lithuania

Denomination: Roman Catholic
Dates: 1831 (founded)
Web: www.kryziukalnas.lt (official website)

The Hill of Crosses is one of the most unique Christian sites in the world. It is, as its name implies, quite literally a hill covered in crosses. There are countless crosses here of every shape and size, all planted in the ground in defiance of over a century of war and tyranny. The hill is renowned throughout the Baltics and has been recognized as a place of sanctity by the Roman Catholic Church. Many Lithuanians visit here annually, both for religious and historic purposes.

From the early 19th century until the late 20th century, Lithuania was in a nearly constant state of either conflict or occupation by other powers. The history of the Hill of Crosses began in 1831 after a failed coup against Russian occupiers led to the slaughter of many Lithuanians and Poles. The first crosses were placed on the hill, where a fortress had formerly stood, in honor of bodies that could not be found or identified.

In the ensuing century, it became tradition to add more crosses to the hill, especially in times of adversity. Many went up in the wake of failed revolutions and the world wars, and continued during the Soviet occupation of Lithuania in the post-war era. Amazingly, the site was left undisturbed throughout this entire period, although there were several close calls during the Soviet era. The hill is now held to be a site of reverence for many of Lithuania's Roman Catholics.

Of Interest: The Hill of Crosses is packed with so many crosses, crucifixes, statues and other Christian symbols that no one really knows how many there are. Recent estimates seem to indicate as many as a hundred thousand. Amazingly, the hill is not under any jurisdiction, though it is nominally cared for by monks from a nearby Franciscan monastery. Any visitor is free to leave an addition to the hill's collection.

CENTRAL EUROPE

134. CATHEDRAL OF ST. MARY MAGDALENE

Aleja Solidarnosci 52, 03-402, Warsaw, Poland

Alternate/Full Name: Metropolitan Cathedral of the Holy and Equal-to-the-Apostles Mary Magdalene
Denomination: Polish Orthodox
Dates: 1869 (completed)
Web: www.katedra.org.pl (official website)

The Cathedral of St. Mary Magdalene is the nominal seat of the Polish Orthodox Church, one of the autocephalous churches of Eastern Orthodoxy. It is also one of the few churches in the city, and one of the most important churches in Poland, to have survived both World War II and the Communist era more or less intact.

Following the Napoleanic Wars, most of Poland came under the control of the Russian Empire. Over the next century, many Orthodox Russians migrated into what was predominantly Roman Catholic Warsaw, which necessitated the construction of new churches. Among these was the Church of St. Mary Magdalene.

After Poland gained its independence following World War I, the independent autocephalous Polish Orthodox Church was formed, and the church re-designated as a cathedral and patriarchal seat. During World War II, while the city of Warsaw was nearly completely destroyed, the cathedral remained largely intact, with only minor damage. The building underwent a series of restorations that were completed in the 1990s.

Of Interest: The Cathedral of St. Mary Magdalene is a magnificent Revival building along the lines of the other great national churches constructed in Central Europe in the 19th century. It is among Warsaw's most beloved landmarks. Although smaller than a typical cathedral of its importance, the green-domed building is no less stunning. The interior is home to a trove of murals and artwork, as well as several iconic paintings. Below the main church is the Chapel of the Passion of Christ, which preserves some older artwork and mosaics from earlier churches.

---

135. ST. JOHN'S ARCHCATHEDRAL

Kanonia 6, 00-278, Warsaw, Poland

Denomination: Roman Catholic
Dates: c. 14th century (completed)
Web: www.warsawtour.pl/en/st-johns-archcathedral-in-warsaw (tourism website)

St. John's Archcathedral is the seat of the Catholic Archbishop of Warsaw. Almost completely destroyed during World War II, the modern building largely dates from the post-war period. Since its reconstruction, the church has become a national monument of sorts to those who died fighting against the Nazis here in 1944. St. John's Archcathedral is part of the city's UNESCO World Heritage Site.

The first cathedral on this site was constructed in the 1300s. For centuries it was used by many Polish monarchs, who had their own private entrance directly into church from the palace. The last Polish king, Stanislaw II, was buried here in 1798. In the years after his death, much of the aging cathedral was reconstructed in grand Baroque style.

Throughout the turbulent first half of the 20th century, St. John's survived right up until 1944. In that year, the cathedral became part of the battleground of the ill-fated Warsaw Uprising. The fighting left the cathedral badly damaged, and what survived was demolished afterwards by the retreating Germans. St. John's Cathedral was incorporated into the Warsaw UNESCO World Heritage Site in 1980.

Of Interest: The Cathedral of St. John is almost completely a post-war reconstruction. When the church was rebuilt, it was constructed along the original Gothic lines, not the more recent Baroque style. However, the feeling is of a more modern building, especially on the interior. A number of prominent Polish figures are buried in the crypt, including several presidents as well as King Stanislaw II.

---

136. WAWEL CATHEDRAL

Wawel 3, 31-001 Krakow, Poland

Alternate/Full Name: Royal Archcathedral of Sts. Stanislaus and Wenceslaus on the Wawel Hill
Denomination: Roman Catholic
Dates: c. 11th century (originally completed), c. 14th century (current building completed)
Web: www.katedra-wawelska.pl (official website)

Wawel Cathedral is one of the most historic churches in Poland. During the years of the Kingdom of Poland it was the country's royal cathedral, with most of Poland's kings coronated here and a large number buried here. Its most famous burial is Stanislaus the Martyr, Poland's first saint. The cathedral also achieved fame in the 20th century as the home church of Karol Jozef Wojtyla, also known as Pope John Paul II, who gave his first mass here in 1946. The Cathedral of Wawel is part of the Historic Center of Krakow UNESCO World Heritage Site.

In the mid-11th century, the Catholic Church was still in competition with the Eastern Church as well as pagan religious practices. During this turbulent period, the Church made little headway expanding into Poland. Stanislaus, born into a well-off aristocratic family, was encouraged at an early age to enter service with the Church. He likely went to Western Europe for his education. A few years after his return to Poland, he received ordination as Bishop of Krakow, possibly the first native-born Pole to receive this honor.

It was during Stanislaus' tenure as bishop that the Catholic Church began to make headway in Poland. Under his guidance, and with the assistance of King Boleslaw II, new churches and monasteries were established throughout the country. He organized new bishoprics and helped the Polish crown achieve recognition from the Church. According to tradition, Stanislaus was also involved in the miraculous, temporary resurrection of a man so that he could bear witness in a court case.

Stanislaus had a good working relationship with the king until a falling out in 1079. The details are sketchy, but the brief version is that Stanislaus had Boleslaw excommunicated. In retaliation, the king killed the bishop with his own hands. This threw the country into revolt, and Boleslaw was forced to flee to Hungary. Stanislaus became a national hero and went on to become Poland's first home-grown saint. He was entombed in Wawel Cathedral, which has been one of the country's most important historic sites ever since.

Of Interest: Wawel Cathedral is a beautiful building with a simple, white gothic structure dating from the 14th century. Two bell towers, architecturally at odds with each other and with the church, sort-of flank one end. One of the towers is built of white brick half-way up and crowned with red brick; the other is crowned with a towering, baroque belfry. The domes which crown the chapels along the side vary in size, shape and decoration, not to mention color, with copper-green on some and gold-leaf on others. The interior is more harmonious, if perhaps less memorable than the flamboyant exterior. The impressive white nave is flanked by numerous chapels which house the remains of sixteen Polish kings, and a dozen other notables. The relic of Stanislaus is kept in a great silver sarcophagus beneath the church's black marble altar.

---

137. JASNA GORA MONASTERY

Ul.o.A. Kordeckiego 2, 42-225, Czestochowa, Poland

Denomination: Roman Catholic (Marian shrine)
Dates: 1382 (founded)
Web: www.jci.jasnagora.pl (official website)

The Jasna Gora Monastery in Czestochowa is home to the most popular Catholic Marian shrine in Eastern Europe. For most of the last six centuries, pilgrims have been flocking to Jasna Gora to see the monastery's famous icon, the Black Madonna. The arrival of the icon at the monastery in the 14th century also makes it one of the oldest major Marian shrines in the world.

The origin of the Icon of the Black Madonna is something of a mystery. According to legend, it was painted by none other than Luke the Evangelist, and the board on which it is painted was supposedly part of a piece of furniture from Mary's house. Scholars who have studied the picture suggest that it is more likely that it was painted sometime between the 5th and 10th centuries and probably came from the Byzantine Empire. The icon arrived in Czestochowa in 1382.

For fifty years the abbey thrived and was a magnet for pilgrims. However, Czestochowa found itself in the path of the Hussites, who overran the monastery and left the icon severely damaged. A few years later it was taken to Prussia where it was restored and kept safe until things calmed down. It was returned to Czestochowa in 1434 to great fanfare. Over the course of the next two centuries massive fortifications were raised around the monastery and icon to protect it from the religious turbulence that was ravaging Europe.

In 1655 a small band of monks and citizens defended the monastery against the vastly superior Protestant army of Sweden. The miraculous and successful defense was attributed to the presence of the Black Madonna. As the legend of the icon grew, the monastery was officially sanctioned as a Christian Shrine by the Papacy. In 1717 the Black Madonna was officially crowned as the Queen of Poland. During the communist years Jasna Gora became a spiritual center of resistance, and was the sight of tremendous celebrations after the fall of the Iron Curtain in 1989. Today Czestochowa is the most important Marian shrine in Eastern Europe.

Of Interest: The Jasna Gora Monastery is one of the most beautiful in Eastern Europe. Laid out on a hill in a densely built-out twelve acre square behind daunting 17th century fortifications, the complex includes the original Chapel of Our Lady, the main basilica which dates from the 1400s, a large monastic compound with cloisters, and gardens. The signature tower and spire dominates the monastery and the nearby town. The spiritual focal point of the complex is the Chapel of Our Lady where the Icon of the Black Madonna is kept. The icon itself is a very old work that dates back at least a thousand years. It features the Virgin Mary in a black hooded robe holding the Infant Jesus clothed in red and clutching at a Bible.

---

138. ST. VITUS' CATHEDRAL

III. nadvori 48/2, 119 01, Prague, Czech Republic

Alternate/Full Name: Metropolitan Cathedral of Sts. Vitus, Wenceslaus and Adalbert
Denomination: Roman Catholic (of interest to Protestants)
Dates: 930 (originally completed), 1929 (current building completed)
Web: www.hrad.cz (official website)

St. Vitus' Cathedral is the architectural centerpiece of Prague Castle, and is a place of religious historical importance to both Catholics and Protestants. The cathedral has ties to Good King Wenceslaus of Christmas carol fame, while Prague Castle was the site of the Defenstration of Prague, which kicked off the Thirty Years War, the bloodiest intra-Christian conflict in history. The St. Vitus' Cathedral is part of the Historic Center of Prague UNESCO World Heritage Site.

Good King Wenceslaus is one of the most famous Catholic rulers in the history of Eastern Europe, though his fame beyond Bohemia is due primarily to his namesake 19th century Christmas carol. Although this holiday song gives little information about the life of this famous ruler, his true story is interesting enough. To start, Wenceslaus I was technically not a king, but rather a 10th century duke whose family ruled over Bohemia, or the modern-day Czech Republic. Wenceslaus' father is believed to have been personally converted to Christianity by the missionaries Cyril and Methodius.

Wenceslaus himself was a champion of the Church, endeavoring to convert the subjects of his kingdom to Christianity in the face of stiff opposition. He was assassinated by agents of his pagan brother,

Boleslaus. Because Boleslaus' motiviations were purely political, the conversion of Bohemia continued and was largely completed during his reign. Wenceslaus was buried in the cathedral which he had founded.

In 1415 the death of Jan Hus led to the First Defenestration of Prague, wherein his followers seized the Catholic leaders of the city and tossed them out of a window of the castle. Violence flared here again in 1618 at when a Protestant tribunal found several Catholic officials guilty of violating Protestant rights and also tossed them out of a window, sparking the Thirty Years War. Together the cathedral and castle are honored for their role in the history of Christianity in Central Europe.

Of Interest: St. Vitus' Cathedral, the royal cathedral of Prague, is a massive Gothic structure which took nearly six centuries to complete. It was built in the traditional cross-style with a pair of massive bell-tower steeples over the entrance. Many of Bohemia's kings were coronated here, and most are buried here in the royal crypt. The chief attraction is the St. Wenceslas Chapel, the earliest part of the Cathedral, built over the site of the saint's tomb. The Bohemian Crown Jewels are kept in a room next door.

---

139. STS. CYRIL AND METHODIUS CATHEDRAL

Resslova 9a, 120 00, Nove Mesto, Prague, Czech Republic

Denomination: Czech and Slovak Orthodox
Dates: 1736 (completed)
Web: www.katedrala.info (official website)

Sts. Cyril and Methodius Cathedral is the most famous non-Catholic church in Prague and the seat of the Orthodox Church in Czechia and Slovakia. It is the westernmost of the patriarchal seats of the Eastern Orthodox Church in the Old World. It is perhaps most famous in history for its connection to the assassination of Reinhard Heydrich, a high ranking Nazi leader who played a key role in organizing the Holocaust.

Historically Prague has been religiously connected to western Christianity. Eastern Orthodoxy had long been kept out of what is now Czechia primarily by the efforts of the Hapsburgs. After the collapse of the Austro-Hungarian Empire in World War I, Eastern Orthodoxy was finally legalized here. The cathedral, originally constructed in the 18th century by the Catholic Church, was acquired by the Orthodox Church for use in the 1920s.

In 1942, at the height of World War II, Czechoslovakian partisans managed to successfully pull off one of the greatest assassinations of the war: that of Holocaust mastermind Reinhard Heydrich. After a three week manhunt, the primary suspects were cornered in this church, where most were killed and the others arrested. They are now remembered as heroes of Czechoslovakia and commemorated at the cathedral.

A few years after the war ended, in 1951, the Czech and Slovak Orthodox Church was established as the 14th autocephalous Church of Eastern Orthodoxy. The Church of Saints Cyril and Methodius became the seat of the Czech and Slovak Church at this time. Today the cathedral counts both the faithful and history enthusiasts among its visitors.

Of Interest: Sts. Cyril and Methodius Cathedral is a stunning Baroque building representative of the grand architecture of the Hapsburg Empire at its height. The building has a number of memorials both inside and outside of the church commemorating the martyrdom of Heydrich's killers. Bullet holes still mark the walls of the church where the Czechoslovakian gunmen fought against the SS following the assassination.

140. CHURCH OF OUR LADY BEFORE TYN

Staromestske nam, 110 00, Stare Mesto, Prague, Czech Republic

Alternate/Full Name: Church of Mother of God before Tyn
Denomination: Roman Catholic
Dates: c. 11th century (originally completed), c. 1450 (current building completed)
Web: www.tyn.cz (official website)

The Church of Our Lady before Tyn is one of Europe's most visually distinctive churches, and arguably the most iconic and memorable building in the city of Prague. Towering over the city's Old Town Square, despite being set back from it, this dark and haunting architectural masterpiece utterly dominates the sea of red-roofed buildings which surrounds it.

At least two prior churches have stood on the spot of the current church, the earliest probably dating back to the 11th century. The current church witnessed a turbulent history even before construction was complete. Begun by the Catholic Church, it was intermittently occupied by the Hussites in the 15th century and the Protestants in the 16th and 17th centuries.

The church became a focal point for Counter-Reformation activities after Catholics retook the city during the Thirty Years War. All traces of Protestant activity were removed and the building fully restored for use by Catholics. A fire badly damaged much of the building in the 17th century, and it took more than two hundred years before repairs and renovations were carried out. Today Tyn Church is one of Prague's definitive pilgrimage churches and the city's most recognizable building.

Of Interest: The Church of Our Lady before Tyn is one of the most distinctive Gothic churches in the world and possibly the most photographed building in Prague. This is perhaps due to the unusually large number spires on the church, some of which protrude from other spires.

Although some of its appointments were damaged or destroyed during the intermittent strife of the various religious conflicts, the church was largely renovated in the 19th and 20th centuries. Tycho Brahe, one of the fathers of modern astronomy, is buried within the church.

---

141. BETHLEHEM CHAPEL & JAN HUS MEMORIAL

Betlemske nam, 255/4, 110 00, Stare Mesto, Prague, Czech Republic (Bethlehem Chapel)

Staromestske nam, 110 00, Stare Mesto, Prague, Czech Republic (Jan Hus Memorial)

Denomination: Formerly Roman Catholic & Public Monument (of interest to Protestants)
Dates: Chapel - 1391 (completed) & Memorial - 1915 (completed)
Web: www.bethlehemchapel.eu & www.prague.cz/jan-hus-monument (official websites)

Bethlehem Chapel is one of the most historic churches in the city of Prague, thanks to its connection with early Reformer Jan Hus. Dating back to the 14th century, Hus served as a priest here before his break with the Roman Catholic Church. While the current chapel is a recreation that dates from the Communist era, the site is considered of particular historic interest for its association with the Hussites.

Jan Hus was born in Bohemia in 1369. In his youth studied for a life in the clergy and became a priest in his early thirties. Influenced by the works of John Wycliffe, he famously preached against the failings of the Catholic Church. He developed a significant following which threatened the Church both politically and religiously. Eventually the Papacy took the threat of the Hussites so seriously that Hus was charged with heresy. He was tried at the Council of Constance, found guilty and condemned to death. In 1415 he was martyred by burning at the stake, his ashes later scattered on the Rhine River.

Jan Hus was appointed as the priest of Bethlehem Chapel in 1402, and it became a major forum for his verbal attacks on the Roman Catholic Church. After his death, the chapel was retained by the Church, coming under the jurisdiction of the Jesuits. It was gutted in the 1780s and repurposed as city housing. During the Communist era, the church was restored as close as possible to its original condition. It is now maintained as an historic site in Hus' honor. The city of Prague erected a massive monument in the Old Town Square in his memory on the five hundredth anniversary of his death.

Of Interest: Bethlehem Chapel largely dates from the 20th century restoration, though portions of the walls and interior sections are original. Some of the magnificent wall paintings date from the 15th century. The immense Jan Hus Memorial absolutely dominates Prague's Old Town Square. It features a bronze statue of Jan Hus, tired but determined, surrounded by the bodies of those Hussites martyred for their faith. Interestingly, there was once a massive column crowned with a statue of the Virgin Mary in the square, but this was torn down after Czechoslovakia gained its independence at the end of World War I in 1918.

---

142. SEDLEC OSSUARY

Zamecka, 284 03, Kutna Hora, Czech Republic

Alternate/Full Name: Cemetery Church of All Saints
Denomination: Roman Catholic
Dates: c. 1400 (completed)
Web: https://sedlecossuary.com (official website)

Sedlec Ossuary is possibly the world's most famous bone church, and one of the most popular tourist destinations in the Czech Republic outside of Prague. When the Black Plague swept through Bohemia in the 14th century, it left in its wake tens of thousands of dead bodies and a number of innovative Cistercian monks with a lot of time on their hands. The ensuing six centuries of labor resulted in one of the most macabre holy shrines in Christendom. Here, in a chapel that was meant only for burials, the skeletons of untold plague victims were reworked into sacred ornamentation. The Sedlec Ossuary is part of the Historic Town Center of Sedlec UNESCO World Heritage Site.

What started as a relatively insignificant event in Czech history later turned the cemetery of the Cistercian Abbey near Kutna Hora into one of Central Europe's most popular places for Christians to go and die in the Middle Ages. In 1278 the abbot of the church went on a pilgrimage to the Holy Land. He returned with a box of dirt from the Hill of Golgotha in Jerusalem, which was then ceremoniously scattered in the cemetery. Knowledge of the special dirt spread, and soon people began requesting burial in the abbey graveyard.

In 1349 the Black Plague reached Bohemia, and the trickle of petitioners for burial turned into a flood. Thousands of hopefuls came here in desperation, most of who died in Kutna Hora, and the monks simply could not handle the influx. Most of the tens of thousands of bodies were simply tossed into mass graves. In 1400, a new church was built on the cemetery grounds, and a chapel was opened up beneath the church to serve as an ossuary to receive the human remains from the graveyard.

Mountains of bones were stacked in the ossuary and forgotten. Centuries later, when the monks finally decided to do something with their strange cache, they discovered that someone had arranged a portion of the bones into artistic patterns. This inspired the monks, and beginning in 1870, with the help of a local woodcarver, they proceeded to cover every square inch of the church with bone decorations and furnishings. The result was an artistic sensation. The Sedlec Ossuary has been drawing in both the faithful and those filled with a macabre curiosity ever since.

Of Interest: The Sedlec Ossuary church and chapel are fairly standard examples of 14th century Gothic architecture. Beyond that, this place is all about the bones. The remains of an estimated forty thousand bodies were used to decorate the ossuary. The resulting variety of designs and uses are staggering. From simple wall decorations to large, complex artworks, there are hundreds upon hundreds of bone constructions to enthrall visitors. Among the highlights are: a pair of monstrances flanking the altar; an innovative reconstruction of the coat-of-arms of the Schwarzenberg family; niches filled with carefully constructed stacks of bones; and a stunning chandelier. Many of the leftover bones were incorporated into a quartet of massive bells which now decorate the four corners of the church.

---

143. ST. STEPHEN'S BASILICA & MATTHIAS CHURCH

Budapest, Szent Istvan Ter 1, 1051, Hungary (St. Stephen's Basilica)

Budapest, Szentharomsag Ter 2, 1014, Hungary (Matthias Church)

Denomination: Roman Catholic
Dates: Basiica - 1905 (completed) & Church - 1015 (originally completed), c 19th century (current building completed)
Web: www.bazilika.biz & www.budacastlebudapest.com (official websites)

St. Stephen's Basilica and Matthias Church are the two great Roman Catholic churches of Budapest. The former is the seat of the Catholic Archdiocese of Budapest; the latter is one of the oldest churches in Hungary, tracing its roots back to the 11th century Hungarian king, Stephen I. Together they are among the most visited sites in Hungary.

St. Stephen's Basilica is a relatively new church as major cathedrals go. It dates back to the 19th century, with only a temporary previous church on the site in the early 1800s. Before that the location was occupied by a theater. Constructed as the Hapsburg showpiece of Budapest, it was not completed until 1905. It currently serves as the co-cathedral of Esztergom-Budapest.

The history of the Matthias Church is much older. King Stephen I personally founded the first church here just over a thousand years ago. During this long, violent millennium, the church was destroyed by the Mongols in the 13th century, occupied by the Turks in the 16th century, and used as a base by both the Nazis and Soviets during World War II.

Throughout the Hapsburg era, the Matthias Church was used for many royal functions and state occasions. The last Austro-Hungarian emperor, Charles IV, was coronated here in 1916. Both the basilica and the church underwent substantial renovations in the post-war years. They are now regarded as two of the most important architectural treasures in Budapest.

Of Interest: St. Stephen's Basilica is among the finest Neoclassical churches in Europe to be completed in the 20th century. Viewed from the front, the bell towers perfectly frame the basilica's immense dome. By law it is the tallest building in Budapest. The basilica's great treasure is the hand of King Stephen I, kept in a reliquary. The Matthias Church is a stunning 15th century Gothic building, with a large portion of it dating from a reconstruction in the 17th century after the church was badly damaged during the Siege of Buda. The entire church was recently restored. The crypt now houses the Ecclesiastical Art Museum which contains, among other things, replicas of the Hungarian Crown Jewels.

---

144. ESZTERGOM BASILICA

Esztergom, Szent Istvan ter 1, 2500, Hungary

Alternate/Full Name: Primatial Basilica of our Lady of the Assumption and St. Adalbert
Denomination: Roman Catholic
Dates: c. 1010 (originally completed),
1856 (current building completed)
Web: www.bazilika-esztergom.hu (official website)

The Basilica of Esztergom is the most sacred church in Hungary, and home to the tomb of Stephen I, its first king, who dedicated his life to spreading Christianity in Eastern Europe. While his home town of Esztergom served as the national capital for three centuries, the cathedral was also the heart of the Church in Hungary. The Basilica of Esztergom is Stephen's greatest religious legacy. Although there is little left of his remains, most of which are now located elsewhere, Esztergom remains the country's most historic pilgrimage destination.

Stephen I was both the founder of the Kingdom of Hungary as well as a champion of the Church. Born sometime around the year 970 into a leading family of Magyar nobles, Stephen was trained both in royal leadership as well as in Christian teachings. When his father died, a power struggle ensued, and the popular Stephen put forth his claim for the crown by Divine Right. Supported by both the Church as well as Christian nobles from Germany, he won the crown and was coronated on January 1, 1001.

Stephen dedicated the nearly forty years of his rule to establishing Hungary as part of the community of Christian nations under the Catholic Church. He both supported missionaries and personally worked towards the conversion of the country. By the time of his death, Hungary had developed into a Catholic state. Apparently it had been his intention to abdicate his throne to his son at an early age so that he could pursue a career with the Church. However, his son's untimely death kept him busy with state affairs. He personally oversaw the construction of the original Basilica of Esztergom in the 11th century, and was buried there after his death.

During the Middle Ages the Basilica of Esztergom served as the royal cathedral of the Hungarian kings. It had a rough history, being sacked by the armies of Bohemia in the 14th century and again by the Turks in the 16th century. After centuries of damage and neglect, the original cathedral was finally demolished and completely rebuilt in the mid-19th century. Throughout the Cold War, the Basilica remained a beacon of religious freedom behind the Iron Curtain. It is Hungary's most popular place of Christian pilgrimage.

Of Interest: Eztergom Basilica is an architectural triumph, if a bit unusual in its layout. The main building is fronted by a colonnade and flanked by two bell towers separated from the church by great archways designed to let traffic pass through. Three great green domes top the structure, including two smaller ones over the bell towers and one enormous one over the church rotunda. The church interior is immense and boasts a number of fascinating features, including a painting of the Virgin Mary by Grigoletti, which is believed to be the world's largest single-canvas painting. The Bakocz Chapel was built at the height of the Renaissance and was saved when the church was rebuilt. The church organ was once played by Franz Liszt. Only bits of St. Stephen are preserved in Esztergom, though most of his right arm can be found in Budapest.

---

145. PANNONHALMA ARCHABBEY

Pannonhalma, Var 1, 9090, Hungary

Alternate/Full Name: Territorial Abbey of Pannonhalma
Denomination: Roman Catholic
Dates: c. 10th century (founded)
Web: https://bences.hu (official website)

Pannonhalma Archabbey is among the largest religious complexes in Hungary, and one of the most spectacular Benedictine abbeys to be found anywhere in Europe. Originally founded in the 10th century, the abbey has witnessed a lot of history, and has a number of connections with Hungary's former monarchy.

The original monastery was founded under the auspices of the early Hungarian monarchs, with substantial donations made by Hungary's first king, Stephen I. During the late Middle Ages it became one of the largest and most influential Catholic abbeys in Eastern Europe. Later, when the Ottoman Turks occupied much of the country, the abbey was only periodically occupied.

Following the departure of the Turks, the Pannonhalma Archabbey was restored to its former importance and glory, undergoing a substantial renovation. It remained active through the end of World War II, when it was closed by the Communists. It was returned once more to the Church after the fall of Communism, and is again an active monastery. The abbey was designated a UNESCO World Heritage Site in 1996.

Of Interest: Pannonhalma Archabbey is a sprawling complex which is believed to be the second largest Benedictine monastery in Europe.

Rebuilt on numerous occasions, with a major overhaul in 1995 for its 1000th anniversary, the complex includes a mix of styles with a heavy focus on Baroque. The abbey is home to one of Europe's great literary treasure troves. Its library contains well over three hundred thousand books and manuscripts, including the oldest known writings in the Hungarian language.

---

146. ST. STEPHEN'S CATHEDRAL

Stephensplatz 3, 1010 Vienna, Austria

Denomination: Roman Catholic
Dates: 1160 (completed)
Web: www.stephanskirche.at (official website)

St. Stephen's Cathedral is the great church of the city of Vienna. For many centuries it was also the chief church of the Hapsburg dynasty. Many of the city's bishops are buried within, as are a few members of the Hapsburg royal family. Over the centuries St. Stephen's hosted many state events. It also enjoys a proud musical tradition; the Vienna Boys Choir frequently performs here, and the funerals of many of the city's great musicians, including that of Mozart, have been held here. Today it is a popular music venue, and the plaza in front is ground zero for street performers and promoters wooing tourists to the city's many nightly concerts.

Christianity arrived in Austria sometime around the 7th century, and in Vienna perhaps a century or so later. By the 12th century Vienna was the largest and most important city in Austria, and St. Stephen's Cathedral was built to accommodate the city's growing Catholic population. In 1440 Vienna became the seat of the Hapsburg family, and the city's religious importance skyrocketed. Throughout the later Middle Ages and the Renaissance Vienna was one of the most important cities in Europe, and it became a critical center of the Counter-Reformation.

Throughout the centuries of Hapsburg rule, St. Stephen's Cathedral served as the defacto church of state. Royal coronations were held here, as were other major state functions. Over the years the cathedral was expanded and embellished many times in order to reflect its national importance. Although not the official site of the royal tombs, a number of important figures are buried here, including Holy Roman Emperor Frederick III. The partial remains of many other royals, as well as thousands of other skeletons, are kept in the crypts below the church.

St. Stephen's enjoyed a number of interesting roles in its long history. During the two sieges of the city by the Ottomans in 1529 and 1683, the cathedral was used as a military command center and observation post by the city's defenders. The towers were also used by a resident team of watchmen who kept vigilance here in order to spot fires. In 1791 it held the funeral of Wolfgang Amadeus Mozart, which was followed up by his burial in a pauper's grave. The cathedral narrowly survived destruction in World War II, although repairs from that conflict are still ongoing.

Of Interest: St. Stephen's Cathedral is a hulking, classical Romanesque-Gothic church with just a hint of something eastern in its architecture. The exterior boasts some very unique features, notably its roof. Rebuilt after the war using steel supports, it is the steepest pitched cathedral roof in the world. This was done in order to better show off the tile mosaics which feature Austria's coat-of-arms. Also here is the fabled 'Giant's Door', the immense arched window that dominates the cathedral's façade. Inside, the brightly checked floor, and the baroque-era embellishments, especially in the chapels, offset the more stern medieval features. There are a number of chapels here, including St. Valentine's Chapel, where the corpse of the famous saint is supposedly kept, along with a piece of the tablecloth used at the Last Supper. Beneath the cathedral are the Bishop's Crypt, where many local clergymen are buried; and the Ducal Crypt, where 78 urns contain the hearts and other body parts of members of the Hapsburg family.

147. MELK ABBEY

Abt-Berthold-Dietmayr-Strasse 1, 3390 Melk, Austria

Denomination: Roman Catholic
Dates: 1089 (founded)
Web: www.stiftmelk.at (official website)

Melk Abbey and its famous library was one of the wonders of Central Europe during the Middle Ages. Established by the Benedictines, this monastery has not only survived the ages, but has grown to such spectacular proportions that is has become a must-visit stop on any tour of the Danube valley. Melk Abbey is believed to have been an inspiration for Umberto Eco's famous mystery novel, *The Name of the Rose*.

The founding of Melk is an interesting story. In the late 11th century, Europe became embroiled in the Investiture Controversy, which centered around the right to appoint Church officials. This pitted the authority of the Papacy against the Holy Roman emperors. In the 1080s, Leopold II, Margrave of Austria, sided with the Papacy. In order to cement his relationship with the Church, and to strengthen the Papacy's strategic position on the Danube, he gifted one of his castles to the Benedictine order.

In the end, Leopold's choice to side with the Pope proved disastrous. The Holy Roman Empire won out, and the margrave died a few years later, his lands much reduced. However, his legacy survived in his gift to the Benedictines. In 1089, a number of monks arrived from Lambach and transformed the castle into an abbey. By the late Middle Ages the monastery's scriptorium was one of the most prolific in Europe, and its library collection among the largest north of the Alps.

By the 18th century the abbey had grown to immense proportions, and a completely new baroque structure as spectacular as any in Christendom replaced the old medieval buildings. Melk Abbey became a national treasure, managing to survive the ravages of both Napolean and the Nazis. It remains to the present day active both as an abbey and a school, and is a popular stop for cruises along the Danube River.

Of Interest: Melk Abbey is home to one of the most beautiful baroque-era churches ever constructed. Standing on a tall hill thick with green forest, the breathtaking gold and white walls of the abbey absolutely shine down on the waters of the Danube River below. The complex is palatial in its grandeur, with the towering copper-domed cathedral in the middle flanked by two long wings that could easily have been designed as annexes for Versailles. An exquisitely rendered marble statue of Jesus carrying the Cross and flanked by two angels crowns the façade. The cathedral interior is similarly magnificent, with walls and columns of marble generously adorned in gold leaf. The ceiling consists of immense frescoes depicting the life of St. Benedict and his ascension to Heaven. The greatest treasure of the Abbey is its massive library collection, highlights of which are on display in some of the galleries.

---

148. ST. PETER'S ABBEY & NONNBERG ABBEY

Kapitelpl. 8, 5020 Salzburg, Austria (St. Peter's Abbey)

Nonnberggasse 2, 5020 Salzburg, Austria (Nonnberg Abbey)

Denomination: Roman Catholic
Dates: St. Peter's - 696 (founded) & Nonnberg - c. 712 (founded)
Web: www.stift-stpeter.at & www.nonnberg.at (official websites)

St. Peter's Abbey and Nonnberg Abbey, both in Salzburg, are legacies of one of the oldest Christian communities north of the Alps. Both of these abbeys date from the early Middle Ages, and each is famous for very different reason. The former is the site of the tomb of St. Rupert, one of the most important Christian missionaries of the Middle Ages. The latter has become known worldwide thanks to one of the greatest musicals in Broadway history, *The Sound of Music*. Both abbeys are part of the Old Town of Salzburg UNESCO World Heritage Site.

The exact date of the arrival of the first Christian missionaries in Austria is unknown. It may have occurred as early as the 5th century. Early missionary activities notwithstanding, Salzburg did not become a major Christian center until the arrival of St. Rupert at the beginning of the 8th century. Rupert, who had already served as Bishop of the City of Worms, moved to the Danube region around 700 where he worked as a missionary for much of his life. He spent his last few years in Salzburg.

Among Rupert's legacies in Salzburg is the Abbey Church of St. Peter, which he founded soon after he came to the area. Although the original building is long gone, Rupert's tomb is still there. About a century later, the growing Christian population of Salzburg required more space, and the larger St. Michael's Church was built. St. Michael's served as the city's parish church for the better part of four centuries.

However, neither of these churches has achieved the level of international fame enjoyed by the Nonnberg Convent. Also founded by Rupert, Nonnberg is home to one of the oldest female monastic orders in Central Europe. But despite this distinction, more than worthy on its own merits, Nonnberg Convent is most famous for being the abbey where Maria von Trapp served as a novice in the early 20th century. For this reason Nonnberg is an incredibly popular tourist destination, visited and photographed by hundreds of thousands of Christian pilgrims and *Sound of Music* enthusiasts every year.

Of Interest: St. Peter's Abbey was founded by St. Rupert, but the current Baroque complex largely dates from the 17th century. Built close to the Monchsberg, the green copper domes of the church's bell towers stand out against the mountainside and the sea of white and yellow buildings of the town. St. Rupert is buried inside of the church near the main altar. Behind the abbey is St. Peter's Cemetery and the church catacombs, which were famously depicted as a hiding place for the Von Trapp family in the film. The Nonnberg Convent is located close to the heart of Salzburg, just down the hill from the Hohensalzburg Fortress. The immense white-brick, black-roofed complex largely dates from the abbey's reconstruction in the 15th century, though there are some remnants of earlier structures. The centerpiece of the abbey is the Church of St. Maria Himmelfahrt. A great time to visit the Nonnberg Convent is in May, especially for music lovers, when the resident nuns perform their famous Gregorian Chants in the evenings.

149. BERLIN CATHEDRAL

Am Lustgarten, 10178 Berlin, Germany

Alternate/Full Name: Supreme Parish and Collegiate Church
Denomination: United Protestant
Dates: 1451 (originally completed), 1905 (current building completed)
Web: www.berlinerdom.de (official website)

Berlin Cathedral is the great church of the city of Berlin. Constructed in the 20th century and substantially renovated following World War II, it is one of the youngest national churches in Europe. Thanks to its location on Museum Island and surrounding open spaces, it is also one of the most visually stunning national churches anywhere. It may also be the largest traditional church building used by mainline Protestants, excluding Anglicans and modern mega-churches, in the world.

Christianity in Germany has seen a tumultuous history since the first church was completed here nearly six centuries ago. The original church, built in 1451, was a Roman Catholic institution. Its replacement in 1538 was barely a year old when Lutherans took it over during the Protestant Reformation. In 1817, the congregation became a United church, made up of multiple Protestant groups.

Towards the end of the 19th century, as Germany reached the height of its colonial era power, the government sponsored the construction of a mammoth new cathedral, one that could rival St. Peter's Basilica in size and splendor. The current Berlin Dom was completed in 1905. The cathedral survived some of the worst ravages of World War II, though not completely. It was damaged both by Allied bombs and in street fighting. Some restoration work took place during the Communist era, but most of the cathedral wasn't fixed until the 1990s. It has since been restored to its original splendor.

Of Interest: Berlin Cathedral is the architectural jewel and Neo-Renaissance masterpiece of Germany's capital. Laid out in a nearly perfect square, its environs are graced by parks and the Spree River, allowing for unobstructed views of the cathedral in almost every direction. The main dome, which takes up the bulk of the roof, is one of the largest in Europe. Four smaller domes crown the corners. The church interior is as breathtaking as any Protestant church building anywhere. Few organs in the world can top the monstrously huge musical machine that fills the niche in the north wall. Tucked away beneath the cathedral is the Hohenzollern Crypt, where many members of the former Prussian royal family are buried.

---

150. ALL SAINTS CHURCH

Schlosspl 1, 06886 Lutherstadt Wittenberg, Germany

Alternate/Full Names: Reformation Memorial Church, Wittenberg Castle Church
Denomination: Lutheran (of interest to Protestants)
Dates: 1346 (originally completed),
1511 (current building completed)
Web: www.germany.travel/en/leisure-and-recreation/spiritual-travel/sights/all-saints-church-wittenberg (tourism website)

All Saint's Church is arguably the world's most important Protestant pilgrimage site. It was here in 1517 that Martin Luther nailed his famous 95 Theses to the door of the church, inadvertently kicking off the Protestant Reformation. Today the church and its famous Theses doors are revered by Protestants the world over. All Saint's Church is part of the Luther Memorials UNESCO World Heritage Site.

Discontent with the Catholic Church in Western and Northern Europe can be traced as far back to the 12th century. Growing anti-Catholic sentiment began to reach alarming levels throughout Europe by the beginning of the 16th century. In 1517 the dam finally burst when Martin Luther, an Augustinian monk, drew up one of the most important documents in history and posted it on the door of the Castle Church. These Ninety-Five Theses were a formal dissertation against the selling of indulgences and other practices, and within months copies were circulating throughout Europe.

After briefly ignoring Luther, the speed and scope with which his ideas spread shook the Church out of its complacency. He was denounced and branded as a heretic, but because he was supported by the powerful Frederick of Saxony, the Church could do little but meet him in debate. However, in 1519 Luther denounced the authority of the Pope outright and the Protestant Reformation was on. From the outset, Wittenberg was a major hotbed of Reformation activity. Oppressed Christians began finding their way to Wittenberg, including Lutherans, Hussites, Anabaptists and others.

After Luther's return to the city in 1522, the various groups were more or less consolidated under his leadership. The first Protestant hymnal was completed here in 1524. Luther continued his efforts until the end of his life in 1546. He was buried in the Castle Church. Interestingly, Wittenberg remained relatively undisturbed during the Thirty Years War, and other than a brief engagement with the Austrians in the 18th century and occupation by Napolean's forces in the early 19th century, Wittenberg has miraculously survived every major European conflict through the present. Today the Castle Church and other Luther monuments are among the most important Protestant pilgrimage sites in the world.

Of Interest: All Saints Church was actually a late addition to Wittenberg Castle. Both the original castle and church were damaged during the Seven Years War and restored in 1892, at which time one of the castle's towers was incorporated into the church as a bell-tower. The famous original wooden doors were replaced with bronze ones. In honor of Luther, the new doors were engraved with a copy of the Ninety-Five Theses. When the church was rebuilt, the interior was reconstructed along its original design. An ossuary topped with an engraved bronze plaque contains the remains of Martin Luther. Also entombed here is Philip Melancthion, Luther's associate. A glass case displays an early copy of the 95 Theses.

---

151. WITTENBERG TOWN CHURCH

Kirchplatz 12, 06886 Lutherstadt Wittenberg, Germany

Alternate/Full Name: Town and Parish Church of St. Mary's
Denomination: Lutheran (of interest to Protestants)
Dates: c. 12th century (originally completed),
1280 (current building completed)
Web: www.stadtkirchengemeinde-wittenberg.de (official website)

The Wittenberg Town Church is the city's second most historical church. Often confused with the All Saint's Church, the Town Church was not the site where Luther nailed his 95 Theses to the church door. However, both Luther and Melancthon preached here during the early years of the Reformation. As such most Lutheran pilgrims to Wittenberg stop here when visiting Wittenberg.

An earlier Town Church stood at city center at least as far back as the 12th century. The current building was constructed in stages beginning sometime in the late 13th century. The church briefly served in a military capacity during the Schmalkaldic War, an early conflict between the Catholics and Lutherans, when cannons were mounted on the bell towers.

After his return from exile, Martin Luther returned to Wittenberg and preached some of his most famous sermons here. The first Christian mass spoken in German rather than Latin was likely delivered here around this time. In the mid-16th century, the Town Church became a Lutheran congregation, with Johannes Bugenhagen as the world's first official Lutheran minister.

Of Interest: The Wittenberg Town Church is a towering structure which dominates the center of the city. Although still an active parish church, some of the interior is given over to exhibits on Luther and the Reformation. The altar piece features traditional Biblical artwork, as well as paintings depicting events related to the Reformation. Some of the church's artwork is controversial, a remnant of an earlier age when Anti-Semitism was prevalent in the region. It includes, among other things, of a depiction of Jews suckling from a pig. There is currently a debate as to whether or not this should be removed. However, in 1988, a plaque commemorating the Jews killed in the Holocaust was added to the site, somewhat offsetting the medieval message.

---

152. LUTHER HOUSE MUSEUM

Collegienstrasse 54, 06886 Lutherstadt Wittenberg, Germany

Denomination: Public Museum (of interest to Protestants)
Dates: 1505 (completed)
Web: https://lutherstadt-wittenberg.de/en/culture/unesco-weltkulturerbe/lutherhaus (tourism website)

The Luther House, the home of Luther in Wittenberg and the place where he probably drafted the 95 Theses, is one of the most visited sites in Wittenberg. Along with All Saint's Church and the Town Church, it is one of the buildings that define Wittenberg as the great pilgrimage city of Protestant Christianity. The house is now run as a museum which chronicles Luther's life and the Protestant Reformation.

The house is actually a large residence originally built for Augustinian monks studying and working at the University of Wittenberg. Luther first moved here as a student in 1507, and remained here until 1521 when he was forced to go into hiding. It was during this period that the famous 95 Theses were composed. After his return to Wittenberg in 1524, the entire building was granted to Luther by the local authorities. He lived there for the rest of his life.

A few years after his death, the residence hall was returned to the university. It subsequently had a long history of mixed uses, including as a hospital during the wars that wracked Germany in the early 19th century. The building was completely renovated in the 1850s, and converted to use as a museum in 1883. The Luther House was included in the Luther Memorial UNESCO World Heritage Site in 1996.

Of Interest: The Luther House, recently enlarged, is among the largest Reformation museums anywhere. A large part of the museum is devoted to the life of Martin Luther, and numerous artifacts associated with his life are on display here. There are also exhibits chronicling the events of the Reformation as well as Luther's family. A popular museum highlight is the former pulpit from the All Saints Church from which Luther once preached, now on display here.

---

153. WARTBURG CASTLE

Auf der Wartburg 1, 99817 Eisenach, Germany

Denomination: Public Site (of interest to Protestants)
Dates: c. 1080 (completed)
Web: www.wartburg.de (official website)

Wartburg Castle, located in the heart of modern Germany, was the secret refuge of Martin Luther during his time in hiding from the Church in 1521 and 1522. Luther, who was given sanctuary in the castle following the Diet of Worms, used his time here to translate the Bible into German. This in turn strengthened support for the Protestant Reformation. Wartburg Castle is one of Germany's most popular castles outside of the Rhineland and Bavaria.

Wartburg Castle was begun in the 11th century as a residence for the ruling nobles of Thuringia. As early as the 1200s, Wartburg seems to have had a knack for finding its way into the spotlight. In 1207 the semi-legendary Sangerkrieg, or minstrel's contest, took place here, featuring some of the most prominent musicians of the age. A few years later, Wartburg Castle was the residence of St. Elizabeth, a Hungarian princess who became famous for her charity.

Wartburg's moment in history began in 1521 following the Diet of Worms. After failing to persuade the Catholic Church of the necessity for reform, Martin Luther was excommunicated and branded a criminal by both the Church and the Emperor. Fortunately Luther had a strong supporter in Prince Frederick of Saxony, who took Martin Luther into custody and then hid him away in secret in Wartburg Castle under the pseudonym Junker Jorge.

Luther remained in Wartburg Castle for the better part of a year, from May 1521 until March 1522. He spent almost all of his time here translating the New Testament of the Bible into German. In the ensuing chaos of the Protestant Reformation, Wartburg was a point of contention between the Catholic and Lutheran forces all the way through the Thirty Years War. Wartburg Castle was named a UNESCO World Heritage Site in 1999.

Of Interest: Wartburg Castle was built in stages over the course of seven centuries. At first glance the castle, which includes several Romanesque buildings as well as the late medieval half-timbered Knight's house, is something of an architectural mish-mash. Because most of the buildings back up sharply against a steep hill, only part of the castle is enclosed by the outer wall. Immediately next to the main gate is the Knight's Building, which was used to house less important knights and occasionally prisoners. Behind that is the Bailiff's Lodge, where Martin Luther stayed hidden under the guise of Junker Jorge. His rooms have been partially preserved and are the historical highlight of the castle.

---

154. FULDA CATHEDRAL

Domplatz Fulda, 36037 Fulda, Germany

Alternate/Full Name: Cathedral of Sts. Salvator and Bonifatius
Denomination: Roman Catholic
Dates: c. 8th century (originally completed), 1712 (current building completed)
Web: www.gcatholic.org/churches/europe/3244 (Catholic website)

Fulda Cathedral is the church of one of the oldest Catholic communities in Germany, as well as the burial site of one of Germany's most revered saints, Boniface. The Roman Catholic Church had little or no formal presence east of the Rhine until the arrival of Boniface in the early 8th century. Boniface, sometimes called the Apostle to the Germans, established the Church in Frisia, Bavaria and in the Rhineland. Because of this the Fulda Cathedral is among the most historic churches in Central Europe.

Boniface was one of the last great Christian evangelists of the early Middle Ages. He was born in England around 672, when Danes, Angles and Saxons were struggling for control of the British Isles. His familiarity with these groups, their languages and customs made him a perfect missionary to spread Christianity to Germany. He began in Frisia in what is now the Netherlands, where he achieved notoriety for chopping down the Donnar Oak, a tree sacred to the pagan Germans.

Under the protection of the Frankish kings, Boniface spent his life traveling east of the Rhine, where he baptized countless new Christians and helped to reorganize existing Christian communities. At the age of 82 Boniface made his last missionary trip to Frisia. While there, he and his companions were assaulted and slain by brigands. As the story goes, when the assailants discovered no gold or treasure, they took out their anger on Boniface's books. One of these, the Ragyndrudis Codex, is now kept in Fulda, and still bears the scars left by the bandits' swords.

Boniface' death became a rallying event for the Christians of Germany. After being buried for a brief period in Frisia, his corpse was reinterred in the church of Fulda Monastery. Throughout the Middle Ages it was one of the great monastic centers of Germany, and it remained a popular pilgrimage destination for the better part of a thousand years. For many years one of the oldest churches in Germany, the monastery church was eventually replaced with the current cathedral. It remains to this day one of Germany's most important historic sites.

Of Interest: Fulda Cathedral occupies the same location that its predecessor, the Ratgar Basilica, had occupied since the 8th century. The current structure was built in the 1700s. A baroque masterpiece, it was built along similar lines to the then recently completed St. Peter's Basilica in Rome. Although damaged by fire in 1905 and air raid bombings during World War II, renovations in the 1950s have restored it to good condition. The cathedral's interior includes some oddities such as its unusual westward orientation and its decorative use of obelisks. The bodies of Sts. Boniface and Sturm are both interred in the crypt, as is that of King Conrad I of Germany, whose successors were later Holy Roman Emperors. Adjacent to the cathedral in the old abbey is a museum housing Christian artifacts, including the damaged copy of the Ragyndrudis Codex.

---

155. CHURCH OF OUR LADY (FRAUENKIRCHE) & ST. PETER'S CHURCH

Frauenplatz 12, 80331 Munich, Germany (Church of Our Lady)

Rindermarkt 1, 80331 Munich, Germany (St. Peter's Church)

Alternate/Full Names: Cathedral of Our Dear Lady
Denomination: Roman Catholic
Dates: Our Lady - c. 12th century (originally completed), 1488 (current building completed) & St. Peter's - c. 8th century (originally completed), 1368 (current building completed)
Web: www.muenchen.de/int/en/sights/churches (tourism website)

The Church of Our Lady, or Frauenkirche, and St. Peter's Church are the major Roman Catholic churches of Munich. The former is the archdiocesan seat of the Catholic Church in Munich, and is locally famous for the legend of the Devil's Footprint. The latter is the oldest surviving church in the city and the point from which Munich has spread outward. Together they are among the most visited churches in Bavaria.

It is not known exactly when Christianity reached Bavaria, though it is possible that the earliest Christian community here may date as far back as the Roman era. Although this is unlikely, there is evidence that a monastic community existed here as early as the 8th century. A church was built on or near the spot of the current St. Peter's Church around the time that Munich became a city in the 12th century. The Old Frauenkirche was also constructed at this time.

The monastery church was destroyed in a fire during the 14th century and was replaced by St. Peter's Church in 1368. A century later, as the city's population grew, a massive new cathedral was planned to replace the Old Frauenkirch. The New Frauenkirch was completed in what was then an impressive pace of twenty years. Both churches were instrumental in keeping Munich a Roman Catholic city during the Protestant Reformation and the Thirty Years War.

According to legend, the founding of the Church of Our Lady was associated with the Devil, who was tricked into financing its construction. A black mark on the floor near the entrance is said to be the Devil's footprint, which he left fuming in frustration when he could not enter the church after its consecration.

Of Interest: The Church of Our Lady is a Gothic masterpiece built of brick rather than stone. Much of the church was destroyed by bombing during World War II, and the current building largely dates from a post-war reconstruction. Its two huge bell towers crowned with onion domes are the most easily recognized landmarks in Munich. A massive tomb houses the body of the Holy Roman Emperor Louis IV. A dark mark on the floor by the main entrance, the so-called Devil's Footprint, is said to have been the spot where the devil looked into the church in anger upon its completion. St. Peter's Church is a towering structure of mixed architectural styles. It is less distinguished on the outside than the Frauenkirche, sporting a single bell and clock tower. However, the magnificent baroque interior boasts an absolutely stunning gold and marble altar that is accounted one of the finest in Germany.

---

156. KONSTANZ CATHEDRAL

Munsterplatz 1, 78462 Konstanz, Germany

Denomination: Roman Catholic (of interest to Protestants)
Dates: c. 7th century (originally completed), 1378 (current building completed)
Web: www.germany.travel/en/towns-cities-culture/towns-cities/constance (tourism website)

Konstanz Cathedral, home to one of the oldest Christian parishes north of the Alps, hosted one of the most important ecumenical councils in the history of the Roman Catholic Church. The Council of Konstanz took place here from 1414 to 1418 in order to address several major issues of the day. The foremost of these issues was what to do about the Hussites, who threatened the religious hegemony of the Church. Jan Hus, the leader of the movement, was condemned to death at the council.

There has been a Christian presence here possibly as far back as the 7th century. An early cathedral once stood here, but this collapsed and was replaced beginning in the 11th century. In the early 1400s, the Roman Catholic Church, rocked by war, schism and heresy, called an ecumenical council at Konstanz to debate the various issues. Among these was the resolution of the schism between Rome and Avignon, as well as the war then raging between the Kingdom of Poland and the Teutonic Knights.

But the biggest problem from the Church's standpoint, and one of the first to be dealt with, was the matter of Jan Hus. Hus, a clergyman from Prague who was openly critical of the Church, had begun to attract a large following which threatened the Papacy's religious and political power in Bohemia. In 1415, Hus was put on trial before the council, found guilty of heresy and executed. His remains were later scattered in the Rhine River.

Konstanz Cathedral remained the seat of the local bishopric until the early 19th century. While continuing to be a Catholic institution, the cathedral has become a pilgrimage destination of sorts for Protestants who come to honor Jan Hus' martyrdom. The Papacy declared the cathedral a Minor Basilica in 1955.

Of Interest: Konstanz Cathedral was among the largest churches in Germany at the time of its completion. It still impresses, and is especially noted for the unusual design of its facade. Relatively narrow but very tall, it almost looks though three square bell towers were placed side by side and then decorated with two additional decorative towers that bulge out from the façade flanking the single entrance. The whole is capped with a balcony and an odd spire. The church interior is a mix of architectural elements focused on a baroque influenced niche behind the main altar. A memorial stone to Jan Hus can be found on the outskirts of the city.

---

157. GUTENBERG MUSEUM

Liebfrauenplaz 5, 55116 Mainz, Germany

Denomination: Public Museum
Dates: 1900 (opened)
Web: www.gutenberg-museum.de (official website)

The Gutenberg Museum in Mainz commemorates Johannes Gutenberg, creator of the printing press in Europe, and the signature product of his career, the Gutenberg Bible. The Gutenberg Bible was the first significant multiple copy book ever printed, and was a major step in making the Holy Scriptures more easily available and affordable to everyday people. The press was also instrumental in helping to launch the Protestant Reformation in Germany and later across Europe.

Johannes Gutenberg was born in Mainz in 1400. A smith and businessman by trade, he conceived of the idea of a printing press sometime in the 1430s. By 1450 he had developed a working press. Among his first jobs was the printing of notices of indulgences for the Roman Catholic Church. In 1454 and 1455, Gutenberg embarked on a major project to demonstrate the true value of his printing press, and that was to create the first printed Bible. The production of a full Bible in a fraction of the time that a monk or scholar could copy one by hand caught on like wildfire, and the age of the printed word was begun.

Just a few decades later, the spread of printing presses across Europe combined with Renaissance thinking led to the rapid spread of new ideas across the continent. This led to an increase of voices speaking out against the Roman Catholic Church, and ultimately to the Protestant Reformation. In 1900, a museum was established in Mainz celebrating Gutenberg's work. The collection was kept safe from bombing during World War II and was moved to its current location in 1962.

Of Interest: The Gutenberg Museum is home to exhibits on the inventor's life as well as a replica of the studio where he first practiced the printer's trade. This includes a working model of the original

15th century printing press. There is also a collection of early printed documents and books, including two priceless copies of the famous Gutenberg Bibles.

---

158. REFORMATION MEMORIALS

Lutherring, 67547 Worms, Germany

Denomination: Public Monument (of interest to Protestants)
Dates: 1868 (opened)
Web: www.worms.de/en/tourismus/sehenswertes (tourism website)

The Reformation Memorials in the city of Worms commemorate Martin Luther's historic confrontation with the Roman Catholic Church in the 16th century. Two years after first professing his views in Wittenberg, Luther formally challenged the Papacy outright at the Diet of Worms. His defiance of the Pope and the Church officially marked the beginning of Protestant Christianity. Unfortunately, the palace where the Diet of Worms actually took place is long gone. However, Worms has made commemoration of the event a city-wide cottage industry.

Worms was one of the first cities of the Rhineland to be introduced to Christianity. Located in the heartlands of ancient Frankish territory, it was one of the most prominent cities of Charlemagne's Empire in the 9th century. During the early days of the Holy Roman Empire, Worms grew prosperous, and was eventually declared a crown city. As such, Worms was eligible to host the periodic Diets (assemblies of the Reichtag), which it did on a half-dozen occasions between the 9th and 16th centuries. Two of these meetings had profound religious repercussions for the Catholic Church.

At the first, in 1122, the Concordant of Worms was issued in which the Church relinquished the right to select its own bishops and abbots within most of the imperial territories. The second and more famous meeting took place in 1521, and is often referred to as *the* Diet of Worms. Here, from January to May, the great showdown between Martin Luther and the Roman Catholic Church took place. After Luther's issuance of the Ninety-Five Theses and Pope Leo Xs counter-issuance of the Exsurge Domine, Luther was summoned to the Diet of Worms to make his case. There, under the auspices of the Holy Roman Emperor, Martin Luther defended and reaffirmed his beliefs.

His trial was only one issue of business of the Diet, but it is without doubt the best remembered. In the end, Luther refused to amend or recant his beliefs and accusations, and the conclave found Luther guilty of heresy. The Edict of Worms, issued in May 1521, affirmed this decision and declared Luther a criminal. The extreme terms of the edict had the opposite effect of their original intent. Instead of intimidating people into returning to the Roman Catholic Church, the Diet actually accelerated the Reformation. Despite the loss of the debate, the Diet of Worms was an undeniable victory for the Protestants which would shake Europe to its foundations for the next three centuries.

Of Interest: Reformation Memorials can now be found throughout the city of Worms. Luther's hearings took place in the Bishop's Palace, but over the course of his four months of testimony he may have spoken at other locations. The city's Trinity Church was built on the site of the Old Town Hall where Luther first spoke in Worms. The early 18th century baroque church features a series of stained-glass windows showing scenes from Luther's trial. The Bishop's Palace where the Diet took place is unfortunately long gone. There is now a garden on the site of the hall where Luther's deposition and subsequent debates took place. A plaque marks the spot where it is believed that he stood when he officially rejected Papal authority. Nearby is the Luther Monument, an enormous outdoor series of statues and commemorative markers depicting the history of the Reformation.

159. COLOGNE CATHEDRAL

Domkloster 4, 50667 Cologne, Germany

Alternate/Full Name: Cathedral Church of St. Peter
Denomination: Roman Catholic (sacred to many Christians)
Dates: c. 9th century (originally completed), 1473 (current building completed)
Web: www.koelner-dom.de (official website)

Cologne Cathedral was one of the architectural wonders of the Middle Ages. From the time of its completion it was the largest church, and building, in the world, until it was surpassed by St. Peter's Basilica in Rome. For a time it was also the tallest man-made structure in the world. In addition to its mind-boggling dimensions, the cathedral is also known for what is within: the Shrine of the Three Kings, one of the oldest and most popular pilgrimage places in central Europe. The shrine, whose centerpiece may be the world's largest golden reliquary, supposedly contains the relics of the Three Wise Men who visited the infant Jesus at the time of his birth. To this day the cathedral is one of the most visited churches in Germany. Cologne Cathedral is a UNESCO World Heritage Site.

The history of Cologne Cathedral begins in the 1st century BC with the Biblical story of the Three Wise Men. These wise men are among the most enigmatic figures in the New Testament. An indelible part of the Nativity Story, virtually nothing is known about them, either of their identity or their homeland. Even the traditional names of the Three Wise Men, Caspar, Melchior and Balthasar, are based on later writings. There is certainly no information on where they were originally buried.

This did not seem to stop hordes of medieval Christians from visiting the relics. Helena, who 'discovered' them during her tour of the Holy Land, had them removed to the Hagia Sofia in Istanbul, where they remained for centuries before being relocated to Milan. Eventually they came into the possession of the Holy Roman Emperor Frederick I, who absconded with them as booty while fighting to expand imperial territory into Italy. They were given in turn to the Archbishop of Cologne, a favorite courtier of the emperor and an influential leader of the medieval Church.

In 1248 Cologne's Old Cathedral, which had been constructed four centuries earlier by the descendents of Charlemagne, was destroyed in a fire. It was decided that a new cathedral would be constructed on a massive and grandiose scale befitting the relics of the Three Wise Men. The new church was one of the largest building projects undertaken in the Middle Ages, and it was not completed for the better part of six centuries.

Despite the seemingly endless construction work, the Shrine of the Three Kings was up and running fairly early. During World War II the cathedral was badly damaged by Allied bombing. Fortunately repairs took only a decade, less than one-sixtieth of the time it took to build the cathedral. Cologne Cathedral is once again one of the architectural wonders of Germany, a great landmark overlooking the Rhine River and a must-see for visitors to Cologne.

Of Interest: Cologne Cathedral is a Gothic masterpiece akin to those constructed in Northern France in the Middle Ages. Among the more notable details are the flying buttresses used to support the cathedral's massive height. Most of the construction dates from the 13th, 14th and 15th centuries, though detail and repair work continued well into the 1800s. The dominant external features of the cathedral are the skyscraping twin spires which have dominated Cologne since the 19th century, and which for a few years made the cathedral the tallest man-made structure in the world. The dimensions of the interior of the cathedral are no less impressive, boasting one of the tallest vaults of any church in the world. The highlight of the church is the Shrine of the Three Kings. This giant golden tomb built for three is the largest Christian reliquary on Earth, impressive despite the questionability of those entombed inside.

160. AACHEN CATHEDRAL

Domhof 1, 52062 Aachen, Germany

Alternate/Full Name: Cathedral of Aix-la-Chapelle
Denomination: Roman Catholic
Dates: 805 (completed)
Web: www.aachenerdom.de (official website)

Aachen Cathedral, built by the Holy Roman Emperor Charlemagne, is the oldest surviving great cathedral in Northern Europe. Upon his death the emperor's body was interred within, along with some important religious and historic artifacts. Charlemagne was probably the most important Christian ruler of all time, and was instrumental in cementing the Catholic Church's hold on Europe for the better part of eight hundred years. Aachen Cathedral is a UNESCO World Heritage Site.

The Christian kings of the Franks began to take an interest in Aachen sometime in the 8th century. King Pippin spent the winter of 765 here, and Aachen was soon made part of the king's personal domains. His son Charlemagne also took a liking to the city, and in 768, shortly after assuming the throne, he decided to make the more centrally located Aachen his royal headquarters. Vast sums of wealth poured into Aachen from Charlemagne's conquests, and soon it was a thriving metropolis. The Palace Chapel, which was later redeveloped into the magnificent Aachen Cathedral, dates from this time.

During his reign, Charlemagne built the largest unified state that Western Europe had seen since the fall of Rome in 476. His military and political efforts on behalf of Pope Leo III resulted in a close relationship between the Franks and the Papacy. In an effort to preserve the friendship of the strongest state in Europe, establish a counterbalance to the Emperor in Constantinople and secure a strong ally against the Moors in Spain, Leo crowned Charlemagne Holy Roman Emperor on Christmas Day in 800. This event marked the beginning of the Holy Roman Empire.

Charlemagne strove to make Aachen, the empire's first capital, a major Christian religious center, and went about acquiring all sorts of relics and holy objects for the city. After his death, Charlemagne was buried here, and shortly thereafter Aachen's brief moment in history as the capital of Northern Europe came to an end. The empire was henceforth run from wherever the Emperor or Imperial Diet happened to be at the moment. However, Aachen's spiritual and symbolic importance remained central to the empire's religious traditions, and from 936 to 1531 every Holy Roman Emperor was crowned here.

Of Interest: Aachen Cathedral was originally the chapel of Charlemagne's palace. While the core of the original building is still intact, the church was vastly expanded in later years. Architecturally it is a pre-Gothic blend of Byzantine and early Germanic styles. The three major elements of the building include the Glass House, which features an immense amount of stained glass; the central dome; and the bell tower and spire. The interior of the church is highly decorative and extensively gilded. The chamber under the main dome borrows heavily from the earlier Byzantine themes and is dominated by a great golden chandelier. Charlemagne's body now rests within a gold and silver reliquary behind the main altar. Among the Cathedral's many other treasures are Charlemagne's Crown and the Cross of Lothair, the latter being a gold and silver plated wooden cross with an engraving of Christ.

---

161. CATHEDRAL OF TRIER & ST. MATTHIAS' ABBEY

Liebfrauenstrasse 12, 54290 Trier, Germany (Cathedral of Trier)

Matthiasstrasse 85, 54290 Trier, Germany (St. Matthias' Abbey)

Alternate/Full Name: High Cathedral of St. Peter in Trier
Denomination: Roman Catholic (sacred to many Christians)
Completed: Cathedral - c. 4th century (originally completed); 1270 (current building completed) & Abbey - c. 10th century (founded)
Web: www.dominformation.de & www.abteistmatthias.de (official websites)

The Cathedral of Trier and St. Matthias' Abbey are among the most ancient Christian pilgrimage destinations in Central Europe. The former was the first cathedral founded in Germany, and the latter is home to the relic of St. Matthias, the apostle who replaced Judas in the earliest days of the Church. For these reasons Trier was the most important Christian city in Germany in the early Middle Ages. The Cathedral of Trier is a UNESCO World Heritage Site.

Trier was the first Gallo-Roman city to be established in Germany. At the height of Roman imperial power, Trier was the largest and most important city on the German frontier. It eventually became capital of Gaul and an imperial residence. Constantine, the emperor who converted the empire to Christianity, resided in Trier for a time. It was under his direction that the first churches were constructed in the city.

After the legalization of Christianity in the 4th century, the Bishop Maximin of Trier wanted to firmly establish the influence of the Church in Germany, and set about the construction of a massive cathedral. In the last years of her life, Helena, mother of Constantine, supported Maximin's efforts, with both encouragement and with funds. She also gifted the new cathedral with the Seamless Robe of Jesus, which she 'discovered' and acquired while visiting the Holy Land.

Trier was a particularly busy Christian place in the late Roman and early Medieval eras. St. Ambrose was born here in the 4th century. Also around that time that the supposed remains of the Apostle Matthias were brought to the city. After the founding of the Holy Roman Empire, the authority of the city's bishops soared when Trier became an electoral seat and they became Prince-Archbishops. This designation survived a thousand years until finally dissolved in the 19th century. Throughout this period, both the cathedral and the abbey survived and thrived as pilgrimage destinations.

Of Interest: The Cathedral of Trier is one of the best surviving examples of early Romanesque architecture. The current building largely dates to the Middle Ages, although there are earlier elements. It is the third major church to stand on the spot, the earlier two having been destroyed by marauding Franks and Normans. It is for this reason that the cathedral has a fortress-like appearance. The interior is a mix of period styles. These range from the main chapel, which preserves some of the original 4th century structure, to the interior of the dome, which is a masterpiece of baroque-era relief work. The Seamless Robe of Jesus, which has somehow survived the centuries, is kept in its own chapel. St. Matthias' Abbey is a much more recent complex, having replaced a number of earlier structures. It houses a number of tombs and treasures. Foremost among those buried here is the Apostle Matthias. Others buried here are the city's early bishops Eucharus and Valerius. Also here is a Reliquary of the True Cross, a golden cross in which is set what is believed to be some of the splinters of the True Cross.

WESTERN EUROPE

---

162. ST. BAVO'S CATHEDRAL

Sint-Baafsplein, 9000 Ghent, Belgium

Denomination: Roman Catholic
Dates: 942 (originally completed), 1038 (current building completed)
Web: www.sintbaafskathedraal.be (official website)

St. Bavo's Cathedral in Ghent is one of Belgium's best known churches thanks to its possession of one of the finest pieces of religious art in Northern Europe: The Ghent alter piece. This absolutely breath-taking series of painted panels, officially known as the *Adoration of the Mystic Lamb*, was already famous before it was the subject of the highly acclaimed film, *The Monuments Men*. The cathedral is a popular destination for both religious pilgrims and artists.

The first church here was established in the 10th century. It grew in stages over the next six hundred years into the present building. Holy Roman Emperor Charles V was baptized here in 1500. St. Bavo's was designated as a cathedral and the seat of the Diocese of Ghent in 1559.

Sometime in the 1420s, brothers Jan van Eyck and Hubert van Eyck were commissioned to create an altarpiece for the church. The resultant twelve-panel product, which features both Biblical and historical scenes, is considered to be Jan van Eyck's masterpiece and one of the greatest artistic achievements of the Renaissance in Northern Europe.

In the 19th and 20th centuries, the Ghent alter piece became the focus of an international tug-of-war, with possession changing hands between several countries. It was seized outright by the Nazis in 1942 and hidden away. Its recovery was made famous by Hollywood in the 2014 film *The Monuments Men*. It has since been mostly recovered, though part of it is still missing, and is kept once again in Ghent.

Of Interest: St. Bavo's Cathedral is a towering Gothic structure with earlier Romanesque elements still evident. The main attraction is the Ghent Altarpiece. It features a number of major Biblical images, but at its center is the stunningly detailed *Adoration of the Mystic Lamb*, showing a crowd gathered to worship the Holy Spirit. The church is also home to a number of other great pieces of religious artwork, notably Peter Paul Rubens' *St. Bavo enters the Convent at Ghent.*

---

163. OLD CHURCH & NEW CHURCH

Oudekerksplein 23, Amsterdam, Netherlands, 1012 (Old Church)

Gravenstraat 17, Amsterdam, Netherlands, 1012 (New Church)

Denomination: Formerly Dutch Reformed & Protestant Church in the Netherlands
Dates: Old Church - 1213 (originally completed), 1306 (current building completed) & New Church - 1408 (completed)
Web: https://oudekerk.nl & www.nieuwekerke.nl (official websites)

The Old Church and New Church of Amsterdam are the city's two most historic churches. Both originally constructed as Catholic churches, the latter was built when the parish grew too large to be accommodated by the former. Both churches were also important centers of the Dutch Reform movement in the early years of the Protestant Reformation in the Netherlands.

Amsterdam's earliest church was a wooden chapel that was constructed in the 13th century. It was later replaced by what is now known as the Old Church. The Old Church served as a Catholic parish church until the late 16th century, when it came under the control of local Protestants and became part of the Dutch Reform Church. Rembrandt was a member of this church, and his wife was buried here.

The history of the New Church is something of an extension of that of the Old Church. It too was repurposed for use by the Calvinists, and eventually became the seat of the Dutch Reform Church worldwide.

It also later became the young nation's de facto royal chapel. Although no longer in active service for religious purposes, the New Church is still used as a concert venue and on rare occasions for royal events. In 2013 it was used for the coronation of the current monarch.

Of Interest: The Old Church is the oldest surviving building in Amsterdam and stands at the center of the old city in the famous red light district. Structurally it is famous for having the largest surviving medieval church ceiling. The floor is lined with gravestones, under which are buried thousands of Amsterdam's citizens. A small shrine to Rembrandt's wife can be found in the church. The New Church was damaged or destroyed by fires on several occasions, with the current building dating largely from the 17th century. There are several prominent burials in New Church, notably that of Michiel de Ruyter, Netherland's national naval hero.

---

164. CHURCH OF OUR LORD IN THE ATTIC

Oudezijds Voorburgwal 40, Amsterdam, Netherlands, 1012 GE

Denomination: Formerly Roman Catholic
Dates: 1663 (completed)
Web: www.opsolder.nl (official website)

The Church of Our Lord in the Attic is arguably the most famous surviving example of the many clandestine Catholic churches that were erected throughout Northern Europe during a time when Christians were at each other's throats. Formerly a Roman Catholic church, it is no longer in active use. It is currently maintained as the Roman Catholic Museum, one of the oldest museums in Amsterdam.

Holland, now known as the Netherlands, was at center stage during the early years of the Wars of Religion in the 16th and 17th centuries. For long a possession of the Hapsburg Empire, the Dutch provinces in the north stood at the crossroads of Catholic and Protestant Europe. The Dutch revolt, which pitted rebellious Protestants against the

Catholic establishment, was one of the early clashes of the Wars of Religion.

In the aftermath of the Dutch Revolt, the Netherlands found itself an independent nation, with large numbers of Catholics and Protestants. Instead of devolving into another round of bloodshed, the practical Dutch instead initiated what was effectively the first laws permitting freedom of religion in Europe. Although those who were not members of the Dutch Reformed Church were forced to practice their faith in private, the Netherlands otherwise became a haven for many faiths.

This was especially true in wealthy and progressive Amsterdam, which was home to a large Catholic population. While they were allowed to continue practicing their faith, the Catholics were forced to conform to religious ordinances; specifically that they remain out of sight. The Dutch Catholics responded by building clandestine churches throughout the city. The most famous of these was the Church of Our Lord in the Attic.

Our Lord in the Attic was originally constructed as a canal house in the early 17th century. During the 1660s, the top three floors were converted into a Catholic church. By the 19th century all religions were allowed to practice openly. A massive new cathedral was constructed in the heart of the city, and the Church of Our Lord in the Attic was decommissioned. In 1888 it was restored for use as a museum and is now a popular city historic site.

Of Interest: The Church of Our Lord in the Attic was designed to avoid undo attention. The building was originally constructed as a canal house. It maintains its original exterior construction: a narrow, six-story, gray brick structure elegantly trimmed in white. To the average passerby it is indistinguishable from the other houses in the neighborhood. The interior is another matter entirely. Taking up the entire three top floors of the building, the small space is a model of architectural efficiency. Two beautiful wooden balconies which run the length of the church help to make up for the minimal seating available on the main floor. Several prominent 17th century Flemish artists contributed to the décor of the church. The church and its ancillary rooms now house a museum with exhibits related to the history of the building and the community that once covertly worshipped here.

165. ST. PETER'S CHURCH

Pieterskerkhof 1A, Leiden, Netherlands, 2311 SP

Denomination: Formerly Dutch Reformed (of interest to Protestants)
Dates: c. 11th century (originally completed), 1570 (current building completed)
Web: www.pieterskerk.com (official website)

St. Peter's Church in Leiden is a late medieval building that served first the Roman Catholic Church and later a variety of Protestant groups. It is one of the most important churches in American history that virtually no American has ever heard of. It was to here in the 17th century that a group of Separatist Protestants fled from England and settled for a time before making the journey to the New World. For that brief period, St. Peter's was home to the Pilgrim Fathers of later Mayflower fame.

There has been a church on the current site of St. Peter's since the 11th century. The current church was Roman Catholic until the Reformation reached the Netherlands. By the early 17th century St. Peter's was largely in use by Reform Christians, including a group from England called the Separatists. The Separatists were generally Calvinist in outlook, but unlike the English Puritans refused to be a part of the state Anglican Church. Fleeing England, they lived in safety in Leiden for a few years, under the leadership of their pastor John Robinson.

The Separatists remained here until 1618, when it was decided to return to England before attempting the dangerous voyage across the Atlantic to the New World. John Robinson and several other members of the congregation remained behind in Leiden with the intention of eventually following their brethren. Many of these did eventually reach Plymouth, but Robinson died in 1625 and was buried in Leiden. St. Peter's remained part of the Dutch Reform Church until becoming inactive in 1971.

Of Interest: St. Peter's Church is a Gothic structure in red brick that is more reminiscent of a school building than a church. This is perhaps due to the extreme width of the façade, replete with immense windows, and the lack of a tower, which collapsed in the 16th century and was never repaired. The interior of the church is known for its forest of white columns that support the main sanctuary. A large plaque on the side of the church commemorates John Robinson and the Pilgrim Fathers. Robinson is buried on the church grounds.

---

166. ST. PIERRE CATHEDRAL

Place du Bourg-de-Four 24, 1204 Geneva, Switzerland

Denomination: Federation of Swiss Protestant Churches (of interest Protestants)
Dates: c. 4th century (originally completed), c. 12th century (current building completed)
Web: www.saintpierre-geneve.ch (official website)

St. Pierre Cathedral in Geneva was one of the most important churches to be associated with the early Reformation. It was here that John Calvin took up the banner of the Reformation as one of the most influential Protestant leaders. His home and church in Geneva became an important gathering center for many Protestants groups. The Cathedral and the nearby King's Cemetery where John Calvin is buried are now among the most popular Protestant pilgrimage destinations in Central Europe.

John Calvin was born less than a decade before Martin Luther posted the Ninety-Five Thesis, and by the time he received his doctorate degree in 1532 the Protestant Reformation was already well underway. Swept up in the anti-Catholic fervor of the time, Calvin found himself on the Protestant side of the religious debate then raging throughout Europe. In 1536 he relocated to the increasingly pro-Reform city of Geneva, where he remained for most of the rest of his life.

After settling down in Geneva, he began to organize his religious ideas along slightly different lines than the Lutherans. Among the major differences was a greater emphasis on humanism as well as a belief in predestination. By the 1550's Calvin's following had grown large enough to become a separate and distinct entity from the Lutherans. John Calvin spent the remainder of his life securing Western Switzerland for Protestantism. It became a haven for foreigners who fled their homelands during the Reformation, including such luminaries as John Knox.

During Calvin's lifetime, Geneva came to be known as the Protestant Rome. In 1539 Calvin married, putting an end forever to his priesthood and finalizing his separation from the Roman Catholic Church. He died in 1564. After his death, Geneva expanded its role as a Protestant stronghold. Today the city is renowned as a bastion of peace and neutrality. Some locals claim that this is due in large part to their Calvinist heritage. Geneva certainly boasts its share of major religious organizations, and is home to the World Council of Churches. The tradition of Calvin remains a treasured part of the city's heritage, and his church is the most revered Protestant place in Switzerland.

Of Interest: St. Pierre Cathedral was constructed in the 12th century as the parish church of the city of Geneva. It was appropriated by the Protestants shortly before Calvin arrived, and later rededicated for use by the Reformed Church of Switzerland. The main building was constructed during successive periods which included several post-Calvin remodelings. It now features a mix of Gothic, Romanesque and Classical designs. The interior of the church houses a number of historical treasures, including the excavated remains of a 4th century basilica and John Calvin's favorite chair. Nearby is the King's Cemetery, where John Calvin was interred at the time of his death. Although he wished to be buried anonymously, his gravesite is marked with a simple stone that reads his initials, J.C.

167. CALVIN AUDITORY & COLLEGE CALVIN

Place de la Taconnerie 1, 1204, Geneva, Switzerland (Calvin Auditory)

Rue Theodore De-Beze 2-4, 1204 Geneva, Switzerland (College Calvin)

Alternate/Full Name: Calvin Auditorium, Notre Dame la Neuve Chapel & College of Geneva
Denomination: Formerly Calvinist Reformed (of interest to Protestants)
Dates: Auditory - c. 5th century (originally completed), c. 15th century (current building completed) & College - 1428 (originally completed), 1559 (current building completed)
Web: https://geneve.com/en/attractions/calvin-auditory (tourism website)

The Calvin Auditory was the forum where John Calvin did much of his public speaking. A popular location for Protestant clergyman of the time, many leading Reformers including Theodore Beza and John Knox lectured here as well. The College Calvin is one of the oldest schools in Geneva and one of John Calvin's most enduring legacies in the city. Originally founded in the 15th century, it was supported by the Reformers in order to make education available for free to the poor of Geneva.

The Chapel of Notre-Dame-La-Neuve was built in the 15th century on the site of a previous church that may have dated back to Roman times. In the 1530s, as Geneva abandoned Catholicism outright in favor of the Reformation, the chapel was repurposed as a Reformist lecture hall.

In the ensuing decades the auditory became a forum for speeches and debates on the Reform movement, with leaders from all over Western Europe attending to hear Calvin preach. In the 1550s, John Knox, the Reformer from Scotland, was a regular lecturer here. In 1559, when Calvin founded the University of Geneva, the auditory temporarily served as the college's first lecture hall. It continued to be used by Reformers for many years, and still hosts worship services.

In 1536, obligatory and free education became a law in Geneva. For many residents this was the first time that their children had ever had the opportunity to attend school. In 1559, John Calvin oversaw the conversion of a former convent school into the College of Geneva. The College of Geneva went on to serve as a public institution for the education of older youths. In 1969, it was renamed the College Calvin in honor of its founder. It continues to serve the city as a post-obligatory secondary education school.

Of Interest: The Calvin Auditory is a 15th century Gothic building which formerly served as the chapel of the city's cathedral. The interior is extremely simple, befitting the Reform aversion to extravagant and distracting trappings. The building was fully restored in the 1950s and is still used for worship. The College Calvin is a beautiful complex of buildings constructed in stages between the 16th and 20th centuries. It remains in use as a public school.

---

168. REFORMATION WALL

Prom. des Bastions 1, 1204 Geneva, Switzerland

Alternate/Full Name: International Monument to the Reformation
Denomination: Public Monument (of interest to Protestants)
Dates: 1909 (completed)
Web: www.geneve.com/en/see-do/500th-anniversary-of-the-reformation (tourism website)

The Reformation Wall of Geneva is one of preeminent European monuments commemorating the Protestant Reformation. Founded on the 400th anniversary of the birth of John Calvin, it honors many of the leaders of the Protestant Reformation that grew out of the Calvinist tradition throughout Western Europe. Part of the campus of the University of Geneva, the Reformation Wall is one of the city's most historic sites.

No other city in the world, except perhaps Wittenberg in Germany, has a more enduring legacy where the Protestant Reformation is concerned than Geneva. Home to John Calvin and a refuge for many early Protestant leaders, Geneva was the center from which the Reformation spread to France, the Low Countries, and to a lesser extent England. The city later went on to host some of the world's most important Protestant organizations, including the World Council of Churches.

In 1909, the city decided to establish a memorial to the early Reformers. A competition was held, with the winning design being awarded to a team of Swiss architects and French artists. Officially known as International Monument to the Reformation, the memorial was completed a few years later. It is probably the best known and most visited of such memorials in Europe.

Of Interest: The Reformation Wall is actually built out of a remnant of Geneva's old city walls. It combines a series of statues and engravings, honoring the early Reformers and their ideas. There are ten Reformers in total depicted: In the center are John Calvin, Theodore Beza, William Farel and John Knox. They are flanked by three others on each side, including the English leader Oliver Cromwell and Roger Williams of Colonial American fame.

---

169. GREAT MINSTER (GROSSMUNSTER)

Grossmunsterplatz, 8001 Zurich, Switzerland

Denomination: Federation of Swiss Protestant Churches
Dates: c. 9th century (originally completed), 1220 (current building completed)
Web: www.grossmuenster.ch (official website)

The Great Minster, or Grossmunster, of Zurich is closely associated with Uldrich Zwingli, a prominent early Reformer who established Protestantism throughout much of Switzerland a few decades before

John Calvin showed up. Zwingli's legacy is tied to the Grossmunster where he preached his fiery sermons and where he was later buried after being killed in battle with the Catholics. Along with the St. Pierre Cathedral in Geneva it is one of Switzerland's most important Protestant heritage sites.

Uldrich Zwingli was a contemporary of Martin Luther and a predecessor of John Calvin. Like Luther he was highly educated and had trained for a life in the Church. He became a minister in 1506, and served in that capacity for twelve years, including as a chaplain to Swiss mercenaries. In 1518 he became the priest of the Grossmunster at which time he began having serious doubts about Catholicism.

Zwingli's transformation into a Reformer was profound and dramatic. By 1520 he had openly challenged the practice of indulgences and the use of mercenaries. A fiery and popular preacher, Zwingli convinced the majority of Zurich's citizenry to follow him. By 1523, the Reformation was in full swing in Zurich. In later years a historic meeting between Zwingli and Luther took place in which a universal Protestant reconciliation was attempted, though unsuccessfully.

In 1525 the Christians of Zurich broke with the Catholic Church outright. Many other Swiss towns and cities soon followed. In October 1531, war finally broke out between Switzerland's Catholic and Protestant cantons. A surprise assault on Zurich led to a devastating defeat for the Protestants. Uldrich Zwingli fell at the forefront of the fighting. His followers never truly recovered from the blow, and though they survived for many centuries, they never again played as prominent a role in Protestantism as the Lutherans.

A few years after Zwingli's defeat, the center of Swiss Protestant activity moved to Geneva, where it was reorganized by John Calvin. However, the former followers of Uldrich Zwingli continued to honor his contribution to the Reformation. The Grossmunster where Zwingli preached and was later buried was eventually appropriated by the Swiss Reformed Church. The Great Minster is still revered as one of the most important sites of the early Protestant movement.

Of Interest: The Grossmunster of Zurich was built in the 12th and 13th centuries. An earlier church that had once stood on the spot was founded by the Holy Roman Emperor Charlemagne. Originally a monastery church, it was relieved of its monks and Catholic clergyman during the early years of the Reformation. The church itself is the size of a small cathedral, with a compact rectangular layout and twin bell-towers crowned with domed steeples that were completed almost three centuries later. The church interior was largely stripped bare of decoration by Zwingli's followers. The Grossmunster did retain possession of a few of its treasures, however, including what is believed to be the Sword of Charlemagne. A Bible that once belonged to Uldrich Zwingli is on display as well. His tomb lies beneath the sanctuary.

---

170. CATHEDRAL OF OUR LADY OF PARIS (NOTRE DAME)

6 Parvis Notre Dame Pl, Jean Paul II, 75004 Paris, France

Denomination: Roman Catholic
Dates: c. 4th century (originally completed), 1345 (current building completed)
Web: www.notredamedeparis.fr (official website)

The Cathedral of Notre Dame de Paris is one of the most storied and famous cathedrals in history. This is due in no small part to Victor Hugo, who immortalized the edifice in his book *The Hunchback of Notre Dame*. Because of this, and because of its convenient location in the heart of Paris, millions of tourists flock to Notre Dame every year. Most visitors to the cathedral are so enthralled by the famous stained-glass windows and the legions of guardian gargoyles that few are aware that Notre Dame is home to one of Christianity's most famous artifacts: a piece of the Crown of Thorns, which is on display only a few days every year. The Cathedral de Notre Dame is part of the Banks of the Seine UNESCO World Heritage Site.

Paris was home to one of the first major cathedrals in France, St. Stephen's, which served as the de facto royal chapel in the early days of the Frankish kingdom and the Merovingian dynasty. By the middle of the 12th century, France had become one of the largest and most powerful Christian kingdoms in Europe. In 1160, the city's bishop,

Maurice de Sully, decided that a new cathedral was needed, and the old one was demolished. So grand were the plans for the new cathedral that the Pope himself came from Rome to witness the placement of the foundation stone.

The building of Notre Dame, one of the largest cathedrals yet constructed, was a marvel of engineering. The bulk of the structure was completed in under a century, practically a record for the Middle Ages. It included many new elements that later came to define Gothic architecture. By the time of its completion in the mid-14th century, the cathedral had already witnessed several major events, including the first meeting of the Estates General, the launching of the Third Crusade and a number of royal coronations.

Notre Dame was a major center of French religious life in the late Middle Ages. As a bastion of Catholicism and of the status quo, Notre Dame de Paris was often a target of vengeful enemies, including the Hugenots in the 16th century and Revolutionaries in the 18th century. On both occasions the cathedral was vandalized. By the 19th century the cathedral was in an advanced state of disrepair.

In 1804 the Pope came to Notre Dame to crown Napolean Bonaparte as the Emperor of France. This momentous event notwithstanding, Notre Dame was quickly fading into historical and architectural obsolescence. Everything changed in 1831, when Victor Hugo published *The Hunchback of Notre Dame*. In the wake of this tremendously successful book, the people of Paris took a renewed interest in the cathedral as a beloved symbol of their city, and a massive restoration effort ensued. It has been one of Europe's top tourism draws for the better part of the last century.

Of Interest: The Cathedral of Notre Dame stands at the heart of the city of Paris. It dominates the Ile de la Cite, the island in the Seine which was where the ancient city was founded. The twin bell towers which flank the cathedral's façade are its most recognizable features and, thanks to Hugo's novel, are famous both for its massive bells and their fictional hunchbacked bell ringer. The exterior is also famous for its flying buttresses which, though not a new idea at the time, were constructed on a size and scale unparalleled at the time. And of course there are the cathedral's memorable guardian gargoyles. The interior of Notre Dame is a classic if dark Gothic masterpiece. The most famous features are the Rose Windows, accounted some of the finest stained glass in the world. The cathedral's primary bell, Emanuelle, is located in the south tower, while the four smaller Marie bells are located in the north tower. The Crown of Thorns is kept in storage except for a few Fridays every year when it is on public display. (Note - In April 2019, just before this book went to press, a massive fire destroyed the roof of the cathedral and collapsed the spire, and also badly damaged much of the interior as well; repairs are already underway and anticipated to be completed in 2024)

---

171. BASILICA OF ST. DENIS

1 Rue de Legion d'Honneur, 93200 Saint-Denis, France

Denomination: Roman Catholic
Dates: c. 7th century (originally completed),
1144 (current building completed)
Web: www.saint-denis-basilique.fr (official website)

The Basilica of St. Denis is one of the great, if less well known, churches of Paris. Originally part of an abbey complex, the basilica was the burial site of St. Denis, the first bishop of Paris. It later became the burial site of many French rulers. The oldest monarch buried here is Clovis I, an early king of the Merovingian dynasty, and who is considered to have been the first true Catholic king in Europe. Architecturally the basilica is noteworthy as being one of the earliest Gothic churches.

Christianity arrived in Paris sometime around the early 3rd century. Denis, the city's first bishop, was martyred by beheading. However, the city became much more open to Christianity following the arrival of the Franks in Gaul in the latter half of the 5th century. Clovis, the leader of the Franks, embraced Christianity, or more specifically Catholicism, the first major monarch in Europe to do so.

The mutual recognition of Clovis' dynasty in France and the religious authority of the Papacy established the Church as the arbiter of Europe's monarchs for the next thousand years. Clovis' kingdom represented a return to normalcy in Western Europe for the first time in the better part of a century. Clovis was arguably the most important Christian ruler in Western Europe between Constantine and Charlemagne. After his death, he was buried in the Abbey of St. Genevieve in Paris. During the 18th and 19th centuries, the abbey was massively renovated, and Clovis' remains were relocated here.

There has been a church on the site of the basilica since the 7th century. The current building largely dates from the early 12th century. After its reconstruction, virtually every monarch was buried there, and many of the earlier kings were reinterred there. During the French Revolution, all of the bodies were removed, dumped in a pit, and desecrated. Later, those parts that survived were reinterred in a common ossuary. Long neglected, the Basilica of St. Denis has been recently restored and is beginning to recapture the interest of pilgrims and tourists.

Of Interest: The Basilica of St. Denis was essentially completed in 1144. Many students of architecture consider this cathedral as one of the prototype Gothic churches that would be constructed throughout Western Europe in the later Middle Ages. Definitive exterior elements include the single bell tower on the right side of the façade and a massive, stained-glass rose windows over the transepts. The basilica's main draw is the impressive number of stunning tombs and reliquaries which are scattered around and beneath the building. Although now mostly empty, these sepulchers once contained the bodies of nearly a hundred French monarchs and aristocrats. A flattering but unlikely effigy lies upon the sarcophagus of Clovis I. Among the other tombs here are those of Saints Denis and Louis IX; Louis XIV (the Sun King); Catherine de Medici and Marie Antoinette.

172. STRASBOURG CATHEDRAL

Place de la Cathedrale, 67000 Strasbourg, France, 67000

Alternate/Full Name: Cathedral of Our Lady of Strasbourg, Strasbourg Minster
Denomination: Roman Catholic
Dates: c. 4th century (originally completed), 1439 (current building completed)
Web: www.cathedrale-strasbourg.fr (official website)

Strasbourg Cathedral is one of the greatest medieval cathedrals to be found north of the Alps. An absolute behemoth of a building, it was the world's tallest man-made structure for a while, and remains to this day among the tallest churches in the world. According to tradition, Strasbourg Cathedral was the site of the first Christmas tree.

The city of Strasbourg has a Christian community which dates back to the Roman era. The site where the cathedral now stands was occupied by earlier Christian structures at least as far back as the 4th century. The current building dates from the later Middle Ages and was completed in 1439. Over the course of centuries the city and its cathedral have witnessed a succession of numerous rulers and faiths.

In 1524, the cathedral was swept up in the Reformation and became a Protestant building. It reverted to Catholicism in 1681. Both Louis XIV the Sun King and Adolph Hitler are among those who have strode into the cathedral as conquerors. In 1539, during one of the cathedral's quieter famous moments, a decorated Christmas tree was erected inside the sanctuary. It is credited with being the world's first such holiday tree.

In the years following the French Revolution, the cathedral was repurposed for a time as a Temple of Reason. Although damaged by bombing, the cathedral survived the ravages of World War II largely intact. The stained glass windows were preserved in underground storage during the conflict. The cathedral has since welcomed a visit by a pope and survived a bomb plot. Along with Cologne Cathedral it is one of the two best known and most visited churches along the Rhine River.

Of Interest: Strasbourg Cathedral is the architectural centerpiece of the city of Strasbourg, now one of the capitals of the European Union. Its 142 meter tall bell tower can be seen for miles in every direction. The absolutely humongous façade is on par with that of Cologne Cathedral and is among the largest anywhere. Although many of the original interior decorations were destroyed or removed following the Protestant Reformation, the building has since been restored. Treasures of the cathedral include spectacular tapestries and stained glass windows, as well as an astronomical clock that dates from the 19th century.

---

173. BASILICA OF SAINT-PIERRE-AUX-NONNAINS

1 Rue de la Citadelle, 57000 Metz, France, 57000

Denomination: Formerly Roman Catholic
Dates: c. 4th century (completed as a Roman school); c 7th century (consecrated as a church)
Web: www.tourisme-metz.com/en/must-see-sights-and-activities (tourism website)

The Basilica of Saint-Pierre-Aux-Nonnains is one of the oldest surviving buildings in France. A fully intact Roman-era building, the basilica has served as a spa, a Benedictine chapel, a royal mausoleum, a church, a warehouse and a concert hall. It is also regarded by some as the birthplace of Christian, and by extension Western, music. The basilica has survived the ravages of dozens of major wars, from the Germanic invasions of the 5th century to the World Wars of the 20th century.

The Basilica of Saint-Pierre-Aux-Nonnains was not originally constructed for use as a church. Erected sometime in the 4th century, it was part of a Roman-era spa when Divodurum, the former name of Metz, was a major military and trade center along the Germanic frontier. It was one of the few buildings in the city to remain standing after the Huns passed through in the year 451. Metz was an important cradle of Frankish civilization. After the conversion of Clovis I to Catholicism, Metz became a Christian stronghold. During the 7th century, the old Roman gymnasium was converted to use as a Benedictine church.

Charlemagne was apparently fond of the old church, and two of his sons were buried there. Around the same time the basilica played an interesting role in European music. According to tradition, Charlemagne desired to promote the preservation of music by devising a way to commit music to a written form. The task fell to musicians in Metz, under the direction and patronage of the Church. Some of the earliest, if not *the* earliest, codified music in Europe was produced here at the basilica.

Amazingly, the original Roman structure remained essentially intact throughout the Middle Ages. Apparently by the 16th century the old edifice was showing its age, and the Church moved out. It then spent over 400 years in service as a warehouse. Thankfully, its historical importance was recognized in the 1970s and the basilica was restored. It is now used primarily as a concert hall, a fitting tribute to its medieval musical heritage.

Of Interest: The Basilica of Saint-Pierre-Aux-Nonnains is one of the greatest surviving examples of late Roman architecture anywhere. The building is essentially intact, and the exterior appears much today as it did nearly 1,600 years ago. It consists of a typical Roman basilica layout, with a long main building approximately four stories tall with a peaked roof. Remains of additional Roman- and Medieval-era structures surround the church, including a colonnade from the church's Benedictine period. The interior is much less Roman in appearance than the exterior, as the whole place was renovated in the 10th century, and again in the 20th century. While still designated as a Basilica by the Roman Catholic Church, the building's use nowadays is for primarily for musical functions and exhibitions.

174. VEZELAY ABBEY

Rue du Chapitre, 89450 Vezelay, France

Alternate/Full Names: Abbey of St. Mary Magdalene de Vezelay
Denomination: Roman Catholic
Dates: c. 8th century (originally completed), 1104 (current building completed)
Web: www.thevezelaybasilica.e-monsite.com (official website)

Vezelay Abbey is one of several churches in France that lay claim to the relic of Mary Magdalene. Exactly how this relic found its way to Vezelay in France is not certain. Nevertheless popular opinion supports the Vezelay tradition, which seems to be unofficially recognized by the Roman Catholic Church. In light of the recent fascination with Mary Magdalene in popular culture, Vezelay is again becoming a popular pilgrimage destination. Vezelay Abbey, where the Basilica of St. Mary Magdalene is located, is a UNESCO World Heritage Site.

The story of Mary Magdalene is one of the most controversial in Christian tradition. Some Biblical scholars believe that most of the various women named Mary mentioned in the Bible, other than Jesus' mother, are all one and the same with Mary Magdalene, while others believe that she may have been as many as three separate people. Moreover, the exact nature of her personal relationship to Jesus has been a topic of great interest in recent years

Whatever the truth is, it is clear that Mary Magdalene was a critically important follower of Jesus of Nazareth. She was with him when he was crucified, and it was to her that He first revealed Himself after the Resurrection. Virtually nothing is known of her later life or death. According to one tradition, her relics were brought to Constantinople at the end of the 9th century. The more popular story supported by the Catholics is that she traveled to France after the Ascension, eventually settling in either Marseilles or Vezelay.

Sometime around the middle of the 11th century, monks visiting St. Maximin's Church in Provence discovered a sarcophagus with markings suggesting the occupant was Mary Magdalene. Overjoyed at the 'proof' that Mary Magdalene had indeed been in France a thousand years earlier, the relics were transferred back to their abbey at Vezelay. The region of Provence was soon dotted with churches and shrines in Mary Magdalene's honor.

Vezelay subsequently became one of the preeminent Christian shrines in medieval France. It was here that Bernard of Clairvaux called for a Second Crusade against the Saracens in 1146. It was also home for a time to Thomas Becket during his exile from England. Over time, Vezelay's claim to Mary Magdalene was challenged. Rival St. Maximin discovered the 'true' tomb still within its walls towards the end of the 13th century in an attempt to reestablish its own claim. But it is Vezelay Abbey which is generally recognized and revered as the site of the Magdalene's burial.

Of Interest: Vezelay Abbey is built on the site of several earlier churches which had been sacked on at least two occasions, first by the Moors and than by the Normans. The current structure was built by Benedictine monks. The church exterior is a Romanesque structure that was badly damaged during the French Revolution. It underwent a substantial restoration in the mid-19th century. The façade is crowned by a bell tower over the right portals. The interior of the church consists of a single long, narrow nave designed to focus the attention of visitors on the front of the main sanctuary and the white marble alcove behind the altar. What is left of Mary Magdalene's relic is believed to be located in a reliquary beneath this altar.

---

175. PLACE DE VIEUX MARCHE

Place de Vieux-Marche, 76000 Rouen, France

Denomination: Public Plaza
Web: https://en.rouentourisme.com (tourism website)

The Place de Vieux-Marche was the site of one of the most famous Christian martyrdoms of the Middle Ages: that of Joan of Arc. At the height of the Hundred Years War, a young, uneducated and inexperienced maiden from the province of Lorraine took command of what was left of the French army, leading them to an unexpected victory at Orleans. In 1431, she was falsely tried and executed in Rouen by corrupt church officials at the behest of the English. Rouen is now full of sites related to its favorite daughter, including the church where she was tried, her prison and the place where she was executed.

Joan of Arc was born in 1412, around the time that the Kingdom of France was close to its nadir. As she entered her teen years, she received a series of miraculous visions from Sts. Catherine, Margaret and Michael in which she was commanded to rally France against the English and restore the crown prince of France to the throne. Aided by a prophecy that a champion would come from Lorraine, she arranged for an audience with Charles VII, during which she convinced him of her divine mission. Charles turned honorary command of the French army over to her. Joan's subsequent campaign to liberate the Loire River Valley was nothing short of miraculous.

Her first and greatest victory came at the city of Orleans, which was then under siege. After weeks of stalemate, the French lifted the siege a mere nine days after Joan arrived. She rode at the forefront of every French charge, and during the final engagement she pulled an arrow from her own chest before continuing to fight. Later, she led the French forces on a march along the Loire Valley. An army sent out by the English to stop the French advance was slaughtered at the Battle of Patay. On July 16, Joan and her army arrived at Reims, and the next day Charles VIII entered the city and was crowned king of France in the ancient cathedral there.

In less than three months, Joan of Arc had accomplished her mission. Throughout the next year she participated in a number of military engagements against the English until she was captured at Compiegne. The English decided to exact a brutal revenge, and through the machinations of corrupt Church officials declared her to be a heretic. The ensuing farce of a trial ended with Joan's condemnation to death. The utterly ungrateful King Charles did nothing to intervene. On May 30, 1431, she was burned at the stake in the main square of Rouen.

At first stunned by the loss, the French peasantry and army soon rallied in her memory. The subsequent and last phase of the war lasted another twenty-two years, but when it was over the English were driven out of the whole of France except for Calais. By the middle of the 15th century, Joan of Arc was the national martyr-heroine of France, and a repentant monarchy spent the next four hundred and fifty years finding endless ways to honor her. The Church also had second thoughts about the whole affair and absolved Joan of any wrongdoing. She was finally canonized in the 20th century.

Of Interest: The Place De Vieux Marche is the central square of Rouen, and many of the sites associated with the final year and death of Joan of Arc are located here. Most notably, it was in this square that Joan of Arc was burned alive in 1431. Her remains were dumped ignominiously into the river. A cross marks the spot in the square where she was martyred. Nearby is the Tour Jean d'Arc, the tower where she was imprisoned and threatened with torture. It is the only surviving remnant of an earlier castle, and Joan of Arc may have spent some or all of her time in another one of the castle's other towers. The existing structure now houses an exhibit on Joan of Arc. The tower also offers excellent views of the city.

---

176. MONT SAINT MICHEL ABBEY

L'Abbaye, 50170 Mont Saint-Michel, France

Alternate/Full Name: La Merveille Monastery
Denomination: Roman Catholic
Dates: c. 8th century (founded)
Web: www.abbaye-mont-saint-michel.fr/en (official website)

Mont Saint Michel Abbey is one of the most amazing architectural and engineering achievements of the Middle Ages. A magnificent complex perched on the top of an immense rock jutting out of the sea off the northern coast of France; it is one of the most awe-inspiring constructions in Europe. It is one of France's most beloved religious institutions, and the sheer immensity and magnificence of the place can inspire awe in even the most jaded of pilgrims. Mont Saint Michel is a UNESCO World Heritage Site.

Mont Tomb, the island upon which the Abbey of Mont-St-Michel stands, has been a place of religious and military importance since Roman times. Evidence suggests that the island was originally revered by the Celts as sacred. After the Romans abandoned the area in the 5th century, Mont Tomb was held by the Britons as a foothold on the continent. It was seized by the Franks in the 7th century as part of their kingdom in Western Europe. In 708 Mont Tomb was re-consecrated as Mont Saint Michel and an abbey established there.

Unfortunately, this was closely followed by the first Viking raids into Northern France. After being sacked and destroyed numerous times over the next two centuries, Mont St Michel was conquered outright by the Normans in 933. During the 11th century, the Normans rebuilt the monastery on a magnificent scale, with both a massive cathedral and daunting fortifications. This proved well during the Hundred Years War, as it was the only French stronghold to remain unconquered north of the Loire River Valley throughout the duration of the conflict.

With the coming of the Protestant Reformation, Mont Saint Michel fell into decline, along with many of the monasteries of Western Europe. During the late 18th century and early 19th century, as France was caught up in the throes of Revolution, the complex was seized and converted into a political prison. In the 1860's, after centuries of neglect, an effort was made to restore the site. Today, Mont Saint Michel is one of the most visited sacred sites in France outside of Paris.

Of Interest: Mont Saint Michel Abbey is among the most dramatic churches ever conceived. Perched at the pinnacle of a solitary rocky outcropping just off the coast of Brittany, the Abbey towers over a small town of residences and shops, all built for the use of the monastic community. Most of the hill is packed with buildings lining narrow streets and alleyways that wind their way up to the cathedral. The abbey itself is a maze of chapels, halls and other buildings, with the cathedral piled on the top of the heap. Because of the steep slope below the structure, the main entrance to the abbey is actually beneath the cathedral. A long flight of stairs disappears into the wall of the abbey and comes up through the floor of the main sanctuary. The layout of the church is so complex that it has been hailed as one of the finest achievements of engineering in the Middle Ages. On the top level there is a broad deck which offers a sweeping view of the bay. The cloister garden offers similarly spectacular views.

---

177. BASILICA OF ST. MARTIN

7 Rue Baleschoux, 37000 Tours, France

Denomination: Roman Catholic
Dates: c. 5th century (originally completed),
1924 (current building completed)
Web: www.basiliquesaintmartin.fr (official website)

The Basilica of St. Martin is at least the sixth church built over the tomb of this popular French saint. Martin, along with his contemporary Hilary of Poitiers, was instrumental in the establishment of Christianity in France. The current incarnation of this church was completed in the early 20th century. The Basilica and its predecessors have traditionally been part of the pilgrimage road to Santiago de Compostela.

Martin of Tours was a contemporary and acquaintance of Hilary of Tours. While Hilary was perhaps more important, Martin was undoubtedly the more colorful of the two. Born in Hungary into a family of Roman aristocrats, his father was a cavalry officer, and Martin was brought up to follow in his footsteps. According to tradition, Martin was leading a force near modern-day Amiens in France when he shared some clothing with a beggar. He subsequently had a vision of Christ, who recognized Martin's generosity. Martin was baptized shortly thereafter, left the army and became a faithful Christian.

He served as a disciple of Hilary in Poitiers, eventually becoming bishop of Tours where he founded a monastery. Because of his military service and his ability to rally people under the Christian banner, Martin is recognized by many as a spiritual guardian of France. After his death, his gravesite in Tours became a pilgrimage destination. An early chapel honoring him was constructed there in the early 5th century.

Because of its popularity, the first chapel was replaced with a larger basilica around 470. This in turn was replaced by successfully larger buildings in the 11th and 13th centuries. In 1562 it was sacked and nearly destroyed by the Hugenots, restored in the 17th century, and nearly destroyed again in 1793 by atheists during the French Revolution. In 1860, the relic of Martin was rediscovered, and a new basilica was completed in 1924.

Of Interest: The Basilica of St. Martin is a modern church of neo-Byzantine design. Only two older church towers, which are not architecturally integral to the new church, are still standing. The basilica interior is impressive, with white-stone walls, magnificent floor mosaics and stained glass windows featuring scenes from the life of Martin of Tours. The crypt where the saint's remains are interred is almost entirely new, with no visible traces of the Roman-era sarcophagus in which he was originally buried.

---

178. CHURCH OF ST. HILARY THE GREAT

26 Rue Saint-Hilaire, 86000 Poitiers, France

Denomination: Roman Catholic
Dates: 1049 (completed)
Web: www.uk.poitiers-tourism.com/eglise-saint-hilaire-le-grand (tourism website)

The Church of St.Hilary the Great was built in honor of Hilary of Poitiers, who was pivotal in the spreading of Christianity throughout ancient Gaul. Although constructed nearly seven centuries after his death, Hilary's relic was relocated here, and the church became an important stop on the pilgrimage roads of the Middle Ages. It is one of several ancient and historic churches in Poitiers, including the city's baptistery, which was actually built by Hilary during the 4th century. The Church of St. Hilary the Great is part of the Routes of Santiago de Compostela UNESCO World Heritage Site.

Hilary of Poitiers was one of the major leaders of the Church in the post-Nicaea era. With Christianity recently legalized he was among the first Christian leaders to be able to work without the threat of imminent persecution. He was a key figure in spreading the Gospel throughout the Roman province of Gaul, and in his later years he served as bishop of Poitiers. Hilary was believed to have been married at the time.

Like most of leading Christians of the time, Hilary was ardently opposed to Arianism. He was also a prominent and prolific theologian, and he was among the earliest Catholics to have received the designation of Doctor of the Church. His death in 368 is believed to have been a peaceful one. It is not known where he was originally buried.

The Church of St. Hilary the Great in Poitiers was not constructed until the 11th century, but the relic of St. Hilary was kept here from the Middle Ages through the French Revolution. Unfortunately, the church was the target of violence several times during its history. In the 16th century it was assaulted by the Hugenots, at which time Hilary's corpse was probably destroyed. It was ransacked again during the French Revolution. While Hilary is no longer interred here, the church is still venerated by Catholics and remembered in France for its historical importance.

Of Interest: The Church of St. Hilary the Great is a magnificent Romanesque structure in a city full of such buildings. Although it has been damaged and repaired numerous times over the years, the core of the church essentially dates back to its original construction in the 11th century. The exterior features detailed carvings incorporated into the masonry work. The interior of the church, which is largely built of white stone and enjoys considerable window exposure, has a light feel unusual for a medieval church. Interior decorations include exquisite masonry carvings as well as frescoes dating back as far as the construction of the original building. While the body of St. Hilary is no longer interred within, a shrine marks the location where his tomb was once located in the crypt.

179. PALACE OF THE POPES

Place du Palais, 84000 Avignon, France

Denomination: Formerly Roman Catholic
Dates: 1309 (completed)
Web: www.palais-des-papes.com (official website)

The Palace of the Popes in Avignon was the seat of the Papacy throughout much of the 14th century, during a period many Catholics refer to as the Babylonian Captivity. Its presence helped to transform the tiny town into a major metropolis. When the Popes departed, they left behind a wealth of architectural treasures, including the palace. At the time of its construction, it was the largest Papal residence yet built, and one of the largest and most heavily fortified palaces in Europe. It still stands in the heart of the city, a glorious reminder of Avignon's brief time as the spiritual heart of the Christian world. The Palace of the Popes is part of the Historic Center of Avignon UNESCO World Heritage Site.

The 14th century was a period of tremendous change for the Roman Catholic Church. Since the beginning of the Crusades, the religious authority, secular influence and material wealth of the Church had grown at a dizzying pace, especially in France and Italy. Rome had become a battleground between factions who sought control of the Papacy as the ultimate political prize. The situation came to a head in 1304. After the death of Pope Benedict XI, the Italian cardinals came under great pressure to elect a French Pope. They selected Clement V, the former French Archbishop of Bordeaux.

The new Pope, strongly attached to his French heritage, was crowned in Lyon in 1305, after which he swiftly moved the Papacy to France. The reign of Clement V is one of the best known, and infamous, in history. Among his first acts was the appointment of several new French cardinals to solidify their voting power in the selection of future popes. Soon afterwards he gave the King of France his blessing in the violent destruction of the Templars. He also oversaw the brutal suppression of the Cathar Heresy. Finally he gave the Papacy a new permanent home in Avignon beginning in 1309.

There were seven popes of the Avignon period, which lasted from 1309 to 1377. During the reign of Benedict XII, the third Avignon pope, construction started on a palace-fortress of magnificent proportions. The work took nearly thirty years and was the most expensive building project in Europe in the 14th century. It virtually emptied the Church coffers and foreshadowed the massive building projects that bankrupted the Vatican a century later. In 1376 the Papacy moved back to Rome, and the palace in Avignon was occupied for twenty-five more years by several French anti-Popes. Four centuries later it was taken over by the state during the French Revolution, and has been a government property ever since.

Of Interest: The Palace of the Popes is an immense structure which towers over the comparatively tiny buildings of Avignon. At the time of its construction it was one of the largest complexes ever erected in Europe, and is among the biggest structures of the Middle Ages to survive more-or-less intact to the present day. From the outside it appears as a massive fortress, and is fairly grim even by Gothic standards. The interior of the palace is a different story. The giant complex contains within its walls the Papal residence and cloister garden, a grand chapel and numerous other buildings. After the departure of the Popes, the palace was badly neglected for centuries. Much of the current state of the interior is the result of contemporary restorations which have been ongoing for decades. The highlights of the palace are its numerous chapels, notably the St. Martin Chapel, which features paintings and frescoes by Matteo Giovanetti. The palace now also houses a museum and a convention center.

---

180. CHURCH OF THE JACOBINS

Rue Lakanal, 31000 Toulouse, France

Denomination: Formally Roman Catholic

Dates: 1341 (completed)
Web: www.jacobins.toulouse.fr (official website)

The Church of the Jacobins in Toulouse was once the heart of a great Catholic monastery. For many centuries the Convent of the Jacobins served as one of Roman Catholicism's great theological centers, and was home for a time to one of Christianity's greatest scholars, Thomas Aquinas. The Church of the Jacobins is the greatest surviving edifice of the Middle Ages in this ancient city, and is famous as the burial site of Thomas Aquinas.

Toulouse has historically been one of Christianity's great theological battlegrounds. It has witnessed religious turmoil almost since Christianity became the official faith of the Roman Empire. When the Visigoths arrived in Southern France in the 4th century, they had already adopted Arian Christianity. Arianism established a particularly strong foothold in Toulouse, the Visigothic capital. At the urging of the Papacy, the Catholic Franks conquered most of the Visigothic kingdom in 507, and by the middle of the 6th century most of the city was Catholic.

Two-hundred years later, Toulouse marked the furthest point of advance of Islam into Western Europe. Toulouse was the rallying point of Christendom, and in 721 the city withstood a siege by superior Muslim forces. The ensuing Battle of Toulouse was a major victory for the Christians. The city became a reliable Catholic stronghold after that, but Toulouse never seemed to forget its antiestablishment roots. During the 12th century the Albigensians used Toulouse as their chief headquarters, leading to the first crusade in continental Europe in 1216. Concerned about future heretical uprisings, the Papacy established one of the earliest Inquisitions in Toulouse.

The Inquisition of Toulouse lasted for four centuries, and to emphasize the importance of Catholicism and the 'correct' practice of Christianity, the Church had the body of Thomas Aquinas interred in the Jacobins Monastery. During the Protestant Reformation, Toulouse again found itself in the spotlight. As Calvinist missionaries penetrated Southern France from Switzerland, many citizens of Toulouse embraced Protestantism, and in 1562 rioting between the Catholics and Protestants ensued. This helped lead to the French Wars of Religion that ultimately ended in the defeat of the Huguenots. But for all of its colorful history, Toulouse now goes on about its religious business quietly. Only the relic of Thomas Aquinas now survives as a reminder of the city's turbulent Christian history.

Of Interest: The Church of the Jacobins is a Romanesque masterpiece with an architectural uniqueness befitting Toulouse's controversial history. Built in the 11th and 12th centuries, the Basilica hardly resembles anything else built in the same period, and many of its artistic touches seem to anticipate future designs. The single carillon bell-tower is located at the crossing point of the basilica, rather than near the entrance. The Convent of the Jacobins features the cells, choir and refectory of a typical monastery as well as a superb cloister garden. The religious highlight of the convent is the Tomb of Thomas Aquinas. However, the body was divided up at the time of the French Revolution. The portion that was left in Toulouse was burned, and what is now buried here are his cremated remains.

---

181. SANCTUARY OF OUR LADY OF LOURDES

1 Avenue Mgr Theas, 65108 Lourdes, France

Denomination: Roman Catholic (Marian shrine)
Dates: 1876 (completed)
Web: www.lourdes-france.org (official website)

The Sanctuary of Our Lady of Lourdes is the reigning champion of Marian shrines in terms of fame. Every year, millions of pilgrims visit the place where Bernadette Soubirous saw eighteen visions of the Virgin Mary in 1858. Most come for the waters of the grotto, which are said to contain healing powers. In fact, several genuine, verified medical miracles have been associated with the shrine, adding to both its mystery and its popularity. Lourdes is one of the most popular Christian pilgrimage destinations in Europe not directly tied to the history of the early Church.

Until the middle of the 19th century, Lourdes was just another small French agricultural town. That all changed on February 11, 1858, when a young girl named Bernadette received a vision of a white-robed Virgin Mary while walking near the Gave de Pau River. Bernadette subsequently received another seventeen visions, some of which instructed her to build a chapel. During one of her later visions a spring spontaneously arose from the ground. This later fed the famous pool associated with the shrine. The local church did build a chapel per Bernadette's request, and soon the place was attracting pilgrims.

By the mid-1870s there were reports of miraculous healings, and the small devout following soon became a swarm of pilgrims. A new basilica was erected in 1876 to accommodate the visitors. Bernadette, exhausted from the constant attention, withdrew to a convent where she died of tuberculosis in 1879. The Basilica at Lourdes eventually began to receive international attention, and the Church and other organizations investigated the site. As it turned out, while the total number of actual healings of a miraculous nature was relatively low, it still had the highest success rate of any similar shrine in the world. To this day there are unexplained cases of miraculous healings at Lourdes.

In 1909, Bernadette's body was exhumed for examination, and in the presence of reliable witnesses appeared to have resisted significant decomposition. This miracle was attributed to the power of the shrine. Subsequent exhumations further reinforced the miracle. Bernadette was canonized by the Roman Catholic Church in 1933. Lourdes is now one of the most popular places of pilgrimage in the world. No other modern-day Christian site has more miracles directly associated with it. Lourdes is especially busy during the summer, when nightly candlelit processions illuminate the way to the grotto.

Of Interest: The Sanctuary of Our Lady of Lourdes might best be described as a fairy-tale cathedral. Rebuilt on a grandiose scale in the 1950's, the basilica exhibits a 19th century charm reminiscent of a Romantic age castle. The white stone of the cathedral stands out amid tree-covered rolling hills. There are actually several churches on the site, the primary one being the Basilica of the Immaculate Conception. The main entrance to the shrine consists of a pair of enormous ramps which lead to the cathedral above and a great gate between them that leads to the grotto below. The Massabielle Grotto, the heart of the shrine, is a smallish cave furnished with an altar, seating, and various artifacts associated with Bernadette's miracle. A niche marks the place where the eighteen visions of the Virgin Mary were seen. Inside the niche is Our Lady of Lourdes, a statue of Mary dressed in white. A plaque marks the spot where Bernadette stood during her encounters. The spring is at the back of the grotto. It is accessible to pilgrims via drinking taps and, for the highly devout, full-fledged baths.

---

182. BARCELONA CATHEDRAL

Pla de la Seu, s/n, 08002 Barcelona, Spain

Alternate/Full Name: Cathedral of the Holy Cross and St. Eulalia
Denomination: Roman Catholic
Dates: c. 4th century (originally completed),
1339 (current building completed)
Web: https://catedralbcn.org (official website)

Barcelona Cathedral is one of the greatest Spanish churches of the pre-Colombian period. Its completion helped to cement Barcelona as one of the leading ports of the Mediterranean, and the cathedral became a great beneficiary of the wealth that poured into the city from Spain's colonial empire in later centuries.

There have been metropolitan churches in Barcelona at least as far back as the Visigothic era. The first city church survived well into the Middle Ages, until much of it was ruined during a Muslim attack on the city in the 10th century. This was replaced by a new cathedral in the 11th century. But as the city's economic importance grew, another even larger cathedral was needed. The current building was completed in 1448.

The cathedral has long had a connection to the Battle of Lepanto, where Christian naval forces heavily defeated an Ottoman force in the Gulf of Patras. Many of the ships that were provided by Spain sailed out of Barcelona. One of the cathedral's chapels was subsequently rebuilt and renamed in honor of the victory over the Ottomans. The

Barcelona Cathedral also serves as a chapel for the Spanish chapter of the Order of the Golden Fleece.

Of Interest: Barcelona Cathedral is one of the largest and most magnificent Gothic Revival churches in Spain. While the exterior is just as imposing as similar cathedrals of the period, it is arguably more graceful and delicate than many of its contemporaries. The cathedral interior is more open feeling than typical gothic structures. A number of important persons are buried within the church, including locally popular saints Eulalia and Olegarius. A crucifix that was present at the Battle of Lepanto is displayed above St. Olegarius' tomb. Thirteen white geese, kept in honor of St. Eulalia, roam freely throughout one of the cloisters.

---

183. BASILICA OF THE HOLY FAMILY (SAGRADA FAMILIA)

Carrer de Mallorca, 401, 08013 Barcelona, Spain

Denomination: Roman Catholic
Dates: 2032 (under construction as of the time of this writing)
Web: https://sagradafamilia.org (official website)

The Basilica of the Holy Family, more commonly known as the Sagrada Familia, is possibly the greatest Christian church construction project that is currently ongoing. Unlike most other cathedrals in Europe, the Sagrada Familia does not stand on the site of a former church, and has been a work in progress since the 1880s. It is anticipated to be completed in 2032.

The Sagrada Familia does not have a long history as Roman Catholic churches go. The idea for a massive, modern cathedral dedicated to the Holy Family came from a local resident named Jose Maria Bocabella after he returned from a pilgrimage to Rome in 1872. Raising funds through private donations, Bocabella oversaw the early stages of the construction throughout the last years of his life.

Work on the church has continued on and off for well over a century. Among those who worked on it was the famous architect Antoni Gaudi, who conceived of a radical, modern design for the church. Much of the construction was completed in the early 2000s, and the cathedral was consecrated in 2010 by Pope Benedict XVI.

Of Interest: The Basilica of the Holy Family is one of the most magnificent works of church architecture on Earth. Though essentially a modern building, its style is unclassifiable. The exterior features dozens of major elements that have a Gothic-like look, especially on the main church building. However the complex is dominated by a forest of absolutely immense spires which look as though they were borrowed from a temple in India. Every inch of the façade is covered in detailed carvings depicting scenes from the Nativity and the Passion. The main entrance is framed by a futuristic gateway reminiscent of an organ. The interior is a kaleidoscope of light and color in symmetrical patterns. Upon its completion, the Sagrada Familia will be the tallest church in the world.

---

184. CATHEDRAL BASILICA OF OUR LADY OF THE PILLAR

Plaza del; Pilar, s/n, 50003 Zaragoza, Spain

Denomination: Roman Catholic (Marian shrine)
Dates: c. 4th century (originally completed),
1961 (current building completed)
Web: www.spain.info/en_us/que-quieres/arte/monumentos/zaragoza/basilica_de_nuestra_senora_del_pilar (tourism website)

The Cathedral Basilica of Our Lady of the Pillar in Zaragoza is one of the oldest churches in the world devoted to the Virgin Mary. According to tradition a chapel stood here as early as the 1st century, and commemorates Mary's miraculous appearance to James the Greater during his missionary travels. It is among the most important pilgrimage churches in Spain, and both Ignatius of Loyola and Teresa of Avila were known to have visited. The Basilica of Our Lady of the Pillar was recently designated one of the Twelve Treasures of Spain.

After the scattering of the Twelve Apostles from Judea, James the Greater travelled to distant Spain, the westernmost province of the Roman Empire. According to tradition, his labors were not going well. One day he prayed along the shore of the Ebro River, asking for help. Legend has it that he invoked the name of Mary during his prayers. In a miraculous vision, she appeared before James and offered him words of comfort. She also instructed him to construct a church on the spot. Interestingly, Mary was probably still alive at the time, making this the only claimed such vision during her lifetime.

As the legend further goes, right around the time of James' vision of Mary, an angel appeared and bestowed upon James a pillar made of jasper, as well as a small wooden statue of Mary. Sometime around the year 41, a few years before his martyrdom in Judea, James completed construction of a small chapel in Zaragoza, and placed the pillar and icon inside where it could be venerated.

The chapel became a magnet for the early Church in Spain. However, at some point prior to the 4th century, the original chapel was destroyed. It was rebuilt as a basilica, and has been rebuilt and enlarged several times since. On an interesting historical note, the Basilica of Our Lady of the Pillar was attacked during the Spanish Civil War. Three bombs were dropped on the shrine, but none of them detonated. This has been taken by devotees as a sign of miraculous intervention for the beloved basilica.

Of Interest: The Cathedral Basilica of Our Lady of the Pillar overlooks the meandering Ebro River. Architecturally breathtaking, it blends Mudejar and Baroque styles and is reminiscent of a mosque, with a great dome crowning the main building and four soaring bell towers at the corners. The current edifice was largely completed in the 18th century, and is at least the fifth church to have stood on the spot. The enormous interior is worthy of a great Marian shrine. Among the works of art and frescoes which adorn the place are several pieces by Francisco Goya, notably *The Queen of Martyrs* which fills the great central dome. The famous wooden icon and the namesake jasper pillar are on display in the Holy Chapel. Although the faithful claim that these are the two-thousand year-old originals, these were probably destroyed in a fire in 1434, and the ones on display are replacements.

---

185. TOLEDO CATHEDRAL

Calle Cardenal Cisneros, 1, 45002 Toledo, Spain, 45002

Alternate/Full Name: Primate Cathedral of St. Mary of Toledo
Denomination: Roman Catholic
Dates: c. 6th century (originally completed); 1493 (current building completed)
Web: www.catedralprimada.es (official website)

Toledo Cathedral is one of the great churches of Spain that was built in the triumphant years following the Christian Reconquista. Constructed over the course of two and a half centuries, it was completed in 1493, a year after the fall of Granada. In the late Middle Ages it served as an important church for the Spanish monarchs, a number of which are buried within its walls.

There has been a Christian presence in Toledo since Roman times. According to tradition, there was an earlier church on this site completed in the 6th century, and that St. Eugene of Toledo may have been involved in its construction. Under the Visigoths, Toledo was the seat of Christianity in Spain. However, following the Muslim conquest in the 8th century, the original church was torn down and replaced with a mosque.

After the Reconquista of the city in the 11th century, the mosque was re-consecrated as a church. It was confirmed as the seat of the Church in Spain in 1088, and remained as such for several centuries. The current cathedral was begun in the 13th century, and even before its completion was a popular place for tombs of the aristocracy and monarchy. It remains one of the most historically important churches in Spain thanks to its connections with the royal family.

Of Interest: Toledo Cathedral is a High Gothic masterpiece, noted for its very distinctive bell tower. The façade is striking albeit somewhat unusually laid out, with an ornate main entrance set back from the two flanking towers and protected by a fence and gate. The lower portions of the towers are built of a dull gray brick, but crowned with ornate Renaissance flourishes in white stone. The main bell tower evokes a hint of Moorish design. The interior houses many great works of art, including *The Disrobing of Christ* by El Greco. A number of monarchs from the pre-Spanish kingdoms of Leon and Castille, and one from Portugal, are entombed within the cathedral.

---

186. MONASTERY OF SANTO TORIBIO DE LIEBANA

CA-885, 39570 Camaleno, Cantabria, Spain

Denomination: Roman Catholic
Dates: c. 6th century (founded)
Web: www.santotoribiodeliebana.es (official website)

The Monastery of Santo Toribia De Liebana, tucked away in a quiet corner of northern Spain, has long harbored one of Christianity's most coveted artifacts: the largest surviving piece of the True Cross. Although critics have expressed pessimism over its authenticity since the 4th century, there is little doubt that the section of wood located at Santo Toribio Monastery is at least a piece of the cross identified by Helena. Whatever the truth of it is, the cross was likely used to crucify somebody on Golgotha. It has been a prized possession of the monastery since the 8th century.

Of the many artifacts associated with the life of Jesus of Nazareth, none are quite as prolific as the Lignum Crucis, otherwise known as the True Cross. There is no way of knowing the fate of the cross upon which Jesus Christ was crucified. In all likelihood it was reused numerous times before being hauled off and chopped up for firewood. There was certainly no practical reason for the Romans to keep it, and it is highly unlikely that the earliest Christians would have been allowed to remove it, or have any place to safely store it if they did.

That didn't stop Helena, the mother of the Emperor Constantine, from finding the True Cross during her tour of the Holy Land in the 4th century. According to tradition, the Romans had constructed a Temple dedicated to the goddess Venus upon Golgatha in the 2nd century in an effort to confound Christian pilgrims who sought to visit their holiest site. When Helena arrived, she ordered the pagan temple torn down. During the excavation, a trio of crosses was discovered buried under the temple, along with a number of crucifixion nails. Helena declared on the spot that these were the crosses used in the martyrdom of Jesus Christ and the two thieves who died with him.

The story goes on to recount how Jesus' cross was identified when it miraculously healed a supplicant who touched it. It immediately became the Church's greatest artifact, and over time became so popular that it was eventually broken apart and dispersed to numerous locations. This process continued throughout the ages, and there are now literally hundreds of fragments of the Lignum Crucis scattered across the world. Sometime in the 8th century, Christian refugees fleeing from Palestine arrived in Spain with a hunk of Helena's Cross. They left it in the safekeeping of the monks of the Santo Toribio Monastery where it has been ever since. Only one small piece of the artifact was subsequently removed. What is left is the largest surviving fragment of Helena's Cross anywhere.

Of Interest: The Monastery of Santo Toribio De Liebana is located in the quiet green hills of Cantabria in Northern Spain. While the monastery was founded in the 6th century, the majority of the compound, including the main gothic cathedral, dates from the 13th century. The cloister was built even later. The dominant external feature is the low bell tower at the center of the complex. The piece of the Lignum Crucis is displayed in a chapel located on the north side of the monastery's church. It is the largest surviving piece of the True Cross identified by Helena in the 4th century. In 1679 the Santo Toribio fragment of the Lignum Crucis was encased in a silver reliquary shaped like a cross. This in turn is kept in a large golden display reliquary.

187. SANTIAGO DE COMPOSTELA CATHEDRAL

Plaza do Obradoiro, s/n, 15704 Santiago de Compostela, A Coruna, Spain

Denomination: Roman Catholic (sacred to many Christians)
Dates: 829 (originally completed), 1211 (current building completed)
Web: www.catedraldesantiago.es/en (official website)

Santiago de Compostela Cathedral is one of only a handful of shrines recognized as an apostolic tomb: that of James the Greater. According to a somewhat confusing tradition, the remains of James were brought here following his martyrdom at the hands of King Herod around the year 44. For a time it was the second greatest Christian pilgrimage destination in Europe after Rome. It is one of the most beloved cathedrals in Spain, and hundreds of thousands of visitors still flock to it every year. The cathedral is part of the Santiago de Compostela Old City UNESCO World Heritage Site. It was also recently designated one of the Twelve Treasures of Spain.

St. James the Greater was one of Jesus' closest followers and, according to tradition, was chosen to bear the Gospel across the Mediterranean Sea to the distant Roman province of Spain. His sojourn there apparently only lasted a few years, after which he decided to return to Judea. In 44 James was seized by the soldiers of Herod Agrippa and beheaded. James' was the only martyrdom of an Apostle to be recorded in the Bible.

Accounts vary as to exactly how his body made it to Galacia in Spain. It is possible that after his death James' followers smuggled his body back to the west for safety. For many years his tomb remained forgotten, until an enterprising Bishop rediscovered it in the 9th century. The town was renamed Santiago de Compostela and a church was erected over the site. The shrine quickly became one of the most popular pilgrimage destinations in Western Europe. A now-famous pilgrim road grew up between France and Spain, known as the Camino de Santiago, or the Way of St. James, in order to accommodate the pilgrimage traffic.

After the Crusades ended and the sacred sites in Jerusalem and Bethlehem were once again too difficult for most Christians to visit, the Tomb of St. James became more important than ever. Pilgrimages to the cathedral peaked in the 15th and 16th centuries as Spain was swept up in the religious fervor of the post-Reconquista period. By the 18th century, Santiago de Compostela had become more of a regional attraction. However, there has been a large resurgence in interest in pilgrimages here, with many people taking long vacations in order to walk at least part of the traditional pilgrim trail.

Of Interest: Santiago de Compostela cathedral was completed in 1211. The great gothic sand-colored façade is one of the most impressive and memorable in Spain, and the site of the towering Cathedral must have been awe-inspiring to visiting pilgrims in the Middle Ages. Large statues of David and Solomon dominate the staircase welcoming visitors. Periodically expanded and renovated over the centuries, the rest of the outer structure exhibits an array of styles from Romanesque to Gothic to Baroque. The cathedral's interior reflects the vast wealth from centuries of pilgrim donations. Among the highlights is the *Portico de la Gloria* by the artist Mateo. The high altar is adorned with gold, including a golden shell which is traditionally kissed by visiting pilgrims. Beneath the altar is the cathedral's focal point, the silver casket which contains the remains of James the Greater. Alongside him are buried Theodorus and Athanasius, two of his associates.

---

188. SEGOVIA CATHEDRAL

Calle Marques del Arco, 1, 40001 Segovia, Spain

Denomination: Roman Catholic
Dates: 1577 (completed)
Web: www.catedralsegovia.es (official website)

Segovia Cathedral, nicknamed the Lady of Cathedrals for its transcendent beauty, was among the last and most spectacular Gothic cathedrals to be constructed in Europe. It absolutely dominates the skyline of its city the way few other cathedrals do. The time of its construction spanned most of the early years of the Spanish colonial empire, and is arguably Spain's definitive church of that period.

The history of Christianity in Segovia is somewhat uncertain, as little is known of it in either ancient times or during Muslim rule. The modern community dates from the Reconquista. Segovia's original cathedral was constructed right near the city's alcazar, or fortress, for security. During the Revolt of the Comuneros in the 1520s, the cathedral was the site of fierce fighting. By the end of the revolt, it was largely in ruins.

Construction on a new cathedral began in 1525. Work continued over the centuries as both Spain's and Segovia's fortunes rose and fell. It was largely completed 1577, though work continued through the late 18th century, just a few decades before Spain's overseas empire started to collapse. The cathedral later endured both the Napoleanic occupation and the Spanish Civil Wars. The Cathedral of Segovia was included as part of the Segovia UNESCO World Heritage Site in 1985.

Of Interest: Segovia Cathedral is one of the most distinctive in Spain. Scores of ornate spires, not to mention the stunning dome, give the entire place a fairy-tale feel. The church, along with its largely independent bell tower, crowns a hill overlooking the city. The absolutely massive tower dominates the skyline and can be seen from the farmlands which surround the city from miles around. Adjacent to the cathedral is a museum housing a number of artworks and manuscripts.

---

189. CONVENT OF THE ANNUNCIATION

Plaza Sta. Teresa, 37800 Alba de Tormes, Salamanca, Spain

Denomination: Roman Catholic
Dates: 1562 (founded)
Web: www.spain.info/en_us/que-quieres/arte/monumentos/salamanca/catedrales_de_salamanca (tourism website)

The Convent of the Annunciation in the picturesque town of Alba de Tormes is the site of the tomb of Teresa of Avila, one of only a handful of woman to be designated a Doctor of the Church and perhaps the greatest female theologian in Christian history. Teresa died at this convent, which she had founded, while traveling through the area in 1582. As of the time of this writing, a new basilica was under construction in Alba de Tormes. It is planned that Teresa will be reinterred here upon its completion.

Teresa of Avila was one of the great female luminaries of the Roman Catholic Church, second perhaps only to Catherine of Sienna. Her father's family converted from Judaism to Christianity under the threat of the Spanish Inquisition. After Teresa's grandfather was condemned for backsliding, her mother made certain that Teresa received a strong Christian education. So great did the Christian teachings take hold of Teresa that she was inspired to seek martyrdom at an early age which, thanks to an astute relative, this did not come to pass.

In adulthood Teresa found her calling as a nun, and she became very well known for her devotions as well as her somewhat unorthodox mystical practices. In her thirties and forties she was prone to visions of Jesus, Mary and angels; she also began to practice self-mortification at this time. In the 1560s Teresa began establishing new Carmelite convents in Spain. Her efforts were supported by both the Papacy and the Spanish Crown, and she went on to found her own Carmelite Order. During this period Teresa also established herself as a profound theologian and a prolific writer.

Teresa died in 1582 after having founded nearly twenty convents. She passed away on the same day that Spain adopted the Gregorian calendar, so that her death is commemorated alternatively on October 5 and October 14. Thirty-five years after her death, she was posthumously awarded a degree from the University of Salamanca. Along with Catherine of Sienna, she was one of the first two women to be awarded the title of Doctor of the Church. She was interred in the Convent of the Annunciation in Alba de Tormes where she died.

Of Interest: The Convent of the Annunciation is somewhat innocuous from the outside. Built of sand-colored brickwork, the main church is not overtly large, and by the standards of the time it was built the façade is relatively simple. There are some sculptures and relief work around the main entrance, featuring angels, saints and coats of arms. The church is flanked by a long wall which encloses the adjoining convent. The interior of the church is more interesting than the austere exterior. The focal point is the niche where the relic of Teresa of Avila is kept. The shrine features beautiful paintings of the life of the saint. Her relic is brought out and paraded through the town every year on her feast day.

---

190. SEVILLE CATHEDRAL

Avenue de la Constitucion, s/m, 41004 Seville, Spain

Alternate/Full Name: Cathedral of St. Mary of the See
Denomination: Roman Catholic
Dates: 1507 (completed)
Web: www.catedraldesevilla.org (official website)

Seville Cathedral is arguably the greatest church constructed in Spain during the post-Reconquista era. By some measures the largest church in Spain and the third largest cathedral in the world, it was built at the height of Spanish power and affluence. Today it is one of Spain's most visited cathedrals and the most popular Christian pilgrimage destination in the Andalusia region.

In the early- to mid-13th century, the Christian conquest of Spain churned its way relentlessly through Andalusia. In 1248 Seville fell, effectively dooming the Muslims in Spain. To celebrate their triumph, and to establish their religious hold on their new acquisition, the victorious Christians began erecting churches all over the city. By the late-14th century, Seville was effectively the southern capital of Spain, and it was decided that the city should be graced by a new cathedral. The city's mosque, which had been badly damaged in an earthquake, was torn down to make way for the new edifice.

When plans for the cathedral finally began to move ahead in 1401, city and church leaders decided that it should be among the largest and grandest churches ever built. Construction began in 1402, and proceeded apace throughout most of the 15th century. In 1492, Christian armies took the Moorish kingdom of Grenada, thereby completing the Reconquista of the Iberian Peninsula. In the wake of the final victory, efforts were redoubled to quickly finish the cathedral. When it was finally completed, it surpassed the Hagia Sofia in Istanbul as the largest church in the world at the time. It remains the third largest church building in the world, and is the architectural glory of the Church in southern Spain.

Of Interest: Seville Cathedral is both enormous and exquisitely rendered. The largest Gothic building on Earth, the cathedral dates almost entirely from the 15th century. Despite being the tallest church in Spain, it is not among the tallest churches globally. However, it more than compensates for this with one of the world's most beautiful bell towers: La Giralda, which was constructed in the 12th century as a minaret for the city's mosque. The cathedral interior represents a pinnacle of Gothic architecture. It has the longest nave in Spain and a mind-boggling 44 chapels. Huge quantities of gold, fresh from the New World, were used to adorn the place, especially the ceilings and the titanic, phenomenally detailed altarpiece designed by Pierre Dancart. The tomb of Christopher Columbus, whose remains were brought to Seville in 1898, is in the cathedral.

---

191. MEZQUITA MOSQUE-CATHEDRAL

Calle Cardenal Herrero, 1, 14003 Cordoba, Spain

Alternate/Full Name: Cathedral of the Assumption of the Virgin
Denomination: Roman Catholic
Dates: c. 6th century (originally completed); c. 16th century (current building completed)
Web: https://mezquita-catedraldecordoba.es (official website)

The Mezquita Mosque-Cathedral of Cordoba is one of Christianity's greatest architectural oddities. It is, in fact, a massive mosque repurposed as a church after the Christian conquest of Cordoba. The result structure is one of the greatest religious architectural mish-mashes of all time: a Gothic-style church enclosed inside a Moorish-style mosque. Because of this the Mezquita draws the curiosity of Christians, Muslims and architecture-lovers alike. The Mezquita is part of the Historic Center of Cordoba UNESCO World Heritage Site.

The history of the cathedral dates back to the Visigothic kingdom in Iberia. The Visigoths built many churches throughout Spain during the years of their rule. This included the great Church of St. Vincent in Cordoba. The Muslim conquest was the beginning of the greatest period of Cordoba's history. The city became the seat of the Umayyad Caliphate in Spain, and the first emir, under pressure to destroy the Christian symbol that was St. Vincent's, wisely decided to purchase the building instead. This placated the local Christian population and made it much easier to use the site for the construction of a new mosque.

The Mezquita arose on the expanded foundations of St. Vincent's. At the time of its completion it was the second largest mosque in the world. It is still the third largest today, and among the most lavishly appointed. For many years it was a major center of Muslim worship in the west. However, in 1236 forces of the Christian Reconquista arrived and captured Cordoba. The magnificent mosque was seized and re-consecrated as a church.

Castillian architects went to work almost immediately. A huge section of the center of the beautiful mosque was gutted to make way for the new construction. A church literally arose amidst the sea of columns which supported the Mezquita's roof. From the 13th to the 18th century, new touches were constantly being added to the complex. The result was one of the most unusual composite religious structures in history. Today the Mezquita is a symbol of sorts of Christian-Islamic coexistence, and receives hundreds of thousands of visitors of many faiths every year.

Of Interest: The Mezquita Mosque-Cathedral has retained virtually all of its original form and magnificence, even accounting for the strange church. The imposing outer walls of the Mezquita enclose beautiful gardens filled with magnificent fountains as well as exotic plant-life from all over Southern Europe and Northern Africa. The interior is a dazzling and confusing blend of Islamic and Christian styles and uses. Hundreds of columns made of marble, granite and stone largely pilfered from earlier Roman buildings support the massive arches and ceiling. After the Reconquista much of the interior was adapted to Christian use, with a new nave and chapels. One of the unique features of the Mezquita is the original prayer niche, which does not point towards Mecca.

---

192. CONVENT OF THE ORDER OF CHRIST

Igreja do Castelo Templario, 2300-00 Tomar, Portugal

Denomination: Roman Catholic
Dates: 1118 (founded)
Web: www.conventocristo.gov.pt (official website)

The Convent of the Order of Christ is one of a string of fortresses built to secure Christian territories from the Moors in the 12th century. It is one of the finest surviving medieval castles in Portugal and one of the few surviving Templar convents in Europe. After their dissolution, many of the surviving Templars found their way to the Convento de Christo, their last major safe haven. The convent also played a small but important part at the dawn of the Age of Exploration. This ancient fortress, little changed since its initial construction more than 850 years ago, is still home to a community of monks and is one of Portugal's most historic religious sites.

The Templars, famous for their role in the Crusades in the Holy Land, also played a pivotal role in the Reconquista of Spain. For their efforts they were rewarded with lands and castles, particularly in the west. In Tomar they constructed a heavily fortified convent, which in 1160 became their headquarters in Iberia. By the mid-13th century virtually the entire peninsula was back in Christian hands. The Templar fortress in Tomar was by now one of their greatest citadels. Unfortunately, the Templars were crushed in 1312 following an edict of the Church condemning them as heretics.

While most of the Templars in Europe were cruelly put to death during the ensuing purge, those of Portugal survived under the protection of the crown. Many surviving Templars from Spain and France also fled here. In order to avoid the wrath of the Church the Templars were reformed as the Order of Christ. The Knights of Christ became loyal supporters of the Portuguese crown. Their fortress in Tomar, renamed the Convent of Christ, was retained as their headquarters.

During the 15th century the Order of Christ helped to lead the first wave of European exploration into new lands. Under the leadership of the order's Grand Master, Prince Henry the Navigator, the Knights of Christ set sail for Africa to establish trading posts and serve as Christian missionaries. The Act of Iberian Union, which joined Spain and Portugal under a single monarchy for a time, took place at the Convent. During the 1550s the Knights of Christ were disbanded in Portugal, and their convent turned over to a related non-militant monastic order. The great fortress continues to serve as a monastery.

Of Interest: The Convent of the Order of Christ is a fortified monastery rather than a typical castle. It is designed around a chapel, rather than having a chapel as an add-on piece. The convent is built on a hilltop guarded by a long towered wall. The main monastery building is loosely modeled after the Temple of Solomon. The round worship hall is typical of Templar architecture. The rotunda is lit by round windows and decorated with paintings and murals featuring biblical scenes. The Templar Church was renovated and expanded several times during the 15th century. Henry the Navigator added a nave to the church in order to make its use as a Christian sanctuary more standardized. He also added a Chapter House and Sacristy. Outside the main convent building is a series of cloisters which also date from around this time.

193. SANCTUARY OF OUR LADY OF FATIMA

N356, 2495-401 Fatima, Portugal

Alternate/Full Name: Sanctuary of Fatima
Denomination: Roman Catholic (Marian shrine)
Dates: 1953 (completed)
Web: www.fatima.pt (official website)

The Sanctuary of Our Lady of Fatima is the most revered Catholic site in Portugal. It stands on the site where a trio of young children witnessed an apparition of the Virgin Mary in 1917. It is among the finest cathedrals constructed in Europe during the 20th century. Although it is perhaps less well known than similar shrines such as the one at Lourdes, the Sanctuary of Fatima attracts comparable crowds. Several million pilgrims visit the shrine every year to venerate the Virgin Mary.

The history of the Marian Shrine of Fatima began with a vision of the Virgin Mary appearing to three children: Lucia Santos, Jacinto Marto and Francisco Marto. As the story goes, the children witnessed the apparition for the first time on May 13, 1917. It was the first of six visions, each occurring on the 13th day of each month from May and October. During the appearances the apparition entrusted the children with three secrets, a combination of warnings and prophecies of future events.

Word of the strange appearances spread like wildfire. The faithful and the curious began to visit Fatima. There was skepticism as well, and the children were imprisoned for a short time before being released due to popular outrage. As proof of the miraculous events, the children announced that a miracle would occur at Fatima on October 13, the day of the final apparition. Tens of thousands gathered in Fatima. Lucia Santos instructed the crowd to watch the sun, and before the eyes of the devout pilgrims, the sun began to dance and change colors.

This miracle was witnessed for many miles around, and cemented Fatima's reputation as a sacred site. To further strengthen the legend of the miracle, no unusual astronomical or weather phenomenon was scientifically recorded on that day. Work began on the Sanctuary about a decade later. The shrine was completed and consecrated in 1953. All three of the children were interred within the Sanctuary. Jacinto Marto, who died from influenza in 1920 at the age of ten, was the youngest person ever beatified by the Catholic Church who did not die as a martyr.

Of Interest: The Sanctuary of Our Lady of Fatima is a stunning structure which dominates a great plaza near the city center. Its appearance is reminiscent of the Basilica of Lourdes and features modern and baroque elements. A tall bell and clock tower looms over the front of the church. On the façade of the basilica, flanking the tower, are enormous pictures of Jacinto and Francisco Marto. Few, if any, other churches in Christianity feature such unique and odd exterior elements. The interior of the main basilica is an impressive if simple white-marble affair. The tombs of the two younger children are within. The focus of the Sanctuary is the small, highly modernistic Chapel of Apparitions which stands on the site where the visions of the Virgin Mary actually took place. A small statue of Mary marks the exact location of the apparition's appearance.

NORTHERN EUROPE

194. ROSKILDE CATHEDRAL

Domkirkepladsen 3, 4000 Roskilde, Denmark

Denomination: Lutheran
Dates: c. 10th century (originally completed), 1405 (current building completed)
Web: www.roskildedomkirke.dk (official website)

Roskilde Cathedral is one of the most storied churches of Scandinavia. Constructed as a Catholic institution prior to the Protestant Reformation, it has served as a Lutheran house of worship since the 16th century. Many of Denmark's monarchs are buried here, a reminder of the time when Roskilde served as the national capital.

There have been churches on the site of the current cathedral since Roskilde first served as the royal seat in the 10th century. An early cathedral was constructed here in the 11th and 12th centuries due to Roskilde's growing importance. It was at this time that a skull believed to be that of 3rd century pope St. Lucius was brought to the cathedral to add to its prestige and to draw in pilgrim traffic.

Over the next few centuries the cathedral was massively expanded, with much of the original building actually replaced. During the 1400s the practice of burying Danish monarchs here began. In 1536, the cathedral was swept up in the Protestant Reformation and was converted to Lutheranism. Despite this it continued to be used by Danish monarchs and remains a royal burial site. The Cathedral of Roskilde was designated a UNESCO World Heritage Site in 1995.

Of Interest: Roskilde Cathedral largely dates from the 13th century expansion, though construction and renovations continued into the 20th century. Primarily a Gothic structure with elements of later architectural styles, the cathedral was famous as one of the earliest major churches constructed with red brick rather than dressed stone.

Approximately forty kings and queens of Denmark are buried here, including Harald Bluetooth, who reigned in the 10th century.

---

195. HELSINKI CATHEDRAL

Unioninkatu 29, 00170 Helsinki, Finland, 00170

Alternate/Full Name: St. Nicholas' Church
Denomination: Lutheran
Completed: 1826 (originally completed), 1852 (current building completed)
Web: www.helsinkicathedral.fi (official website)

Helsinki Cathedral is the chief church of Finland's capital city and the seat of the Lutheran Diocese of Helsinki. Built during a period when Finland was part of the Russian Empire, the construction of the cathedral was heavily influenced by Eastern Orthodox designs and is one of the most architecturally unique Protestant churches to be found in Northern Europe.

The Church of Finland was the last of the major national Lutheran churches of Scandinavia to be established. It was founded in 1809, the same year Finland was absorbed into the Russian Empire. The Helsinki Cathedral was constructed a few decades later. In order to appease the Russian government, the magnificent new church was dedicated to Tsar Nicholas I and named the St. Nicholas' Church.

After revolution ravaged Russia in 1917, Finland became an independent state, and the church was re-designated as Helsinki Cathedral. Unlike so many other major churches in Eastern Europe, the cathedral escaped damage during World War II thanks to the fact that the Finns pulled out of the conflict before Helsinki was seriously threatened. Because of this the Helsinki Cathedral is one of Northern Europe's best-preserved national cathedrals.

Of Interest: Helsinki Cathedral is one of the largest traditional Protestant church buildings in Europe. Its architecture evokes eastern styles, with a Greek cross layout and a massive dome surrounded by four smaller domes. Twelve massive statues of the Apostles line the roof of the church, three on each side. The original altarpiece of the church was donated by Russia, a relic of the Tsarist era. The crypt beneath the church is used for special events.

---

196. TURKU CATHEDRAL

Tuomiokirkonkatu 1, 20500 Turku, Finland

Denomination: Lutheran
Dates: c. 13th century (originally completed), 1300 (current building completed)
Web: www.turunseurakunnat.fi/portal/en/turku_cathedral (official website)

Turku Cathedral is one of the oldest surviving churches in northeastern Scandinavia and the seat of the Lutheran Diocese of Finland. Regarded as the mother church of Lutheranism in Finland, the building has been around since the late Middle Ages and has witnessed a number of important events in Finland's history. Originally a Catholic church, it has served as a Lutheran institution since the arrival of the Protestant Reformation in the 16th century.

Finland was among the very last places in Europe to see the introduction of Christianity. It was probably established here sometime before the city of Turku was established, possibly as early as the 1100s. A wooden church was constructed here in the 13th century but was replaced almost immediately by a permanent stone structure which was completed in 1300.

Lutheranism arrived in Finland around the same time that it arrived in neighboring Sweden in the 1530s. Turku Cathedral was seized and re-consecrated for use by the Lutherans. For many years it was part of the Lutheran Church of Sweden, in which it remained until the 19th century when Finland established an independent Church. Today it is honored as one of Finland's most important architectural and historical treasures.

Of Interest: Turku Cathedral is one of the oldest buildings in Finland, though much of it dates from a 19th century restoration that followed a fire which destroyed much of the city in 1827. Built largely of red brick, the building appears less medieval and more post-Reformation, with an outsized bell and clock tower that seems somewhat out of place. A number of prominent early leaders are buried here, including Queen Karin Mansdotter of Sweden and national religious hero Bishop Hemming the Blessed.

---

197. RIDDARHOLM CHURCH

Kungliga Slottet, 107 70 Stockholm, Sweden

Denomination: Lutheran
Dates: c. 13th century (completed)
Web: www.kungligaslotten.se/english/royal-palaces-and-sites/the-riddarholmen-church (official website)

Riddarholm Church was formerly the chief church of the city of Stockholm and the state church of Sweden. Begun as a Catholic monastery, it was later repurposed as a Protestant institution, but remained one of Sweden's most important churches. Almost all of the monarchs of Sweden from the 17th century onward are buried here, as well as a few earlier ones, including Gustavus Adolphus, champion of the Protestant cause during the Thirty Years War.

The earliest church on the current site of Riddarholm was a monastery dating back to the 13th century. Swedish monarchs were interred here as far back as Magnus III in the Late Middle Ages. After the Protestant Reformation arrived in the mid-1500s, Riddarholm became a Lutheran church but remained the official church of the monarchy.

In 1632, Sweden's greatest king, Gustavus Adolphus, was killed at the Battle of Lutzen. Adolphus was one of the most important Protestant commanders fighting in Germany during the Thirty Years War, and his death was a grievous loss to the Lutheran side. His body was returned to Sweden and interred at Riddarholm. In 1807 Riddarholm

Church was decommissioned as an active church but was maintained as a royal burial site.

Of Interest: Riddarholm Church is a magnificent medieval structure that dominates the heart of Stockholm. Although no longer active, the church is well maintained due to its importance as the burial site of Swedish monarchs. Most of those that ruled from the 17th through the 20th centuries are entombed here. The most magnificent sarcophagus is that of king and Thirty Years War hero, Gustavus Adolphus. The walls are decorated with many coats-of-arms representing deceased members of the Royal Order of the Seraphim.

---

198. NIDAROS CATHEDRAL

Bispegata 11, 7012 Trondheim, Norway

Denomination: Lutheran
Dates: c. 1300 (completed)
Web: www.nidarosdomen.no (official website)

Nidaros Cathedral is the most historic church in Norway. The burial site of king and saint, Olaf, many Norwegian monarchs have been coronated and/or consecrated here. The cathedral also serves as the seat of the Preses of the Lutheran Church in Norway. The Nidaros Cathedral is the final destination for travelers along an ancient pilgrimage route known as St. Olaf's Way.

It is unknown exactly when Christianity first arrived in Norway. However, the process of converting the country was largely completed in the early 11th century during the reign of King Olaf II. While few details are known, the achievement was recognized by the Roman Catholic Church by canonizing him barely a year after his death. Construction of the cathedral at the site of his tomb began a few decades later in 1070.

The cathedral has had a rough history, having been almost completely destroyed by fire in 1708 and badly damaged by a number of other fires on other occasions. Like most other Catholic churches in Scandinavia, the Cathedral of Nidaros became a Lutheran institution following the Protestant Reformation in the 16th century. Every year on July 29th the cathedral celebrates the anniversary of St. Olaf's death.

Of Interest: Nidaros Cathedral is a hulking Gothic church with Romanesque elements that largely dates back to a massive reconstruction and renovations in the 18th and 19th centuries. The façade of the cathedral is memorable for its geometric designs and unusually large number of statues. The body of St. Olav is buried somewhere beneath the cathedral. While the exact spot is not known, a small piece of his leg is preserved in a silver reliquary in the church.

---

199. URNES STAVE CHURCH

FV331, 6870 Ornes, Luster, Sogn og Fjordane, Norway

Denomination: Lutheran
Dates: c. 1132 (completed)
Web: www.stavechurch.com/urnes-stavkirke (official website)

The Urnes Stave Church is one of the oldest, largest and most visited of Norway's famous stave churches. When Christianity arrived in Scandinavia, it found a land rich in lumber and people highly skilled in carpentry and woodworking, which led to one of the most unique forms of Christian architecture: the stave church. A surprising number still survive to the present day, a testament to the skill of medieval Scandinavian woodworkers. The Urnes Stave Church is a UNESCO World Heritage Site.

In the mid-12th century, when much of Norway was Christianized, there was a lack of large churches to serve sizeable congregations, especially in the more rural areas. Lacking skilled stoneworkers, as were common in the rest of Europe, they turned instead to carpenters and the great forests that had long provided them with the lumber. By the end of the 12th century, Scandinavians had developed the stave church.

Stave churches first appeared in the area around Sogn Og Fjorden in southern Norway. The oldest of these, and possibly the first ever constructed, was the Urnes Stave Church. This church was the largest yet built and was a prototype for future stave construction. So sound was the engineering of the building and quality of the materials that the church has survived to the present day essentially intact, with only a few minor renovations. It is treasured today as one of Norway's most revered historic sites, and receives hundreds of thousands of visitors every year.

Of Interest: The Urnes Stave Church is located on the outskirts of Luster in an inspirational setting of lakes, forests and snow-capped mountains. The church itself is a classic example of early stave architecture, featuring steep-sloped roofs climbing to a single point. Much of the Urnes Stave Church dates from its original construction in the 12th century, though some parts date from later renovations. Although it lacks many of the embellishments, such as roof ornamentation, that would later be a hallmark of stave church construction, there are some beautiful exterior details, such as the exquisite scrollwork on and around the church doors. The interior is rich with excellent woodwork and hand-carved furniture, including precision-cut posts and beams as well as intricate wall carvings.

---

200. HALLGRIM'S CHURCH

Hallgrimstorg 101 Reykjavik, Iceland

Denomination: Lutheran
Dates: 1986 (completed)
Web: https://en.hallgrimskirkja.is (official website)

Hallgrim's Church is the most iconic building in the city of Reykjavik and one of the quintessentially futuristic churches of the modern era.

Although only 75 meters in height, its unique design makes the church appear much taller than it is. It is easily the most recognizable man-made landmark in Iceland. It is named in honor of one of Iceland's favorite sons, the poet Hallgrimur Petursson.

Hallgrimur Petursson was a 17th century writer and minister who helped to establish the Lutheran Church in Iceland. He grew up in a religious family, with his cousin serving as Lutheran bishop. He pursued religious studies in Copenhagen and later served in a variety of capacities with the Lutheran Church in Iceland. By the time of his death he was famous for his writings, especially for his compilation of Christian hymns.

From the time of Reformation until the 20th century, Iceland was a colony of Lutheran Denmark, and its citizens were generally required to adopt the Lutheran tradition. Iceland gained its independence after the First World War, but the population largely retained its Lutheran character. In recognition of this, the capital embarked on the construction of the magnificent Hallgrimskirkja. Construction was postponed until after World War II, commencing in 1945. It was completed in 1986.

Of Interest: Hallgrim's Church is a stunning piece of modern architecture. It is completely dominated by its jaw-dropping bell tower, which the entire church architecturally feeds into. Huge pillars sweep down from its sides like a tremendous pipe organ in brilliant white stone. Close to the top of the tower is an observatory offering excellent views of the city. The interior of the church is perhaps a bit less interesting, but the pipe organ with its strange display and pipes jutting out at odd angles is a unique and beautiful work of modern art in and of itself.

---

201. WESTMINSTER ABBEY

20 Deans Yd, Westminster, London SW1P 3Pa, England

Alternate/Full Name: Collegiate Church of St. Peter at Westminster
Denomination: Church of England

Dates: c. 7th century (founded), 1519 (current building completed)
Web: www.westminster-abbey.org (official website)

Westminster Abbey has long served as England's royal church (its official designation is 'royal peculiar'). It has been an important place of pilgrimage since the Middle Ages. The majority of England's monarchs have been both coronated and buried here. Thanks to its location in the heart of London, as well as the sheer number of historical celebrities buried here, it is among the most visited churches in the world. Westminster Abbey is a UNESCO World Heritage Site.

The Collegiate Church of St. Peter at Westminster began life long before the Church of England broke off from the Papacy in the 16th century. Earlier churches have stood on the site as far back as the 7th century. It may have been founded by one Mellitus, the Bishop of London at the time. In 1042, Edward the Confessor was crowned King of England. The last king of the Saxon dynasty, he went on to be the only English monarch to be canonized. He had a reputation as a secular champion of the Church, and was responsible for rebuilding and enlarging Westminster Abbey. It was consecrated in 1065, just before the Normans arrived.

After William I conquered England in the next year, the abbey was appropriated by the Norman rulers and their successors, by whom it has been used for coronations, funerals and other royal occasions ever since. Originally a monastery of the Benedictine order, the abbey's proximity to the governmental center of England made it both incredibly influential and wealthy, and the position of Abbot of Westminster became one of the most important in the British Isles.

The 16th and 17th centuries were a period of great turbulence for Westminster Abbey. In the 1530s, when King Henry VIII broke the Church of England away from the Papacy, he ordered all monastic orders dissolved, and all monasteries seized, looted and, in many cases, destroyed. However, perhaps due to a sense of history and sentimentality, the king had Westminster Abbey declared a cathedral in order that he could spare the building. This proved fortuitous, as Westminster remains one of the world's most popular tourist destinations.

Of Interest: Westminster Abbey is in surprisingly good shape considering its age. Despite numerous restorations and a few additions, much of the Collegiate Church dates from the original 11th century construction. The architectural details of the church, as magnificent as they are, are generally overlooked by most visitors who are simply too awed by the sheer number of historic figures and celebrities buried within. Sixteen British monarchs are interred here, including Edward the Confessor and Elizabeth I. A short list of Westminster's other tombs include those of Robert Browning, Geoffrey Chaucer, Charles Darwin, Charles Dickens, George Handel, Thomas Hardy, Rudyard Kipling, Isaac Newton, Laurence Olivier, William Pitt and Alfred Tennyson, not to mention many of the abbey's prominent clergymen.

---

202. ST. PAUL'S CATHEDRAL

St. Paul's Churchyard, London EC4M 8AD, England

Denomination: Church of England
Dates: c. 7th century (originally completed), 1697 (current building completed)
Web: www.stpauls.co.uk (official website)

St. Paul's Cathedral is the great church of the city of London, and architecturally one of the most spectacular in the English speaking world. Designed by renowned architect Christopher Wren after the Great Fire of London, it is among the greatest landmarks in a city of great landmarks. It is the home church of the Bishop of London and has been the scene of many important historic events and royal functions over the last four centuries.

There has been a church on the site of the current cathedral since the 7th century. Along with most of the rest of medieval London, the prior structure burned down in the catastrophic Great Fire of London in 1666. Fortunately one of the greatest architects of all time was on hand to oversee its reconstruction. Christopher Wren, who helped to plan the rebuilding of many of the city's grander structures, paid particular attention to the cathedral. It was undoubtedly his crowning achievement.

By the early 19th century, St. Paul's was used to host major state occasions, most notably funerals of prominent citizens. These have included Arthur Wellesley, the Duke of Wellington, and Admiral Horatio Nelson, both heroes of the Napoleanic Wars. The cathedral also was a symbol of defiance during World War II, surviving the Blitz largely intact. An image of the cathedral wreathed in smoke but undamaged became one of the most famous photos of the war. The funeral of Winston Churchill, one of the largest state funerals of all time, took place here in 1965.

Fully restored after the war, St. Paul's Cathedral became popular as a venue for state events. These have included, among other things, the Jubilee birthday celebration for Queen Elizabeth, the longest reigning monarch in British history, as well as the memorable wedding of her son Charles to Diana Spencer. Its beauty, its history and its burials make it one of London's top tourism sites.

Of Interest: St. Paul's Cathedral is among the most jaw-dropping churches in the British Isles. Christopher Wren outdid himself with this soaring masterpiece in white, crowning it with one of the largest and tallest domes on Earth. Even today the cathedral stands out starkly against the buildings that surround it. The gargantuan façade mixes Baroque and Classical styles that may be unmatched by any other Protestant house of worship. The church interior is home to a number of famous burials, though not quite so many as at nearby Westminster Abbey. Among these are the aforementioned Duke of Wellington and Lord Admiral Nelson, composer Arthur Sullivan of Gilbert & Sullivan fame and the church's architect, Christopher Wren. If you would see his monument, look around you!

---

203. WESLEY'S CHAPEL & WESLEY HOUSE

49 City Road, London EC1Y 1AU, England

Denomination: Methodist
Dates: 1778 (completed)
Web: www.wesleyschapel.org.uk (official website)

Wesley's Chapel is an historic church in London that was constructed under the direction of John Wesley, founder of Methodism. It is considered by many to be the mother church of Methodism, and is one of the world's most important Methodist pilgrimage destinations. The grounds, which include the Wesley House, are also home to the Museum of Methodism as well as the graves of John Wesley and other early leaders of the Methodist church.

In 1725, John Wesley, a graduate of Christ College at Oxford and an ordained Anglican deacon, began to have ideas concerning reforming the Anglican Church, which was at that time little more than a schismatic offshoot of Catholicism under the leadership of the British monarchy. Over the next few years he began to develop his ideas of Methodism, which downplayed the importance of church ceremony in favor of a variety of ideas borrowed from Luther and Calvin. However, like Luther, it was not originally his intention to break from the mainstream church of his day.

Wesley undertook an energetic ministry that was famous for its impassioned sermons. He preached in London for a time, and then in Georgia in the American colonies at the request of the Governor. Eventually, his style and ideas aroused the ire of the Church of England, and he found himself ostracized. By 1739, he had all but broken with the Church of England. Over the course of his life Methodism became solidly established both in England and in America.

For much of his ministry, John Wesley worked out of a former cannon foundry near London's Moorgate. In the 1770s Wesley built a new church for the Methodists which later came to be known as Wesley's Chapel, the possessive specifically honoring Methodism's founder. He preached there for over a decade, and was buried on the site at the time of his death in 1791. Of post-Wesley interest, Margaret Thatcher was married here in 1951.

Of Interest: Wesley's Chapel is among London's most historic churches constructed after the time of Christopher Wren. It is actually a small complex which includes the chapel as well as Wesley's house on a small courtyard on City Road. The simple but elegant chapel looks much today as it did in Wesley's day, though the current communion rail was donated by Prime Minister in the 20th century. The house is similarly preserved, looking as it did when Wesley lived here. There are also exhibits on Wesley's life here. John Wesley is buried in the crypt beneath the church. His wife is buried across the street at Bunhill Fields.

---

204. SALVATION ARMY HEADQUARTERS & ABNEY PARK CEMETERY

101 Queen Victoria Street, London EC4P 4EP, England (Salvation Army Headquarters)

215 Stoke Newington High Street, London N16 0LH, England (Abney Park Cemetery)

Denomination: Methodist & Public Cemetery
Dates: Salvation Army – 1865 (founded) & Cemetery – 1840 (established)
Web: www.salvationarmy.org.uk & www.abneypark.org (official websites)

The Salvation Army International Headquarters and the Abney Park Cemetery in London are both closely tied to the life of one of the most famous Protestant missionary leaders of all time: William Booth. Booth, who founded the Salvation Army in London in 1865, became famous for his work with the city's poor and those with substance abuse issues. He is honored today as one of the great theologians of the 19th century.

William Booth was born in 1829 and grew up in the Methodist tradition. He became a Methodist minister, but had difficulty finding a permanent position. He subsequently became a street evangelist preaching and working among the city's poor. In 1865 he established his first mission in London's East End. The mission was renamed the Salvation Army in 1878, and within a decade its missions had spread throughout the major cities of the British Isles and to the United States.

By the time William Booth died in 1912 he had become one of the most famous men in the world. His funeral was one of the largest in

London's history. He was buried in Abney Park Cemetery. This public burial ground became known for the many Christian missionaries, evangelists and abolitionists who are buried here. Among these were Booth's wife, other early leaders of the Salvation Army and members of the London Missionary Society.

The Abney Park Cemetery was originally the site of the Manor of Stoke Newington, formerly a suburban village outside of London. In 1840 the estate was donated for use as a public park after the 17th century manor house was demolished. Burials took place within the park as far back as its opening, but the magnificent Victorian landscape did not formally become a cemetery until the 1880s. It is currently designated for Non-Denominational use.

Of Interest: The Salvation Army World Headquarters remains in London to this day. It houses the International Heritage Center, a museum and the archives of the Salvation Army. On display are exhibits on the history of the organization including everything from the iconic uniforms to the instruments of the SA's marching bands. Abney Park Cemetery is a popular outdoor space in London and its cemetery a favorite place to be buried. The Abney Park Chapel, completed in 1840, dominates the cemetery. Famous burials in the Salvation Army plot include William Booth, his wife Catherine Booth, Bramwell Booth and George Railton.

---

205. BRITISH LIBRARY

96 Euston Road, London NW1 2DB, England

Denomination: Public Library
Dates: 1753 (founded)
Web: www.bl.uk (official website)

The British Library is one of the oldest and largest national libraries in the world. Over the course of two and a half centuries it has amassed a collection of hundreds of millions of items from books and manuscripts to artwork and music recordings. As many of these items were collected during the Colonial era, when the British Empire spread across much of the world, the library now houses an enormous number of antiquities from around the globe.

At the height of British colonial power, when archaeological expeditions and related pillaging reached its crescendo, a great premium was placed on artifacts of Christian interest. From individual donations to acquisitions of huge collections, thousands of historic Christian documents were amassed at the museum over the course of decades. The British Library is now home to one of the largest collections of historic Christian books and manuscripts to be found in the world.

The highlight of the collection, from a Christian standpoint, is the Codex Sinaiticus. This Greek Bible, which dates to the early 4th century, is possibly the world's oldest surviving nearly-complete Bible. It is believed to be one of the original Bibles commissioned by the Roman Emperor Constantine, and may have even been worked on by St. Jerome. It was discovered at St. Catherine's Monastery in Egypt in the 19th century.

Of Interest: The British Library's collection of Christian writings is absolutely staggering. The main attraction, the Codex Sinaiticus, is kept here nearly in its entirety (there are a few pages kept at St. Catherine's Monastery in Egypt, the Russian National Library and the Leipzig University Library). Also kept here are several copies of the original Gutenberg Bible printed in the 15th century; one of the earliest Bibles in English translated and hand-written by William Tyndale; and George Handel's original hand-written musical score of the incomparable Christian choral work, *Messiah*.

206. ST. GEORGE'S CHAPEL

Windsor Castle, 2 The Cloisters, Windsor SL4 1NJ, England

Denomination: Church of England
Dates: 1354 (completed)
Web: www.royal.uk/st-georges-chapel (official website)

St. George's Chapel is the church of Windsor Castle, and one of the great treasures of the Church of England. Like Westminster Abbey in London, St. George's is technically a Royal Peculiar under the direct authority of the reigning monarch of the United Kingdom. It is also the official church of the Order of the Garter, as well as the site of many royal burials.

St. George's was founded in the 14th century by King Edward III. Construction started in 1348, the same year as the Order of the Garter was established, and the church has served the order's chapel since its completion. Over the centuries, the chapel was significantly expanded and embellished, especially in the years after the English Civil War. Much of the current building dates to the reign of Queen Victoria.

Throughout its history, the Chapel of St. George has been the site of many royal events, including numerous weddings and funerals. Most recently the chapel hosted the highly publicized wedding of Prince Harry to Meghan Markle. Every June St. George's also hosts an annual gathering of members of the Order of the Garter.

Of Interest: St. George's Chapel is a Gothic masterpiece that has grown significantly since its initial construction. It is located in the Lower Ward of Windsor Castle and makes up a significant portion of the castle's skyline. The most famous exterior features of the chapel are a series of fantastical statues that line the roof. These statues, known as the Queen's Beasts, were erected in honor of the Royal Supporters of England. The current statues actually date from the 1920s, replacing those that had been removed more than two centuries earlier. The chapel interior is decorated with the heraldic devices of the members of the garter of the Order. There are over fifty members of the royal family and other aristocrats buried here. Although Edward III was not buried here, nearly a dozen of his successors are. Among these is Henry VIII, who founded the Church of England in the 16th century.

---

207. CANTERBURY CATHEDRAL

Cathedral House, 11 The Precincts, Canterbury CT1 2EH, England

Alternate/Full Name: Cathedral and Metropolitan Church of Christ at Canterbury
Denomination: Church of England
Dates: 597 (originally completed), 1077 (current building completed)
Web: www.canterbury-cathedral.org (official website)

Canterbury Cathedral is the seat of the Church of England and, for most of the Middle Ages, it was also England's greatest pilgrimage shrine. Canterbury Cathedral houses some of England's oldest Christian treasures, including the relic of St. Thomas Becket, a 12th century champion of the separation of church and state. While the hordes of Chaucer emulating pilgrims to Canterbury are long gone, many tourists still visit every year to see this most beloved of English religious sites. Canterbury Cathedral is a UNESCO World Heritage Site.

Canterbury and its great cathedral enjoy one of the longest and greatest traditions of pilgrimage in Northern Europe. In 597 Augustine of Canterbury was sent to England by the Church in order to see it through the dark times of the early Saxon occupation. Basing himself in Kent, he established a new Archbishopric in Canterbury with himself as the first Archbishop. A local church was made available for his use, and he soon began the work of converting it into a cathedral. The construction took centuries, during which time the site was looked after by the Greyfriars, the first monastic community in England.

Canterbury Cathedral's great moment in history took place in the late 12th century, when Henry II, in an effort to reduce the influence of the Papacy, had his close friend Thomas Becket appointed as the

Archbishop. To his surprise, Becket insisted on an independently functioning church. This enraged Henry, and Thomas Becket was subsequently assassinated by four of Henry's knights. Becket's martyrdom made him an instant hero to England's masses, and his tomb at Canterbury Cathedral was soon swarming with pilgrims. In order to appease his subjects, the English monarchy rushed to formalize Thomas Becket's canonization.

For centuries Canterbury Cathedral was England's most important religious center. The annual pilgrimage caravan that descended on the cathedral became the subject of Geoffrey Chaucer's famous 14th century book *The Canterbury Tales*. When Henry VIII declared England's independence from Rome in the 16th century, authority of the new Church was vested in the Archbishop of Canterbury. Virtually overnight, Canterbury found itself at the center of one of the world's largest Christian denominations. Nevertheless the Archbishop is still considered a successor of Augustine, of which there have now been over a hundred. Today Canterbury Cathedral is one of England's most important Christian holy sites.

Of Interest: Canterbury Cathedral is a sprawling Gothic building that was largely completed in 1077. The overall design features an atypical cross-shaped layout, with what is effectively a second transept. Its lofty design and intricately detailed exterior masonry suggest something other than Gothic. A large monastic compound and cloister is adjacent to the cathedral. Canterbury Cathedral's interior features high vaulted ceilings supported by great pillars. However, its light colored walls, extensive lighting and numerous windows give it a much lighter feel then typical of the period. The main site of interest is the Tomb of Thomas Becket. A marble plaque identifies the location where the saint was murdered. Another plaque marks the spot where Pope John Paul II knelt in prayer with the Archbishop of Canterbury. Thomas Becket's body lies under a simple stone slab that is merely labeled 'Thomas' in large red letters.

---

208. ST. MARTIN'S CHURCH

1 North Holmes Road, Canterbury CT1 1QJ, England

Denomination: Church of England
Dates: c. 5th century (originally completed), c. 6th century (current building completed)
Web: www.martinpaul.org (official website)

St. Martin's Church enjoys the distinction of being the oldest church in continual use in England, and by extension the oldest church in continual use in what was formally the British Empire. Although it can't be accurately dated, part of the structure dates from the Roman occupation of Britain in ancient times, and the current building largely dates from the 6th century. The Church of St. Martin is a UNESCO World Heritage Site.

The arrival of Christianity in the British Isles in the Roman era is heavily shrouded in legend. It was supposedly introduced by Joseph of Arimethea in the 1st century and spread by St. Patrick in the 5th century. There were certainly parishes and churches established throughout the country by the time Augustine of Canterbury began his missionary work here in the 6th century. It was under his direction that Canterbury became an important Christian center.

St. Martin's Church, or at least its predecessor, was among these very earliest churches, and was standing before the Romans abandoned the island around 410. Much of the building was rebuilt and restored in the late 6th century for the use of the Christian Queen Bertha. It has remained more or less the same since this period, a fact confirmed in the writings of Bede. The Church of St. Martin is one of the great architectural treasures of England.

Of Interest: St. Martin's Church was a large and impressive structure by the standards of its day, but today seems much smaller and intimate. The stonework is some of the finest in England that survives from that nation's Dark Age. Part of the outer wall incorporates remains of the earlier Roman building. The bell tower dates from a later period.

A statue of St. Bertha, the aforementioned Christian queen, is kept inside.

---

209. ST. MARY'S CHURCH

Church Gate, Lutterworth LE17 4AN, England

Denomination: Church of England
Dates: c. 13th century (completed)
Web: www.lutterworthchurch.org (official website)

St. Mary's Church in Lutterworth was closely tied to the early Reformer John Wycliffe. It was here in the mid-14th century that Wycliffe offered an early challenge to the authority of the Catholic Church. Wycliffe also worked here while translating the Bible into English, something that had not yet been done. St. Mary's Church is part of John Wycliffe's legacy, for he preached here and was later buried her, at least for a while before his body was exhumed.

John Wycliffe was born into a prosperous family sometime around the year 1325. Little is known of his early life, other than the fact that he was enrolled at Oxford around the time he turned twenty. He was apparently a keen student with diverse interests, choosing to study theology and philosophy with an eye towards a career in the Church. He spent the better part of a quarter of a century studying and teaching at Oxford, becoming one of the most renowned scholars of his day. However, Wycliffe became increasingly disillusioned with the Church, which he saw as having grown stagnant and corrupt.

Beginning in 1366 John Wycliffe became involved in a series of events that ultimately led to his break with the Church. It began when he was replaced as the head of Canterbury Hall at Oxford by a monk who had better political connections to the Archbishop of Canterbury. It worsened over the next decade, during which time he began to quietly preach the rejection of the Papacy as the supreme authority over all Christians. Despite his beliefs he received an appointment to the Church in Lutterworth in 1374. Two years later he began to make his teachings more vocal, and the Church took notice.

In 1377 the Papacy issued a Bull condemning Wycliffe's teachings. Nevertheless for the next seven years he pursued an ever-increasing stream of verbal attacks against the corruption of the Church. Protected by John of Gaunt and other important officials in England, the Church could do little in retaliation but issue condemnations. Throughout this period Wycliffe also worked diligently in translating the Bible into English as he believed that the only true religious authority was Holy Scripture.

In the final years of his life he gained a large following known as the Lollards. By the time of his death in 1384 he had won over many to his ideas and earned the wrath of the Papacy. Strangely, he was never excommunicated. However, in an effort to discourage other proto-Protestants in the decades after his death, Wycliffe was formally declared a heretic in 1415. His body was exhumed, cremated, and his ashes scattered in a nearby river. Nevertheless his ideals lived on among the Lollards in England, and these ultimately bore fruit during the Reform movement of the 16th century.

Of Interest: St. Mary's Church dates back to the 13th century and is still in use as the town's parish church. It was built in a late-gothic style that was popular in England at the time. The bell tower was rebuilt in the 18th century after being damaged during a storm. The interior of the church is simple with a very traditional feel. The highlight of the church is a series of medieval-era wall paintings that were uncovered during a restoration in the 19th century. Among these is a picture of the Final Judgment. There are also paintings of King Richard II and his wife, as well as a picture of John of Gaunt. An old cemetery can be found behind the church, with gravestones dating back to the 17th century. It is believed that John Wycliffe was once buried in this graveyard, but his body is long gone and it is uncertain exactly where the site of his grave once was.

210. NEW ROOM

36 The Horsefair, Bristol BS1 3JE, England

Denomination: Methodist
Dates: 1739 (completed)
Web: www.newroombristol.org.uk (official website)

The New Room is a chapel in Bristol which has the distinction of being the world's first purpose-built Methodist Church. It was constructed in 1739 under the direction of Methodism founder John Wesley. Originally not intended to be a church but rather a meeting house, it was later expanded for use in worship. Along with Wesley's Chapel in London it is one of the most important Methodist churches in England.

John Wesley conceived of the idea of Methodism following a brief and somewhat unsuccessful tour as a minister and missionary from the Church of England to the American colony of Georgia. Sensing something lacking in his faith, he embraced several new principals which he incorporated into his existing Anglican practices. In 1739 he had the New Room built as a meeting space for those who agreed with his ideas and wanted a place to share an adjunct worship.

Within a few years, Methodism became a fully independent Christian institution, and the New Room was expanded for full use as a church. In its early years the upper rooms of the church were also used as a residence for clergy, including John Wesley, who stayed here for the better part of two decades. After his death the church was passed on to a group of Calvinist Methodists. It remained in use by that group until the 1920s, when it became part of the mainstream Methodist Church.

Of Interest: The New Room was originally built as a multi-purpose facility, incorporating both a meeting house and facilities for its staff. Although it has been expanded and renovated since its completion, it essentially looks as it did at the end of the 18th century. The old minister's quarters in the upper rooms now house a museum with exhibits on the history of the chapel, the Methodist Church and Wesley. A statue of a horse mounted John Wesley guards the front of the church.

---

211. DURHAM CATHEDRAL

The College, Durham DH1 3EH, England

Alternate/Full Names: Cathedral Church of Christ, Blessed Mary the Virgin and St. Cuthbert of Durham, Shrine of St. Cuthbert
Denomination: Church of England
Dates: c. 7th century (originally completed), 1739 (current building completed)
Web: www.durhamcathedral.co.uk (official website)

Durham Cathedral is one of the most seen churches in England outside of London, though many people don't realize that they have seen it. Architecturally it is considered one of the finest surviving examples of Norman church architecture. Religiously it is the site of the tomb of Bede the Venerable, England's greatest home-grown theologian, as well as that of his fellow saints, Cuthbert and Oswald of Northumbria. However, it is perhaps most famous for its use as a major shooting location for the *Harry Potter* films. Durham Cathedral is a UNESCO World Heritage Site.

Bede the Venerable is a Doctor of the Catholic Church, the only native-born Englishman to be so designated. Born sometime around 672, evidence suggests that he was from a noble family and was raised in a monastery. He became a deacon of the Church at a very early age, and by his late twenties he was well educated in both theology and secular studies. Bede's writing career spanned most of the second half of his life. He authored approximately sixty books, including works on everything from history to literature to music.

Although Bede did write religious commentaries, most of these were based on earlier works or translations. His major contribution was in the writing of religious histories. In addition to being hailed as the Father of English History, his works inspired other authors across

Europe to prepare historical texts of the faith. His contemporary Cuthbert, who also went on to become a saint, was with Bede when he died. At some point in the ensuing centuries Bede's writings began to take on epic proportions among the monks of England, and he was eventually canonized. Bede became such a popular figure that in the 11th century his remains were stolen by pious thieves who were seeking a relic for their own church.

Durham Cathedral, one of the most magnificent churches in Northern England was constructed by monks in the Middle Ages to house the relic of St. Cuthbert. It was rebuilt by the Normans in the decades after their conquest of England. At some point during or after its completion the remains of Bede were placed therein. The cathedral survived the dissolution of the abbeys and the purges under Henry VIII; it was used as a prison during the English Civil Wars, when nearly two thousand Scotsman starved to death inside; and over the last two decades it has become a popular site for shooting period-piece movies.

Of Interest: Durham Cathedral was a destination in the Middle Ages for pilgrims seeking to venerate the tombs of Bede and Cuthbert. Now, thanks to the movies, it has become a huge draw for Harry Potter enthusiasts. It also draws architecture enthusiasts, who come to gape at what is probably the world's best preserved Norman era church. Essentially an early version of a Romanesque cathedral, Durham features a strange double-cross floor plan, with the chapels of Bede and Cuthbert forming the second cross-section. Great bell towers flank the façade while the central tower over the transept dominates the city skyline. The interior is in nearly pristine medieval condition, which is perhaps why it is popular as a filming location. In the 18th century a rose window was added after part of the abbey was demolished. The oak benches date from after the English Civil War, as the Scottish prisoners burned the earlier ones in order to keep warm. The bodies of Bede and Cuthbert lie in sarcophagi at the east end of the cathedral.

212. YORK MINSTER

Deangate, York YO1 7HH, England

Alternate/Full Name: Cathedral and Metropolitan Church of St. Peter in York
Denomination: Church of England
Dates: 627 (originally completed), 1472 (current building completed)
Web: https://yorkminster.org (official website)

York Minster is one of the great religious institutions of Northern England. For over a thousand years it has been the seat of an archbishopric, first with the Roman Catholic Church and later with the Anglican Church. Rising above the ramparts of one of the greatest surviving walled cities of Europe, it continues to dominate York's magnificent medieval skyline.

Christianity reached Northern England as early as the late Roman era. There has been a church on the site of the current cathedral at least as far back as the 7th century. Throughout the Middle Ages York Minster saw many hard times, and has been badly damaged or destroyed on at least three occasions. The current building was not consecrated until 1472.

The city's archbishops, which in Great Britain were second in importance only to those of Canterbury, often found themselves embroiled in national politics. This was especially true during the War of the Roses and the Protestant Reformation in England. This led to York Minster's being damaged several more times in its history. York Minster is among the most visited churches in England outside of London.

Of Interest: York Minster is one of the largest cathedrals in Northern England and one of the most important in the country. Rising above a sea of red-roofed houses, it dominates the entire city of York in a way few other churches in the British Isles can match. One of the largest Gothic cathedrals anywhere, it boasts a number of unusual structural features. For one thing, the cross is at the center of the nave, as opposed to closer to the eastern end, and is crowned with a great square tower rather than a dome. Because of this it is among the most easily recognizable churches in England. Although much of the original Catholic décor was stripped away after the Reformation, the interior remains packed with gothic detail and many tombs. Among these are the tombs of many of the cathedral's bishops and archbishops, as well as William of York, a popular local saint.

---

213. ST. GILES' CATHEDRAL

High Street, Edinburgh EH1 1RE, Scotland

Alternate/Full Name: High Church of Edinburgh
Denomination: Church of Scotland
Dates: c. 9th century (originally completed), c. 15th century (current building completed)
Web: https://stgilescathedral.org.uk (official website)

St. Giles' Cathedral is the great church of Edinburgh, the chief house of worship of the Church of Scotland and the spiritual headquarters of the worldwide Scottish Reform community. Originally a Catholic church, it was seized by the Protestants and converted to Reform usage in the 1550s. The Chapel of the Order of the Thistle, a Scottish knightly order, is located here. St. Giles' Cathedral is part of the Old Town of Edinburg UNESCO World Heritage Site.

Several years after the Reformation began in Central Europe, the idea of Protestantism began to spread to Scotland. During the 1540's a priest named John Knox left the Catholic Church and devoted himself to the Protestant cause in Scotland. Because the Catholic Church had been dealt such a heavy blow by Henry VIII in neighboring England, the Papacy was at first in no condition to deal with the Scottish reformers. However this changed during the reign of the very devout Catholic, Queen Mary.

Around 1546 John Knox was captured and enslaved for two years. However, he eventually made his way to Geneva where he sought shelter among the Calvinists. He remained in exile there until 1559, when he deemed it necessary to return to Edinburgh. In 1560 the Scottish Parliament declared Protestantism to be the officially recognized religion of the State. John Knox became the minister of the St. Giles Cathedral and the leader of the Scottish Protestants. By the time of his death in 1572, Knox and his associates had solidly established the Church of Scotland, a Reform institution along Calvinist lines.

After the overthrow of King James II in 1690, the Church of Scotland became separated from the government politically, but remained the nation's most important Christian institution. Presbyterian churches throughout the world continue to recognize the Church of Scotland as their ancestral church. St. Giles' Cathedral is still the parish church of the city of Edinburgh, and because of its historical importance retains the honorary moniker of Cathedral. Today it is one of Scotland's most visited churches and welcomes hundreds of thousands of pilgrims every year.

Of Interest: St. Giles' Cathedral dominates the famous Edinburg street known as the Royal Mile. The current building dates from the 15th century, being largely completed just in time for the Reformation. The brown-brick cross-shaped structure is topped by the easily recognizable crown steeple. The large vaulted interior is typical of its period of construction. St. Giles is home to the chapel of the Order of the Thistle, which was rebuilt in the early 20th century. Its use is reserved for members of the Order and the British monarch. Most of the stained-glass windows in the church date from the 19th and 20th centuries. One of the most famous is the Burne-Jones window which depicts a trio of Biblical heroines. The Tomb of John Knox is outside of the Church, ignominiously paved over by a parking lot.

214. GLASGOW CATHEDRAL

Castle Street, Glasgow G4 0QZ, Scotland

Alternate/Full Name: High Church of Glasgow, St. Mungo's Cathedral
Denomination: Church of Scotland
Dates: c. 6th century (originally completed), 1136 (current building completed)
Web: www.glasgowcathedral.org (official website)

Glasgow Cathedral is one of the oldest intact churches in Scotland, and one of the oldest cathedrals in the United Kingdom. Dating from the Middle Ages, the cathedral was associated with both St. Mungo and the founding of the city of Glasgow. It has also achieved a measure of literary fame thanks to its mention in the book *Rob Roy* by Walter Scott.

Christianity was introduced to Glasgow and Scotland by St. Mungo sometime in the 6th century. According to legend, Mungo was related to King Lot and thus distantly tied to the Arthurian legends. He is believed to have founded the first church in Glasgow, and was later buried in or near this church. Mungo is honored to this day as the patron saint of the city. During the Middle Ages, the church, which had become a popular pilgrimage destination, was replaced with the current cathedral.

In the 15th century, the cathedral was used for a few years to hold classes for the newly founded Glasgow University. The cathedral remained under the jurisdiction of the Roman Catholic Church until the 16th century. Following the turbulent period that followed in the wake of the Protestant Reformation, care of the cathedral was taken over by the city, and it has been used by a succession of Protestant congregations ever since. It is currently used by the Church of Scotland.

Of Interest: Glasgow Cathedral is a venerable Gothic structure that, except for a few restorations, looks more or less as it did at the time of its completion. The very ancient stones, dark with age, give the cathedral a particularly brooding appearance, especially from the front. The interior is a medieval masterpiece, with dark stones, dark woodwork and an intricately designed ceiling, all of which give the church a mystically medieval feel. Inside the church is preserved one of only a handful of rood screens to have survived the Protestant Reformation. The tomb of St. Mungo is in the crypt beneath the church.

---

215. LLANRHYCHWYN CHURCH

Trefriw LL27 0YJ, Wales

Denomination: Church of Wales
Dates: c. 6th century (originally completed), c. 13th century (current building completed)
Web: www.walesonline.co.uk/all-about/churches-in-wales (tourism website)

The Llanrhychwyn Church is the oldest surviving church in Wales, and one of the oldest buildings standing in Great Britain. According to tradition, it was originally established in the 6th century by the legendary Welsh figure Rhychwyn, who also founded the town, making it one of the oldest known Christian parishes in Wales. The church is still occasionally used for worship.

Christianity arrived in Wales as early as the Roman era, but it was not until the sixth century that churches and abbeys started to become widely established throughout the area. According to legend, a prince at the time had a number of sons who helped to found churches throughout Wales. Among these was one Rhychwyn, who built the church at Llanrhychwyn. Rhychwyn and his brother Celynin both went on to become saints of the Catholic Church.

Records concerning the church are limited, but it seems to have been rebuilt and renovated in stages over the course of many centuries. Much of the current building probably dates back to the 13th century, though there are some surviving elements that are far older. It is now part of the Church of Wales, though it is only rarely used for worship. Local farmers look after the church.

Of Interest: The Llanrhychwyn Church is a tiny stone building that both looks and feels ancient. Set amidst a church yard, some of the graves here are very old, and some of the oldest are no longer marked. The church interior consists only of a small sanctuary barely large enough to seat a few dozen people. The beautiful exposed roof beams are among the oldest still in use in Great Britain.

---

216. ST. PATRICK'S CATHEDRAL

43 Abbey Street, Armagh BT61 7DY, Northern Ireland

Denomination: Church of Ireland (sacred to Roman Catholics)
Dates: 445 (originally completed), 1549 (current building completed)
Web: www.stpatricks-cathedral.org (official website)

St. Patrick's Cathedral in Armagh is one of two cathedrals in that city with the same name. One is a Roman Catholic church, while the one discussed here is part of the Church of Ireland in the Anglican communion. Both cathedrals honor Ireland's patron saint, Patrick, who first established Christianity in Ireland at Armagh in the 5th century.

The origins of the cathedral date back to the late Roman era. An early stone church was constructed in Armagh sometime around the year 445, with work possibly overseen by St. Patrick himself. Armagh was the center of Christianity in Ireland at the time, and remained so despite the regular destruction and reconstruction of its churches. Most of the current building dates from the 16th century.

Despite its Catholic roots, the cathedral was incorporated into the Anglican Church in the years following the Reformation. It has served as the seat of the Archdiocese of Armagh in the Church of Ireland ever since. All the while, Armagh never lost importance to the Catholics, who built a new cathedral for themselves in the city in the 19th century. Nevertheless the Anglican St. Patrick's Church is still historically honored by both Christian denominations.

Of Interest: St. Patrick's Church is a stately Gothic structure typical of such buildings constructed during the British occupation of Ireland in the Colonial era. Because the church was destroyed so many times, most of the current structure dates from the 16th century. Despite being an Anglican building, the church houses a significant amount of iconic artwork and statuary that dates back to its Roman Catholic roots. Buried in the cathedral is St. Eithne, a 5th century saint who, according to tradition, was baptized by St. Patrick himself.

---

217. DOWN CATHEDRAL

35 English Street, Downpatrick BT30 6AB, Northern Ireland

Alternate/Full Name: Cathedral Church of the Holy and Undivided Trinity
Denomination: Church of Ireland (sacred to Roman Catholics)
Dates: c. 10th century (originally completed), 1826 (current building completed)
Web: www.downcathedral.org (official website)

Down Cathedral is the site of the tomb of Patrick, Ireland's beloved patron saint. The tradition of Patrick's missionary work is legendary, and his feast day is among the most celebrated in the world. After the division of Ireland most of the places associated with this champion of Catholicism were left in Protestant English territory. Nevertheless, Downpatrick still draws pilgrims from all over the British Isles, and is one of Ireland's top Christian sacred sites.

Ireland's most famous saint and evangelist was not actually Irish. Born in the late 4th century in Western England, Patrick was kidnapped by Irish raiders at a young age and sold as a slave to an important Druidical leader. During his time in captivity he developed both a great faith in God as well as a mastery of the Celtic language and customs. He escaped slavery at the age of twenty-two, and then spent a dozen years recovering and studying in the Monastery of Auxerre. After years of theological training, Patrick decided to put his familiarity with the Celts to good use.

Patrick traveled to Ireland as that country's first truly successful missionary. He settled at Armagh where he established a church, monastery and an early seminary. He traveled throughout Ireland teaching the Gospel, and by the time of his death the majority of Ireland had been converted to Christianity. According to tradition, Patrick died in the year 493, well past his 100th year. He was laid to rest in Down, and at some later point the town was renamed Downpatrick in his honor.

The date of the first church in Downpatrick is uncertain, but a cathedral has existed on the site at least as far back as the 10th century. Over time the church was repeatedly destroyed by Vikings, Normans and Protestants. From 1539 through 1789 the Cathedral lay in ruins. Oddly, it was a visit by the famous Protestant minister John Wesley that spurred interest in Down Cathedral's restoration. The current building was completed in 1826. Catholic pilgrimage to the shrine has increased in recent years, though this trend may see a set back once the United Kingdom leaves the European Union.

Of Interest: Down Cathedral dates back less than two centuries, but looks far older. It is memorable for its simple beauty and setting amidst Ireland's rolling green hills. Many of its architectural elements hearken back to earlier more romantic styles. Unlike most Catholic saint shrines, the grave of Patrick is actually located outside the cathedral and is marked by a tremendous granite boulder. The tradition of the tomb dates back to the 7th century, and later legends add that St. Brigid and St. Colmcille are also buried at the site. An ancient High Cross which stands guard nearby was once located in the marketplace marking the road to the church. Found in pieces scattered throughout Down, it was reassembled and erected just outside of the cathedral in 1897.

---

218. CHRIST CHURCH CATHEDRAL & ST. PATRICK'S CATHEDRAL

Christchurch Plaza, Wood Quay, Dublin 8, Ireland (Christ Church Cathedral)

St. Patrick's Close, Wood Quay, Dublin 8, Ireland (St. Patrick's Cathedral)

Denomination: Church of Ireland
Dates: Church - c. 11th century (originally completed), c. 13th century (current building completed) & Cathedral - c. 12th century (originally completed); c. 1270 (current building completed)
Web: https://christchurchcathedral.ie & www.stpatrickscathedral.ie (official websites)

Christ Church Cathedral and St. Patrick's Cathedral are the two great historic cathedrals of Dublin. Founded as Roman Catholic institutions in the Middle Ages, they are now the seat of the Diocese of Dublin of the Church of Ireland and the national seat of the Church of Ireland, respectively. Together they are among the most visited churches in Ireland.

Christ Church is the oldest church in Dublin, dating back to the 11th century. Strongbow, a nobleman who was instrumental in the English conquest of Ireland in the Middle Ages, was an early patron of the church. Many English monarchs left their stamp on this church, including Henry VIII, who oversaw its conversion to his newly formed Anglican Communion.

The Cathedral of St. Patrick was founded not too long after Christ Church Cathedral. However, St. Patrick's was accorded a nearly equal status, and was also designated as a cathedral during the Middle Ages. In the 16th century it became part of the Anglican Communion. Interestingly, St. Patrick's was selected to serve as the seat of the Church of Ireland rather than Christ Church.

Throughout their history, the two cathedrals presented something of a controversy, since both were considered seats of the Diocese of

Dublin. However, seniority and most official functions were assigned to Christ Church Cathedral up until the 19th century. Today they sort of split the duties of the senior cathedral of the Church of Ireland, with one serving as the seat of the diocese and the other as the seat of the national church.

Of Interest: Christ Church is a stately Gothic structure that evokes a mysterious medieval atmosphere, though much of this is due to retro embellishments that actually date to the 19th century. The crypt houses some very interesting treasures, including, for some reason, 17th century punishment stocks. St. Patrick's Cathedral is the largest church in Ireland, and though also primarily Gothic in design has a more colorful, lighter feel than its contemporary. This is especially true in its famous Lady Chapel. St. Patrick's is also home to several historic treasures, including an ancient Celtic Cross which was associated with St. Patrick's Well. Among the tombs found here is that of Jonathan Swift of *Gulliver's Travels* fame, who served as the Dean of the Cathedral in the early 18th century.

---

219. ST. PETER'S CHURCH

West Street, Drogheda, County Louth, Ireland

Alternate/Full Name: St. Peter's Roman Catholic Church
Denomination: Roman Catholic
Dates: 1793 (originally completed), 1884 (current building completed)
Web: www.saintpetersdrogheda.ie (official website)

St. Peter's Church in Drogheda is one of Ireland's most famous churches as it is the burial site of Irish born saint Oliver Plunket. His death is well remembered, as he was the last Catholic to be martyred for his faith in England. His shrine in Drogheda is the most important saint's tomb in Ireland proper, as St. Patrick is technically buried in Northern Ireland.

Oliver Plunkett was the most prominent Catholic in the British Isles at a time when much of Europe was embroiled in fierce religious wars. He spent time as a student and professor in Rome, and remained in exile there following Oliver Cromwell's conquest of Ireland. Upon his return in 1670, Plunkett found the Church in disarray. He set about restoring the clergy and founded a Jesuit College. Unfortunately, it was destroyed three years later when persecutions against Catholics were renewed.

As Primate of Ireland, he spent most of the 1670s traveling throughout the country in secret where he did his best to help his fellow Catholics. Plunkett was finally captured in 1679, imprisoned in Dublin Castle and accused of plotting against England and the Protestants. He was tried several times, with the first two trials resulting in no conviction. However, at his third trial in 1681 he was found guilty of high treason and brutally executed.

After his death, his relics, which were split up after he had been drawn and quartered, were moved around Europe several times. They were at first interred in England, then moved to a monastery in Germany. Most of his body was eventually laid to rest at Downside Abbey in England. His head made its way to Rome for a while, than back to Armagh in Ireland. Finally a new church was completed in Drogheda, where Oliver Plunkett had established his school, and where his head has been kept ever since.

Of Interest: St. Peter's Church is a Neo-Gothic structure that largely dates back to the reconstruction of the 19th century. It is noted for the single elegant bell tower and classic rose window which grace the main façade. The shrine of Oliver Plunkett is fascinating but fairly gruesome. The chapel features a towering, steeple-like reliquary. At its base, in a glass case, is the severed head of Oliver Plunkett. Not a skull, but his actual preserved head: overall an interesting tribute to the last Catholic to be martyred in the British Isles.

---

220. KNOCK SHRINE

Main Street, Knock, County Mayo, Ireland

Alternate/Full Name: Sanctuary of Our Lady of Knock
Denomination: Roman Catholic (Marian shrine)
Dates: 1880 (completed)
Web: www.knockshrine.ie (official website)

The Knock Shrine is the most popular Marian site in the British Isles. Like Lourdes, it is famous for a miraculous appearance of the Virgin Mary in the 19th century. Unlike Lourdes, there were many witnesses to the event. After years of inquiries, Catholic authorities confirmed the miraculous vision as genuine and Irish pilgrims began to swarm to the site. The Knock Shrine is Ireland's most popular Catholic pilgrimage shrine.

On the evening of August 21, 1879, a certain Mary McLoughlin, a servant in the household of one of the town's clergymen, was strolling past the church on her way to visit a nearby acquaintance. As she walked past, a strange site caught her eye: several small figures appeared upon the church gable dressed in Biblical garb. Thinking at first that they were decorations or statues recently added to the church, she didn't give the matter a second thought, and continued on her way.

However, she returned a short while later with a friend, and it was then that they realized that something was amiss. Both witnessed the figures as though as in a vision. Amazed, they began to gather others to see the strange sight. Within the hour more than a dozen people had witnessed the strange vision. Based on the appearance of the strange figures, the townsfolk concluded that they were the Virgin Mary and her husband Joseph, along with John the Apostle and a lamb sitting quietly on an altar.

The vision lasted well into the night. That might have been the end of it, but a Church-sponsored inquiry into the matter concluded that the vision had been real, though it was unclear exactly what its purpose was. The story of the vision became an overnight sensation.

Even Queen Victoria took an interest, personally requesting a report on the strange occurrence.

Knock soon began attracting pilgrims, growing in popularity throughout the early 1900s. By the mid-20th century Knock was receiving so many pilgrims that a new church, the Basilica of Our Lady, was built to accommodate them all. Even Pope John Paul II made a visit to Knock. It is currently ranked among the world's most popular Marian shrines.

Of Interest: The Knock Shrine consists of a large white modern structure that incorporates elements of an earlier church, known as the Church of the Apparition. The basilica is laid out in an unusual circular pattern with the main entrance facing the plaza. A tall, narrow steeple rises from the center of the building. Among the exterior architectural elements of the building are stones from the original church, which pilgrims traditionally touch when visiting. A fifty-foot cross towers above the plaza in front of the basilica. The focus of the interior of the church is a series of statues which recreate the original vision. The centerpiece of the tableaux is an altar with the Lamb of God standing upon it. A cross rises from the altar, and the whole is surrounded by angels. A trio of figures stands to the altar's left, and includes Joseph the Carpenter and John the Apostle. The Virgin Mary, crowned in gold, stands between them.

LATIN AMERICA

221. STATUE OF CHRIST THE REDEEMER

Parque Nacional da Tijuca-Alta da Boa Vista, Rio de Janeiro, Brazil

Denomination: Public Monument
Dates: 1931 (completed)
Web: https://en.cristoredentoroficial.com.br (official website)

The Statue of Christ the Redeemer is arguably the world's most famous Catholic icon anywhere. Standing upon the crown of Corcovado Mountain overlooking Rio de Janeiro, it is the most recognized symbol of Christianity in all of Latin America. So spectacular is the site of Christ the Redeemer looming over the city that the ocean view of Rio de Janeiro is consistently rated one of the most beautiful in the world. Today it is one of the most popular tourist destinations in Latin America and a must-see for every visitor to Brazil.

The city of Rio de Janeiro was founded in 1565, and the Catholic Church arrived soon afterwards. As capital of Brazil for the better part of several centuries, Rio was one of the most important centers of Catholicism in the Americas. In the mid-19th century a local priest came up with the idea that the city should have a major shrine, and suggested the idea of constructing a Christian monument on the top of Corcovado Mountain. Although the idea for such a monument was locally popular, it was rejected by the government owing to Brazil's strict laws regulating the separation of church and state.

The effort was revived three decades later, and this time there were no objections from the governmental authorities. Fundraising began in 1921, and construction commenced a year later. The monument would be in the form of a statue of Jesus Christ, the largest that had yet been raised anywhere on Earth. Construction took a mere nine years, and was dedicated on October 12, 1931. It was an overnight success, and immediately became a national treasure. At the beginning of the 21st century the statue received a coveted place on the list of the world's New Seven Wonders, virtually guaranteeing that it will remain one of the world's must-see Christian sites for generations to come.

Of Interest: The Statue of Christ the Redeemer thoroughly dominates the skyline of Rio de Janeiro. Standing at just under forty meters in height, its perch on the seven hundred meter peak of Corcovado makes it even more imposing. A design competition resulted in the choice of Jesus with his arms open wide as if to embrace the entire world. The statue's symbolic cross-like appearance is impossible to misinterpret. The statue is constructed of steel-reinforced concrete and finished with limestone. In 2006, a chapel was added to the site to accommodate the pilgrims who desired to hold religious celebrations such as baptisms and weddings there.

---

222. CATHEDRAL OF BRASILIA & SANCTUARY OF DOM BOSCO

Esplanada dos Ministerios lote 12, Brasilia, Brazil, 70050-000 (Cathedral of Brasilia)

SEPS Quadra 702 Asa Sul, Brasilia, Brazil, 70330-710 (Sanctuary of Dom Bosco)

Alternate/Full Name: Metropolitan Cathedral of Our Lady of Aparecida
Denomination: Roman Catholic
Dates: Cathedral - 1970 (completed) & Sanctuary - 1963 (completed)
Web: https://catedral.org.br & http://santuariodombosco.org.br (official websites)

The Cathedral of Brasilia and the Sanctuary of Dom Bosco are two of the ultra-modern churches that grace the ultra-modern skyline of Brazil's capital city. Both constructed in the 1960s, the former is the seat of the Roman Catholic Church in Brasilia, and the latter honors the priest and utopian visionary John Bosco, a saint popular in Brazil.

Together they are among the most popular tourist spots in Brazil's capital.

In 1960, Brazil moved its national government from aging and overcrowded Rio de Janeiro to Brasilia, a new city that was being constructed closer to the heart of the country. The entire capital was being built from the ground up, from its government buildings to its churches. In anticipation of a surge in the area's Catholic population, the Roman Catholic Church established a brand new Archdiocese, complete with a brand new cathedral, here. It was completed and dedicated in 1970.

John "Dom" Bosco was a 19th century Italian born priest who was famous for his work with abandoned children as well as his dream of an idyllic city. Active both in missionary work and politics, he became popular among common people well beyond Italy. Bosco was canonized in 1934. When Brazil built its new capital city of the future, the Catholic Church took the opportunity to build a church here in his honor. The shrine was completed in 1963.

Of Interest: The Cathedral of Brasilia is a modern architecture masterpiece reminiscent of Disney's Space Mountain. Supported by more than a dozen massive boomerang-like structures, it soars above a grand plaza adorned with strange bronze statues and an odd egg-shaped baptistry. The massive stained glass windows completely circle the sanctuary in one gigantic work of art, while statues of angels dangle from the ceiling. The Sanctuary of Dom Bosco represents one of the greatest exercises in the use of color in any church anywhere. From the outside the building appears like a large, boxish frame for scores of immense windows. These windows, all stained glass predominantly in varying shades of blue, are what give the church its magic. During the day, they bathe the church interior with a mystical blue light. At night, a huge golden chandelier illuminates the interior and makes the whole structure glow blue on the outside. Dom Bosco is honored with a statue on display in the sanctuary.

223. BASILICA OF THE NATIONAL SHRINE OF OUR LADY OF APARECIDA

Avenida Dr. Julio Prestes-Ponte Alta, Aparecida-SP, Brazil, 12570-000

Denomination: Roman Catholic (Marian shrine)
Dates: 1834 (originally completed), 1980 (current building completed)
Web: https://www.a12.com/santuario (official website)

The Basilica of the National Shrine of Our Lady of Aparedica is the most famous Marian shrine in the Americas and possibly the second most popular in the world after Lourdes in France. The shrine commemorates an 18th century miracle and is credited with many other miracles since. As many as seven million visitors make the pilgrimage to Aparecida annually, making it the most visited Christian shrine of any denomination in the Western Hemisphere.

In 1717, a statue of the Virgin Mary was netted out of water during a fishing expedition near the small village of Guarantinequeta. The previously unsuccessful outing suddenly yielded a great quantity of fish, just in time to prepare a banquet for a visiting nobleman. The immense success of the fishing trip was attributed to the Virgin Mary. One of the fishermen, Felipe Pedroso, kept the icon and brought it back to his village where it was soon venerated.

Later, other miracles were attributed to the statue, and word began to spread. A chapel was erected in nearby Porto Itaguassu to accommodate the pilgrims flocking to see the icon. A larger church was built nearby in Aparecida, where the icon was moved in 1745. Eventually, the flood of religious visitors necessitated a full-fledged cathedral, and in the 1830's and 1840's a massive new church was constructed to accommodate the statue. It continued to reside here throughout the 19th and 20th centuries.

In the early 1900s the Catholic Church formally recognized the Shrine of Our Lady of Aparecida as a full-fledged Marian site, and in 1908 the cathedral was designated as a basilica. In 1929 the Virgin of

Aparecida officially became the patron saint of Brazil. In the 1980's, an even bigger cathedral was built to accommodate the crowds. Today the Shrine of Our Lady of Aparecida is among the most visited Christian sites in the world outside of Europe and the Holy Land.

Of Interest: The Basilica of the National Shrine of Our Lady of Aparedica is one of the largest buildings in Latin America. Unlike many newly built Christian shrines it was not constructed on the site of an earlier church, but rather near the old one. It is laid out with a traditional cross-shaped sanctuary, and features an absolutely massive clock tower and one of the largest domes in the Americas. The church interior has seating for tens of thousands of pilgrims. Hundreds of enormous windows keep the basilica well lighted. The focal point is the Shrine of Our Lady of Aparecida, where the famous statue is kept. This statue of Mary, believed to have been the work of a monk named Frei Agostino de Jesus, probably dates back to the middle of the 17th century. Over the centuries it has been refurbished, adorned in gold-trimmed robes, and topped off with a crown. It is displayed daily.

---

224. CATHEDRAL BASILICA OF OUR LADY OF PEACE & SAN FRANCISCO CHURCH

Potosi, Junin, La Paz, Bolivia
(Cathedral Basilica of Our Lady of Peace)

Plaza Mayor de San Francisco, Sagarnaga 173, La Paz, Bolivia
(San Francisco Church)

Alternate/Full Name: Basilica of San Francisco
Denomination: Roman Catholic
Completed: Cathedral - 1692 (originally completed); 1925 (current building completed) & Church - 1581 (originally completed); 1758 (current building completed)
Web: www.boliviatravelsite.com/tourist-attractions/la-paz/cathedral-and-plaza-murillo (tourism website)

The Cathedral Basilica of Our Lady of Peace and the San Francisco Church are the major historical Catholic churches of the city of La Paz in Bolivia. The former is the seat of the Roman Catholic Archdiocese of La Paz, while the latter traces its roots to a convent of the original Spanish settlement. Both churches are designated as basilicas.

The Catholic Church arrived in what is now the city of La Paz in the mid-16th century with the founding of the San Francisco Convent. The first church at the convent was completed in 1581. A diocese was established here in 1605, and the city's first cathedral was completed in 1692. Due to deterioration, this cathedral was replaced by a new building in 1925. It became the seat of an Archdiocese in 1943.

The original church of the convent collapsed in the early 17th century. Construction on the new San Francisco Church began in 1743 and was completed in 1758. The rest of the convent was rebuilt in the 1950s. Pope John Paul II visited the city in 1989, and was present when the finishing touches were put on the cathedral.

Of Interest: The Cathedral Basilica of Our Lady of Peace is a huge baroque structure with a very broad façade that makes the church appear less tall than it actually is. The bell towers are relatively short but wide, crowned by intricate black domes that match the massive main dome. The bells in each tower are exposed in the style of an old Spanish colonial mission. One unusual feature of the interior are the unusually square pillars which support the soaring nave. The San Francisco Church is also baroque, but with a much older feel than the cathedral. The façade is particularly ornate, with scrollwork reminiscent of Moorish design. The interior has a very medieval feel, with the exception of the front of the church which is completely dominated by an absolutely breathtaking golden altar piece.

225. CONVENT OF ST. DOMINIC

Jiron Camana 170, Cercado de Lima, Peru

Alternate/Full Name: Basilica and Maximus Convent of Our Lady of the Rosary
Denomination: Roman Catholic
Dates: c. 16th century (originally completed), 1766 (current building completed)
Web: www.peru.travel/en-us/where-to-go/lima (tourism website)

The Convent of St. Dominic is the site of the tomb of St. Rose of Lima, the first Catholic saint to be born in the New World. One of the first major saint shrines in the Americas, it is the most popular Christian pilgrimage site in Lima, and one of the most sacred Catholic sites in South America. The Convent of St. Dominic is part of the Historic Center of Lima UNESCO World Heritage Site.

Isabel Flores de Oliva was born in Lima in 1586. Her nickname, Rosa, was attributed to a miraculous vision of Isabel's head in the form of a rose by one of her family's servants. This later became her confirmation name. Rosa became a devout Catholic at an early age, and by her teens was determined to lead a life of the Spirit. Her early endeavors included extreme fasting and, to a lesser extent, self-disfigurement that included head shaving. In later years she also became a recluse.

Her efforts attracted the attention of the local Dominican convent, who invited her to join without a family donation. Rosa was famous throughout Lima for her acts of charity. She sold her own hand-made embroidery and home-grown flowers to raise money for the poor of Lima. By the time of her death in 1617 she had become a beloved daughter of the Spanish colonies. She was buried in the convent, along with Toribio de Mogrovejo and Martin de Porres, all three of whom were later recognized as saints.

During the Colonial Era, Lima was adorned with some of the largest early churches and monasteries in the New World. The Convent of St. Dominic was established by monks in the late 16th century.

Later also referred to as the Convent of Santa Rosa, the monastery rose to prominence when it became associated with Rose of Lima. After her death, the Convent of St. Dominic became a major Catholic pilgrimage shrine.

Of Interest: The Convent of St. Dominic consists of a complex of buildings of various architectural styles. While large, the main basilica is not particularly tall, but does have an absolutely stunning baroque bell tower. The interior houses a wealth of beautiful artwork. An effigy of St. Rose of Lima can be found within the church. However, her tomb is elsewhere on the convent grounds.

---

226. CUSCO CATHEDRAL & CHURCH OF THE SOCIETY OF JESUS

Plaza des Armas, Cusco, Peru

Alternate/Full Name: Cathedral of Santo Domingo, Cathedral Basilica of the Assumption of the Virgin & Jesuit Church of the Companions of Jesus
Denomination: Roman Catholic
Dates: Cathedral - 1654 (completed) & Church - 1668 (completed)
Web: www.cuscoperu.com/en/travel/cusco/temples-convents (tourism wesbsite)

Cusco Cathedral and the Church of the Society of Jesus in the mountain city of Cusco are two of the most spectacular early churches in South America. Flanking two sides of the city's great central plaza, these churches, along with yet a third church, completely dominate the city's main square, the Plaza des Armas. Together they are part of the City of Cusco UNESCO World Heritage Site.

Cusco was the capital of the expansive Incan Empire when it was discovered by Spanish conquistadors in the 16th century. The Spanish, under the leadership of Francisco Pizarro, followed in the footsteps of Cortez in Mexico, and in no time flat the Incan Empire was laid waste. Many of its greatest monuments were torn down, soon to be replaced by public buildings and churches. The first church to be built was the Church of the Triumph, constructed on the site where a small garrison of Spanish Conquistadors held off a vastly superior army of Incan warriors.

By the time of its completion in the mid-16th century, the Catholic population of the city had grown so large that plans were made for the construction of a massive cathedral. Around the same time, a group of Jesuit priests began to draw up plans for their own church, to be located close to the cathedral. In their eagerness they designed a church that rivaled the cathedral in size and magnificence, which did not sit well with the city's bishop. Nevertheless construction on both edifices proceeded apace.

In an effort to forestall the Jesuits, the bishop appealed to the Vatican to intervene. But it took so long for the message to reach the Pope and his reply returned to Peru that the exterior of the Jesuit church was all-but-completed before it could be stopped. Both of these massive churches were completed quickly thanks to easy access to enormous quantities of pre-quarried stones taken from the old Incan city. Fortunately, the Incan ruins were so expansive that large areas survived the Spanish pillaging. Both churches are now considered historical treasures of Peru's colonial Christian heritage.

Of Interest: Cusco Cathedral is one of the most intact examples of early Spanish Colonial church architecture in South America. The bulk of the cathedral is the original construction and dates from the 16th and early 17th centuries. The exterior is a blend of several architectural styles, including a bit of both Gothic and Baroque, whose dominant feature is a broad façade flanked by a pair of bell towers. The cathedral's interior is home to a great wealth of art and artifacts, including a giant altar made from solid silver. The cathedral also doubles as an art museum, and is home to the city's largest collection of art from the Spanish colonial era. The Church of the Society of Jesus, while a bit smaller, is perhaps even more architecturally impressive. Also built in Spanish colonial style, the exterior boasts even more intricate stonework than the cathedral as well as a magnificent dome, outdoing its rival on both counts.

---

227. LAS LAJAS SANCTUARY

Santuario de Las Lajas, Potosi, Nanno, Narino, Colombia

Alternate/Full Name: Shrine of Our Lady of Las Lajas
Denomination: Roman Catholic (Marian shrine)
Dates: 1756 (originally completed), 1953 (current building completed)
Web: www.colombia.travel/en/what-to-do/pacific/pasto/experiences/las-lajas-sanctuary (tourism website)

The Las Lajas Sanctuary in Colombia is among the most fantastic churches in one of the most magnificent settings to be found anywhere on Earth. Clinging to the side of a bridge-spanned gorge, the most talented of Hollywood's set designers would be hard pressed to match this soaring masterpiece in white marble. Because its fame is overshadowed by larger and more popular shrines elsewhere in Latin America, and also because of its isolation, the Sanctuary of Las Lajas is among the best kept architectural secrets of the Roman Catholic Church anywhere on the planet.

Spanish conquistadors and settlers arrived in Colombia at the turn of the 16th century, and the Catholic Church arrived soon afterwards. However, while churches and cathedrals were quickly erected in Cartagena and other cities along the Gulf of Mexico, the Pacific Coast was long neglected. Moreover, for the better part of two and a half centuries, Colombia lacked a great pilgrimage shrine such as those that existed in Mexico and Peru.

That changed in 1754, when a native Colombian woman named Maria and her daughter Rosa sought shelter from a storm under a great rock called Las Lajas, which means the flat stone. As the lightning flashed, Rosa noticed what looked like a great painting of the Virgin Mary over the rock. Rosa, who was mute, shouted out when she realized what she saw. A few years later, a blind man named Fray Juan undertook a sacred journey from Ecuador to Colombia. Unaided he made his way up the western coast of the Pacific Ocean, collecting donations as he went.

When he arrived at Las Lajas, where the miraculous image was still imprinted on the rock, he decided to build a chapel. According to tradition, he regained his sight when it was completed. This original church stood on the spot where the two miracles occurred for nearly two centuries, during which time it became the most popular Christian pilgrimage destination in Colombia. In the 1950s the Sanctuary of Las Lajas was recognized as a sacred site by the Roman Catholic Church. The old chapel was removed and replaced with the magnificent new basilica which is known today.

Of Interest: The Las Lajas Sanctuary is one of the most architecturally unique and jaw-dropping sites in Christendom. Constructed to incorporate the Las Lajas Stone, the Sanctuary church is built precariously on the side of the steep gorge of the Guaitara River. A series of bridges, tunnels and stairways connect the sanctuary to the nearby hillsides and to the river below. The overall effect of the delicate white stonework amidst green-covered mountains, white-water rapids and tumbling waterfalls makes the place look like the set of Rivendell from *Lord of the Rings*. Constructed in a modern-baroquish style, one side of the church is adjacent to the mountainside, which actually forms the church's front wall. This was done so that the miraculous painting could be incorporated into the church without removing it from the mountain. A number of niches in the rock wall are put to clever use displaying statues and icons.

---

228. METROPOLITAN CATHEDRAL

Plaza de la Constitucion S/N, Centro, Cuahtemoc,
Mexico City, Mexico, 06000

Alternate/Full Name: Metropolitan Cathedral of the Assumption of the most Blessed Virgin Mary into Heavens
Denomination: Roman Catholic
Dates: 1532 (originally completed), 1813 (current building completed)

Web: www.gcatholic.org/churches/northamerica/3165 (Catholic website)

The Metropolitan Cathedral of Mexico City was the largest cathedral built in the New World during the Colonial era. Begun by the conquistador Hernando Cortez on the ruins of an old Aztec temple, the Metropolitan was the first cathedral constructed in Central America. It is also the headquarters of the Catholic Church in Mexico, one of the largest dioceses in the world. The Metropolitan Cathedral of Mexico City is part of the Historic Center of Mexico City UNESCO World Heritage Site.

The history of the Metropolitan Cathedral began in the bloody aftermath of the Spanish conquest of the Aztec city of Tenochtitlan. In 1521 the Spanish took Tenochtitlan by siege, and what wasn't destroyed in the siege he ordered destroyed. Among those buildings destroyed was the immense step pyramid Templo Mayor. In 1524, it was decided that the site of the temple would be cleared, and its foundation and materials used for the construction of a church.

As the capital of the fastest growing Catholic colony in the Americas, it wasn't long before the Spanish authorities decided to replace this early church with an even more magnificent cathedral. Work began in 1573 with the expansion of the existing church, and continued for the better part of two and a half centuries. However, the construction of the cathedral was plagued with difficulties almost from the start, difficulties that were attributed by local superstition to bad luck associated with the destruction of the old Aztec Temple.

Among the problems encountered was the belated discovery that the foundations lay on top of soft ground. Other problems included a major flood which halted construction in the 1600s, a fire which damaged much of the cathedral interior in the 1960s, and the tragic death of the cathedral's bell ringer in 1947. The Metropolitan Cathedral briefly served as a royal chapel during Mexico's imperial period, and witnessed the coronation of the emperor Maximillian I. The cathedral remains to this day the heart of Christianity in Mexico.

Of Interest: The Metropolitan Cathedral dominates the Plaza de la Constitucion in the heart of Mexico City. Most of the cathedral dates from the 16th and 17th centuries, though much of the structure is newer due to the constant renovations of later periods. Virtually nothing is left of the original church. One of the largest colonial Gothic structures, the Metropolitan boasts one of the world's broadest facades, including two massive bell towers as well as a secondary façade adjoining the tabernacle building. The towers are home to an impressive twenty-five bells, including the famous Mute bell, which was silenced in 1947 after the death of the bell ringer. The interior of the cathedral is a labyrinth of stunning art and architecture. There are two main altars and one of the best collections of chapels in the Western Hemisphere: sixteen in all, each representing one of the cathedral's religious fraternities. A number of important tombs can be found throughout the cathedral, including that of Juan de Zumaragga, the first Archbishop of Mexico and one of the earliest major Church figures in the New World.

---

229. BASILICA OF OUR LADY OF GUADALUPE

Plaza de las Americas 1, Villa de Guadalupe,
Mexico City, Mexico, 07050

Denomination: Roman Catholic (Marian shrine)
Dates: 1532 (originally completed), 1976 (current building completed)
Web: https://virgendeguadalupe.org.mx (official website)

The Basilica of Our Lady of Guadalupe is one of the most important and popular Marian Shrines in the Americas, second only to the Basilica of Aparaceda in Brazil. One of the busiest churches in the world, it is claimed that in December of 2009, the Basilica of Our Lady of Guadalupe witnessed the largest number of pilgrims ever to gather at a Catholic shrine in a single two-day period ever, with crowd estimates of over a million. This church is so popular that a second basilica was constructed next door to the first in order to accommodate devotees.

Half a century after Columbus discovered the New World, Catholicism was still taking root in the Americas. Throughout the

Spanish domains there were as yet no great home-grown miracles. That changed in 1531, when a peasant named Juan Diego experienced a vision of the Virgin Mary in the desert outside of Mexico City. The apparition of Mary instructed Diego to construct a church on the spot.

The peasant rushed off to the local bishop, who inquired for proof of the event. Thankfully Mary made a second appearance, and she instructed Diego to return to the bishop with roses from a nearby rose bush. By the time he found the bishop again, the roses had transformed into a picture of the Virgin as Diego had seen her in his vision. The picture, which was likely beyond a peasant's ability to produce, was accepted as miraculous proof of the claim.

Construction of a church began shortly thereafter. Juan Diego has become a figure of some controversy, as no reliable, contemporary records of his life exist. Nevertheless he was designated as a saint in 1990. The church that he founded has since grown into an immense, two basilica complex which dominates the eastern suburbs of Mexico City. As for the icon of Mary, all scientific investigations to date have failed to rule out its authenticity.

Of Interest: The Basilica of Our Lady of Guadalupe consists of two huge churches dominating an immense plaza known as the Villa de Guadalupe. The original basilica was founded in 1531, and was rebuilt and expanded several times. The current structure largely dates from the early 18th century. In the 1970s it was decided a new basilica would be constructed. However, the old building was not demolished, and after years of repairs is now once again open to the public. The New Basilica, while lacking the architectural appeal or historical important of its predecessor, is now the religious center of the shrine. A strictly modern affair, the circular building looks like a cross between a soccer stadium and a circus tent. The interior is similarly modern, and more functional than inspirational. Nevertheless its design allows for large crowds to come and worship and venerate the 16th century icon, which is prominently displayed in the new Basilica.

230. SANCTUARY OF ATOTONILCO

Calle Principal, Atotoniclo, Guanajuato, Mexico, 27700

Alternate/Full Name: Sanctuary of Jesus of Nazareth of Atotonilco
Denomination: Roman Catholic
Dates: c. 18th century (completed)
Web: www.visitmexico.com/en/actividades-principales/guanajuato/enter-the-sanctuary-of-jesus-nazarene (tourism website)

The Sanctuary of Atotonilco is one of the great architectural and artistic legacies of the colonial Spanish Empire in Mexico. Nicknamed the Sistine Chapel of Mexico, the sanctuary is home to one of the greatest collections of Christian mural art in the Western Hemisphere. Painted over the course of several decades, murals cover nearly all the available interior space. The church is also famous for its healing waters and is also associated with the Mexican War of Independence.

According to tradition, the church traces its origins to a vision by a priest named Neri. Father Neri was inspired to found a church on the site while resting there after a long journey. He spent almost four decades overseeing its construction before his death in 1776. The sanctuary was largely completed by the end of the 18th century.

Ignacio Allende, one of the great military leaders of the Mexican independence movement, attended church here and was married here. In 1810, the sanctuary became an early rallying point for the revolutionaries. For a time the rebels used an icon of the Virgin Mary taken from the church as their banner. Because of its association with the revolution the sanctuary is honored as an important historical site. The Sanctuary of Atotonilco is a UNESCO World Heritage Site.

Of Interest: The Sanctuary of Atotonilco is a hulking Baroque structure, with an exterior perhaps more reminiscent of a castle than a church. The interior is another story. The place is a treasure trove of murals and artwork. Thousands of paintings fill the place, depicting Biblical scenes and people that span nearly every major story of the New Testament. Among the most memorable is a stunning mural depicting The Last Supper. The centerpiece of the shrine is a statue of Jesus tied to a column and bloodied. It is paraded through the community every year.

---

231. HAVANA CATHEDRAL

156 Empedrado, Havana, Cuba

Alternate/Full Name: Cathedral of St. Christopher
Denomination: Roman Catholic
Dates: 1777 (completed)
Web: www.arquidiocesisdelahabana.org (official website)

Havana Cathedral is Cuba's national cathedral and one of the most historic and distinctive buildings in the capital. One of the most magnificent Roman Catholic churches to be found on any island in the Caribbean, it is one of the best examples of Spanish Colonial Baroque architecture in Cuba. The Havana Cathedral is a UNESCO World Heritage Site.

Christianity was temporarily introduced to Cuba in 1492 when Christopher Columbus discovered the island during his first voyage. The first permanent settlement, and the first Catholic parish on the island, came a few decades later. Although Havana had a small church as far back as the 16th century, the cathedral was not built until the 1700s. Construction took place under the auspices of the Jesuits until they were expelled from Cuba in 1767.

The cathedral was completed in 1777, and immediately became one of the most important centers of Roman Catholic worship in the Caribbean. From around 1796 to 1898, the corpse of Christopher Columbus was interred here. Despite the nation's current communist rule, the Cathedral of Havana remains in active use.

Of Interest: Havana Cathedral is a large baroque structure which dominates the heart of the Old City. From the front the façade looks more like an oversized Spanish mission than a traditional cathedral, and is flanked by a strangely mismatched pair of towers, clock to the left and bells to the right. The interior looks more traditionally baroque, with a wealth of beautiful artwork and statuary, including a locally famous statue of St. Christopher. Unfortunately the body of Christopher Columbus has been gone for over a century.

---

232. OUR LADY OF THE ASSUMPTION CO-CATHEDRAL

38 Ciro Frias, Baracoa, Cuba

Alternate/Full Name: Baracoa Cathedral
Denomination: Roman Catholic
Dates: 1807 (originally completed), 1905 (current building completed)
Web: www.cuba.travel/en/destinations/baracoa-guantanamo/what-to-do (tourism website)

Our Lady of the Assumption Co-Cathedral is a 19th century church that is home to one of the most historic religious artifacts in the Americas: the Cruz de la Parra. This cross, assembled by Spanish sailors, was erected on the spot where Columbus first set foot upon the shore of Cuba in 1492. The cathedral both commemorates this event and serves as the seat of the Diocese of Guantanamo-Baracoa.

The city of Baracoa stands at the easternmost end of Cuba. According to the most accepted account, it was here that Christopher Columbus first set foot on the island. Though neither Columbus nor any of his crewmembers remained long at the site, it was given a name: Porto Santo. To mark their claim of the island for both Spain and the Roman Catholic Church, Columbus had a wooden cross constructed and erected here.

Amazingly, despite being left out in the open for decades, the Cruz de la Parra managed to survive. It was in fact the only cross left behind by Columbus to remain more or less intact. Though recent scientific research indicates that the cross was made from native wood and did not come from Europe, carbon dating did place it's completion around 1500. It is thus the oldest verified Christian artifact in the entire Western Hemisphere.

Of Interest: Our Lady of the Assumption Co-Cathedral is largely a replacement of an earlier church that was destroyed by fire in the 19th century. Architecturally it is a modern if somewhat uninspired take on traditional Spanish Colonial construction. However, pilgrims do not come here for the church, but rather to see the historic Cruz de la Parra, which has been kept in the city for over five centuries. It is currently on display in the church in a wooden and glass case. A replica has been erected outside of the church on the spot where the original cross stood for decades.

---

233. BASILICA CATHEDRAL OF SANTA MARIA LA MENOR

Callejon de los Curas, Santa Domingo, Dominican Republic, 10210

Denomination: Roman Catholic
Dates: 1541 (completed)
Web: www.godominicanrepublic.com/poi/churches/santo-domingo/catedral-primada-de-america (tourism website)

The Basilica Cathedral of Santa Maria La Menor and the city of Santo Domingo are generally recognized as the birthplace of Christianity in the New World. For a while Santo Domingo served as the headquarters of the Catholic Church in the New World, and the cathedral its chief place of worship. For many years the cathedral also had the added attraction of the tomb of Christopher Columbus. Santa Maria La Menor remains to this day one of the most important Catholic churches in the Caribbean, and is an all-but-mandatory pilgrimage stop for Christian tourists to the island. The Cathedral of Santa Maria La Menor is part of the Colonial City of Santo Domingo UNESCO World Heritage Site.

The early history of the church was closely tied to the voyages of Christopher Columbus. He first set foot in the New World in 1492 in what later became the Dominican Republic. His claim to the island on behalf of Spain and the Church set the stage for five hundred years of the dominance of Catholicism in Latin America. The city of Santo Domingo was founded a few years after Columbus' first voyage, and for many years it was a major center of Catholic activities and missionary efforts. Santa Maria La Menor was completed in 1540, becoming the first full-fledged cathedral in the Americas.

The importance of Santo Domingo began to wane by the end of the 16th century, as larger and more strategic cities were built by the Spanish in Cuba, Mexico, Panama, Columbia and Peru. Santo Domingo nevertheless remained a key transit center, and often served as a base for various conquistadors. Throughout the colonial period the city became a battleground between Spain, France and England, and was frequently troubled by pirates. However, the church survived largely intact.

At nearly five-hundred year-old the Cathedral of Santa Maria La Menor still remains almost unchanged from the time of its original construction save only repairs and the occasional refurbishment. The cathedral is one of the most popular tourist sites on the island and among the most visited churches in the Caribbean, and overall is considered to be one of the most historically important churches in Latin America.

Of Interest: The Basilica Cathedral of Santa Maria La Menor is an excellent example of 16th century Spanish-colonial architecture. It was one of the larger churches in the Americas for the better part of a century. The façade is constructed of coral limestone. The interior of the church houses an impressive collection of artifacts and treasures. The tomb of Christopher Columbus once stood on a spot just inside of the main entrance. The main altar is primarily constructed out of silver. Other treasures of the church include furniture, artwork, and jewelry. At the time of this writing a museum was under construction within the cathedral to house and display many of the artifacts.

234. CATHEDRAL OF SAN JUAN BAUTISTA & SAN JOSE CHURCH

151 Calle del Cristo, San Juan, Puerto Rico, 00902 (Cathedral of San Juan Bautista)

Calle del Cristo, San Juan, Puerto Rico, 00901 (San Jose Church)

Alternate/Full Name: Metropolitan Cathedral of St. John the Baptist
Denomination: Roman Catholic
Dates: Cathedral - 1540 (completed) & Church - 1532 (completed)
Web: https://catedral-san-juan-bautista.business.site & www.iglesiasanjosepr.org (official websites)

The Cathedral Basilica of San Juan Bautista and the San Jose Church are the oldest parish/congregation and the oldest church on American soil, respectively. Parts of the latter can be dated back to 1532. Ponce de Leon, of Fountain of Youth fame, was interred here for nearly three centuries. Together these two churches are among the most popular tourist destinations in Puerto Rico.

San Juan was one of the very first permanent European settlements in the Americas, and it was here that the Spanish constructed some of the earliest Catholic churches in the New World. One of these, the Iglesia de San Jose, was started by Dominican monks in 1532. While the Church of San Juan Bautista was actually completed first, it was destroyed in 1540 by a hurricane. It was soon replaced by a full-fledged stone cathedral.

The famous Spanish explorer Ponce de Leon was closely associated with both churches. He served as governor of Puerto Rico and was instrumental in the construction of both buildings. De Leon was buried in the San Jose church from the mid-16th to the mid-19th century before being removed to the cathedral.

Following the Spanish American War, Puerto Rico became a territory of the United States. Overnight these became America's oldest churches. One of the cathedral's congregants, Carlos Manuel

Rodriquez Santiago, rose to prominence in the Roman Catholic Church in the 20th century and is currently on his way to becoming a saint. He died in 1963, and in 1997 was beatified by Pope John Paul II. In 1966, the San Jose Church was added to the San Juan National Historic Site. It was designated a UNESCO World Heritage Site in 1983.

Of Interest: Both the Cathedral Basilica of San Juan Bautista and the San Jose Church look much as they did upon their completion nearly five centuries ago, and are classic examples of early Spanish Colonial church architecture. There are three points of primary interest within the cathedral. The first is the immense, carved marble tomb of the explorer and colonial governor Ponce de Leon. The others include the beautiful statue and shrine of the Virgin of Providence, and the Reliquary of Carlos Manuel Rodriguez Santiago, who locals hope may one day become a saint. The San Jose Church sanctuary is adorned with artwork, some of which was rediscovered during a recent renovation. Ponce de Leon's grandson is buried beneath the church, and the family's coat-of-arms is still on display here.

---

235. SPANISH TOWN CATHEDRAL

Red Church Street, Spanish Town, Jamaica

Alternate/Full Name: St. Jago de la Vega Cathedral, St. Catherine's Parish Church
Denomination: Anglican
Dates: 1655 (originally completed),
1714 (current building completed)
Web: www.jnht.com/site_spanish_town_cathedral.php
(official website)

The Spanish Town Cathedral is the oldest Anglican church in the Caribbean and one of the oldest non-Catholic churches in the Americas. Built on the site of an earlier Spanish-built Roman Catholic church, it is also one of the oldest surviving buildings on the island of Jamaica, and is one of that country's major historic tourist destinations.

Jamaica was originally a Spanish colony in the early 16th and 17th centuries during which time the island was Roman Catholic. When the British arrived and captured Jamaica in 1655, the Catholic priests were removed from their posts and the island converted to the Church of England. The Anglican parish founded here is one of the oldest in the world outside of the British Isles.

The original Catholic building was torn down in the 17th century and a new church built in its place. This in turn was badly damaged by a hurricane in the early 18th century. Most of the current structure dates from a reconstruction in 1714. It is now counted among the most historic buildings on the island of Jamaica.

Of Interest: The Spanish Town Cathedral is architecturally somewhat unusual, with an odd layout and a red brick mishmash of styles including elements ranging from Gothic to American Colonial. The grounds of the church are enclosed by a brick wall. The uppermost structure of the bell tower is a more recent reconstruction that looks as though it were borrowed from a turn-of-the-century beachside hotel. However the lush greenery surrounding the cathedral, which includes swaying palm trees, does give it an exotic feel.

---

236. ST. PETER'S CHURCH

Queen Street, St. George's, Bermuda

Alternate/Full Name: Their Majesties Chappell in St. George's
Denomination: Anglican
Dates: 1612 (originally completed),
1620 (current building completed)
Web: www.stpeters.bm (official website)

St. Peter's Church on the island of Bermuda is the oldest Anglican Church in the world outside of the British Isles. Although the church has been damaged and repaired on a number of occasions, the parish has been continuously active since its founding. It is the oldest non-Catholic church in use in the New World.

Throughout the 16th century, the majority of the Americas were colonies of the Spanish and Portuguese empires, and by extension territories of the Roman Catholic Church. When the British finally decided to establish their own colonies, they set up the island colony of Bermuda as a stepping stone. With the first colonists at the beginning of the 17th century came the island's first house of worship. This was the Church of England's first toehold outside of the home islands.

The initial building, quickly constructed, soon needed to be replaced. The permanent structure, more or less as it exists today, was completed in 1620. St. Peter's remained Bermuda's primary place of worship until the Hamilton Cathedral was consecrated in the 1890s. St. Peter's Church is a UNESCO World Heritage Site.

Of Interest: St. Peter's Church is a stately structure of somewhat indeterminate though clearly colonial architectural style. Despite being positioned on a hill at the top of a dramatic flight of steps, the church is somewhat plain, even modernish in appearance. However, the interior is an entirely different matter. Constructed from hewn and dark stained wood, it is one of the most exotic looking Anglican churches anywhere. It almost looks like a movie set of a 19th century mission church in the South Pacific. The whitewashed interior walls are covered in plaques and memorials commemorating parishioners and events in the history of the church.

NORTHERN AMERICA

---

237. ALL SAINT'S CATHEDRAL & ST. PAUL'S CHURCH

1330 Cathedral Lane, Halifax, Nova Scotia, B3H 2Z1 (All Saint's Cathedral)

1749 Argyle Street, Halifax, Nova Scotia, B3J 3K4 (St. Paul's Church)

Alternate/Full Name: Cathedral Church of All Saints
Denomination: Church of Canada
Dates: Cathedral - 1910 (completed) & Church - 1750 (completed)
Web: www.cathedralchurchofallsaints.com & www.stpaulshalifax.org (official websites)

All Saint's Cathedral and St. Paul's Church are the most historic Anglican churches in the province of Nova Scotia and among the most famous Anglican institutions in all of Canada. The former is the seat of the Anglican Diocese in Halifax as well as the largest Anglican cathedral in Canada. The latter is the oldest surviving Anglican church in Canada, and one of Nova Scotia's most popular historic sites.

The Church of St. Paul was the first Anglican parish formed in Canada outside of Newfoundland. The parish was established in 1749 and the church completed the following year. A number of British heroes of the Seven Years War and the American Revolution were buried here in the late 18th century. St. Paul's became the seat of the first Anglican Diocese outside of the British Isles in 1787. It was designated as a National Historic Site of Canada in 1981.

The Cathedral of All Saints was constructed around the turn of the century in order to accommodate the growing population of Halifax. This need was especially pressing after one of Halifax's other major churches, St. Luke's, burned down in 1905. The cathedral was completed in 1910, at which time it became the seat of the Diocese of Nova Scotia and Prince Edward Island.

Of Interest: All Saint's Cathedral is an imposing Neo-Gothic structure that is among the largest churches in Canada. Interestingly, the cathedral does not have a distinctive bell tower or spire of any sort. Because of this it looks more like an immense collegiate chapel that might be found on the grounds of a private school or university. St. Paul's Church is a beautiful old Georgian building typical of, but somewhat larger than, standard churches of the period. It is architecturally distinctive due to the fact that the church is predominantly painted white while the belfry is a dark grey with green roofing. There are a number of beautiful monuments both inside and outside of the church commemorating members from the late 18th and early 19th centuries.

---

238. CATHEDRAL BASILICA OF OUR LADY OF QUEBEC

16 Rue de Buade, Quebec City, Quebec, G1R 4A1

Denomination: Roman Catholic
Dates: 1633 (originally completed), 1843 (current building completed)
Web: www.holydoorquebec.ca/en/cathedral (official website)

The Cathedral Basilica of Notre Dame de Quebec was one of the first churches in Canada and the first truly major church of any denomination in non-Latin North America. It was also the first cathedral in North America outside of the Spanish domains to be designated as a full basilica. The Cathedral of Notre Dame de Quebec is a religious and historic treasure to all Canadians, and is one of Canada's most visited churches. The Cathedral of Notre Dame de Quebec is part of the Historic District of Old Quebec UNESCO World Heritage Site.

Quebec City was founded in 1608 as the first permanent European city in North America outside of Latin America. The city's earliest chapel was built in 1633 and was the first Francophone parish outside of continental France. In the 1640s the original chapel was expanded into a full-fledged cathedral in order to accommodate the establishment of the Archdiocese of Quebec in 1658. It remained the most important French Catholic diocese in North America throughout much of the 17th and 18th centuries.

At the end of the French and Indian War in 1763, Canada was ceded to England. However, the territory of Quebec was permitted to retain its French language and culture as well as its religious beliefs. Thus the Cathedral of Notre Dame de Quebec was not taken over by the Anglican Church, as many local residents undoubtedly feared would happen, and it remained Catholic. This status was formalized in the 1950s when the Vatican designated the Archbishop of Quebec as the Primate of Canada.

Notre Dame de Quebec was heavily renovated in the years following the Seven Years War, and again in the 19th and 20th centuries, the last time after a fire which had severely damaged the interior. Today the cathedral is the center of Catholicism in Canada and a popular destination for French Canadian pilgrims. It is also one of the most popular tourist sites in this heavily touristed city.

Of Interest: The Cathedral Basilica of Notre Dame de Quebec dominates the city skyline from its perch inside the old city walls. Virtually nothing remains of the original 17th century building, and much of what stands today dates from the 20th century reconstruction. The elegant exterior is easily recognized with its cross-capped steeple which is the highest point in the city. The cathedral interior is one of the finest examples of neo-baroque architecture in Canada. It is richly decorated, with a heavily gilded main altar and canopy. The stained-glass windows are some of the most magnificent in Quebec. Beneath the cathedral is a crypt containing the tombs of many prominent clergyman and other leaders of Quebec. The tomb of the city's first bishop is located in its own chapel.

239. BASILICA OF SAINTE-ANNE-DE-BEAUPRE

10018 Avenue Royale, Sainte-Anne-de-Beaupre, Quebec, GOA 3CO

Denomination: Roman Catholic
Dates: 1606 (originally completed), 1946 (current building completed)
Web: https://sanctuairesainteanne.org (official website)

The Basilica of Sainte-Anne-de-Beaupre is one of Canada's most important Roman Catholic shrines, and is famous for many miracles of healing which have attracted countless pilgrims from around the world. Just outside of Quebec City, it is among Canada's most visited churches. In addition to the many year-round visitors, there is an annual pilgrimage trek to the basilica that begins across the border in Connecticut.

A chapel was established on the current site of the church as early as the 17th century. A larger church was constructed here in the 19th century. According to tradition, as the foundation was being prepared, a worker who suffered from rheumatism was miraculously cured of his disease. This was followed by other miracles of healing, and by the time the church was completed, it had already become a popular destination for pilgrims.

Sadly, the church was destroyed in a fire in 1922. However, work on a new building began almost immediately. Planners took advantage of this opportunity to construct a much larger church that could accommodate many more visitors. After a brief halt during the Great Depression, work resumed, and the basilica was completed in 1946. In the decades since Sainte-Anne-de-Beaupre has resumed its position as one of the most popular healing shrines in the Americas.

Of Interest: The Basilica of Sainte-Anne-de-Beaupre is a hulking Gothic-Romanesque structure in brilliant white stone. A golden statue of St. Anne, framed by two massive spires, crowns the façade. The interior of the church houses a large collection of items, such as crutches, left behind by those who have experienced miraculous healing at the shrine. Next to the church is a chapel commemorating the Stations of the Cross.

---

240. FIRST PARISH CHURCH

19 Town Square, Plymouth, Massachusetts, 02360

Denomination: Unitarian Universalist (of interest to Protestants)
Dates: 1621 (originally completed), 1899 (current building completed)
Web: http://firstparishplymouthuu.org (official website)

The First Parish Church in Plymouth holds the title of oldest continuously active Protestant congregation in the United States. Founded in England in 1606, the congregation was established by Puritan Separatists before they travelled to America in search of religious freedom. Although there are rival claims to America's oldest congregation, it is the story of the church at Plymouth that has captured the nation's imagination and is celebrated every year at Thanksgiving.

The adventure of the Pilgrims began in the town of Scrooby, England in the early 17th century. During this period, residents of Scrooby, under the leadership of William Brewster, established a new church which was based on Puritan teachings but otherwise separate from the authority of the Church of England. The congregation of the new church was formally organized in 1606. However, faced with difficulties and persecution, the Separatists decided to leave England.

After briefly residing in the Netherlands, the congregation opted to relocate again, this time to the newly explored lands of North America. In 1620, they crossed the Atlantic on the Mayflower, and in November made landfall in what is now Massachusetts. After exploring the area, a colony was established at Plymouth. In the first few months worship services were held on board the ship, then later in a makeshift church in the colony's fort.

The Puritans at Plymouth ultimately went on to build a series of four more church buildings, with the current one being completed in 1899. The congregation, which has remained continually active as a Congregationalist church for over two hundred years, eventually adopted Universalist Unitarianism. The church was added to the National Register of Historic Places in 2014.

Of Interest: The First Parish Church is a stately Romanesque building of dark brick that stands at the heart of the historic district of old Plymouth. Immediately behind the church is Burial Hill, home to the gravesites of some of the most famous of the Pilgrims, including William Brewster. Plymouth Rock, an integral part of the congregation's history, can be found enclosed and on display in a monument by Plymouth Harbor a few blocks to the northeast.

---

241. OLD NORTH CHURCH & OLD SOUTH MEETINGHOUSE

193 Salem Street, Boston, Massachusetts, 02113 (Old North Church)

310 Washington Street, Boston, Massachusetts, 02108 (Old South Meetinghouse)

Denomination: Episcopal & Formerly Congregational
Dates: Church - 1723 (completed) & Meetinghouse - 1729 (completed)
Web: http://oldnorth.com & www.oldsouthmeetinghouse.org (official websites)

The Old North Church and the Old South Meetinghouse are, to many Americans, the nation's most patriotic churches. Together they played a key role in the early stages of the American Revolution, the former for its role in the Battle of Lexington and Concord, and the latter for its role in the Boston Tea Party. Both churches are located along Boston's famous tourist route known as the Freedom Trail and are designated as National Historic Landmarks.

The earliest church to be formed in Boston was founded in 1630 as the First Church of Boston. By the late 1660s the congregation had grown too large for one building, and a second was established. The Old South Meetinghouse was completed in 1729. Following the Boston Massacre of 1770, it became a regular meeting place for anti-Royalist factions in the colony. In 1783, the Old South Meetinghouse became the rallying point for the mob that later marched on the harbor and perpetrated the Boston Tea Party.

Among those who regularly visited the church at the time were John Hancock, Samuel Adams and Benjamin Franklin. After the American Revolution, the meetinghouse remained in use for almost another century. It is now maintained as an historic site and museum, with only one service held here every year. The church was designated as a National Historic Landmark in 1960.

Meanwhile, in 1688, the Episcopal Diocese of Massachusetts was formed with its headquarters in Boston. The diocese constructed the Old North Church as its place of worship. It served the Anglican community of Boston for fifty years before it soared into the stratosphere of American history. In 1775, local patriots used the church as a signal tower. Dissidents under the direction of Paul Revere hung lanterns in the steeple warning the American militia in the surrounding countryside of an imminent attack.

The entire event, including the role of the church, was immortalized in the Henry Wadsworth Longfellow poem *Paul Revere's Ride*. Since that historic night, the Old North Church has achieved a near mythical status in American culture. Maintained by the congregation as a regular place of worship, it has been visited by dignitaries, politicians, presidents and even British royalty. The church was designated a National Historic Landmark in 1961.

Of Interest: The Old North Church dates from 1723, though its steeple, which was destroyed twice, dates from the 1950s. It closely resembles the second steeple, which was designed by famous American architect Charles Bulfinch. Inside can be found what is believed to be one of the original lanterns hung on the night of Paul Revere's ride, as well as what is considered to be the most accurate bust of George Washington ever made. Beneath the church is a crypt with the bodies of several heroes of the American Revolution. The Old South Meetinghouse building largely dates from the reconstruction after the 1872 fire. No longer active, it currently houses a museum, with an exhibit on the Boston Tea Party, a model of Boston during the Colonial era, and John Hancock's writing desk.

---

242. TRINITY CHURCH & ST. PAUL'S CHAPEL

75 Broadway, New York, New York, 10006 (Trinity Church)
209 Broadway, New York, New York, 10007 (St. Paul's Chapel)

Denomination: Episcopal
Dates: Church - 1846 (completed) & Chapel - 1764 (completed)
Web: www.trinitywallstreet.org (official website)

Trinity Church is New York City's most historic church, an impressive claim in a city which boasts so many spectacular churches. It has close associations with the American Revolution and several of the Founding Fathers, most notably Alexander Hamilton, first Secretary of the Treasury. St. Paul's Chapel in Lower Manhattan is the oldest standing house of worship on the island of Manhattan. Completed in 1766, it has witnessed many moments in American history, from George Washington's inauguration to the terrorist attacks of 2001.

The Anglican Church in New York was one of the most important religious institutions in the American colonies in the 17th and 18th centuries. Formally established in the 1690s, the Anglicans constructed the first Trinity Church in Lower Manhattan. The original church stood until 1776 when it was destroyed in a fire during the British occupation of the city. During the Revolution, church members were predominantly Loyalist, though some, including Alexander Hamilton, supported the revolution. Trinity Church still pays a token rent to the crown based on a three century old charter, more out of tradition than out of requirement.

After formal separation from Britain took place in 1789, all of the Loyalist clergymen were removed from their posts, and Samuel Provoost became the first Episcopal bishop of New York. A new church was completed in 1790. Trinity Church retained its prominence as one of America's most influential churches throughout much of the

19th century. It was rebuilt again in 1846 after being badly damaged by winter weather the previous year. In 1976 Queen Elizabeth II made a state visit to Trinity Church at which time she ceremoniously collected the back rents. The church featured prominently in the 2004 film *National Treasure*. Trinity was designated a National Historic Landmark in 1976.

St. Paul's Chapel was established when the congregation of Trinity had grown too large and a new church was required to serve those members who lived further north of what was then the city center. After the Revolution, St. Paul's Chapel enjoyed a moment in the spotlight as the church George Washington attended when New York temporarily served as the national capital. He worshipped here on the morning of his inauguration in 1789. A number of heroes of the American Revolution are commemorated with memorials here.

St. Paul's Chapel enjoyed a long and distinguished history for over two centuries before it was once again thrust into the national spotlight on September 11, 2001. Located just a few blocks from the World Trade Center, it was the second closest church to Ground Zero and was used as a command center for the rescue and recovery efforts in the months after the attacks. A service was held here in 2006 on the fifth anniversary of the attacks, attended by prominent political figures including President George Bush. St. Paul's Chapel was designated a National Historic Landmark in 1960.

Of Interest: Trinity Church is one of the most recognizable buildings in Lower Manhattan. Once the tallest building in New York, it is now dwarfed by modern skyscrapers. Its location on Broadway at the end of narrow Wall Street makes it one of the city's most famous photo ops. The graveyard surrounding the church is one of the oldest on the island of Manhattan. Among those buried here are Alexander Hamilton, first Secretary of the Treasury, and Robert Fulton, world renowned naval engineer. St. Paul's Chapel and its graveyard take up an entire city block between Broadway and Church Street. The front of the church actually faces Church Street, but since it is set in the graveyard far back from the street the only way to tell is from immense steeple that is largely obscured by trees. The chapel is home to numerous memorials, from the American Revolution to September 11th. A highlight is the president's box, where Washington sat when he worshipped here.

243. ST. PATRICK'S CATHEDRAL

611 Fifth Avenue, New York, New York, 10022

Denomination: Roman Catholic
Dates: 1878 (completed)
Web: www.saintpatrickscathedral.org (official website)

St. Patrick's Cathedral is one of the most awe inspiring churches in the United States. It is the seat of New York City's Catholic archbishopric and one of the best known historically Irish parishes in America. Moreover, thanks to its incomparable location on Fifth Avenue in the heart of Midtown in New York City, it is possibly the most visited church in the United States.

The first Catholic parishes were established in New York in the 18th century. However, it wasn't until 1808 that New York became the seat of a Catholic diocese and received its own cathedral. The first cathedral, now known as Old St. Patrick's Cathedral, was completed in 1815, and served as the bishop's seat for most of the 19th century. Meanwhile, further north in Manhattan, the site where the new cathedral now stands was home to a Jesuit community and later to Trappist monks.

After the end of the Napoleanic Wars, the Trappists left and the site went into disuse for several decades. In 1830s, Catholic immigrants from Ireland began pouring into New York, and the site was revived for use by the Church. By the 1850s, the Catholic population of New York had grown so large that the city was named an archbishopric, and in 1858 construction began on a massive new cathedral on the site of the old monastery. The new building was completed and dedicated in 1879.

St. Patrick's Cathedral became a beacon for the large numbers of Catholic immigrants arriving in New York at the turn of the century. It has been the site of many important city events over the years, including several Papal visits. St. Patrick's Cathedral sponsors New York's annual St. Patrick's Day Parade, one of the largest such celebrations in the world. It was designated as a New York City Landmark in 1966, and received National Landmark status as well as being added to the National Register of Historic Places in 1976.

Of Interest: St. Patrick's Cathedral is one of the largest churches in the world, and was the biggest church in the Western Hemisphere at the time of its completion. Its massive façade looms over Fifth Avenue, where New York's St. Patrick's Day Parade takes place every year. The interior features one of the highest vaulted ceilings in the United States, one of the largest organs, and stained glass produced by Tiffany & Co. A number of archbishops and cardinals are interred inside the cathedral, as well as Haitian hero Pierre Toussaint, whose body was relocated here in 1990, nearly a century and a half after his death.

---

244. AMISH COUNTRY

2209 Millstream Road, Lancaster, Pennsylvania, 17602

Denomination: Anabaptist
Dates: 1719 (founded)
Web: www.mennoniteinfoctr.org (official website)

Amish Country in Lancaster, Pennsylvania is home to one of America's most unique Christian communities. Part of the Anabaptist tradition that emerged in Central Europe during the Protestant Reformation, the Amish and related groups such as the Mennonites began settling in the area in the decades leading up to the American Revolution. They are famous for avoiding both obscurity and modernity, stoically maintaining their traditions and cultural independence in the modern era. Their efforts have resulted in one of the world's most unique Christian communities.

The first Anabaptists began arriving in America in the 18th century after being worn down by years of persecution at the hands of more aggressive Christian denominations in Europe. Many of these settled in the hills of Pennsylvania, the colony best known for its religious tolerance. Although they came from Germany and were German-speaking, the Anabaptists have been mistakenly referred to as the Pennsylvania Dutch since their arrival in America.

Very little has changed in Pennsylvania Dutch Country over the last two and a half centuries. The residents have traditionally shied away from technology, luxury, politics, wars and anything else that distracts from their simple lifestyles. This was true even during the American Revolution and American Civil War, despite the fact that both wars saw battles on Lancaster's doorstep.

When most people think of the Pennsylvania Dutch, they generally think of the Amish. But there are, in fact, several different groups living in the area ranging from the traditional Amish to more modern Mennonites. Because of the traditions of the Amish, Lancaster is a time capsule of German-American life of an earlier time. Visitors and pilgrims from all over come to Pennsylvania Dutch Country not just to gawk and shop, but also to admire what may be one of the most enviable examples of sincere Christian lifestyles among any denomination anywhere in the world.

Of Interest: Amish Country does not feature a single site, monument or tomb that distinguishes it as a pilgrimage destination. The rolling hills filled with quaint architecture and horse driven buggies is the destination. The Mennonite Information Center is a good first stop for most pilgrims to the area. In addition to visitor information, the center doubles as a Christian/Amish education facility. Next door to the information center is a full-sized reproduction of the Biblical Tabernacle, the tent which housed the Ark of the Covenant during the Israelites' journey to the Promised Land.

---

245. ST. JOHN'S EPICOPAL CHURCH & WASHINGTON NATIONAL CATHEDRAL

1525 H Street NW, Washington, DC, 20005
(St. John's Episcopal Church)

3101 Wisconsin Avenue, Washington, DC, 20016
(Washington National Cathedral)

Alternate/Full Name: Cathedral Church of St. Peter and St. Paul in the Diocese of Washington

Denomination: Episcopal
Dates: Church - 1816 (completed) & Cathedral - 1990 (completed)
Web: http://stjohns-dc.org & www.cathedral.org (official websites)

St. John's Episcopal Church and the Washington National Cathedral are the most famous Episcopal institutions of Washington, D.C. The former is well known thanks to its location on Lafayette Square directly across the street from the White House, earning it the nickname "Church of the Presidents". The latter is America's de-facto national church. It is one of the largest church buildings in the world, and is usually the place that hosts state events that require a church. A number of prominent Americans are also buried on the site.

In the early days of the American republic, the majority of government leaders were active members of the Episcopal Church, an offshoot of the Church of England that broke away after the American Revolution. After acquiring land convenient to the White House, St. John's Episcopal Church was constructed between 1815 and 1816. James Madison attended services there soon after its completion. This started a tradition of presidential visits that has continued with every sitting president.

During the presidency of John Tyler, one of the pews was rented in perpetuity for exclusive presidential use. Some presidents prayed here more regularly than others, notably Abraham Lincoln, who came here frequently during the years of the American Civil War. St. John's was named a National Historic Landmark in 1960 and was added to the National Register of Historic Places in 1966.

The earliest plans for Washington DC included a site for a national church building. In 1893, the Episcopal Church received a commission from the federal government to establish a national cathedral. Ground broke in 1907 in a ceremony presided over by then President Theodore Roosevelt. The first chapel opened in 1912. After World War I, construction was overseen by military hero and leader General John Pershing. Construction continued on and off for the better part of the 20th century.

During World War II, the partially completed cathedral was designated by Congress as the National House of Prayer. It has since been the site of many national prayer services, as well as three presidential funerals: those of Eisenhower, Reagan and Ford. Woodrow Wilson was buried here in 1924. Other notable burials include World War I hero Norman Prince, Helen Keller and her teacher Anne Sullivan. The National Cathedral was added to the National Register of Historic Places in 1974.

Of Interest: St. John's Episcopal Church is a distinguished Greek Revival building on Lafayette Square in full view of the White House. It is home to a small trove of Americana, from the American eagle standing beside the pulpit to the church bell cast by Paul Revere. What many come to see, however, are two pews: the presidential pew and the pew in the back where Abraham Lincoln used to sit. One of the church windows was designed as a memorial to the wife of President Chester Arthur. Washington National Cathedral is one of the largest and most stunning buildings in a city full of large and stunning buildings. Its white brick façade, replete with two enormous square bell towers, is reminiscent of Notre Dame in Paris. The cathedral interior is cavernous, with a forest of immense white columns supporting a soaring ceiling over the nave. President Wilson is buried off to the side in the main sanctuary, while Helen Keller and other prominent Americans are interred in the crypt beneath the cathedral.

---

246. JAMESTOWN CHURCH

1368 Colonial Parkway, Jamestown, Virginia, 23081

Denomination: Formerly Episcopal
Dates: 1639 (originally completed), 1907 (current building completed)
Web: www.nps.gov/jame (official website)

The Jamestown Church is one of the claimants of being America's oldest church, and it enjoys several distinctions. Jamestown was the site of the first permanent English-speaking Christian parish in North America, not counting the lost Roanoke colony; and the church bell tower is the second oldest Christian structure in the United States after the San Miguel Chapel in Santa Fe.

The Jamestown colony in Virginia was the first surviving English colony in North America. Predating the Plymouth colony of Massachusetts by over twelve years, Jamestown was a crown-sponsored effort, and its earliest citizens were members of the Church of England. The first church was constructed in Jamestown in 1617. This was the first Protestant church erected in what would later be the United States.

Among its earliest members were Reverend Robert Hunt, America's first English minister, and Captain John Smith of Pocahontas fame. By the 1630s a larger and more permanent church was needed. This church was completed in 1643. It stood for more than a century before being abandoned and falling into disrepair. Only the original church tower survived.

In 1907, a recreation of the church was constructed based on excavations of the first and second churches as well as the designs of other early colonial churches. The church was included as part of the Jamestown National Historic Site in 1940. It was added to the National Register of Historic Places in 1966, and designated a Virginia Landmark in 1983.

Of Interest: The Jamestown Church is a very unusual structure. Both the original surviving tower and the 1907 recreation of the main building are built of red brick, with unfinished red brick interior walls. The entrance to the church is through what remains of the tower, possibly the oldest English-built structure still standing in the United States. The main sanctuary is decorated throughout with commemorative plaques. The church is surrounded by a small cemetery where many of the early settlers are buried. Among the memorials here are statues to Captain John Smith and the famous Native American princess, Pocahontas.

247. EBENEZER BAPTIST CHURCH

101 Jackson Street, Atlanta, Georgia, 30312

Denomination: Baptist
Dates: 1929 (completed)
Web: https://ebenezeratl.org (official website)

Ebenezer Baptist Church was one of the organizational centers of the Civil Rights movement and one of the most historic churches of the 20th century. The home church of Dr. Martin Luther King Jr., it is part of the Martin Luther King Jr. National Historic Site, which includes the King home and gravesite. Hundreds of thousands of pilgrims visit the Ebenezer Baptist Church every year to pay their respects to this most beloved of American ministers.

Martin Luther King Jr. was born in Atlanta, Georgia in 1929 on the eve of the Great Depression. Ebenezer Baptist Church, the church with which King was most closely associated, was completed the same year. King arrived in a world fraught with economic hardships and terrible racial hatred and violence. These difficulties, a lingering legacy of three centuries of slavery and another century of segregation, had a profound impact on King's early life.

King earned his PhD in theology at the age of twenty-six. He followed up with some pastoral work at the Ebenezer Baptist Church, but was soon deeply involved with the civil rights movement. By the 1960s, Martin Luther King Jr. had established himself as one of the world's most popular Christian leaders. His triumphant moment came in 1963 during the famous March on Washington, when he delivered the *I Have a Dream* speech, one of the greatest oratories in American history. The following year he was awarded the Nobel Peace Prize.

Unfortunately, like many of history's greatest Christians, Martin Luther King Jr. died a martyr, the victim of an assassin's bullet. His funeral was a major event, both in the African-American community and in America at large. King was laid to rest a few blocks from his home. Ebenezer Baptist Church and the Martin Luther King Jr. gravesite were added to the National Register of Historic Places in

1974, named a National Historic Landmark District in 1977 and finally a National Historic Site in 1980.

Of Interest: Ebenezer Baptist Church is part of the Martin Luther King, Jr. National Memorial Site which covers several city blocks just east of downtown Atlanta. The church is a modest red brick building that evokes King's own modesty and his down-to-Earth faith and message. Much of the early neighborhood has been preserved, including the King house a few blocks away. Martin Luther King, Jr. and his wife are buried in a magnificent memorial tomb close to the church. A major museum across the street, run by the National Park Service, features a multitude of exhibits and artifacts on the life of Martin Luther King Jr. and the Civil Rights movement.

---

248. CATHEDRAL BASILICA OF ST. AUGUSTINE

38 Cathedral Place, St. Augustine, Florida, 32804

Denomination: Roman Catholic
Completed: 1565 (originally completed), 1797 (current building completed)
Web: www.thefirstparish.org (official website)

The Cathedral Basilica of St. Augustine is the oldest Catholic parish in America as well as the oldest cathedral site in the country. Between the 16th and 18th centuries, Spain tried numerous times to build a permanent cathedral here. By the time they succeeded, more than two hundred years had passed since the first attempt was made, making it one of the longest church building projects in American history.

Spanish conquistadors arrived in Florida in the mid-16th century, working their way as far north as St. Augustine, which roughly marked the northern end of the Spanish Empire in the New World. To secure the colony, a fort and a church were built. The work was fast and slipshod, and the result was less than stellar. In 1586, the original structure was destroyed in a pirate raid led by Francis Drake.

The Spanish colonists quickly built a new church. This second structure, completed in just a few months, was even worse than the first one. In 1599, it burned to the ground. In the 17th century, funds were finally appropriated for a larger, more permanent structure. Designed by better architects and built from more solid timber, this cathedral lasted for nearly a century before being destroyed during a British raid in 1702. Finally, in 1793, construction began on a permanent masonry structure.

The Cathedral of St. Augustine was completed in 1797. Ironically by then the St. Augustine colony had considerably dwindled. The city did not recover until after Florida was acquired by the United States in 1819. In 1976 the cathedral was designated as a minor basilica, more than four hundred years after its first incarnation was completed. The Cathedral of St. Augustine was named a National Historic Landmark and added to the National Register of Historic Places in 1970.

Of Interest: The Cathedral Basilica of St. Augustine actually had another fire in 1887, and although the original shell survived, most of the cathedral as it exists today dates from restorations in the 19th and 20th centuries. The current building was constructed with coquina stone, used due to its fire-proof nature. The bell tower is unusual in that the interior is partially exposed. This was done in part to give the tower a more Spanish missionary feel, but also so that some of the oldest bells still in existence in the United States would be visible.

---

249. SAN MIGUEL MISSION

401 Old Santa Fe Trail, Santa Fe, New Mexico, 87501

Denomination: Roman Catholic
Dates: 1610 (originally completed), 1613 (current building completed)
Web: http://sanmiguelchapel.org (official website)

The chapel of the San Miguel Mission is the oldest, partially intact church standing in the continental United States of America. The fact that this four century old adobe mission predates anything constructed by the Spanish along the Caribbean coast or by the English or Dutch along the Eastern Seaboard is nothing short of amazing. It is almost a fluke of history that this chapel, constructed by an expedition exploring the area in the early 17th century, is still standing. Because of this, it is regarded as both a state and national treasure.

The territory of New Mexico was established by Spain in 1515, less than a quarter of a century after the discovery of America. It was a further twenty-five years before the Spanish explorer Coronado formally claimed it, and another century before its territorial capital was established at Santa Fe. In 1610 a parish was founded. A mission chapel was completed and in use here even before the Puritans founded the Plymouth colony in 1620. It was Santa Fe's chief church, and the most important religious institution in the American southwest until the early 19th century.

The San Miguel Mission played a small role in the Pueblo Revolt that took place at the end of the 17th century. In 1680, the area's Pueblo inhabitants sought to drive the Spanish out of New Mexico. There were numerous causes of the uprising, the primary ones being the poor living conditions of the Pueblos and the repression of their native religion. The rebellion was a success, and most of the Spanish colonists were driven out for the better part of the next decade.

The mission was badly damaged at this time, and more than half of the Franciscan monks living in New Mexico were put to death. The Spanish returned in 1692, retook Santa Fe and rebuilt the mission a few years later. The San Miguel Mission was listed on the National Register of Historic Places and included in the Barrio de Analco Historic Landmark District in 1968, and listed on the New Mexico State Register of Cultural Properties in 1972.

Of Interest: The San Miguel Mission does not appear to be nearly four centuries old. All that is still standing of the original mission is the chapel, which was once part of a much more extensive compound. Evidence of the greater mission remains only in the form of vestigial walls. The chapel interior is very plain, with only a single wooden-frame entrance and a handful of small windows. The most noteworthy feature of the chapel exterior is the small bell tower over the entrance. A number of brick supports, built in later years, buttress the foundation and outer walls of the chapel.

250. SALT LAKE TEMPLE

50 N. West Temple, Salt Lake City, Utah, 84150

Denomination: Latter Day Saints
Dates: 1893 (completed)
Web: www.lds.org/church/temples/salt-lake (official website)

The Salt Lake Temple is the world headquarters of the Church of Latter Day Saints, America's largest home-grown Christian denomination. The temple is the centerpiece of Temple Square, a complex which consists of dozens of buildings including the famous Mormon Tabernacle. The Salt Lake Temple is a must see for Mormons, many of whom make at least one pilgrimage to Salt Lake City during their lifetimes.

The early years of the Church of Latter Day Saints were a turbulent period, when the Mormon community was forced to relocate on several occasions in the 1830s in 1840s. After the death of the church founder Joseph Smith in 1844, most of the community decided to pull up stakes and relocate to a completely new territory far away. Three years later, under the direction of Brigham Young, thousands of Mormon settlers headed west across the Great Plains and Rocky Mountains, finally settling beside the Great Salt Lake.

In 1853 Brigham Young laid the cornerstone for the Mormon Temple. It took forty years to build, during which time Salt Lake City grew into a thriving community. At the time of its completion, the Temple was one of the largest buildings in the American west. As the number of Mormons has grown into the millions, Temple Square became a sprawling complex. Today the Salt Lake Temple is a major pilgrimage destination, with hundreds of thousands of Mormons and other tourists visiting annually.

Of Interest: The Salt Lake City Temple is an inspiring structure towering nearly seventy meters over the surrounding square. The tallest point is capped with a golden statue of the angel Moroni. An oval reflecting pool and surrounding flower gardens complete the Temple's setting. Overall the temple structure seems to be evocative of what the ancient Temple of Solomon might once have looked like. The interior is strictly off-limits to non-Mormons. However, for those non-Mormons who are curious there is a beautiful model of the temple interior on display. The tomb of Brigham Young and other important Mormon heritage sites are located in and around Temple Square.

OVERVIEW OF CHRISTIAN DENOMINATIONS & DIVISIONS

As of the time of the writing of this book, there were well over two billion Christians living on Earth, making it by far the world's largest religion. However, Christianity is by no means a monolithic faith. Over the course of two thousand years it has fractured into a dozen or so major denominations and countless sub-denominations. While there is certainly no need to address every last one of these, a brief refresher on the major denominations and their primary divisions is in order.

Ancient Non-Orthodox Churches (founded 1st through 3rd centuries)

In the early centuries of Christianity there was little central organization of the Church, and as a result the Christian faith flourished in numerous forms. These groups included the Ebionite Christians, the Arian Christians, the Gnostic Christians and many others. It wasn't until the Council of Nicaea in the 4th century that an 'orthodox' form of the Christianity came into existence. Some of these ancient churches died out on their own, some were absorbed into the new universal Church, and the rest were treated as heresies and destroyed over time. These ancient Churches were largely gone by the early Middle Ages.

Ancient Catholic-Orthodox Church (founded 1st century, formalized 325 AD)

The Mother Church of pretty much all modern Christians, this group represented the Christian 'main-stream' such as it was in the 1st through 4th centuries. It traces its roots back to the missionary work of the Peter, John and, perhaps most importantly, Paul. These Christians formally crystallized into the Church at the Council of

Nicaea in 325 AD, eventually absorbing or destroying virtually every other Christian group by the early Middle Ages.

Church of the East (established in 424 AD)

In the 5th century, the Catholic-Orthodox Church underwent its first major schism as many Christians in distant Asia broke away and formed the Church of the East. Also known as the Persian Church or the Nestorian Church, Christians from this group became dominant in Mesopotamia and Persian, spreading as far away as China and India. Over time the Church of the East fragmented into more than half a dozen smaller churches including the Assyrian Church of the East. The nominal leader of the Church of the East is the Patriarch of the Church of the East, with its traditional seat in the ancient city of Ctesiphon, the modern city of Al-Mada'in, Iraq.

Oriental Orthodox Church (established in 451 AD)

Less than three decades after the first schism of the Church, a second schism, this one much more serious, took place. Following the Council of Chalcedon, Christians from Armenia to Egypt broke away from the Catholic-Orthodox Church over a doctrinal dispute. The Oriental Orthodox Church has survived to the present day as the world's fourth largest Church. While it has avoided further major schisms, it is organizationally made up of a half dozen independent Churches that are in communion with each other. In addition, the Oriental Orthodox Church claims the ancient patriarchal seats of Alexandria, Antioch and Jerusalem. The six Churches in the Oriental Orthodox communion are:

Organization	Current Seat of Church	Head of Church
Coptic Orthodox Church of Alexandria	Cairo, Egypt	Pope of the Church of Alexandria
Ethiopian Orthodox Tewahedo Church	Addis Ababa, Ethiopia	Primate of the Ethiopian Church
Eritrean Orthodox Tewahedo Church	Asmara, Eritrea	Primate of the Eritrean Church

Syriac Orthodox Church of Antioch	Damascus, Syria	Patriarch of the Church of Antioch
Armenian Apostolic Church	Etchmiadzin, Armenia	Catholicos of All Armenians
Malankara Orthodox Church	Kerala, India	Catholicos of the East

Eastern Orthodox Church (split from Rome in 1054 AD)

In 1054 the Catholic-Orthodox Church was shattered by the 'Great Schism'. This event split the bulk of Christianity in two, dividing the Greek-speaking Orthodox Church in the East from the Latin-speaking Catholic Church in the west. The Eastern Orthodox Church, the second largest branch of Christianity in the world, claimed four of the original five patriarchal seats, with the Patriarch of Constantinople acting as the nominal head of the entire Church. While there has been no additional major schism within Eastern Orthodoxy, it has fragmented into fifteen patriarchates and nearly two dozen sub- and self governing-patriarchates, all in communion with each other. The fifteen Churches in the Eastern Orthodox communion are:

Organization	**Current Seat of Church**	**Head of Church**
Ecumenical Patriarchate of Constantinople	Istanbul, Turkey	Patriarch of Constantinople
Patriarchate of Alexandria	Alexandria, Egypt	Patriarch of Alexandria
Patriarchate of Antioch	Damascus, Syria	Patriarch of Antioch
Patriarchate of Jeruslaem	Jerusalem, Israel	Patriarch of Jerusalem
Russian Orthodox Church	Moscow, Russia	Patriarch of Moscow and All Rus
Serbian Orthodox Church	Belgrade, Serbia	Patriarch of the Serbian Orthodox Church
Bulgarian Orthodox Church	Sofia, Bulgaria	Patriarch of All Bulgaria

Romanian Orthodox Church	Bucharest, Romania	Patriarch of All Romania
Georgian Orthodox Church	Tbilisi, Georgia	Patriarch of All Georgia
Church of Cyprus	Nicosia, Cyprus	Archbishop of Cyprus
Church of Greece	Athens, Greece	Archbishop of Athens and All Greece
Orthodox Church of Albania	Tirana, Albania	Archbishop of Tirana and All Albania
Polish Orthodox Church	Warsaw, Poland	Archbishop of Warsaw and All Poland
Orthodox Church of Czechia and Slovakia	Prague, Czechia	Primate of the Czech and Slovak Orthodox Church
Orthodox Church in America	Oyster Bay Cove, New York	Primate of the Orthodox Church in America

Roman Catholic Church (split from Constantinople in 1054 AD)

After the Great Schism of 1054, the surviving Church in Western Europe came to be known as the Roman Catholic Church. The largest surviving descendent of the original Church established at the Council of Nicaea, the Roman Catholic Church currently numbers over a billion members. Based in the city of Rome, it lays sole claim to the ancient Patriarchal seat of Rome. In later years many other Churches broke away from the Roman Catholic Church, but the core institution has remained intact. The bulk of Catholicism uses Latin Rites and follows the leadership of the Pope at the Vatican. However, there are a few small churches in the east that are semi-autonomous and typically use a Greek liturgy that are in full communion with the Roman Catholic Church.

Late Medieval Non-Catholic Churches (founded 12th through 15th centuries)

In the Late Middle Ages and Renaissance era, Western Europe saw a revival of interest in Christianity outside of the jurisdiction of the Roman Catholic Church. A number of groups tried to break away from Rome, but these were systematically crushed. Nevertheless with each attempt the outcry against the Papacy grew louder, ultimately leading to the Protestant Reformation of the 16th century. Among the more prominent breakaway movements were the Cathars in France, the Lollards in England and the Hussites in Bohemia. None of these denominations have survived to the present day in any substantial way, though some were absorbed into the Protestant Reformation movement of the 16th century.

Lutheran Church (broke away from Rome in 1521 AD)

The Lutherans were the first major group to successfully break away from the control of the Roman Catholic Church in Europe. Named for Martin Luther, whose publishing of the famous 95 Theses was the final spark that ignited the Reformation, the Lutherans effectively created the framework for the establishment of Protestant congregations. While there is no single global Lutheran organization, there are many national and liturgical Lutheran sub-denominations. The Lutheran Church serves as the state church of several Scandinavian countries.

Anglican Church (broke away from Rome in 1534 AD)

The Anglican Church began as the Church of England, which broke away from the control of the Papacy under the leadership of King Henry VIII. While Henry's motives were not particularly Reform-minded, the defection of England provided a major boost to the Protestant Reformation. Over time Anglicanism spread to every corner of the globe along with the British Empire. The Anglican Communion was formally established in 1867, with branches around the world, including the Episcopal Church in the United States. The seat of the Anglican Communion is the Archbishopric of Canterbury, though the nominal head of the Church remains the reigning monarch of the United Kingdom.

Reformed Church / Calvinism
(broke away from Rome in 1536 AD)

The Calvinists were the second major group to successfully break away from the control of the Roman Catholic Church in continental Europe.

The teachings of John Calvin, which developed into Reform theology, took root in Switzerland, the Low Countries, Scotland and, for a time, France. Since its inception Reform Christianity has splintered into hundreds of branches and denominations, which include such groups as the Presbyterians and Congregationalists. While there is no central governing body for Reform Christians, many Reform organizations are in communion with each other through the World Communion of Reformed Churches and the World Council of Churches, based in Geneva, Switzerland.

Other Mainstream Protestant Churches (founded 16th through 19th centuries)

In addition to the three major branches of Protestant Christianity, a number of other important main-stream Protestant churches came into existence in the years following the Reformation. Among the major groups are the Anabaptists, which originated in Central Europe in the 16th century; the Baptists, which primarily developed in the American colonies in the 17th century; and the Methodists, which grew out of the Church of England in the 19th century. Modern Evangelical churches are often classified in this category.

Other Churches

In addition to the above, there are a number of churches that, for a variety of reasons, are generally not considered to follow a traditional form of Christian beliefs, and are thus not considered true Protestants. These include such organizations as the Church of Latter Day Saints, which recognize the Book of Mormon as an authoritative religious writing; the Church of Christian Scientists, which recognizes a different Sabbath Day, does not celebrate typical Christian holidays and generally rejects modern science; and the Universal Unitarian Church, which integrates Christian beliefs with those of other faiths. Messianic Judaism, in which Jewish practices are integrated with Christian beliefs, is also typically included in this category.

CHURCHES BY CURRENT DENOMINATION

ROMAN CATHOLIC		
1. Church of the Holy Sepulchre	Jerusalem, Israel	Joint Jurisdiction
2. Church of St. Anne	Jerusalem, Israel	
6. Abbey of the Dormition	Jerusalem, Israel	
6. Coenaculum	Jerusalem, Israel	Israeli Government Jurisdiction
9. Church of All Nations	Jerusalem, Israel	
10. Chapel of the Ascension	Jerusalem, Israel	Muslim Jurisdiction
12. Tomb of Lazarus	Al-Eizariya, West Bank	Muslim Jurisdiction
13. Church of the Nativity	Bethlehem, West Bank	Joint Jurisdiction
14. Chapel of the Shepherd's Field	Bethlehem, West Bank	
17. Basilica of the Annunciation	Nazareth, Israel	
19. Church of the Transfiguration	Mt. Tabor, Israel	
20. Church of the Beatitudes	Tabgha, Israel	
21. Church of the Primacy of St. Peter	Tabgha, Israel	
21. Church of the Multiplication	Tabgha, Israel	
22. Ruins of Capernaum Archaeological Site	Capernaum, Israel	Joint Jurisdiction
24. Shrine of Our Lady of Lebanon	Harissa, Lebanon	Maronite Catholic
28. Chapel of St. Ananias	Damascus, Syria	Maronite Catholic

41. Church of St. Peter	Antakya, Turkey	Turkish Government Jurisdiction
47. Basilica of Bom Jesus	Goa, India	
48. St. Thomas Basilica	Chennai, India	
51. Mother House of the Missionaries of Charity	Kolkata, India	
52. Ruins of St. Paul's Cathedral	Macau, China	Chinese Government Jurisdiction
53. Myeongdong Cathedral	Seoul, South Korea	
55. Basilica of Santo Nino	Cebu City, Philippines	
56. Quiapo Church	Manila, Philippines	
66. Basilica of St. Augustine	Annaba, Algeria	
66. Ruins of the Basilica of Peace	Annaba, Algeria	Algerian Government Jurisdiction
67. Basilica of Our Lady of Peace	Yamousoukro, Ivory Coast	
72. Kisantu Cathedral	Kisantu, DR Congo	
88. Dubrovnik Cathedral	Dubrovnik, Croatia	
89. Cathedral of St. Domnius	Split, Croatia	
91. St. Peter's Basilica	Vatican City	
92. Sistine Chapel	Vatican City	
93. Basilica of St. John Lateran	Rome, Italy	
94. Basilica of St. Paul Outside the Walls	Rome, Italy	
95. Basilica of St. Lawrence Outside the Walls	Rome, Italy	
97. Church of the Jesuits	Rome, Italy	
97. Church of St. Ignatius of Loyola	Rome, Italy	
98. Church of St. Mary and the Martyrs (Pantheon)	Rome, Italy	
99. Christian Catacombs of Rome	Rome, Italy	Italian Government Jurisdiction

101. Basilica of St. Francis of Assisi	Assisi, Italy	
103. Florence Cathedral	Florence, Italy	
104. Basilica of St. Dominic	Bologna, Italy	
105. Arian Churches of Ravenna	Ravenna, Italy	Italian Government Jurisdiction
106. Basilica of St. Anthony of Padua	Padua, Italy	
107. St. Mark's Basilica	Venice, Italy	
108. Basilica of St. Peter in the Golden Sky	Pavia, Italy	
109. Church of Santa Maria Delle Grazie	Milan, Italy	
110. Basilica of St. Ambrose	Milan, Italy	
111. Turin Cathedral	Turin, Italy	
112. Monte Cassino Abbey	Mont Cassino, Italy	
113. Basilica of St. Thomas the Apostle	Ortona, Italy	
114. Basilica of St. Nicholas	Bari, Italy	
115. Cathedral of Syracuse	Syracuse, Italy	
116. Salerno Cathedral	Salerno, Italy	
117. St. Paul's Cathedral	Mdina, Malta	
117. St. John's Co-Cathedral	Valletta, Malta	
118. Church of St. Paul's Shipwreck	Valletta, Malta	
132. Vilnius Cathedral	Vilnius, Lithuania	
133. Hill of Crosses	Sialiai, Lithuania	
135. St. John's Archcathedral	Warsaw, Poland	
136. Wawel Cathedral	Krakow, Poland	
138. St. Vitus Cathedral	Prague, Czech Rep.	
140. Church of Our Lady before Tyn	Prague, Czech Rep.	

141. Bethlehem Chapel	Prague, Czech Rep.	Czech Republic Jurisdiction
142. Sedlec Ossuary	Kutna Hora, Czech Rep.	
143. St. Stephen's Basilica	Budapest, Hungary	
143. Matthias Church	Budapest, Hungary	
144. Esztergom Basilica	Esztergom, Hungary	
145. Pannonhalma Archabbey	Pannonhalma, Hungary	
146. St. Stephen's Cathedral	Vienna, Austria	
147. Melk Abbey	Melk, Austria	
148. St. Peter's Abbey	Salzburg, Austria	
148. Nonnberg Abbey	Salzburg, Austria	
154. Fulda Cathedral	Fulda, Germany	
155. Church of Our Lady	Munich, Germany	
155. St. Peter's Church (Frauenkirche)	Munich, Germany	
156. Konstanz Cathedral	Konstanz, Germany	
159. Cologne Cathedral	Cologne, Germany	
160. Aachen Cathedral	Aachen, Germany	
161. Cathedral of Trier	Trier, Germany	
161. St. Matthias' Abbey	Trier, Germany	
162. St. Bavo's Cathedral	Ghent, Belgium	
164. Church of Our Lord in the Attic	Amsterdam, Netherlands	Dutch Government Jurisdiction
170. Cathedral of Our Lady of Paris (Notre Dame)	Paris, France	
171. Basilica of St. Denis	St. Denis, France	
172. Strasbourg Cathedral	Strasbourg, France	
173. Basilica of Saint-Pierre-Aux-Nonnains	Metz, France	French Government Jurisdiction
174. Vezelay Abbey	Vezelay, France	
176. Mont St. Michel Abbey	Mont Saint-Michel, France	
177. Basilica of St. Martin	Tours, France	

178. Church of St. Hilary the Great	Poitiers, France	
179. Palace of the Popes	Avignon, France	French Government Jurisdiction
180. Church of the Jacobins	Toulouse, France	French Government Jurisdiction
182. Barcelona Cathedral	Barcelona, Spain	
183. Basilica of the Holy Family (Sagrada Familia)	Barcelona, Spain	
185. Toledo Cathedral	Toledo, Spain	
186. Monastery of Santo Toribio de Liebana	Cantabria, Spain	
187. Santiago de Compostela Cathedral	Santiago de Compostela, Spain	
188. Segovia Cathedral	Segovia, Spain	
189. Convent of the Annunciation	Salamanca, Spain	
190. Seville Cathedral	Seville, Spain	
191. Mezquita Mosque-Cathedral	Cordoba, Spain	
192. Convent of the Order of Christ	Tomar, Portugal	
219. St. Peter's Church	Drogheda, Ireland	
222. Cathedral of Brasilia	Brasilia, Brazil	
222. Sanctuary of Dom Bosco	Brasilia, Brazil	
224. Cathedral Basilica of Our Lady of Peace	La Paz, Bolivia	
224. San Francisco Church	La Paz, Bolivia	
225. Convent of St. Dominic	Lima, Peru	
226. Cusco Cathedral	Cusco, Peru	
226. Church of the Society of Jesus	Cusco, Peru	
228. Metropolitan Cathedral	Mexico City, Mexico	
230. Sanctuary of Atotonilco	Guanajuato, Mexico	

231. Havana Cathedral	Havana, Cuba	
232. Our Lady of the Assumption Co-Cathedral	Baracoa, Cuba	
233. Basilica Cathedral of Santa Maria La Menor	Santo Domingo, Dominican Republic	
234. Cathedral Basilica of San Juan Bautista	San Juan, Puerto Rico	
234. San Jose Church	San Juan, Puerto Rico	
238. Cathedral Basilica of Our Lady of Quebec	Quebec City, Canada	
239. Basilica of Sainte-Anne-de-Beaupre	Sainte-Anne-de-Beaupre, Canada	
243. St. Patrick's Cathedral	New York City, New York	
248. Cathedral Basilica of St. Augustine	St. Augustine, Florida	
249. San Miguel Mission	Santa Fe, New Mexico	

ROMAN CATHOLIC, MARIAN SHRINES		
36. House of the Virgin Mary	Selcuk, Turkey	Joint Jurisdiction
90. Basilica of St. Mary Help of Christians	Brezje, Slovenia	
96. Basilica of St. Mary Major	Rome, Italy	
96. Shrine of Our Lady of Divine Love	Rome, Italy	
137. Jasna Gora Monastery	Czestochowa, Poland	
181. Sanctuary of Our Lady of Lourdes	Lourdes, France	
184. Cathedral Basilica of Our Lady of the Pillar	Zaragoza, Spain	
193. Sanctuary of Our Lady of Fatima	Fatima, Portugal	
220. Knock Shrine	Knock, Ireland	

223. Basilica of the National Shrine of Our Lady of Aparecida	Aparecida, Brazil	
227. Las Lajas Sanctuary	Narino, Colombia	
229. Basilica of Our Lady of Guadalupe	Mexico City, Mexico	

EASTERN ORTHODOX		
1. Church of the Holy Sepulchre	Jerusalem, Israel	Greek Orthodox; Joint Jurisdiction
13. Church of the Nativity	Bethlehem, West Bank	Greek Orthodox; Joint Jurisdiction
15. Monastery of the Temptation	Jericho, West Bank	Greek Orthodox
16. Church of St. Photini	Nablus, West Bank	Greek Orthodox
18. Church of St. Gabriel	Nazareth, Israel	Greek Orthodox
22. Ruins of Capernaum Archaeological Site	Capernaum, ISrael	Greek Orthodox; Joint Jurisdiction
27. Church of St. George	Madaba, Jordan	Greek Orthodox
30. Convent of St. Thecla Ma'Lula	Maaloula, Syria	Greek Orthodox
31. Ruins of the Church of St. Simeon Stylites	Deir Semaan, Syria	Greek Orthodox; Syrian Government Jurisdiction
33. Church of the Holy Wisdom (Hagia Sophia)	Istanbul, Turkey	Greek Orthodox; Turkish Government Jurisdiction
34. Church of St. George	Istanbul, Turkey	Greek Orthodox
35. Ruins of the Basilica of St. John	Selcuk, Turkey	Greek Orthodox; Turkish Government Jurisdiction
37. Church of the Holy Wisdom	Iznik, Turkey	Greek Orthodox; Turkish Government Jurisdiction
38. Cave Churches of Cappadocia	Nevsehir, Turkey	Greek Orthodox; Turkish Government Jurisdiction

39. St. Nicholas Church	Demre, Turkey	Greek Orthodox; Turkish Government Jurisdiction
40. St. Paul's Church	Mersin, Turkey	Greek Orthodox; Turkish Government Jurisdiction
62. Cathedral of Evangelismos	Alexandria, Egypt	Greek Orthodox
63. St. Catherine's Monastery	Feren, Egypt	Greek Orthodox
77. Cave of the Apocalypse	Patmos, Greece	Greek Orthodox
78. St. Andrew's Cathedral	Patras, Greece	Greek Orthodox
79. Monasteries of Meteora	Kalabaka, Greece	Greek Orthodox
81. Church of the Holy Wisdom	Thessaloniki, Greece	Greek Orthodox
119. St. Basil's Cathedral	Moscow, Russia	Russian Orthodox
120. Novodevichy Convent	Moscow, Russia	Russian Orthodox
121. Cathedral of the Annunciation	Moscow, Russia	Russian Orthodox
121. Cathedral of the Dormition	Moscow, Russia	Russian Orthodox
122. Smolny Cathedral	St. Petersburg, Russia	Russian Orthodox
123. St. Alexander Nevsky Monastery	St. Petersburg, Russia	Russian Orthodox
124. St. Isaac's Cathedral	St. Petersburg, Russia	Russian Orthodox
124. Church of the Savior on Spilled Blood	St. Petersburg, Russia	Russian Orthodox
125. Trinity Monastery of St. Sergius	Serfius Posad, Russia	Russian Orthodox
81. Church of St. Demetrius	Thessaloniki, Greece	Bulgarian Orthodox
82. Alexander Nevsky Cathedral	Sofia, Bulgaria	Bulgarian Orthodox
83. Rila Monastery	Rila, Bulgaria	Bulgarian Orthodox
85. Monastery of the Patriarchate of Pec	Pec, Kosovo	Serbian Orthodox
86. Church of St. Sava	Belgrade, Serbia	Serbian Orthodox
87. Ostrog Monastery	Ostrog, Montenegro	Serbian Orthodox

128. People's Salvation Cathedral	Bucharest, Romania	Romanian Orthodox
129. Metropolitan Cathedral	Iasi, Romania	Romanian Orthodox
126. St. Sophia's Cathedral	Kiev, Ukraine	Ukrainian Orthodox
127. Kiev Monastery of the Caves	Kiev, Ukraine	Ukrainian Orthodox
84. Dormition of the Theotokos Church	Labove e Kryqit, Albania	Albanian Orthodox
134. Cathedral of St. Mary Magdalene	Warsaw, Poland	Polish Orthodox
139. Sts. Cyril and Methodius Cathedral	Prague, Czech Rep.	Czech and Slovak Orthodox
42. Jvari Monastery	Mtskheta, Georgia	Georgian Apostolic Orthodox
25. Church of St. Lazarus	Larnaca, Cyprus	Church of Cyprus
80. Monasteries of the Holy Mountain	Mount Athos, Greece	Eastern Orthodox (general)

ORIENTAL ORTHODOX		
1. Church of the Holy Sepulchre	Jerusalem, Israel	Armenian Apostolic; Joint Jurisdiction
13. Church of the Nativity	Bethlehem, West Bank	Armenian Apostolic; Joint Jurisdiction
3. Cathedral of St. James	Jerusalem, Israel	Armenian Apostolic
43. Etchmiadzin Cathedral	Etchmiadzin, Armenia	Armenian Apostolic
44. Khor Virap Monastery	Pokr Vedi, Armenia	Armenian Apostolic
45. St. Thaddeus Monastery	Qareh Kelisa, Iran	Armenian Apostolic
61. St. Mark's Cathedral	Alexandria, Egypt	Coptic Orthodox Church of Alexandria
64. Monasteries of St. Anthony and St. Paul the Anchorite	Zafarana, Egypt	Coptic Orthodox Church of Alexandria
65. Sts. Sergius and Bacchus Church	Cairo, Egypt	Coptic Orthodox Church of Alexandria
65. Hanging Church	Cario, Egypt	Coptic Orthodox Church of Alexandria

69. St. George's Cathedral	Addis Ababa, Ethiopia	Ethiopian Orthodox Tewahedo
69. Holy Trinity Cathedral	Addis Ababa, Ethiopia	Ethiopian Orthodox Tewahedo
70. Church of Our Lady Mary of Zion	Aksum, Ethiopia	Ethiopian Orthodox Tewahedo
71. Rock Hewn Churches of New Jerusalem	Lailbela, Ethiopia	Ethiopian Orthodox Tewahedo

ANGLICAN		
201. Westminster Abbey	London, England	Church of England
202. St. Paul's Cathedral	London, England	Church of England
206. St. George's Chapel	Windsor, England	Church of England
207. Canterbury Cathedral	Canterbury, England	Church of England
208. St. Martin's Church	Canterbury, England	Church of England
209. St. Mary's Church	Lutterworth, England	Church of England
211. Durham Cathedral	Durham, England	Church of England
212. York Minster	York, England	Church of England
215. Llanrhychwyn Church	Llanrhychwyn, Wales	Church of Wales
216. St. Patrick's Cathedral	Armagh, N. Ireland	Church of Ireland
217. Down Cathedral	Downpatrick, N. Ireland	Church of Ireland
218. Christ Church Cathedral	Dublin, Ireland	Church of Ireland
218. St. Patrick's Cathedral	Dublin, Ireland	Church of Ireland
4. Christ Church	Jerusalem, Israel	Episcopal Church in Jerusalem and the Middle East
7. St. George's Cathedral	Jerusalem, Israel	Episcopal Church in Jerusalem and the Middle East
7. Garden Tomb	Jerusalem, Israel	Episcopal Church in Jerusalem and the Middle East

46. St. Francis Church	Kochi, India	Anglican Church of South India
49. St. Mary's Church	Chennai, India	Anglican Church of South India
50. St. Paul's Cathedral	Kolkata, India	Anglican Church of North India
57. St. Andrew's Cathedral	Singapore	Anglican Church of South East Asia
59. St. Paul's Cathedral	Melbourne, Australia	Anglican Church of Australia
60. Christ Church	Russell, New Zealand	Anglican Church of New Zealand
68. Cathedral Church of Christ	Lagos, Nigeria	Anglican Church of Nigeria
73. All Saint's Cathedral	Nairobi, Kenya	Anglican Church of Kenya
74. Christ Church	Zanzibar City, Tanzania	Anglican Church of Tanzania
76. St. George's Cathedral	Cape Town, South Africa	Anglican Church of South Africa
235. Spanish Town Cathedral	Spanish Town, Jamaica	Anglican
236. St. Peter's Church	St. George's, Bermuda	Anglican
237. All Saint's Cathedral	Halifax, Canada	Church of Canada
237. St. Paul's Church	Halifax, Canada	Church of Canada
241. Old North Church	Boston, Massachusetts	Episcopal
242. Trinity Church	New York, New York	Episcopal
242. St. Paul's Chapel	New York, New York	Episcopal
245. St. John's Episcopal Church	Washington, DC	Episcopal
245. Washington National Cathedral	Washington, DC	Episcopal
246. Jamestown Church	Jamestown, Virginia	Episcopal; American Government Jurisdiction

PROTESTANT, LUTHERAN		
150. All Saint's Church	Wittenberg, Germany	Evangelical Church in Germany
151. Wittenberg Town Church	Wittenberg, Germany	Evangelical Church in Germany
194. Roskilde Cathedral	Roskilde, Denmark	Church of Denmark
130. St. Mary's Cathedral	Tallinn, Estonia	Estonian Evangelical Lutheran Church
131 Riga Cathedral	Riga, Latvia	Evangelical Lutheran Church of Latvia
131. St. Peter's Church	Riga, Latvia	Evangelical Lutheran Church of Latvia
195. Helsinki Cathedral	Helsinki, Finland	Evangelical Lutheran Church of Finland
196. Turku Cathedral	Turku, Finland	Evangelical Lutheran Church of Finland
197. Riddarholm Church	Stockholm, Sweden	Church of Sweden
198. Nidaros Cathedral	Trondheim, Norway	Church of Norway
199. Urnes Stave Church	Ornes, Norway	Church of Norway
200. Hallgrim's Church	Reykjavik, Iceland	Evangelical Lutheran Church of Iceland
5. Church of the Redeemer	Jerusalem, Israel	Evangelical Lutheran Church in Jordan and the Holy Land

PROTESTANT, REFORMED		
167. Calvin Auditory	Geneva, Switzerland	Calvinist Reformed; Swiss Government Jurisidction
166. St. Pierre Cathedral	Geneva, Switzerland	Federation of Swiss Protestant Churches
169. Great Minster (Grossmunster)	Zurich, Switzerland	Federation of Swiss Protestant Churches
213. St. Giles Cathedral	Edinburgh, Scotland	Church of Scotland
214. Glasgow Cathedral	Glasgow, Scotland	Church of Scotland

163. Old Church	Amsterdam, Netherlands	Dutch Reformed; Netherlands Government Jurisdiction
165. St. Peter's Church	Leiden, Netherlands	Dutch Reformed; Netherlands Government Jurisdiction
75. Great Church (Groote Kerk)	Cape Town, South Africa	Dutch Reformed
241. Old South Meetinghouse	Boston, Massachusetts	Congregational; American Government Jurisdiction

PROTESTANT, OTHER TRADITIONAL		
203. Wesley's Chapel	London, England	Methodist
204. Salvation Army Headquarters	London, England	Methodist
210. New Room	Bristol, England	Methodist
130. St. Olaf's Church	Tallin, Estonia	Baptist
247. Ebenezer Baptist Church	Atlanta, Georgia	Baptist
244. Amish Country	Lancaster, Pennsylvania	Anabaptist
149. Berlin Cathedral	Berlin, Germany	United Protestant
163. New Church	Amsterdam, Netherlands	Protestant Church in the Netherlands
58. Ebenezer Church	Ebenezer, Australia	Uniting Church in Australia
240. First Parish Church	Plymouth, Massachusetts	Unitarian universalist
250. Salt Lake Temple	Salt Lake City, Utah	Latter Day Saints

OLDEST CHURCHES IN THE WORLD

CHURCH	LOCATION	YEAR BUILT	NOTES
CHURCH RUINS			
32. House Church of Dura Europas	Dura Europas, Syria	c. 232-256	Oldest remains of any church ever verified (not purpose-built)
Megiddo Church	Tel Megiddo, Israel	c. late 3rd century	Oldest remains of a purpose-built church
Aqaba Church	Aqaba, Jordan	c. 293-303	Oldest remains of a purpose-built church (alternate)
SURVIVING NON-PURPOSE BUILT CHURCHES			
98. Church of St. Mary and the Martyrs (Pantheon)*	Rome, Italy	126	Built as a pagan temple; consecrated as a church in the 7th century
89. Cathedral of St. Domnius*	Split, Croatia	305	Built as a mausoleum; consecrated as a church in the 7th century
173. Basilica of Saint-Pierre-Aux-Nonnains	Metz, France	c. 380	Built as a school; consecrated as a church in the 7th century
CHURCHES WITH SURVIVING ANCIENT CAVE/ GROTTO ELEMENTS			
64. Monastery of St. Anthony*	Zafarana, Egypt	c. 298-300	Cave of St. Anthony from 4th century
12. Tomb of Lazarus	Al-Eizariya, West Bank	c. 4th century	Cave of St. Lazarus from 1st century
17. Basilica of the Annunciation*	Nazareth, Israel	c. 4th century	Grotto of the Annunciation from 1st century

77. Cave of the Apocalypse*	Patmos, Greece	c. 4th century	Cave of St. John from 1st century
41. Church of St. Peter	Antakya, Turkey	c. 4th-5th century	Cave of St. Peter from 1st century
30. Convent of St. Thecla Ma'Lula*	Maaloula, Syria	c. 5th century	Cave of St. Thecla from 1st century

PURPOSE-BUILT CHURCHES WITH MINIMAL SURVIVING ORIGINAL ELEMENTS			
91. St. Peter's Basilica*	Vatican City	c. 319-333	Portions of original Christian necropolis beneath church
93. Basilica of St. John in Lateran*	Rome, Italy	324	Traces of original building and artwork still exist
Church with 100 Doors (Panagia Ekatontapiliani)*	Parikia, Paros, Greece	326	A handful of elements can be traced back to the 4th century
21. Church of the Primacy of St. Peter*	Tabgha, Israel	c. 4th century	Incorporates an original stone known as the 'Table for Christ'
70. Church of Our Lady Mary of Zion*	Aksum, Ethiopia	c. 4th century	Traces of original building still exist
110. Basilica of St. Ambrose*	Milan, Italy	386	Part of the original floor plan is still in use
96. Basilica of St. Mary Major*	Rome, Italy	c. 422-432	Part of the 5th century structure and mosaics still exist

PURPOSE-BUILT CHURCHES WITH SIGNIFICANT SURVIVING ORIGINAL ELEMENTS			
161. Cathedral of Trier*	Trier, Germany	c. early 4th century	Original core of the church preserved
43. Etchmiadzin Cathedral*	Etchmiadzin, Armenia	c. 301-303	Significant surviving original elements with later renovations

Basilica of Santa Maria in Trastevere*	Rome, Italy	c. 340	Original floor plan and some of the original structure preserved
Basilica of San Lorenzo*	Milan, Italy	c. 390-402	Reconstruction dating to the 6th century remains at core of structure

PURPOSE-BUILT CHURCHES ESSENTIALLY INTACT FROM ORIGINAL CONSTRUCTION			
33. Church of the Holy Wisdom (Hagia Sophia)	Istanbul, Turkey	537	Original church is still intact, though with significant later additions
63. St. Catherine's Monastery*	Feren, Egypt	c. 548-565	Original chapel still intact, with later additions to the monastery
13. Church of the Nativity*	Bethlehem, West Bank	565	Not the original 4th century building, but 6th century building still standing

CHURCHES OF RAVENNA HONORARY MENTIONS			
105. Orthodox Baptistry	Ravenna, Italy	c. early 5th century	Surviving structure of an early basilica; the baptistry is intact
105. Archbishop's Chapel	Ravenna, Italy	495	Part of the Archbishop's Palace
105. Arian Baptistry	Ravenna, Italy	c. 5th-6th century	Surviving structure of the Church of Spirito Santo; the baptistry is intact
105. Basilica of Sant'Apollinare Nuovo*	Ravenna, Italy	c. early 6th century	Significant portions intact with later renovations
105. Basilica of San Vitale*	Ravenna, Italy	547	Original construction essentially intact
105. Basilica of Sant'Apollinare in Classe*	Ravenna, Italy	549	Significant portions intact with later additions and renovations

OTHER HONORARY MENTIONS			
Church of St. Adrian at the Roman Forum	Rome, Italy	29 BC	Formerly the Curia Julia which housed the Roman Senate; served as a church from 630 until 1920
36. House of the Virgin Mary*	Selcuk, Turkey	c. 1st century	6th century house with 1st century stone foundation; a chapel is inside
99. Christian Catacombs	Rome, Italy	1st, 2nd, 3rd centuries	Numerous catacombs contain some early purpose-built worship areas

Currently still in use as a Christian place of worship

About the Author

Howard Kramer is the creator and author of *The Complete Pilgrim*. He first took an interest in religious sites in his early twenties when traveling through Italy after college. In the three decades since he has traveled to nearly thirty countries and forty American states, visiting and photographing hundreds of the world's greatest churches, cathedrals, synagogues, temples and other places of religious interest. Howard has been writing about religious sites for the better part of the last decade, and *The Complete Pilgrim* is the culmination of years of his work and passion.

Made in the USA
Las Vegas, NV
27 November 2020